CONFESSIONS OF A MAVERICK MIND

A PSYCHOLOGIST SHARES STORIES AND ADVENTURES, ESSAYS AND ARTICLES, AND POEMS AND SONGS

Mark Steinberg, Ph.D.

ISBN: 1500828246
ISBN 13: 9781500828240
Library of Congress Control Number: 2014914557
CreateSpace Independent Publishing Platform
North Charleston, South Carolina

CONTENTS

II ESSAYS AND ARTICLES 237

III POEMS AND SONGS.............477

INTRODUCTION

The writings in *Confessions of a Maverick Mind* are an amalgam of my chronicles and creative inspirations over the past decades. I have always loved writing and reading. As a child, I found knowledge, companionship, fantasy, and escape in literature. I was encouraged in the arts and humanities in my formative development, exposed to creative writing instruction and journalism in school, and praised for my efforts and skills using expressive language.

Writing poses a difficult set of challenges. Among other skills and attributes, it requires self-discipline, an organized mind, a tolerance for being alone and for being rejected, and a confident commitment that what one has to say is valuable. I developed these characteristics slowly and gradually as I matured in adulthood. It is likely that my decades as a professional practicing in the neurosciences helped me to focus and communicate lucidly and persuasively. It is also very clear to me that I needed to develop a degree of humility in order to accept criticism and refine my efforts in expressive language.

Without doubt, I was given a genetic gift of verbal expression and the ability to use written communication as a tool to learn, teach, produce insight, mentor, motivate, inspire, and connect with others. My parents, teachers, and elders recognized and encouraged these talents. For a good part of my early life, I rejected my strengths and even scoffed at what I considered my impractical and abstract "talents." In my self-doubt and search for identity, I felt taunted by a world that needed and valued pragmatic, hands-on skills: the manly qualities of mechanical ability that I lacked. For many years, I felt that academic skills—and writing in particular—were superfluous and that creativity and literature were indulgences.

How mistaken and callow I was! Through God's grace and the wisdom that comes with maturity and humility, I began to understand that people are given different talents and gifts and that it is a duty and privilege to develop and use them. My career as a cutting edge neuropsychologist, my family, and the many people who have blessed and challenged me have served as inspirations to recognize and apply my abilities.

If I could fix cars, program computers, stitch wounds, or build skyscrapers, I might have taken on those challenges. As it stands, I forge ideas, nurture insights, heal traumas and maladies, and solder words and phrases. I have learned increasingly to love and treasure these gifts and practices.

People often tell me that I identify, encapsulate, and express their experiences, yearnings, and conflicts with precision and empathy that makes them feel rewarded and validated. This is music to my ears and a continuing source of encouragement. I hope that you will feel validated, amused, and encouraged as you read these pages.

I

STORIES AND ADVENTURES

CONFESSIONS OF A MAVERICK MIND

Once upon a time, before the advent of cell phones, but after the end of World War II, a son was born to a Jewish couple in the Bronx. This middle-class professional couple lavished upon their first-born child much love and attention and some of the trappings of material abundance that they themselves had lacked as children. As things evolved in those baby boom years, the accouterments of city life were nonetheless relatively modest for this family: a one-bathroom walk-up apartment, occasional dinners out, public schools, summer camp, and an economical car.

So began my journey.

Whatever my parents lacked in parenting expertise, they compensated in values, high expectations, aspirations for their children (my brother came along years later), and intense and encouraging preoccupation with the development of the mind.

It became apparent during toddlerhood that I was an exceptional child. Though it may sound immodest, most people noticed that I was curious, active, and extremely bright. I tested in the upper gifted range in preschool and was a teacher's pet throughout elementary school, attaining superior levels of achievement until the onset of a rebellious adolescence.

Less clear and more confounding was the development of uncanny creativity tethered by psychological quirks and instabilities. As I grew, I became more brilliantly cerebral and more deeply disturbed. A collision course was inevitable, and in late adolescence, the speeding trajectories of ambition, creativity, emotional need, and rebellion came together in chain-reaction accidents of mental and social breakdown and physical illness. These crises accelerated from puberty on and became dramatic and debilitating in late high school and in my early college years.

There were years of rehabilitation, therapy, academic catch-up, physical reconstitution, and what seems, in retrospect, a spiritual cleansing and preparation. All the while, my mind was active, searching, comparing, evaluating, and training itself in the recognition and precise perception of intricate patterns and recapitulations that are woven into the fabric of life. These idiosyncratic ways of thinking often manifested in creative and iconoclastic expression of ideas. It was clear to me and to others that I was "different." Eventually, I turned my fierce determination to developing and highlighting the positive differences and to minimizing, compensating, and repenting for the negative ones.

One of my most significant differences was the manner in which my mind worked. On the one hand, I was very logical and analytic, perhaps lawyerly in applying my facility for reasoning, arguing, and deduction. On the other, I was artistic, blessed with a mind flooded with imagery and intuition, my impressions and inventions unbounded by time, space, or sequence. It is true that many people have gifts of language and logic, and others bear extraordinary talents in designing, constructing, or modifying concrete three-dimensional objects. Some people have combinations of these abilities, and they are able to blend left-brain and right-brain capacities into wondrous manifestations of brilliance. I had elements of both, though it would be many years beyond these early decades of angst when these elements would integrate, mature, and flourish.

Perhaps it was the deconstruction of my mind and spirit during adolescence that propelled me toward the study of psychology; perhaps it was the desire to figure out myself and my problems or the genuine intrigue of mental mysteries that spurred me to refinement and achievement. My path might also be explained by reductionist genetics: What else could a person with few practical skills do? As a friend proverbially and insightfully quipped, "Unemployable Jewish comedians make great salesmen, teachers, and psychologists."

Not surprisingly, my natural interests, practical limitations, and the need to find a career led me along the avenues of liberal arts and social sciences. I became increasingly interested in psychology and specifically in how the brain interacts with and influences behaviors, beliefs, feelings, perceptions, and physical health. Depending upon one's view, serendipity and/or inevitability steered me into the orbits of several accomplished geniuses, leaders in the fields of psychology and neuropsychology. In reaction to the heat generated by their innovative brilliance, my brain was dry tinder, waiting to be ignited.

Even before the honing of professional skills and my demonstrated competence in healing, I conducted my own longitudinal experiment in the perceptions, expressions, and integration of the mind. My laboratory, canvas, and theater played out amid the convoluted ambiguities of daily life. Problems, people, and the ironies throughout life formed the sources for my methods and material. Eventually I learned to sort out, distill, and deftly manipulate the content and context of my ever-expanding experience and insight.

In many ways, I was stereotyped, yet in many other ways, I was atypical. A *paradox,* in other words, but nonetheless one that was dissectible, analyzable, but not quite explicable. As my diverse qualities became more apparent and extensive, the character of paradox became more familiar. Acquisitive by nature and habit, I was driven to obtain material things and security. At the same time, I was governed by an intense and pervasive devotion to God and spiritual matters. Physicality and hedonism became longstanding personal habits, and I rigorously practiced body discipline and self-regulation. Yet my favorite recreation was the freewheeling exercise of my mind in exploring and inventing new combinations of ideas and expression and molding them into creative projects. My preferred media were language (oral and written), humor, and the mosaic integration of technology with internal mental connections and imagery. At some point, I coined a term to describe the creative, logical, relational, and multifaceted engine I experienced as my mind: I became a *maverick multimediast.*

A curious word: *multimediast.* Certainly, I was no maven in the arts or technology. Indeed, my fascination with gadgets and technologies was tempered by limitations in mechanical ability and indiscriminate frustrations with building, assembling, or fixing things. Most comfortable in the world of ideas, I learned to function and negotiate in the slower-moving and more obstructive three-dimensional world. I learned to accept these limitations, and grew in humility and the marveling appreciation for the gifts of others. I joked self-effacingly that the males in my family were born with a genetic condition called *decadigislexia* (Latin for "ten meaningless fingers")—thus my inability to use my hands to fix things. Such quips elicited many quizzical expressions, quick laughs, and temporary excuses to avoid the traditional "manly" tasks of repairing things around the house.

My fascination with multimedia grew by leaps and bounds as technological innovations burgeoned and accelerated during the vibrant high-tech days of the twenty-first century. The click of a button could summon vast mélanges of sensory display: music, video, text, design, special effects, phantasmagoria that blended reality and fantasy. Digital technology could shrink or expand the vicissitudes of time and space. The capacity of the human brain to invent, combine, and synthesize seemed limitless; but this presented challenges to organize and utilize such a vast array of tools and images that could easily overwhelm. Internet globalization blew the lid off communication and privacy. Skype could bridge physical boundaries and cyberattacks could unfortunately intrude on economic and emotional boundaries. It became time to rethink where, how, and when the thoughts of an individual were contained and where, when, and how the perceptions of others, furtive or obvious, would be permitted to penetrate these boundaries. Traditional markers of mental disorders would bleed into commercial offerings, combining images, sounds, and special effects that could eerily simulate illusions. The nefarious invasions of institutional and rogue intelligence could permeate what was once the sanctity of privacy. Whereas those with loose associative minds are subject to intrusive thoughts, persistent unwanted voices, and the anxieties caused by these takeovers, increasingly the "normal" population must deal with computer viruses, identity theft, online profiles of pretension, and the admixtures of real and sham composites and digital legends. Such is the price of progress, as easy access and technical tools facilitate the acting out of human impulses and ambitions.

The progress of technology was indeed maverick. Geniuses and innovators worked to make lives easier and more fun and also to make money by helping people in areas where they wanted things, teaching them how to achieve what they desired, creating their acquisitive impulses, supplying these things, and fulfilling their real and imagined "needs." This movement dovetailed with my personality, for I had always been the maverick, a misfit beset with ambition, frustration, and good intention. Unfortunately, I was too disorganized in thinking and in patching together my ideas. Keeping track of notions and images required an intensive memory. Either my head was too small or my brain too busy and primitive for the ideas I wanted to assemble. Pictures had to be copied and physically cut and pasted. Melodies and harmonies had to be revisited on vinyl disks. Books had to be stored and their ideas and connections indexed in the mind. Even a burgeoning mind was limited by sequential and serial access before the external storage of ideas became digital and random access and montage could flow freely from technology and the wonders of the Internet. Calligraphy was an art that laser printers would quickly reform, making style available electronically to anyone with a keyboard. Before computers, art seemed separate from science. The combination and permutation of ideas often required manual accounting and visual-motor efficiency to make personal creativity manifest.

Alas and hallelujah! I did not invent or innovate with products; I consumed, experimented, and used them in combination with my creative and problem-solving mind. In 1984, the release of the first Macintosh unfurled a revolution. As a person with sloppy handwriting and no programming skills, I embraced the Macintosh as my muse. A memory of 128K and a simple linear screen smile became a watershed in history!

Moreover, this early innovation was both personal and professional. Experienced as I was in working with people with disabilities and learning disorders, the early Macintosh facilitated new methods and capacities for communication and expression, interaction and learning, and creativity and autonomy. Who knew then about the imminent advent of e-mail obsession, tablet communication for autistics, computer wristwatches and Google glass, commands by eye movements and brainwaves, Bluetooth, YouTube, tweets, Facebook, etc.? Would telepathy remain a science fiction fantasy, or would it become prescience to the manifest future? Even in the early days, technology and media were evolving collaterally with, or perhaps as a projection of, the neuroscience of mind architecture and operations.

In parallel with the explosion of technology, this Bronx-born maverick was developing a career and expertise in neuropsychology. I was using computers to train human brains—a marvelous and healing synergy of digital technology, biological brain plasticity, and the inherent timing mechanisms of the universe! Imagine: using neuroscience and technology to adjust brain timing through natural learning! The applications seem limitless for the betterment of health, well-being, productivity and creativity, and community and social compassion. Maverick multimedia had become blessing and joy!

A psychologist and innovator, I find myself on the twenty-first century frontier of excitement, laden with the burdens of aging, but brimming with energy and maturity. I'm rapt with the possibilities of transformational healing; where cause-and-effect can become nonlinear and the relationships between content and context can be composed and modified as in a creative score. This maverick views choice, complexity, and flexibility as means to an end.

And what is that end? Well in the end—which is never final, but only a way station for appreciating the past and then looking ahead—whichever end you are looking at or from, you cannot hide or minimize the connections among humans and their experiences. It's all about the human "condition" with its frailties, anomalies, and mysteries. Old school, really. Technology and media won't change that. You can Photoshop your images and even your memory, to an extent. But human beings still need the nourishment and prana (breath or life-force) of relationships, connections, validation, compassion, intrigue, and hope.

Confession reveals vulnerability and humility. The revelation of one's innermost sensitivities, longings, and quirks should be heard as baring, not boasting. It is disclosure with trust and some embarrassment and shame. It is honest. Confession wants someone to hear and accept. It is afraid of judgment, but brave and desperate enough to reach out and connect. Confession wants absolution from secrecy and loneliness.

Confession wants a parent to the child, a soothing and reassurance through release. Even mavericks need connection. A chronicle of connections lies herein, providing URLs for the soul. Are you there, at the other end?

MAVERICK CONFESSION

These are the confessions of a busy maverick mind,
Expressions of experience in hopes that you will find
The patterning of lives so different in degree,
But similar in kind.

Linear in focus, yet always multitasking,
Split between the answers and the questions that need asking.
Weaving new material with fabric from the past,
Integrating future with the memories that last.

What is the grand purpose, then, of making wisdom rise?
Does it gain in truth or merely camouflage the lies?
Spinning yarns of history attempts to make things whole.
Confession bares the mystery that haunts the very soul.

WHEN GOD TAKES AWAY

Living with Loss and Surrender

All of us experience loss. Things, people, circumstances come and go, sometimes slipping unnoticed or not missed in the course of busy and changing lives. Loss that is suffered, however, has a different character. This is the ripping away of what we protect, cherish, covet, need, and think we deserve. The real and meaningful losses we experience take a toll on our identity and challenge our beliefs about fairness, rightness. At its core, loss threatens our abilities and confidence about survival.

There are many losses throughout life, of course; it is the natural order of things. Losing a loved one is among the most difficult to bear—a family member, friend, pet, someone you knew or identify with and who enriched you with meaning and humanity. One of the most difficult sufferings is the loss of a child.

On Memorial Day weekend in 2013, we lost our son, Neal. He was twenty-six years old. He died from an accidental drug overdose. The police came to our door in the middle of the night to respectfully deliver the tragic news, sentries of a nightmare for any parent. Instantaneously, we were transported into that unenviable group of parents who grieve and suffer and try to make sense of the unexpected and insensible.

How can I bear such a loss? How can I continue with my duties, swimming in a world of overwhelm, swallowing the salty tears and flailing to connect reality with pretense? What shall I say to others? What will they say and think? Is it right for me to burden them with this grief, and is it deceptive or isolating to withhold it? What will happen with my heartache and sorrow, and how might God use it for good?

Why did this happen, God who loves me and loves my son? Why did you take Neal from us at this time? In your natural order, children outlive their parents, difficult as that painful finiteness is, too. Why this exception? How shall I placate my analytical mind's unanswerable questions, and who will soothe my emotional angst?

In the midst of agonizing loss, vulnerability takes center stage, stark and unrehearsed. The carousel of emotions and coping skills spins aloof, and I'm incompetent at jumping on or off: hurt, despair, confusion, numbness, relief, misery, grief, love, self-pity, rationalization, anxiety, fear, fatigue. Those common and reliable escapes—denial and anger—don't fit me well. I am loathe to wear them, like some old fat clothes that no longer fit, or the garish sports jacket that I wore in college when I was so full of myself.

I am plainly hurt, sensitive, and needy—exposed to the grim reality that what I hold most dear can be, has been, and, in varying measure and timing, will be taken away. This life that I cherish, act in and out, and pretend is my own exists in a context that has greater control than I can ever exert. The painful reality of loss asserts its sobering reminders that all I "own" is temporary. In the bigger picture, I am truly not even my own.

Loss is a natural, inevitable, and unpleasant aspect of life. It is far less predictable than we'd like, and it often strikes with sudden terror, leaving us exposed, shocked, and needy. Given the universality and intermittency of loss, we would think to take it in stride, at least much of the time. But that is not the case, even with "minor" losses; to lose something meaningful feels deeply personal and threatening. When something is taken away, the experience cuts to the core of vulnerability, control, security, comfort, entitlement, and the organization of the world we take for granted.

There are no curricula for loss, no courses to teach how to give things up. Our culture exalts "getting" more and holding on to it. This market structure operates on an economy of material growth and confidence, catering to pragmatic needs but insensitive to emotions and the needs of the spirit. Even death has its proper associated industries.

Despite its unanimity, loss remains a private matter, leaving each of us to mourn, resent, pine, wish, regret, and adjust as best we can. There are support groups for processing, close ones for comfort, and "replacements" for some losses. You can get a new car or pet, but you can't bring back the dead. Whether the loss is minor (such as a wallet) or tragic (as in the death of a loved one), no replacement, substitution, distraction, or opportunity teaches the practical and spiritual skills of *giving up.*

Loss means giving up. Many people view giving up as an act or attitude of resignation or cowardice. To give up can connote a reprehensible loss of motivation or a failure to participate and compete. Giving up can seem a flaw in moral character, in the fiber necessary for adaptation and survival. However, when God takes away something valued, giving up is a choice we can make in response to God's sovereignty. When faced with loss, even devastating, irreversible, irreplaceable loss, we can choose to respond in deference to God's will and with deference and neediness to the one who knows and can meet all needs. This process is called *surrender.*

Surrender is weakness and vulnerability leaving the soul and spirit. It is the renunciation of control and the capitulation to a force or will greater than one's own.

My wife grieves with me. She wails and laments that Neal will never have a wife or children, never know the challenges and rewards of a developing career, never experience the mixed blessings of aging. My heart echoes these laments, and my mind reflexively reviews the "coulda, shoulda, woulda, if only" thought loops that intrude in the aftermath of this tragedy. I know I did all I could for my son, yet the inexorable finality of losing him exacerbates my helplessness and the smallness of my power and competence in the universe. What is left for me when the exercise of "figuring this out" leaves only repeated fatigue and frustration?

I must yield to God's will and omniscience, for he is my strength and comfort. Accepting what happened and adjusting to life without my son and his future does not mean forcing away my pain and suffering. I know that God feels my feelings because he is the Creator of those feelings. I trust God to comfort me and to bring about healing in his own time. My best efforts are put toward recognizing and yielding to his sovereign will.

It is difficult to think about what happens when you are gone; such thoughts don't compute with worldly reasoning, and it can be scary, especially without secure belief and reassurance about the hereafter. It is so overwhelming and confusing to experience and organize the thoughts and feelings of outliving a child. Yet life is a process of acquisition and loss, and the passion and security of attachment can only be ultimately disappointing. It is a great conundrum that fulfillment and peace appear through blessed involvement and, necessarily, through letting go.

Taking things for granted suits the natural mind, and this part-time illusion helps the nervous system relax and function. Eventually, everything in the material world goes away—but when loss strikes home, it is a traumatic challenge to the processes of attachment and surrender, these life experiences in the earthly and spiritual realms that God wants us to know and resolve through dependence upon him.

Oh, how hard it is to lose, to suffer, to accept and adjust, to yield and surrender to a world that doesn't follow one's plans and desires! For loss that comes unpredictably but inevitably with its trail of hurt and trauma, its specter of fear and vulnerability, it is the salve of surrender that gives the comfort, peace, and security that heals beyond expectation or understanding. And to whom is it safe to surrender? It is the one whose capacity and caring infinitely reaches beyond even the imagination and aspirations of his creations.

I suppose that in time the sharp pains of loss will abate and the open wounds will heal. Memories will soften and somehow fit with the passage of life. The agony will subside to a lessening and perhaps even occasional dull ache or pang, a reminder of injury that never quite disappears, but that can become manageable. Hopefully…

I miss my son with a love beyond reason and words. I want him back—something I cannot have. Each day has multiple reminders of the stark change: I cannot call him or hear from him, give him advice, or respond to his frustrations and complaints. I cannot provide him food and comfort, watch him perform, share an Internet link, argue his ideas, or join him for a ride. The change is sudden and permanent. It is reality become chimera: disappearance appearing as the new normal. It is shocking, disorienting, and pushing the limits of my reason and belief.

I have coped with loss many times in my fractured life, recovered well from the hurt, numbness, and sense of exposure and threat. I have many blessings, including a wholeness and stability that stand up well to challenge and trauma. From decades of personal and professional experience, I know that trauma is cumulative, so that those individuals most affected by life's multiple insults, injuries, and stresses will have the hardest challenge to accommodate the next tough surprise. Thus, I am charged with the responsibility of leadership, solace, and healing for my loved ones who also grieve and suffer greatly.

For this calling I am ready. I know our God is a God who provides comfort and that his grace is sufficient for me. With the discipline of prayer, I defer my spotty understanding to the occasional glimpses of wisdom far too vast and magnificent for me to apprehend. Just as I accept the night as the earth turns even while I'm not making it do so or seeing the other side, I know by experience that the sun will shine on me again. Without full grasp of this process, I stop to marvel and renew my faith that I will be blessed again.

Hope and faith may seem like clichés. But they are as real and necessary as oxygen. God gives and he takes away: the good and the bad, as perceived by man—but God works his own sovereign plan. And so, when struck with tragic loss, I suffer and mourn and work to heal, aided by faith and hope and dependence on a loving, omnipotent God who sees all that has been and will be and who knows everything. I choose the path of surrender, a lifelong practice of releasing my stubbornness and desires to God's will, letting him lead me to greater acquisition and grace. Hope and humility become the surrender that leads to clarity, perseverance, and peace.

When God takes away, he closes doors, often unexpectedly. In his providence, new doors open and opportunities unfold to discover and live out what God has in mind. Loss can be an opportunity to turn disappointment and longing regarding the past into hopeful longing and eagerness about the present and future. With God, the future is brighter. Surrender allows us to let go and move more fluidly toward what God has in store.

How does this manifest in practical ways? How do the daily hardships get handled, the overwhelm settled, the healing accelerated, the work done? How do I abide affliction, conquer fear, and carry on with triumph? And how can *you*?

Stay tuned.

Neal Randall Steinberg
1986–2013

1993
Written after a camping trip in the Sierra Nevada mountains with Tree Climbers, my church group of fathers and sons.

HEALTH CARE REFORM

Benefits for Mental Health, Substance Abuse, and a Prescription Plan

My back is killing me. I smell bad, and my beard is not pretty. Who knows what a shower will wash away, but I know that a hot shower will liberate me substantially from the misery of three days in the wilderness. I just returned from camping with my two sons—seven thousand feet up in the Sierras, and I feel as though I've climbed every one of them.

Above my aching body, my mind is peaceful. My boys had a great time, and I have the secure feeling one gets from a sound investment. Through this camping experience, I paid another premium on family health insurance—the kind money really can't buy. I was counting on these experiences to insure my children against the ravages of drug addiction, the emotional injuries that are often part and parcel of growing up, the accidents of rebellion, and the pernicious malady of family and social alienation. There are no guarantees, of course, but I believed it was a wise investment. Dollar for dollar, I was certain, it would beat anything in the form of preventive family mental health care.

This "primitive" form of health care has reformed a number of ideas I've held about being a dad. Yes, there was a cost, a cost I was happy to pay: I lost several days of work. But there was a precious payoff. I spent time reacquainting myself with my children and with my own aging process. I discovered how arduous canoeing is when one is out of shape; memories of my agility in this pursuit have submerged beneath my own weight.

I marveled at the relative value of a flashlight over a computer when one is in the forest. Some things remain unchanged: I still prefer beds to sleeping bags, and I still deplore guns. Some things have changed for the better: my ability to sleep well in unfamiliar places has improved, as has my prowess with a bow and arrow. Perhaps this is because I can concentrate more now and am better able to focus on the relevant. Thus, I paid more attention to my boys and noticed salient changes confronting the images I retained about the younger children that they used to be. These differences manifested through their current fears. We spent a lot of time with fears, the boys and I, stereotypically following a traditional male prerogative of challenging nature to reflect both our strengths and weaknesses. I'm not sure we conquered anything, but we did experience and discuss our respective fears out in the open. Our fears were different, but the defenses were the same. The grip of apprehension was familiar, but how we shared our trepidations varied.

Five-year-old Jeremy surprised me with his anxiety in the water. He was frightened in the canoe, edgy, and mortified at the prospect of a motorboat excursion. (This is the same child who, two summers ago, gleefully egged me to higher speeds riding on the Jet Ski.) In addition to his shaky "water legs," Jeremy was also rattled by his fear of incompetence. Many of our activities were too demanding on his five-year-old strength and coordination: aiming a BB rifle, stretching a bow, paddling a canoe.

My poor Jeremy had succumbed to the grip of despair that he expressed with sorrowful statements such as "I'm acting like a real wimp today" and "I'm a loser at everything" and "Nobody cares about me. God doesn't care about me." It was clear that there was a crisis in the wilderness, and there was no hospital emergency room in sight. In this unsterile environment, I needed to bandage his self-esteem, which was ruptured and bleeding at the source. Of course, I reassured him and used this opportunity to explain how important and valuable he was to me and to God.

Seven-year-old Neal ambushed me with his question, "Dad, what are you afraid of?" I fielded his inquiry with a smug and clichéd paternal reflection of embarrassed wisdom, commonly experienced by adults when their children ask them where babies come from. In a quick moment, I returned from reverie to the wooded thicket where my son waited for an answer. This was a father-son heart-to-heart, one of many such communications that I hoped to encourage by dealing a straight answer.

"I'm afraid that you will grow up and no longer want to be with me, that we will lose the closeness we now enjoy," I responded. The gulp in my throat gradually transformed into an apprehensive abstraction. "On the other hand, I also worry that you *won't* grow up, and that I will have to take care of you when you should be independent.

"I also fear—if you really want to know the truth—that I will somehow lose the love or presence of the people who really matter to me.

"I worry that I might get sick..."

"Dad," Neal replied with a mixture of sympathy and consternation, "what I mean is, what *animals* are you afraid of?"

Caught by surprise, I sheepishly admitted that I was not particularly frightened by animals and that I worried more about other matters. Neal didn't miss a beat in pursuing his prey, who had just become ensnared in a classic developmental trap. "Then I suppose it would be okay if we got a rattlesnake for a pet."

As I gazed at my son, pondering his unnerving fascination with reptiles and winning debates, he continued the spirit of the discussion with his seven-year-old concerns: "I'm afraid of the dark, like especially that someone is in my room at night. And also, I'm afraid of the black widow spider, not a *whole* lot, but just..."

I listened, absorbed in my son's trust and in the reality of this spinning web of bonding; it was the fabric of identity, confidence, and assurance weaving strand by experiential strand. This was the stuff of protection and prevention, I believed, the housing of health and emotional sustenance.

Over a parallel circuit, my mind processed the flow of anxieties unleashed by Neal's question. The concrete-associative fears of a child's thinking scurried through the foreground against a patina of adult memories and abstractions. My fears…yes, a thousand iterations of the apprehension that life will accidentally puncture my invincibility and, in so doing, irretrievably damage my ability to recover and repair.

The double whammy of aging and responsibility for the welfare of my family has increased the desire for security. I wanted a hedge, a safer risk than the unknown. My mind developed a multisensory fantasy: I pictured a wall of hedges, an impenetrable thorny thicket behind which I crouched, watching colorful balloons rise into the sky; they could not burst, even as they approached and cleared the sharp hedges. Simultaneously, I heard the inane jingle of an insurance commercial: "Insurance is lo-o-ove…" (It's not insurance; it's love.) "Insurance is ca-a-aring…" (We'll bet you so many dollars a day until you die that you don't die.) "Contact your Roulette Insurance agent today!"

In thinking about the future of my children's well-being, I wandered to images of the past. My father loomed large, like a giant poster in my chamber of relationships. He was my model, and he was brave. Oh, the man was riddled with fears, common and idiosyncratic. Yet he was brave by being himself, pressing through life with a hodgepodge of anxieties and quirks that rendered him more vulnerable to attack. I am not as brave as my father, but I may be smarter. Perhaps, in this hubris, I've simply had the benefits of his mistakes and learned through the innocence and faith of his generation. My father grew up through two world wars—but I had wars of a local kind through my growing up. The trauma of my adolescence is not forgotten. Like an incipient threat, I was vigilant for its contagion in the pattern of my sons' development and the denouement of our relationships.

I folded away the sleeping bags, contemplating the future and the prospect of health coverage. I've discovered anew that there are valuables that money itself cannot buy. I will spend, hope, complain, and follow the expected procedures of parental duty. Only a father, however, can provide a particular core of invaluable insurance benefits, particularly those involving mental, emotional, and spiritual health. It is a prescription plan to avoid pharmaceuticals. This kind of health care reform—where families have protection against the ravages of maturation—should indeed be universal.

1995
Written after my first wife, Barbara, was diagnosed with breast cancer.

SURVIVING THE OLDERNESS

Fugue in A-Sharp Minor

What has been will be again, what has been done will be done again; there is nothing new under the sun.

Ontogeny

My youngest son, Jeremy, is five. He returned from an afternoon at the park with yet more horror stories of being teased by the older kids. Jeremy persists in hanging around with older children, despite the obvious advantages they have over him by virtue of their advancement over his coordination, size, and (by implication) social standing.

As he says, "It's a jungle gym out there." Perils of the wilderness arise from nature. Perils of the olderness arise from mature.

Cast your bread upon the waters, for after many days you will find it again.

This dichotomy of inclination and desire, poignantly expressed by Jeremy's angst, reflects a human irony: we cherish the stimulation and recognition attainable in the larger arena—the little fish in the big pond, so to speak. But we also need and depend upon the security and ego strength that come from familiarity, personal leadership, and the easy reward of exercising the skills we have mastered to the point of admiration.

This vacillation is played out on so many stages of development: the growth and excitement of challenge alternating with the familiar flexing of mastery and authority.

Through Jeremy's survival in the olderness, I experience life passionately and vicariously. My heart trills the octaves of emotion; the soprano of excitement and anticipation yields to the strident tenor of confidence—then, the sudden tumble through the bass depths of despair. The confusing facial foliage that hides Jeremy's humiliation glistens bittersweetly with remembrances of the olderness of my own yearnings.

I am determined to be wise—but this is beyond me. Whatever wisdom may be, it is far off and most profound—who can discover it? So I turned my mind to understand, to investigate, and to search out the wisdom and scheme of things...

Phylogeny

Vivid memories flood me. My forays into the world beyond my parents led to unknown, varied, compelling, and often unpredictable responses. The maze of the olderness was complicated. Leaving behind my parental roots—sturdy trees I could climb for support and for a secure vantage from which to survey the environment—I repeatedly entered the labyrinthine temptations of the olderness. Everything was new and, therefore, surprising. The novelty alone was stimulating; excitement fed upon itself to entice me further. Fear hibernated beyond my senses, at least temporarily. People took me seriously, as if I could summon to the game board a new character who must be given his turn. Alas, the experiential dice inevitably sabotaged me. I became hurt, lonely, rejected, devastated. Characters in the olderness revealed themselves as predators—and the ego-less, dangerous night would envelop me. My piece would be permanently (it turned out not forever, but repeatedly) banished from the playing board.

...a time to embrace and a time to refrain...

Lost in the olderness, defenseless, without a retrievable foothold on worthiness, only the pain of my wounds sustained consciousness. I stumbled in retreat toward the sanctuary of my family, hopeful for succor, steeped in my humiliation, mindful that the nurturance I craved would not settle the score. *I must achieve victories in the olderness!*

As a father has compassion on his children…

The time machine is playing *Significance and Security* in the present. Jeremy is recovering from the latest bout of self-pity; I watch my solace drip automatically into his anguish. This parental potion heals, and injustice magically dissolves. Jeremy is fortified; he is ready once again to combat the mendacious ways of the olderness. He will prepare to engage by making up his own rules. This is indeed a wily strategy. He will ordain cause and effect so that he may win. Watch out olderness! You are about to discover Jeremy's rules, a pervasive and persuasive armamentarium of illogic and need. You will defer, you must submit, you could at least accept… please?!? But the olderness is complex and unyielding…and its lure is irresistible.

Who is like the wise man? Who knows the explanation of things?

I couldn't understand the teasing. To this role of the stooge, I became accustomed. But the sense of isolation was onerous. Although the term "second-class citizen" was well beyond my ken, it was the embodiment of my role. I was tolerated according to conditions over which I felt no control and had only partial understanding. I was often tricked yet smart enough to see it coming. Like a prescient Huck Finn attending his envisioned funeral, this mental agility encouraged me to facilitate the games in which I was the inevitable victim. The olderness made room for me—as a cheerleader for my own demise.

At least I was involved in the fray and tumult where it really counted. I was surviving in the olderness! Soon, however, the other players tired. The game dispelled, along with my connection to its players. I was not included in their other concerns. Discarded, dejected, once again hung out to dry…

...tears streaming in a profusion of guileless sorrows. Why won't they play with me? Nobody likes me-e-e-e-e...Gr-r-r-r-r!!! An angry swipe of indignation. I wince at Jeremy's ire as he girds in protection. I'll show them. It's all my lousy brother's fault. They like him instead of me. He makes fun of me. He copies me. I wanna be with them and do what they do, but they won't let me. Why not? It's not fair. I'm a person too. He plays with them, but they won't play with me. He plays with the bigger kids, and they won't play with me. This big kid took my ball and wouldn't let...

...me have the ball, despite the double-teaming on him while I was free right under the basket. What's the ***matter*** *with him?!! Doesn't he see me? Maybe he knows I'm here and thinks I can't score. Or maybe he's freezing me out on purpose, just like...*

...when they ran me around, tossing my ball (shoes, jacket, book, toy...) among them, taunting, daring me to assert some dominant skill of interception. They paused, waited, hovered over my reactions as if fueled by my frustration. ***Let's play embryo—Steinberg's helpless in the middle; watch him kick!***

Stop kicking the furniture, son. That won't help you with the older kids. Let's talk about it. *What's there to talk about?* The way it works is this: you play with the big boys, they make the rules. Usually, they take advantage. I know it's not fair. They won't listen to me either; they'll just pretend and be polite while I'm there (maybe). Why don't you play with the smaller kids, the ones around your age...

...less fun than being with the bigger kids. It's boring 'cause they can't do what I can do. Anyway, I like to do special stuff, and the big kids would appreciate it if only they'd let me and pay attention to me. Nobody has room for Jeremy! But they only want to tease me, and I...

...don't think it's fun to tease the younger kids. The big kids tease me, and they seem to get a lot of fun that way. But I don't get fun from teasing kids like me or younger. Is there something wrong with me? I'm not interested in the kids who are interested in me. I am interested in the bigger kids and what they do—but they like to tease me, and I don't like that and don't want to do that to others. But I still want to be with the bigger kids; I hate it when they treat me mean! What's the matter with me? What do the older people know that I just don't get?

(Put on your big kid stuff)

Stomping clownishly in my father's enormous wing-tipped shoes... imagining how big I would be for my feet to fill those shoes and walk purposefully...to...work?...in the mechanical trenches of routine and ordinariness? Where is ***his*** *olderness? Where is the olderness* ***then*** *(toward which I scamper headlong)? What has my father conquered? Where were his tears...*

...when I needed them? They were sometimes there for sustenance and security. Sometimes, I was left to fend for myself. I often wondered whether this was planned parenthood on the part of my mother and father, or simply the result of their preoccupations or ignorance of my impending traumas. Increasingly, I sought to tread my trails in the olderness unchaperoned. I ruminated about whether this was the natural path or simply a reflection of my deviance. Over time, I grew more wary, less sensitive to the thorns and thistles, quicker to swathe injuries, craftier in evading traps. I accumulated skills, defenses, and weapons. Self-preservation and exploration became more efficient. At times, I had fun in the olderness. Still I pondered, as I stalked solitarily, *was I becoming more civilized or more beastly?*

(Put on your big kid stuff)

The commissioners glared at me during the oral examination for my license. Membership restricted—would they let me join the club? I glanced diffidently at the man questioning me. Irrelevant thoughts meandered into consciousness: *His tie is insignificant; it's not a sign. You can't tell from his expression what he's thinking.* Sure, I'm nervous, *but look at his feet...he's sitting in an open position. Those shoes remind me of...*

...my father, on his day off, would frequently visit libraries in Manhattan. These large, majestic structures held fascination for me; they contained innumerable books (which I enjoyed) and mysterious hallways and corridors (which I loved). I coveted any opportunity to visit these palaces, especially with my dad. Proudly accompanying my father (whose omnipotence included finding his way here by subway!), I alternated between the studious pretense of reading advanced tomes and the adventure of exploring the nooks, crannies, and connecting arteries in these intriguing buildings. Unaware that the stairwells of the Donnell Library above the ground floor were locked on the stairwell side (these were meant for emergency fire exit), I ventured into one and became immediately imprisoned behind the cavernous thud of the heavy door. *I tug, yank, and scream to no avail. This fire door has a foot-square window of wire-enmeshed safety glass located well above my head. In a state of panic, I launch running jumps to raise my eyes level with the window for fleeting seconds. Several glimpses of my unresponsive father make me feel like a drowning victim. Thrashing, flailing, pounding against the unrelenting door. If only somebody could catch the attention of…*

…"Dr. Steinberg," the commissioner began, as he fired another challenging question, "What would you do if a patient came to you with…"

…cancer! This nonkosher word does not belong in our vocabulary. It must be a myth, like Santa Claus. Unwelcome and nonexistent in my world, it nevertheless has stubbornly invaded—my wife's body. This philandering disease intruded upon my safe and limitless world, an assailant who robbed me of illusions of competence, bullied me away from the embrace of oneness, and who shackled me with alienation, hurt, and embarrassment.

…a time to be born and a time to die…

Gazing dreamily at my wife, I see the memory of our first child, Neal, in the hospital nursery. He gapes at me with that peaceful just-born stare that bonds us in future closeness. With the magnets of time, we will cling and repel. Time will propel him, too, into the olderness. Will his parents be there to guide him? Will his mother live to see him as a…

…teenager, that's what I wanna be. 'Cause teenagers have fun, and they can do all sorts of brave and wild things (Neal drones on) like cool stuff and rock 'n' roll and going places without their parents and not having parents always watching how…

I am cast aside. It is Yom Kippur; after the synagogue service, there is little to do but wait for the sun to set on this surreal day of deprivation. On the tarred schoolyard ground, Alan is apparently unconscious but is softly whimpering. He fell from atop a schoolyard fence where he ventured between our stickball games. Alan is much older, a teenager; in fact, I look up to him with adulation and marvel as he embodies a picture of my potential. But now I am looking down on him, uneasy with this new development. Defensively, I decide momentarily that Alan is faking, that he will suddenly arise with color in his face and an animated grin that says, "Gotcha!" But he is pale, and softly moaning, "Momma…" Abruptly pinched by reality, I realize that Alan is seriously hurt. I feel paralyzed, but must act. Shaken, I must get help; it is time to venture into the olderness…

(Put on your big kid stuff)

…so I run, out of the schoolyard, accelerating into the world of the olderness. Breathless and scared, I flee, mindful of fear and adrenaline chasing me. I must get help, they must notice me in the olderness, I must alert them that youthful essence languishes in the schoolyard. My perception narrows in panic, and rules of the olderness recede. I sprint into the street amid unconcerned traffic, a random car bears down on my path, the inevitable terror escalates, and I jump…

…up and down to raise my eyes level with the window in the desperate hope that someone (my father?) will notice my helplessness and imprisonment in a library stairwell. Don't let this be a terrible metaphorical ending to a childhood of intellectual isolation. Someone must take action! I need help from…

…above…

…the car hood, which has screeched angrily to a resentful pause at least a foot beyond my intersecting leap. Heart pounding louder than the driver's horn, driven by the heel of his hand, I am driven by my heels and toes and the panic…

…and the next day is a swirl of timeless confusion, fear, and grief. The smears of dirt on Alan's cheek glare in my mind against the whiteness of the ambulance as they entomb him in its mystery and sirens. I cannot separate the tears and smears on Alan's face from my own when I find out he has died. Yet, I feel separated; all the while I, too, am moaning, Mom…

…and I want to retreat from the olderness, to locate and climb into the arboreal reaches of my family tree of security. That place of magic, where fascination parades unfettered with danger. A place of love and total acceptance where all things work out well. We are supposed to live happily ever after in this fusion of child and adult states, where I am a secure child.

(Put on your big kid stuff)

But now I have a wife who may die if the doctor…

"Steinberg, we'll let you know," the commissioner said in abject nondisclosure. *I stared vacantly at this grown-up whom I needed to satisfy and please, so much in the character of…*

…my father! He appears to notice…yes, he's headed toward the locked library door! With curious and incredulous attention, he moves toward me, a flicker of rescue between my fatigued and frantic jumps. The door opens, and I can catch my breath. Time to gather myself. Composure is a new acquaintance, a foreigner with mysterious allure. Deliverance has strangely accelerated my descent into cool aplomb.

(Put on your big kid stuff)

I was just exploring. Nothing serious. I'm glad you came and opened the door, Dad, but you really didn't have to worry. I was just waiting for you to finish reading so we can…

"Sir! You can see your wife now." A call from the present pokes at my numbness. I have been sequestered in prayer, and the words pouring upon me about multiplying mutant cells clutter like so much dandruff outside a busy brain. In the doctor's presence, I studiously try to comprehend his scientific dribble about the nature of cancer. In my private Piagetian translation, I assimilate these technical words into the fabric of my existing thinking. *Repel the Philistines!* We are hostage negotiators (my mind tells me), and the terrorists hold my wife. (*Anything* to make this more human! But how can you combat *multiplying* terrorists?)

...be fruitful and increase in number...

It is *terrifying*!

(Put on your big kid stuff)

How can God let this happen? Surely he knows how much I need my wife, how much our children need their mother, how overwhelming is the olderness. HE MADE THE OLDERNESS!! (Better yet, in cosmic appeal) God *knows* the difference between good and bad cells...

He causes his sun to rise on the evil and the good, and sends rain on the righteous and the unrighteous.

The olderness engulfs me with its wicked ways. Heaven seems far away and inscrutable...

...because he is kind to the ungrateful and the wicked.

A tumor is eating my wife, and it's hard to make dinner conversation.

Jeremy has a problem that he finds difficult to discuss. This is understandable, and, without many words, the message gets across. He feels left out because he has not yet learned to ride a bicycle unassisted. Afternoons at the park hold the specter of his barely contained chagrin over this puerile insufficiency. The olderness has many weeds, and this day at the park may overgrow Jeremy's developing and precarious balance.

Teaching a child to bicycle offers rending and poetic similarities to the push-and-pull process of parenting toward independence. The child, of course, must learn balance and must eventually embark on solo operation. The parent must also balance support with letting go. Too little success will injure the child, both physically and motivationally. Too much support breeds resentment, a stifling dependence, and rebellious desire to break…

…away from the constraints and limits of riding within usual boundaries, I pedal ferociously down Sheridan Avenue, a familiar half-mile stretch of sidewalk whose every bump and crack I know as intimately as the contours of my own elementary body. This time, I would test the limits of kinesthetic knowledge and stretch physicality past its natural confines. Resisting the reflexive instinct to brake at the last building before the bottom of the hill on Sheridan, I choose instead to experience a climbing velocity. What a thrill it will be to whiz past the corner I have known only in the sobriety of cautious slow motion! Frozen by determination and the brisk fatalistic wind in my ears, I hunch over the handlebars, legs askew from the pedals, as I speed off the curb into the churning traffic. Fleeing the grasp of gravity and adult-imposed limits, I charge into the olderness, pursuing freedom and the Icarus of unencumbered flight.

He rebuked the Red Sea, and it dried up; he led them through the depths as through a desert.

The car screeches to an agonizing halt just inches from my involuntary swerve. Jerking the handlebars to the right at the last instant saves me from collision, but catapults me to a lacerating impact with the street as my bicycle abandons me. I lie bruised and dazed in the gutter, thankful to be alive, but wondering if the army of motorists may still harm me. In the fog of disbelief and encroaching pain, I stagger among onlookers to the safety of the curb. Feeling sheepish and guilty over my Mister Magoo–like caper, I retreat under the castigating gazes of the olderness. With some concessions to reality, I have again miraculously survived.

Remember, son: In traffic, if it's a tie, you lose.

He wavers precariously a few precious yards down the driveway; I hesitate for an eternal second before lunging from behind to grab Jeremy's bike, lest he tumble. I catch up with him, winded. Like some reverse rickshaw caricature, we plod forward: Jeremy oscillating the handlebars like a cornered sniper and I, thumping my feet as brakes. I am his breathless father, acting as training wheels, and we both know this cannot continue.

Gr-r-r-r-r!!! I can't do it…I'll never be able to do-o-o-o-o it, o-o-o-oh!!!…I am moved and mortified by this unabashed blend of despondency and whining complaint. I provide consolation and encouragement. Hesitantly, I reflect that the ripening of his skills will bring self-tests beyond my forbearance and awareness. There are stickers and thorns out there in the olderness. Tires deflate in the middle of nowhere, bicycles sometimes mysteriously steer their own courses, and no matter how hard the imagination may try (I learned), the bike can't fly.

Until he masters bicycling, Jeremy must find equilibrium with the crowd in some other manner. With his feelings as balance beams, he discovers the tilted scales taunting him in the olderness.

When the teasing gets out of hand and I am told about my children's merciless group escapades at the park, I question each of them about the heartless one-upmanship. I hold Neal to a higher standard of behavior because he is older. Hoping to spare Jeremy the ignominious spurning by a clan that includes his older brother, I emphasize for Neal the importance of setting a good example.

As we talk, Neal discloses his remorse over the teasing and his awareness of his role in rejecting others and perpetuating torment. I praise him for showing this side of himself, and I suggest that he might take the lead in sharing these feelings with the group of friends. He grimaces. "Nah, my friends would think I'm an imbecile if I talked about my feelings."

...a time to be silent and a time to speak...

I am shocked by this stark revelation. How I have underestimated the depth of my son's experience and his capacity to discern and tolerate the backlash of the olderness! He is struggling with the ageless dilemma of integrating the hunting instinct with emotional sentience. To cope, the tough veneer and cavalier put-down are unconsciously summoned to bind the affect and anxiety—by this common temptation, the olderness seduces wanderers to attack by machete. Then, the olderness redoubles its flora, enveloping its pilgrims in forests of emotional confusion. How can I lead him through this thicket, lest the fronds of the olderness camouflage traps and hinder his progress? My meditation deepens, and response is occluded by a choking memory of...

...dust swirling up from my feet stamping the batter's box in mock determination. I am a ten-year-old summer camp all-star. As a hedge against striking out, I crouch in protective anticipation, reducing the strike zone further. The umpire is college All-American athlete/camp counselor Stan; he is vending unwelcome field chatter. "Very little human being up at the plate. Tiny strike zone because he's so small. Hardly any batter." *I cringe crimson, wanting to swing at his head—"very little human being"—and I am weakened in the knees and about to cry. My hero has disparaged me. I am crushed and hopeless. My only recourse is to act tough and smash the ball way out into the olderness. But I am consumed with feeling! Where shall I cry out? My hero has forsaken me with his insolent banter. They would tease me and call me an imbecile if I expressed my distress. But I am human and have these strong feelings. Now, amid public disgrace, I am choking on this dust...*

...for he knows how we are formed, he remembers that we are dust.

(Put on your big kid stuff)

...and the dust returns to the ground it came from...

Recapitulation

As for a man, his days are like grass, he flourishes like a flower of the field; the wind blows over it and it is gone, and its place remembers it no more.

After forty-plus years surviving the olderness, I gaze longingly for a glimpse of milk and honey in the promised land. All I see, however, is milk and cereal, a messy breakfast before our sojourn to their promised land—a baseball field, site of my pledge to teach my boys, hopefully, some skills for flourishing in the olderness.

They will need body skills and interpersonal skills, mastery of some craft or trade to ply, a measure of faith, dogged persistence, humor, and a respect for the unexplained convolutions and dangers in the olderness. In their feisty youth, they experiment and compete exuberantly (often with each other), as they cut their teeth in multilayered preparation.

Be happy, young man, while you are young, and let your heart give you joy in the days of your youth...So then, banish anxiety from your heart and cast off the troubles of your body, for youth and vigor are meaningless.

As it always has, the olderness lies in surreptitious control, and sometimes, to gain advantage, my sons join forces and conspire…

…to play a trick on Grandma (World's Most Caring and Gullible Babysitter). I set the game plan with my brother. It goes like this: I'll perch on the windowsill, and you call Grandma in a panic. When she comes, tell her hysterically that I'm threatening to jump, but when she tries to come and grab me, hold her back. We'll both tell her that if she comes any closer I'll jump. She'll be hysterical, but she won't dare to rescue me. It'll be fun to see how she reacts, and besides, when we tell her that the only way to get me down is to give us extra dessert, she'll give in…

…to gain footholds with the most accessible generation. The olderness is so challenging, we are kept so often under the ruling thumb of mere survival that we forget to be…

...grateful! They got the mutant terrorists (for now; there are always more in the olderness, you know). My wife has healed, the threat repealed. *Whew...*

...heals all your diseases, who redeems your life from the pit and crowns you with love and compassion, who satisfies your desires with good things so that your youth is renewed like the eagle's.

My children sit on the couch, as we slump toward the previews of the next episode in a popular television series. They are captivated by the commercial drama and allurement for next week's viewing. Rapt and spellbound, they naïvely echo the ritualistic refrain, "Dad, is it to be continued?"

"Yes, it's to be continued."

"For how long, Dad?"

"Until the end of the season."

"But, why, Dad? Why, until the end of the season?"

"Because life goes on, children."

...from everlasting to everlasting...

Maybe, even past the end of the season.

There is a time for everything, and a season for every activity under heaven...

Ecclesiastes 1:9
What has been will be again, what has been done will be done again; there is nothing new under the sun.

Ecclesiastes 3:1
There is a time for everything, and a season for every activity under heaven...

Ecclesiastes 3:2
...a time to be born and a time to die...

Ecclesiastes 7:23–25
I am determined to be wise—but this is beyond me. Whatever wisdom may be, it is far off and most profound—who can discover it? So I turned my mind to understand, to investigate, and to search out the wisdom and scheme of things…

Ecclesiastes 8:1
Who is like the wise man? Who knows the explanation of things?

Ecclesiastes 11:9
Be happy, young man, while you are young, and let your heart give you joy in the days of your youth.

Ecclesiastes 11:10
So then, banish anxiety from your heart and cast off the troubles of your body, for youth and vigor are meaningless.

Ecclesiastes 11:1
Cast your bread upon the waters, for after many days you will find it again.

Psalm 103:3–5
…and heals all your diseases, who redeems your life from the pit and crowns you with love and compassion, who satisfies your desires with good things so that your youth is renewed like the eagle's.

Psalm 103:13
As a father has compassion on his children…

Psalm 103:14
…for he knows how we are formed, he remembers that we are dust.

Psalm 103:15–16
As for a man, his days are like grass, he flourishes like a flower of the field; the wind blows over it and it is gone, and its place remembers it no more.

Psalm 103:17
...from everlasting to everlasting...

Matthew 5:45
He causes his sun to rise on the evil and the good, and sends rain on the righteous and the unrighteous.

Luke 6:35
...because he is kind to the ungrateful and the wicked.

2004
Written when I resumed exercising and hired a personal trainer.

LEXISUCTION

Knocking Out the Pneuma

For those of you interested in human life-span development, I offer the latest in personal improvement. My fifty-one-year-old body (age and size-balanced) is rejuvenating with the aid of a personal trainer down at the athletic club. Twice a week, she punishes me for my gourmet indulgences with a circuit of weighted muscle repetitions and cardiovascular challenges designed to synapse my utterly ingrained neurological predilections. Though habit may be borne of repetition, I covet the pet name for my trainer as "Abacus." An attractive forty-two-year-old white woman of impeccable shape and condition, she seems, nevertheless, a bit pokey on the counting regimes. I, of course, an experienced wizard at the calculus of abdominal exercises, could only have developed these "abs of sausage" through geometric sleight-of-hand with the numbers. We all have talents, and I was always much better with numbers than with diets. And the discipline of "May I have a word with you?" developed both my relational skills and my vocabulary, not to mention the appellation and tissue tag of "thunder thighs." So, shortcuts and short ribs are my fortes.

Back to the regime: Though I fancy cardio as romantic interlude expressed, my trainer measures my devotion differently. She holds my wrist gently and persistently for pulse, as I sweat increasingly to please her. As we ascend into triple digits, I develop the hots—literally—and require a sortie to the water fountain.

As far as I can tell, there are no dirty old men at this health club. The dues are high enough to sustain the rampant infusion of chlorine in the water spas, and, so, the caucuses of aging arthritic mavens exchanging economic wits and waning testosterone around the severe machines are carcass-clean.

One of the Jack LaLanne types notices the blotches on my trainer's skin and feels compelled to comment upon and detract from her near-perfect image. She explains that she has a disease called scleroderma. She turns her intense eyes upon me as if in reprimand for my predictably scurrilous and sneaky slowdown in reps while she defends herself against any misinterpretation that she might be the victim of abuse.

"No, those are not bruises," she explains to the elder inquirer. "They're an occasional symptom of a medical condition called scleroderma.

"Hey!" I exclaim, as we return to our enclaved duo-dance around the weight machines. "I'm the one being abused!"

She laughs, never slowing from the tug on her invisible leash. I follow her around the cavernous weight room like a circus puppy. If only she would command me to lie down. Instead, she hands me a set of barbells and challenges me to defy gravity fifteen times once again, as she watches me sweat to earn her smile.

I tell her, "I didn't even notice those skin blotches until he said something. What I notice about you is that you're sprightly. That's what you project."

"Thanks," she responds. "I'll have to look up that word, but it sounds like a compliment."

"Yes, it is," I murmur, hoping this will win me some points and slow down the merciless depletion of my energy. She moves ahead with my next contortion, and I must continue to expunge calories as I strive for conversation and distraction.

"I'm thinking of having lexisuction." She bites at this gambit.

"What?"

"You know, that procedure where they suck the puffy words out of you."

She watches me.

"They remove the large deposits of inflated vocabulary, so you shrink in size." I clasp my love handles with a poker face. "For instance, after the procedure, 'adipose' becomes 'fat'—get it? Smaller..."

She smiles wryly and puckers her cheeks. She reeks of corporeal confidence, her college degree in exercise physiology enhancing her allure and my respect. "I didn't know that vocabulary was stored that low in the body." Smirk.

"Well, haven't you ever met anyone with his head in his ass? It's a great stretch and wonderful for the figure of speech, too." Smirk back. Touché!

She laughs, tosses her hair back, and I feel enthralled and inferior. Such is the fate of one who uses too much butter and words like "spavined" and "limmer" and "susurration" in the course of discourse. Part of my childhood trauma was discovering that not everybody enjoyed reading the dictionary. While the others read comics and watched cartoons, I stuffed myself with three- and four-syllable words. Rehearsing for spelling bees and buffets, I ingested more than letters. I loved words, and I could always see them dancing before me, waiting for my firm embrace in capture of their order and articulation. My tongue became a hunter, searching for meaning, seeking to suck the semantics out of new prey. I pounced and pronounced, articulating here, turning phrases there, hoarding new words for the inevitable occasions when I would immobilize my audience with top-shelf lexis. Words were my survival weapons. Is it any wonder that the years had helped me amass a storage system? Ah, but am I weighted down by excess in the mind as well as in the body?

I proselytize mental fitness, so ought I not trim my speech to measure correctly to the situation? The Bible says it's not what goes into a man's mouth that makes him clean or unclean; it's what comes out of it. I point this out to my svelte trainer-priestess after her confessional demand for my food intake over the last twenty-four hours. She motions to the treadmill and mentions that I can read a thesaurus while I work out on it.

If we are what we eat, I must lay off the fruitcake.

Now we are sitting on the edges of benches, and she is modeling stretches that look so inviting. When I try them, I can lift only some parts of my body. (Dictionaries and encyclopedias are heavy. So are cookbooks. They chronicle many meals.) The stretches are so easy for her; she could balance on a tennis ball. This is embarrassing and uncomfortable for me, coaxing my body through space and half a century of time, muscling up in defiance of gravity, and ever on the alert for those weapons of ass destruction, bleachers and straight-backed chairs. I am posturally challenged, flexibly impaired, and definitely a disadvantaged leaner.

I will have to do the lexisuction soon, for I cannot work much harder at this. Despite my athletic history and my stubborn willpower, time and gravity are winning. The hardbodies around me taunt through self-absorbed grimaces and grunts and reflections of flat midriffs in a landscape of spandex. That memory fades and jades with age is not so bad, considering that youth has no memory at all. Youth does generally have good humor, and you can make young people laugh by reminding them that eventually they will look like you.

Irony is neither compensation nor consolation for my excesses, and I do need a strategy. Our society *pounds* us regularly with quick bytes and bites, so the words are short, the portions long, and the message is to consume more. Personal responsibility notwithstanding, I am not immune. I get it—including the commercial messages. Gravity and selfishness practice together, and I grow lazier. Somehow, I must cut down on what goes in and out of my mouth.

In the short-term, perhaps abbreviation is the answer. Radical vowel bypass, period. Eat less, say less, spell less, don't inflate with fancy foods, wide-mouthed portions, or those vowels that stretch your lips and use up so much oxygen.

This might make me more like others, physically and linguistically. Not that I need it, but I might be spared distinction from the spelling-impaired. Kierkegaard said, "The society that exalts philosophy but scorns plumbing will have both bad philosophy and bad plumbing."

I say, "The society that exalts fast food and sports heroes but scorns spelling and good language will have bad fast food and sports heroes and bad spelling and language."

If I do push this lexisuction idea, perhaps the food industry will reduce its preposterous addictive inflation and the sports industry will stop flogging us with models unachievable.

In the meantime, I had better abbreviate my philosophy and my exercise, and go grab some lunch. I just hope I can find a comfortable chair.

2003
Written after a visit to my mother, whose stroke had left her with aphasia.

IT'S JUST APHASIA GOING THROUGH

Some Life Passages Cannot Find Words

Recovering from her strokes and the death of my father, Mom is doing rather well. She has gradually adjusted to certain life limitations in her eighth decade, and is finding her way around obstacles and through the help of friends, gadgets, and her own ingenuity and perseverance. She is the center of attention among our family and group-of-friends connections, and she invokes Dad's presence through her memories, conversations, and consultations with him, past and present.

"Daniel, why did you have to leave me?" she complains in front of the portrait of him she painted. "We were having such a good argument!" My father's smile shimmers unwaveringly from the canvas, frozen in time, yet iridescent with the climate of expressions we knew from weathered experience with him.

"There's so much to do," Mom continues. "You hardly helped me then, and now you're not here to help at all." After a poignant pause, Mom looks toward me and, with moist sclera, says wistfully, "Dad would have liked that movie we saw. He was always complaining about the lack of good movies. Hmm..."

She speaks of Dad in the past and in the present, the former appropriate and the latter understandable. There is no future for my father, and this reality is so bruisingly tangible as we sit in her kitchen the day before the "unveiling," a religious ceremony we will hold at the cemetery, six months after his death. It is the occasion of my visit. Mom's transition to a life without him is gradual, and I notice her upswing when she talks about things in the future—plans for a visit, buying something for the house, selling her paintings, and, of late, her project to bring hot coffee to the senior center.

She looks forward to her time at the senior center and appreciates the services provided and the opportunities for interchange with people. Abashedly, she confides in me her "fussy" desire for hot coffee, thus far absent at the senior center. Mom decided to take action on her own to remedy the situation. She called local stores to locate an item featured in a newspaper ad she clipped. An ideal solution for her need, this item was called the "Vacuum Flask" thermos, offered by the Signatures Company, out of Perris, California.

Unfortunately, several strokes have left my mother with more than her share of senior challenges in word recall. This came into play when she called the local Walgreen's and asked if they had vacuums on sale. She had forgotten the word "thermos."

"Vacuums?" intoned the clerk. "I don't think we sell vacuums. You lookin' for a big vacuum or a small one?"

"A small one," said my mom, "for coffee."

"Coffee?"

"Yeah, you know, to keep coffee warm."

"Ma'am, I don't know whatchu want, but we don't have anything like that."

Undaunted, my mother called the Target store.

"Hello, I'm looking for a vacuum, a small one."

"How small, ma'am?"

"One I can sit with in my lap."

"In your *LAP*?"

"Yes," my mother continued, "to hold in my lap."

"Why you want to hold a vacuum in your lap?"

Frustration lapped at her patience, as my mother answered this doltish inquiry:

"So I can drink from it."

"You want to drink from a vacuum?"

"Yes, haven't you ever used a vacuum to keep coffee warm?"

"I-I-I don't think I can help you. Maybe you should call Sears." Click.

Next…

"Hello, I'm interested in a vacuum."

Silence. "Appliances, may I help you?"

"Yes, I need a vacuum, please."

"An upright or one with attachments?"

"Well, I'm not sure," Mom faltered. "What kind of attachments?"

"Suction hoses, wide hard bristles," came the reply.

"I don't think so. That might hurt my dentures."

"Excuse me?"

Confusion engulfed Mom, as the salesman questioned impetuously. She was not used to such obstacles in purchasing an ordinary item. Mom was always an excellent communicator, a savvy consumer, and competent at getting things done.

"What do you want to use this vacuum for?"

"For liquids."

"Ah, so you want a wet vac?"

"Look, mister, I don't know what's so complicated. I just want a vacuum for hot or cold liquids, like coffee or iced tea," declared Mom.

"How much liquid?"

"A cup, maybe two."

"Ma'am, couldn't you just use a sponge?"

Mom hadn't thought of this—wouldn't think of this—sponges, suction hoses…What had this world come to? It was bad enough that she sometimes became confused and forgot what she meant to say. Now the personnel at stores were unable to help her with simple commodities!

She quit haggling with store personnel, and chose instead to wait for her mail-order "Vacuum Flask" to arrive from Perris, California. In the meantime, she would tolerate the tepid and insipid coffee offered at the senior center along with their generous human services. More pressing at the moment were her plans for my father's unveiling and her increasing anxiety about the event.

This Sunday would bring far-flung family members and some close friends together in a temporary ad-hoc support group in honor of my father—kind of like an all-star squad or an Olympic "Dream Team" of personal relations. Only with relatives, you never know: "Dream Team" sometimes is more like "Bad Dream Team." As my father used to say, "Relatives are like fish: after a few days, they begin to smell." This was a ceremony to honor my father, yet all in the family were ambivalently fond and fearful of him. When people die, they still exert power and influence. This is scary for what it says about them and us. It was hard to think of my dad without entertaining his probable sarcastic contribution to any topic at hand. His memory lives in quotes, italicized comments, double entendres, and put-downs. He is available to those who knew him at almost any moment in the merry-go-round of daily life. Now, he would again take center stage, briefly, smelling perhaps, the relatives standing above him, praying and catching a fragrance of his wit and devotion in the humid Florida air.

When I asked, Mom confided in me her worry about proceedings at the unveiling. She fretted obsessively about preparations at the restaurant where we would head from the cemetery. Would they have enough tables? What if fewer people showed up than she had planned? Aunt Lu called to say she *might* be able to get to the cemetery, but certainly not the restaurant, because Uncle Hy (my mother's brother) was close to death, tethered to an oxygen tank. And, how many people could John David transport in his car? Did everyone know directions?

Though I suspected that Mom had troubling emotions beyond the logistics anxieties, she was open to getting rid of the ones she mentioned. I treated her with TFT (Thought

Field Therapy), and her nervous fretting disappeared. When I subsequently asked her how she felt, she replied, "Well I'm not thinking about the situation, so I guess I must be better and rid of the problem," proving, once again, that logic is developmentally more evolved than the apex problem! My mother has been through several TFT treatments, and she gets it—not only about the treatment efficacy, but about our human preoccupation with having a "story line" that fits our mold of reality (and our place in it) and our tendency to fester in distress and helplessness because of problems due to perceived external circumstances.

My mother is easy to treat and even easier to love. Whenever I complete a treatment with her, it ends with the following:

Me: "How do you feel now?"

Mom: "Fine, I feel fine."

Me: "Is *anything* bothering you right at this moment?"

Mom: "No, I feel good."

Me: "Are you still Jewish?"

Moments of such poignancy could not be staged without the backdrop of our character quirks and history; even then, they are usually unrehearsed. These moments arrive in the garb of good-natured ridicule and proverbial punch lines, and we learn to cherish their sweet punctuation upon the striving and suffering sentences of our lives. Words give them voice, yet their timing and impact are ineffable. A good time, a memorable moment—*how long does it last?*

Thermos. Mom chuckled as she repeated the word. As if drumming it into the humor lobes will preempt future casualties of memory. She had called my brother in the midst of her purchasing debacle, and he had gently supplied her with the lost word. *Thermos, Mom, you want a thermos. Oh, that's right, and thank you.*

Thank you, not only for the missing word and closure, but for another family legacy, destined for the intrigues of the Steinberg Survival Guide. There are words for the containers that hold hot and cold liquids and words for those that whisk away the dusty dirt we wish to hide, but there are no adequate words to describe the containers that hold the delicious metamorsels of ironic experience.

Listening to my mother's story had left me speechless. I could hardly contain myself. My pride in Mom swelled, as did my gratefulness that her recovery had regained faculties of mind and humor enough that she could recount the thermos/vacuum story. I looked at the newspaper clipping of the "Vacuum Flask" thermos and marveled at this story my mother told as I drank my good cup of coffee. This was better than Abbott and Costello.

The next day we headed to the cemetery. I secretly prayed that it would go well for my mom. In a fleeting moment, a thought surprised me: this occasion was for me, too. It would likely be an emotional rendezvous with my father. He always had to have the last word in life, and he prepared us for his death by regular admonitions about how it would be too late posthumously to enjoy the times we weren't enjoying with him while he was alive. The words and logic are peculiar, but that epitomized my father. He was right, too, for a scant few months after his departure, we regard him ambivalently, honoring him as though he were here, yet reiterating his absence. We reminisce about his marked idiosyncrasies and speak of how he would react to situations as if he were present—yet, we privately bask in the security that he is not here to dominate and chastise us. He's not around to hear all the things I want to tell him that I couldn't tell him when he was alive because he wouldn't listen. Dad was always right, even about this—a reflection that made my head swim, as we headed for the grave site. What would I say to my father in summary? Do he and eternity listen?

The plot thickened—at the cemetery. First of all, my father's grave looked different. The last time I'd seen it, we were lowering his casket into the ground. Now there was a headstone, a marker for him differentiated only by his engraving. In Steinberg tradition, a story secretes behind this plump groundswell with the fabric waiting to be unveiled with prayer. My father, we recall, was always fussy about salutation. Once a doctor, always a doctor, he decreed. An easy way to incense him was to address him as "Mister" Steinberg. It was *Dr.* Steinberg, or you invited him to pull out your teeth (and, remember, that a retired dentist was under no obligation!). The headstone engravers had foolishly omitted his middle initial. So, the stone had to be replaced with one bearing the middle initial *J*, for it is Daniel *Jacob* Steinberg, in truth, who lies beneath this ground.

We stood gathered in prayer and remembrance. I felt moved and quite uncomfortable. A tear streamed in quiet lonely slalom down my cheek, and I couldn't wipe it or tap it away. I escaped into my schizoid internal poetry:

A casket, a flask it
Is just a body basket,
Contains a body dead to hold
The liquids once warm, now grown cold
Vacuum in which life grows old,
We all fall down.

The rabbi finished, arcing his arm and complaining about an injury that might curtail his racquetball side career. Back to life and the mundane concerns of protocol. For we, above ground, have stomachs that need to hold hot and cold liquids. And my mother had prepared for this occasion by placing reservations at a restaurant.

The Florida sun framed portraits of antiquity, as the aging character of my family came into view. The relatives I hadn't seen in a quarter century looked much as I would expect, had I been able to conjure up their images. They had more wrinkles, as did the development of our individual lives. It seemed odd to notice how they had aged, because, around them, I could never outgrow feeling like a child.

Time flies like an arrow. New York flies like a Florida brunch. So we gathered at the deli. Cousin Melvin, whom my mother hadn't seen since she helped him out when he was in high school, was a garrulous and vibrant man. Trying earnestly to catch up on family ties and ingratiate himself with the clan, Melvin wasn't too clear on the rosters, and the faces of our heritage were not etched finely in his memory. He mistook me for Uncle Hy's son.

"So, how is your dad?" he intoned solicitously in a gratuitous attempt to express concern for my uncle who wavered absently near death with his oxygen tank. This social faux pas was irrevocable, as my family members watched in horror to witness my reaction. Poor Melvin had dug himself a relative grave of misplaced identity.

"He's…resting," I responded with sober sensitivity, hiding my disbelief at how well Melvin exemplified the brazen social calumny that qualified him as a true member of my family.

The muffled snickers yielded to the familiar and familial revelry of a loud and ethnic delicatessen brunch. Amid much chitchat, there was hardly anything left to say. My mother conducted herself with aplomb, gratitude, and elegance. My father's honor was preserved. Dignity prevailed all the way around, as family members kept grievances, complaints, and *kvetching* tendencies to themselves.

Aging brings an unmistakable mixture of pride and humility. We're proud that we are still around; yet we exist with the incipient scars and lurking awareness that, sooner or later, we are next. And, we have nothing much to say about it. After all, it's just aphasia going through.

2006
Written after a scolding from my spa maintenance man.

CHEMICAL ABUSE

J'accuzi moi pour l'addiction et l'addition

I am a chemical abuser. I know this because my spa repairman told me. It came as a shock—no, not the kind of chemical shock you put in your spa to cleanse it, but an emotional shock when I realized he is right. My secret is out in the open—actually, in the yard—and there is little I can do about it. My chemical of choice is perfectly legal, and it's not sold in bars or drugstores, but, rather in pool-supply stores. My chemical problem is…well, chlorine.

Chlorine?

Yes, I am a chlorine abuser. I put too much of it, too frequently, in my spa. I claim the innocent motive of wanting cleanliness, an aromatic euphoria, the ability to succumb to what might be called artificially induced relaxation. Whereas some people might seek to allay anxiety, my nemesis is *algae.*

Marvin, the spa guy, is here to do an intervention. He really puts the screws to it, and I mean literally. The spa doesn't work, and the culprit is a faulty heat exchanger. Actually, as Marvin would tell it, the culprit is me.

"But I just paid you hundreds of dollars to put in a new heat exchanger less than six months ago!" I clamor plaintively. Marvin remains unruffled. I've heard him irritated when he didn't know I was listening; he can be as disdainful as the rest of us about the customers we serve, thinking them (me) stupid simply because lack of knowledge or bad habits require the services of pros. Well, I'm a suburban softy, unable to manipulate a tool or fix anything mechanical, my hands smooth and soothed when I can soak them in a working spa, my body a pampered float.

Not today, however. Marvin explains unemotionally that my spa bears the telltale signs of chemical abuse. Like a physician discussing liver function, Marvin rambles on about the decrepit degradation I cause by my habit. I feel the turgid conflict between shame and angry resentment. My mood turns to one of frustration and despair. *What if Marvin is right?* Could I be haplessly, wantonly poisoning my beloved spa, denigrating and decimating the innards upon which I rely to cleanse, refresh, and heal me?

Perhaps, after all, I *am* an addict. I do love sloshing into the warming drink, a chemicalized liquid that drains my pain. The pulsating jets are my mosh pit, thrusting me among the pressurized waves of recreation and carefree repose. Candidly, I do experience withdrawal: whenever I travel, I seek out my addiction at health clubs, else I miss the warm, necessary, accustomed relief and, thereby, suffer pain. I'm drawn to the communal public happy hour, shamelessly shared naked, no less. My excuse is that my back hurts, as though I have a monkey on it—and I do!

Marvin is unflappable as he shakes his head in disapproval at my abuse of crack chlorine.

"You have to learn to stop reaching for the little white crystals—as if they will solve your problem," he intones.

"But, Marvin," I plead, "what do I do when the spa *stinks*?"

Marvin offers no answers that satisfy, no weight-watchers scale to measure out the portions. He simply advises moderation.

"Use less," he advises plainly.

I am aghast. This is a Jones I've faced for years, a problem I've failed to surmount.

"Wh-what do other spa owners do," I stammer, "when the spa smells and the algae anxiety hits?"

I am expectant, supplicant, that perhaps he will relieve me, release me from my dilemma. But Marvin just picks up his tools and calmly shakes his head.

"You need to go easy on the white rocks. It's getting to be a costly habit. You're eroding and ruining your spa."

Spaseebo. (Russian for thank you.)

Without any flourish, he just walks away. What recourse do I have? Cognitive therapy—Shall I rehearse in reframing the problem? *Sure, it stinks, but this is just nature's way of balancing the environment. After all, you're recycling nitrogen—just relax.*

Perhaps a medicinal cure—decongestants?

No-oo-oo! I could even do group therapy—there is room in my spa…but we need the white crystals to make it refreshing. I am chemically dependent! My recovery depends on a fix—from the repairman.

I need Marvin—he is my liaison, after all, to the dealer, the resource to supply the parts to get my spa working again. I *need* him. Despite his admonition and my self-remonstration that I am a mature professional who does not have to succumb to the lectures of the spa repairman, I know that the craving will return. When I lift the cover and that murky mildew soup stench wafts up, that primordial smell of microorganisms—a pox on literature, elegant food, and sexy perfume—then, I am at the mercy of my algae angst. In a mindless swirl of aquaddiction, I reflexively reach for the potion to quell the swill.

I will administer the therapy by tapping—a few gentle taps on the chlorine bottle—and, very quickly, the gaseous elixir will erase the miasma.

So, I remain a chemical abuser. *Je n'accuse pas de personne, mais J'accuse seulement moi et le Jacuzzi.*

1994
This story occurred in my dream one night in 1994 in Minneapolis, the night before I delivered a professional presentation. The dream occurred in French. I later translated it into English (mostly).

QUELQUECHOSE POUR RIEN:

L'Histoire du Restaurant Francais Albert

(Something for Nothing:
The Story of Albert's French Restaurant)

About a generation ago, there was a fellow growing up in New York who was very much enamored of the activities and adventures available in this grand and endless city run by adults.

Along with his natural curiosity and enjoyment of pleasure, he was energetic, self-motivated, and attracted to people, places, and happenings that made him feel grown up. In fact, Nayeev (which was his name) possessed the idea that childhood was a kind of prison sentence that was lifted when you proved that you could do things well enough on your own, and when your body, voice, manner, words, air of confidence, and dress convinced the adults that you were worthy of serious consideration and inclusion. Of course, Nature (with whom Nayeev had a love/hate relationship) controlled much of his progress in these developments, but Nayeev figured he could help things along by virtue of his own determination and practice. Besides, Nature had given him a little head start; his maturation included advantages like having body hair at a relatively early age and knowing the meaning of fancy words like "precocious."

So, Nayeev's quest for maturity and independence geared him to look for the truths that would unlock him from the limitations and vulnerabilities of childhood. His parents also wanted him to grow up, and they, too, went about the business of showing Nayeev what life was all about, as they knew it. Naturally, their perspective was different from Nayeev's; for example, his mother, who was a teacher, cultivated a rewarding career out of telling people what they didn't know and showing them how well she could do those things. She was outstandingly well intentioned. Nayeev admired her ability and basked in her love and affection; however, it was hard for Nayeev to participate, learn, and try things while his mother was running the show. He reveled with her in descriptions and testimony about his impending stature as an independent adult, but inwardly, Nayeev suspected he would have to secede from his family in order to realize those desires.

Auspiciously, Nayeev had two loving and omnipresent parents. As a male, he looked to his father for an admixture of direction, advice, permission, acceptance, and example. Although his father was responsible and kind, for Nayeev he was an enigma who complicated life with a frustrating combination of self-sufficiency and avoidance. He knew so much, yet did so little—a kind of New York Zen approach to life. Nayeev envied his father's keys to independence, and he longed for an early parole.

His father, who was a dentist, often contradicted himself and spoke in riddles. He would ask people to please shut their mouths and open their mouths. He told Nayeev that his problems came from being backward—his feet smelled and his nose ran. His father had other peculiar forms of expression, such as the bumper sticker on the old car, which read, "I was born at night, but not *last* night." In New York, such as it was, these expressions were not deemed particularly offensive. Like many in his generation, Nayeev's father had ambitions, which were pursued diligently when circumstances permitted. One of his ambitions was to get a parking space directly in front of the apartment building in which they lived. Alternate-side-of-the-street parking made leaving your car in the same space for more than a day very costly in terms of fines. There was avid competition for parking, and Nayeev's father had neither the time nor patience to play musical cars. So the family car was parked in a garage two miles away. Whenever the family went for a drive (usually on weekends), Nayeev had to accompany his father on walks to and from the garage. It was during these forays that Nayeev's father imparted much of what wisdom he could to Nayeev.

Not surprisingly, Nayeev tried to take the subway on weekends whenever he could (without his parents) into Manhattan to do grown-up things—these were opportunities to show off his wisdom and, invariably, to glean useful additional tidbits of worldliness. One of his favorite pastimes was eating in restaurants. Dining out was a wonderful activity that suited several of Nayeev's important needs. First, he loved to eat, and he had a voracious appetite. Nayeev was an active, athletic adolescent who exercised vigorously. From his muscular body, you could never tell that he had a hollow leg until you saw how much he ate. Second, eating was something that had to be done regularly anyway, and there were many, many restaurants of every price, flavor, quality, and style in New York. Third, food had always been very important in Nayeev's family and culture; appetites, attitudes, idiosyncrasies, and behaviors involving food had assumed the status of ritualistic fetish within the family. Fourth, food acquisition was a rather strategic operation for Nayeev's parents, and these survival skills were passed along through the generations. Nayeev's mother religiously devoted herself to the preparation of traditional foods, even those in which family members did not have much interest. There was never a shortage of protein or preservatives at her table. She bore a legendary reputation for winning arguments against butchers and grocers; her tongue was sharper than their knives. Nayeev's father was a temperate man, imbued with the talent and experience of endurance eating. (Undoubtedly, the family lineage contained adept hunters and gatherers; however, evolution produced interesting variants of this behavior in contemporary New York City.) The dentist was a master at the buffet table, blithely passing the initial salads, indifferently appraising the appetizers, jousting judiciously with the Jell-O, haggling half-heartedly with potatoes or pasta, engaging numerous entrées, and *always* reserving room for dessert. Through years of festive celebrations, Nayeev studied his father's techniques until he, too, could take whatever was dished out, slicing through the gauntlet of caloric opposition. Endurance eating was a manly sport of quiet and thrifty determination, requiring steadfast practice at resplendent feasts and mealtime leftovers alike.

Following in his father's image, Nayeev resolved to grow out of the "big eyes," about which his father taunted him, and to seek and find and know "what good is"—as the dentist used to say. In matters of the mouth, his parents knew! Nayeev could tolerate many an insult, but he could neither bear nor parry the accusation of not knowing what good is.

With this background, Nayeev's sojourns from the household usually involved taking the D subway train in search of worthy places to eat. Indeed, Nayeev prepared, compared, and compiled his experiences into a personal teenage restaurant guide for New York City. It was this fastidiousness that led him to discover Albert's French Restaurant.

The *Village Voice* newspaper featured an ad touting Albert's French Restaurant as Greenwich Village's oldest landmark. Nayeev noticed the Eiffel Tower logo and the bold print proclaiming **All the Steak You Can Eat** for the modest price of $5.95. (Even a generation ago, this was a good deal.) Flooded with saliva and insight, Nayeev perceived immediately the advantages of an excursion to Albert's. He could savor tasty food, eat much of it (after all, adolescents usually have more appetite than money), flaunt his savoir faire in a place of ambiance, heartily relish in his private knowledge of what good is, and—who knows—perhaps meet interesting people. With certainty, Nayeev anticipated impressing Albert's French staff with the number of steaks he could elegantly consume, all for $5.95! Plus a generous tip, of course, which was a vital punctuation to his message that adolescents like he ought to be welcomed at such adult establishments. Nayeev knew from experience that he would enjoy dessert following however many steaks he could devour; he gloated in his expectation of amazement on the waiter's face. Although he was anxious to get away from his parents, he was comforted by the pride his father would take in Nayeev's gustatory conquest. At $5.95 plus, this would be a steal...*Allez à l'Albert's! Quelquechose pour rien, enfin!*

Subways had long been an ambivalent womb for Nayeev. He loved the subterranean security, the familiar rocking as the train barreled down the canal, rebirthing him into the stunning stimulation of Manhattan. After tiring forays, the subways rescued him, whisking him back to his "boroughed" nest in the Bronx. There was another aspect to the subways, one that poked at Nayeev with sharp labor pains: crowded lives competing for space, air, and comfortable position. Subways could be used for freedom, anonymity, and mobility; alternatively, they were traps—labyrinthine tunnels for the tunnel-visioned commuters who roamed the mazes between office and apartment like well-trained rodents...the treadmills and mazes of New York life. Many evenings, Nayeev had kept himself awake with prayers and oaths that he would escape the subway destiny. He steeled himself against adversity, and avoided the impingement of urban blight and filth by telling himself it was all temporary—his passage on these trains was limited by contempt for the mindless conformity, the anomie, the smell of urine wafting shamelessly, a crass public transportation aftershave.

Knowing that his dues-paying efforts and thrusts toward maturity would eventually bring suburban rewards, Nayeev savored the liberty offered by the dirty rambling train as he rode downtown toward Albert's French Restaurant. He was hungry! His appetite for good food was vast, and for gratifying experience it was almost insatiable. Albert's would be perfect! *C'ést magnifique.* A hospitable place to practice etiquette and to exercise his French and his mandibles. As he fumbled his fingers over the *Village Voice* ad in his pocket (no doubt wrinkling the Eiffel Tower), Nayeev visualized the dining room with waiters bustling by; he imagined the feel of soft, pliant linen draping his lap as he strained alertly to translate the brisk and melodic French lyrics dancing in the background. Nayeev anticipated that when the romance he believed to be his birthright arrived, it would dress often in linen and candlelight, ornamenting its sensory splendor with mood music and rich sauces. He could picture a gelatinous steak stretching impudently across a modest-size plate showing pastels of impressionist hand-painting. As his stomach rumbled in rhythm with the subway racket, Nayeev succumbed to the warm image of onion soup submerged under an avalanche of Gruyère. Ah, the comforting expectation of Gruyère, crisply tanned and taut, beckoning to be tongued, as it stretched long, sinuous limbs of aromatic ecstasy over flavorful, warm fluid. Nourished by his fancy, Nayeev brushed past the sideshow of cheap snack stands littering the station and emerged from the windswept roar of the subway.

Greenwich Village teemed with activity. At first encounter, the quaint and smaller architecture struck Nayeev as handsomely artificial—as though he had entered a dollhouse world where the more petite scale of the streets and buildings made people seem to move even faster. Suppressing the din of a distant jackhammer, car horns blared aggressively, accosting pedestrians at every turn. Nayeev had often wondered how New Yorkers could walk so fast, since everybody seemed boxed in by other people and cars. Manhattan had the feel of an amusement park designed by Rod Serling before he settled into *The Twilight Zone.* Nayeev imagined the streets as boardwalks, shuttling the crowds in ricochet among dangerous vehicles and all varieties of esoteric displays, hidden in their mysteries behind narrow entrances and exorbitant prices. Amid so much entrancing stimulation, one could easily notice nothing and blend impassively into this predatory metropolis. Inured and desensitized, New Yorkers swarmed in solitary vigilance, coveting avaricious and paranoid fantasies behind gruff and formidable miens. New Yorkers invariably thought fast and acted defensively and acquisitively. Nayeev was used to this; he was one of them. In this pullulating culture where possessions were dear and expenses outrageous, everyone looked out for a deal. The hustle was everywhere; those on the move and those on guard veiled a common motivation: anticipate something for nothing. *Quelquechose pour rien, monsieur!*

Surrounded by stifling anonymity, Nayeev could relax and revel in the sheer expanse of his opportunities in Manhattan. He felt at home in the Village. Its diversity and indifference allowed him to feel purposeful, autonomous, even artistic in his pursuit of riper versions of what good is. Nayeev hurried toward Albert's, and he unobtrusively descended the stairs to the half-basement entrance. Once inside, he waited tensely for recognition and seating. Such moments were excruciating. The glint of first acknowledgment by the proprietor would communicate instantly whether he was accepted as a customer or subjected to hostile dismissal, the fate of all assumed restroom invaders. Potty was tough in New York. Nowhere in the world were things more expensive, including waste. Biological relief was restricted to paying customers. It was as if business owners had collectively, and with the support of the NRA (National Restroom Association), lobbied some unofficial ordinance into the New York City Sanitary Code:

> No person shall relieve himself of biological material in any building or commercial establishment selling to the public or offering for purchase or consumption any goods or services, overpriced or otherwise, unless such person has made a financial transaction sufficient for the proprietor to recover the costs of maintaining said facilities. It is illegal for any person (blood relatives exempted) to excrete in any public or commercial property without expressed consent of the owner and substantial profit to the establishment thereof, with the exception of the subways, which are deemed unrestricted by the sanitary provisions of this code. Penalties for violation include, but are not limited to, harsh eviction from said premises, hostile stalking and humiliation, and punishment by incarceration for up to seven days in a NYC Transit Authority lavatory.

Relieved over passing inspection by the maître d'hôtel, despite a stiff, almost disgruntled greeting, Nayeev followed obsequiously to his table.

A hunky-looking waiter shuffled to Nayeev's table; almost reluctantly, feigning great effort, he mumbled, "Bonjour, my name is Jock." Somewhat startled, Nayeev echoed, "Jock, er, Jacques?" The waiter shot back, "Yeah, dat's right, 'Szzhock'… what can I get ya?" Nayeev detected the unmistakably distasteful New Yawk accent. It sounded rather tweedy *en francais.*

After a briefly obliging glance at the menu, Nayeev smiled triumphantly at the waiter. He had rehearsed his order many times before arriving at Albert's. Hesitating momentarily, Nayeev decided to place his order in English. No need to invite annoyance from an obviously disinclined waiter. "I'd like French onion soup, and the New York steak, please, medium. No potatoes, please." Bearing the burden of an unusual allergy to potatoes and its peculiar social stigma, Nayeev resigned himself to the raised eyebrows and irritatingly repetitive questions elicited by his routine inquiries about the presence of potatoes in the recipe and his need to avoid them. This *garçon* did not react. He merely finished writing on his pad and brusquely walked away.

Something was odd: after a few minutes of unnerving self-consciousness, Nayeev noticed the casual touching among the waiters. They seemed to linger around each other, paying only secondary attention to their tables. Each of them was quite muscular, and the coquettish French outfits accentuated more discomfiting incongruity. Nayeev knew the telltale signs of weightlifters, and these "guys" obviously worked out. Less familiar with the rituals and flirtations of homosexuals, he nevertheless quickly awakened to the parody of Albert's French Restaurant. Evocative memories surfaced of his father's reaction to blatantly gay affectation. The dentist would wink and snicker, "I think he can be had." As if this pronouncement were some wise conquest of perception or potentiality…Nayeev certainly did not want to "have" or "be had." Absorbed in the pursuit of "what good is," he had come upon a disconcerting twist. It would be difficult to impress the staff at Albert's with his sophistication and maturity, and the risks were—

Interrupted in his musings by the appearance of the waiter with his food, Nayeev mumbled a weak appreciative thanks. Adult realities were encroaching, just as his stomach begged more stridently for attention. Nayeev decided to focus on eating and to make the best of a delicate situation. The steak was small but appetizing, and Nayeev began his work with gusto. Several bites into his meal, however, Nayeev reluctantly realized that this was below his standards for what good is. He wondered what his father would think of *biftek Albert* as he decidedly masticated the remains of his first steak. Invoking his father's tacit mental encouragement, Nayeev beckoned for the waiter.

"I'm ready for another steak, *monsieur.*"

Hovering above Nayeev, the waiter remained immobile for a seeming eternity. The tense paralysis ended when he stiffly removed Nayeev's plate. Silently, with obvious disinterest and a haughty, stoic air, the waiter strutted into the kitchen.

It was nearly twenty minutes later that "Jock" returned with a second steak. Nayeev's startled reaction curled the waiter's lips into the tiniest of sarcastic smiles as he receded from the table, leaving Nayeev to contemplate a pathetically tiny and shriveled steak. Feeling duped, Nayeev nonetheless embarked on the shameful task of getting his money's worth. This second helping had little edible surface. Inwardly aghast at his fortune, Nayeev debated with himself about sending the steak back, but decided not to make a scene. Beneath his indignation, Nayeev relented to the possibility that this was a fluke not worth fussing over. Besides, he would soon be done with this morsel and ready for a third and juicier rendition.

Nayeev's self-consciousness raced his mind toward new absurdities of fantasy. He stabbed half-heartedly at his gristly steak, peering with cross-eyed surreptitiousness the coterie of waiters ogling him. Nayeev the Ripper attacking a poor, fatty, defenseless steak! Nayeev felt guilty and simultaneously sheepish and angry about so ridiculous a phantom accusation. His paranoia heightened by the tacit attention of the waiters, Nayeev imagined himself the nightly feature on the Gay News Channel: *Borough boy can't get enough meat—mutilates cow in full view of witnesses.* Nayeev watched the waiters watching him, and ruminated over the peculiar nature of voyeurism in New York. He tried to comfort himself with the intellectual reassurance that this was a *garçon* pastime, practiced long before and long after his appearance at Albert's. This, however, led him to more elaborate and uncomfortable thoughts, culminating in his conjecture that the city was experiencing a new predatory mutation: the serial service witness. An archetypal shadow to the blatant, quirky capitulations of the urban disinhibited, the serial service witness lurked in the dreams and meanderings of ordinary citizens, spectating the subtlest faux pas. Committing repetitive acts of senseless random observation, such witnesses often appeared in the guise of service workers: waiters, bus drivers, teacher aides—even the seemingly innocent and obtuse parents of wayward friends could moonlight as serial service witnesses. The chief contribution of the serial service witness was to conspicuously ogle behavior that was none of his business. In a society with little moral restraint and lots of fear, the serial service witness was perhaps the last defense against anomie. During the course of a single day, one serial service witness could embarrass and disarm multiple nervous, inappropriate thoughts and acts. *The nose-picking police,* thought Nayeev, *moonlighting and always on the scene, donating their abundant ocular guilt as stage lighting for uncivilized productions.*

Nayeev chomped unenthusiastically on the remains of his steak. As if to stave off unpleasantness, he dutifully motioned to the waiter and ordered another steak. The response was an icy stare that made Nayeev's heart begin to pound. Feeling like a dog locked in a prefight stare with a determined attacker, Nayeev repeated his request; his voice wavered noticeably, and Nayeev was flushed with a morbid sense that he had betrayed his maturity with sham etiquette covering his despicable greed.

Inattentive to Nayeev's supplicant expression, "Jock" simpered at him. "Another steak?" Speechless, Nayeev watched helplessly as the waiter removed his plate and dignity. *Mon Dieu et sacre bleu, tout les deux!*

Now Nayeev was rattled. His veneer was stripped, exposing a hungry kid. Ringing in his ears was his father's version of "I told you so." Besides not knowing what good is, Nayeev had left himself open to disgrace by suckering. In a sense, he was being "had" by these gay waiters, unwittingly a victim of slick advertising, adult ruses, and his own appetite. His mortification subsided under mischievous and self-righteous anticipation. So they thought he was a foolish kid, so what...he could still avenge this chagrin by consuming more steak. After all, it was *All You Can Eat!*

With glum acknowledgment, Nayeev watched "Jock" set his third steak down with a thud, unmuffled by the tablecloth. Along with the waiter's insouciant gaze, the pathetic brown lump faced him defiantly. This had to be a joke, thought Nayeev, as "Jock" swaggered away. *False advertising* screamed his mind, though his intention crumpled in defeat. Sorry, kid (ha, ha!). With piteous irony, Nayeev remembered another of his father's à propos jokes. A man complains about the terrible food at a restaurant: "The steak is like shoe leather, the coffee tastes like dishwater, the pie is like rubber...and to top it off, what small portions they give you!"

Nayeev surrendered his plate to the smirking waiter. Most of the inedible steak remained, a visible signal that Nayeev wished no longer to engage with the miscreant policies of this kitchen. "Jock" returned again, this time with amazing quickness, and disdainfully cast a gooey dessert in front of Nayeev. He punctuated his contemptuous service by flourishing a check at Nayeev's hand. "*Merci,*" offered "Jock" facetiously, and he tromped off, much to the relief of both of them.

Dejectedly, Nayeev shuffled down Sixth Avenue and turned west on Eighth Street. He was anxious to quickly and coolly distance himself from the episode at Albert's. Haunted by the specter of serial witnesses reviewing his embarrassment,

Nayeev tried to blend into pedestrian traffic. The street people leered at him through their aggressive neediness. "Spare some change, buddy?" and "Eh, gotta cigarette?" came the muffled pleas. Nayeev felt sick and alone. His stomach was fine, but his childhood was back with a vengeance. He brushed aside the beggars with the assertive grace of a basketball guard cutting to the hoop, but his face was vacant and weak, his heart removed from the color of the night. As he passed through the gauntlet of beggars, his mind translated their brusque implorations: *Quelquechose pour rien; something for nothing! Quelquechose pour rien; something for nothing! Quelquechose pour rien; something for nothing! S'il vous plait!!!*

Nayeev fulminated at the salty tide of welfare mentality. It seemed to him that life was mercilessly deriding, full of promises undelivered at maturity. In this charade of temptation, advertisement, and fatuous demands, he felt hopelessly puerile. The grown-up world was full of deception and disappointment. Perhaps his parents' mode of skepticism and retreat was wise after all. This churlish thought made Nayeev almost retch. *Could there be no escape?*

Nayeev walked through the lecherous New York evening in stony numbness. The sidewalks were garnished with stores, sensory esplanades studded with neon appeals. He approached a franchise sandwich shop, drawn by its glaring yellow sign: **Blimpie's—World's Second Best Taste Treat!** Galvanized by the guilty admonition of his parents ("don't eat that garbage"), Nayeev wondered with adolescent prurience what the world's first best taste treat could be. He wandered past the Blimpie's, knowing better than to ask. Half a block beyond, the subway entrance bellowed for his descent.

Entombed in the cavernous din and echo, the platform stretched in a slightly curved downtown frown. From the gullet of the subway tunnel, steel girders pitched the tracks from the dank palate of the ground above. Nayeev observed these steel subway teeth arched in a lurid municipal smile, separating uptown from downtown, braced against an avalanche of desperation in the teeming city above. Nayeev absent-mindedly strolled the platform, watching some kids younger than himself doggedly yank the coin return on a candy machine. A moment later, he was distracted by the whooping of three youths as they hopped over the turnstile, just as the thundering train emerged from its tubal lair. Louder than the subway's roar, Nayeev could hear the thrumming grow deafening in his head: *Quelquechose pour rien; something for nothing! Quelquechose pour rien; something for nothing! Quelquechose pour rien; something for nothing!*

2000
Written after a family trip to Florida and the Bahamas to celebrate my parents' fiftieth wedding anniversary.

TIP-TAPPING ACROSS AMERICA

The Cost of Excess Baggage: Tip unto Others, Tap unto Thyself

I have an incredible tale to tell. Knowing my reputation as a storyteller, I can only assure you that I lead a charmed life. From this Camelot flow adventures that raise admiration and suspicion. It is my calling to relay these truths; make of them what you will.

The story begins in the middle of a busy life as a healing practitioner. However, I lead a double life as a family man. Indeed, I am a double family man, and this is where it gets interesting and stressful. It was on the occasion of stretching to reach my family across the country that I became tapped out. This is my saga of tip-tapping across America.

Now you may wonder what on earth tip-tapping is, and I will explain. First, you must consider that much of this time was not spent on "earth" as it were, but in the air, on the air, and on the water. We will come back to that. Second, my parents live in Florida, and it was on the occasion of their fiftieth wedding anniversary that my immediate family and I traveled from the golden state of California to the otherworld across our nation to celebrate and pay due respects.

The prospect of spending ten days away from home promulgated my full indulgence in overpacking. This is a failing of mine under most circumstances; but add to this flaw the itinerary of a short ocean cruise and the obligation of a TV appearance en route back to California, and—well—there was every reason to anticipate and justify a baggage transfer simulating migration.

The "just-in-(suit)case" mentality that spawned my frenetic closet-cleaning also emptied my wallet of quite a few large bills to grease the palms of those carrying the luggage. I greased so much that it amazes me that only one piece of luggage slipped behind—but that, again, will unfold in the telling.

Suffice it to say that the journey across America and beyond spawned much opportunity to quell the pervasive anxiety and sporadic trauma with lots of timely tapping. Between the tipping and the tapping, my fingers were busy, and it seemed as though I was treating everyone. Well, not exactly everyone…

A Take-off on Parody

A stunning example of omission occurred early in our trip on an airplane en route from Atlanta to Fort Lauderdale. Before departing the gate in Atlanta, a passenger on our crammed jet experienced a "medical emergency"—that is, she fainted. I discreetly told a flight attendant that I was a doctor and offered my assistance. Apparently, I was not discreet enough, for my older son Neal (aka the Apex Kid), contorted in his embarrassed anguish and grumbled, "Oh, no, not the Callahan Techniques! Dad, you don't get it; she needs a *doctor*! You're going to kill her with that tapping!"

Meanwhile, as far as we could tell, an older woman passenger had fainted for a few moments and then regained her composure. The originating problem was not clear, but she recovered consciousness, claiming she was okay and did not need the oxygen the paramedics expeditiously wheeled down the aisle to her. After coercively receiving the oxygen anyway, she was then forced to leave the plane and go to a local hospital—despite her protestations that she was fine and did not want to get off the plane.

"Sorry," prattled the captain. "Now that you've had medical intervention [oxygen], I can't assume liability. You may be fine, but you'll have to get off the plane and go to the hospital."

What a cute development! I vacillated between relief and horror. A passenger has a momentary spell (or panic). My offer of tapping assistance goes unnoticed (except for the anxiety it creates in another passenger, my son), the victim receives unwanted medical attention; then she is forced to abandon her flight against her will because of the liability invoked by the unwanted medical intervention…

As comedian Yakov Smirnoff used to say, "What a country! In the store, they sell baby powder. In America, you just add water. Everywhere else, it takes nine months."

On Delta, you just add oxygen! I figured it was just as well. Why should I expose myself and others to liability and the prospect of leaving the gate with less than an hour delay? Finger-tapping could lead to finger-pointing, and, as my son intimated, that's if the lady would live!

They wheeled her off the plane over her muted objections. I was tapping my fingers in amazement as we waited to take off.

Cough It Up Again

We landed in Florida at 11:00 p.m., and then the work began. Eight suitcases besides the carry-on pieces. Off the baggage conveyor, into the shuttle; off the shuttle in some godforsaken lot where the bugs played night games under a freakish span of fluorescent lights. The humidity draped over me like a wet towel, as my wallet slipped effortlessly through tired, sweaty fingers. Here's a five, there's a ten, load my bags and tell me when…I can get to sleep and escape this groaning bad dream.

We rented a van, and the porter could just barely fit our luggage in it. He earned his tip, and I tapped on the steering wheel as the nighttime highway floated by. Twenty miles to go, then a check-in with more greasy greenbacks, but not even any greasy food available at this hour.

On this ride, another hardship rose to the occasion. The Apex Kid asserted his phlegmatic objections—Neal had a hollow and persistent cough, the kind of hyperactive visitor that interrupts conversations and announces that you have serious company for awhile.

Poor kid! He was really suffering. Indeed, we all were under the humid weather and the onus of fatigue. Four people in a room, exhausted, and nobody could sleep. Parental concern and responsibility were giving way to delusions about putting a bag over his head. The interesting part was coming: tomorrow we would face the grandparents with a sick child. I could envision the tacit disapproval and the sarcastic predictions of pneumonia.

The sun rose on a family of travelers determined to have fun and celebrate my parents' half century of union. My wife and I sipped bad hotel coffee and watched our children scarf down cereal from tiny boxes. Accustomed to the family-size cereal boxes, the proportion seemed wrong as they gobbled the measured contents quickly. They were quite involved for brief moments in satiating their hunger, but it was like watching them have a conversation with toy soldiers.

At last, we were ready to greet the day, but I glanced at the clock and thought of California, mostly asleep—the two places I still wanted to be.

How Long Can It Last?

The following day was the big event: my parents' fiftieth wedding anniversary celebration. The affair was held at an elegant restaurant. The food was fabulous, its toxic effects so well disguised in taste sensations that I didn't even suffer the inevitable exhaustion for hours.

The children were well behaved, indeed a delight and pride noticed by the geriatric crowd. When you're a child, it's not easy to humor the old folks—and age prevailed over youth at this gathering. Indeed, it was a veritable cardiac unit. My family and the restaurant staff were the only ones without heart conditions (and I didn't give the staff long, working amid that scrumptious and tempting food).

The challenge for me was social diplomacy with relatives I hardly recognized. Their aging was secondary to the vague registration I had of them anyway. It was embarrassing to slip into the gaze and smiling grip of several wrinkled and perfumed admirers who accosted me and queried, "Do you remember me, Mark?"

"How could I forget you?" I feigned, immediately recovering with, "Barbara would *love* to say hello to you!" as I reached for my wife. "Honey, look who's here!" (Deftly turning) "This is my wife, Barbara."

"Hello, Barbara, I'm Cousin Elsie. Nice to see you. I remember when Mark was little, even when he had freckles like your son. Your children are wonderful; you both look great. Mazel tov!"

"Elsie, thank you. Glad you could join us; great to see you!" Relieved, I wondered how many times this charade had been replayed over the years, and I reflected upon the family amnesia that beset me. Did I not care about remembering these people, or was it a genetic cognitive flaw? I was left to conclude that family makes you stupid, one way or another.

The time came for me to toast my folks with a few *bon mots.* I stood before the room of well-wishers and introduced myself by reminding them that since I was not yet retired, I specialized professionally in eliminating negative feelings in minutes.

"And people invariable ask, 'Yes, but how long does it last?' So, this past week, as I thought often of my blessed parents, I found myself replying absent-mindedly, 'Fifty years; can you believe it?' And in the moment, my patient would say incredulously, 'Doc, you gotta be kidding!'

"And I would continue, 'I'm not kidding; the time goes so fast, you hardly remember the painful parts.'

"'Painful parts?'

"'Like my father always says—all those years…and I've got the scars to prove it!'

"'SCARS?!' in a high-pitch echo.

"'We're talking about commitment here, about tapping into something far more fundamental than what most people call love. I mean this goes beyond feeling good.'

"'I-I-I don't know, Doc…,' from the increasingly traumatized patient.

"'Oh, pshew, I was talking about my parents' fiftieth… remember, I told you it was coming up?'"

The patrons appreciated this droll anecdote. To my surprise, the hyperactive photographer approached me and asked if I would treat him. Crossing boundary lines is risky, but nowhere more fun than in marketing.

It was a wonderful party. Despite the idiosyncrasies of my extended family, the general spirits of celebration and congratulations were preserved, and my parents were truly honored and feted for the remarkable longevity of their union. In love, as in cure, we can never be sure how long it will last. Many passions have evaporated in divorce or toxins, the latter less recorded but just as costly. In many regards, my parents were fortunate, their commitment to be revered.

Still, the ingénue in me could not refrain from fantasizing about the possibilities of launching a new trend for the golden years: early bird heart rate variability tests—it would make a lot of people last longer.

A Nagging Cough—How Long Can This Last?

After the party, we settled down to the realization that Neal was sick and headed for a bout with bronchitis. For a period of time, my parents cast glances askance, but eventually they pressured us to take him to a doctor. Relenting, we visited a local medical office, and we waited the obligatory hour before my son was examined. Since the doctor only spends a few minutes attending, they make you wait so you'll think you got your money's worth.

"It looks like a respiratory infection, certainly," the doctor confidently claimed. "Whether or not that cobblestone texture at the back of his throat is allergies…we'll have to see when the infection clears up. I'll write you a prescription for an antibiotic. Remember to drink plenty of fluids."

I should have expected this, of course: drugs and drinking. It's what the physicians always recommend. They never recommend sex, though, I chuckled silently to myself. Probably wiser in this case, since my son was only thirteen.

"Are you sure it's a bacterial infection?" I asked.

The doctor regarded me with that momentary disbelief that accompanies any question of the physician's absolute omniscient authority.

"Well," she replied, matter-of-factly, "even if it's a virus, the antibiotic will kill off any secondary infectious bacteria. It becomes a breeding ground in there, you know."

And with that statement and half a flourish, she scribbled out the prescription and handed it to my wife. As an afterthought, she added, "We could be sure by doing lab work. That is, if your son wants to let us draw blood." She looked at us with a hint of impatience and a mischievous challenge lurking beneath her demeanor.

Neal regarded me for a cue on when to show panic. Immediately, his face flooded with displeasure. I looked at him and then at the doctor, whose impassive expression said she had seen this rerun many times.

"I think it's a good idea; I'd like to know," I ventured. My wife assented, and, for a long few moments, we just sat there. I brooded silently over how pointless was this exercise. Visiting the doctor was the *right* thing to do, the responsible act, a vapid attempt to disguise our negligence as parents for allowing our son to get sick in the first place. At least my parents would approve of this swipe at protection, and they would want all possible details. For no logical reason, my mind drifted toward a half-recalled line from Macbeth: "For we are now already so steeped in blood, that we may as well proceed toward its conclusion."

"All right, Dad," my stoic son offered, as he held his arm out toward the doctor. She approached with a syringe, and it was over with little fanfare.

A Tap on the Hand Is Worth Two in the Ambush

We tried valiantly to make the best of our crowded quarters—four members of a suburban bourgeois family, barely sidestepping each other in a hotel room. Three hours ahead of ourselves and already short on sleep, we politely tripped over the baggage that edged us nearly into the corridor. The one bathroom...well, I won't even get into that; suffice it to say that before getting out of bed during the night, I thought twice... and three and four times, actually, for it was nearly impossible to sleep with Neal hacking away. Barbara had exiled him into bed with me, while she wrestled slumber in the other bed with eleven-year-old Jeremy.

I tossed and turned and rotated and vacillated between sympathizing with poor Neal and plotting something featuring a pillowcase. Mostly, I felt exasperated and sorry for myself. My mind wandered, but not far enough that I could escape my frustration at this restive imprisonment with my ever-so-close family. I thought of the impending Caribbean cruise, of work, of home. I considered writing a letter to occupy my mind and restlessness. All this jumbled together in a senseless fusion of images. I contemplated tapping to relieve my pent-up state, and Roger Callahan came to mind. RJC was a peaceful image, the unflappable supervisor peering over my amygdala, reminding me I could have tapped much earlier. The reassuring Mister Roger...Jolly Roger...God help me with this insomnia and the damned infernal coughing of the consumptive offspring beside me. My mind whirled. Dr. Allahcan, what's going on? *I'm losing it, that's what's going on!* Fatigue has addled me into an Islamic slip!

Unwittingly, I hosted a refrain from that Pointer Sisters song, *Yes, you can can, Yes, you can, Allah can can, Yes he can, If you can't, Callahan can, Yes he can can, Allah can...*

Jeesh! I pulled my hands over my head, as if to drag the dark down over my rambling semiconsciousness. Neal hacked into a rhythmic fit, and I reflexively reached over to rest my hand on his back, a helpless reassuring gesture. Then, it occurred to me: surrogate treatment. I could tap myself while touching him. Hopefully, I could harness the energy to quell his cough. Ambush TFT to the rescue!

Thankfully, the guerrilla healing worked. Within about twenty minutes after tapping, he settled into a blissful wheezing rhythm. Suspiciously, I awaited the cacophony of phlegm, whose absence kept me lingering at the brim of awareness for several dreamy minutes. Relative silence was golden, three thousand tired miles from my golden state.

Choking on Medicine

We had filled the prescription and had given Neal one dose of antibiotics. His cough was much better the next day, diminished to the fading, half-hearted presence that healing often leaves in its trail, as residual inflammation dries up. The miracles of antibiotics notwithstanding, I have never known a single oral dose to be sufficient. However, we had tapped into something extraordinary.

Neal continued to improve without any more medicine. My parents were placated, but I felt a bit guilty about secrets: the ambush TFT and the abandoned antibiotics. I decided to keep the healing a mystery, since it is hard to convince people anyway when certain ideas are entrenched. Speaking of incredulity, I called the physician to check on the lab results, and we engaged in a conversation that defied my boundaries of logic and science.

"How did the blood work turn out?"

"It was inconclusive."

"What do you mean, 'inconclusive'?"

"It looks like he should take the antibiotics."

"Why?"

"We can't say for sure whether it's a bacterial or viral infection..."

"Well, were there any identifiable bacterial strains that could cause his cough?"

At this point, the doctor became impertinent. "What is it you're trying to say? What do you want to know?" she demanded.

Not one to back down, I countered, "I want to know if the lab results showed any bacteria that might be responsible for my son's cough. That's why we drew his blood, right?"

"Dr. Steinberg, I don't know why you're giving me such a hard time. If it were my child, I would give him the antibiotics."

"I appreciate your advice, and I don't perceive myself as giving you a hard time. I simply want to understand the basis for your statement that the blood work was 'inconclusive' and why I should continue to give him antibiotics if there are no bacteria that warrant them. Was there anything abnormal in the results?"

"No."

"Then what was inconclusive?"

"His blood work was completely normal." I could sense this statement forced through gritted teeth. Then she repeated, "If it were my child, I would give him the antibiotics."

"Thank you, doctor."

Thank God for science—and all that imitates it. Sometimes, medicine and its philosophy are too much to swallow in one gulp.

Making Waves

We moved out of the hotel on the day our ship left port from Fort Lauderdale. Like a wizened gunslinger, I poised with my hand at my hip as the bellhop surveyed our luggage with raised eyebrows. Out of the hotel, to the dock at the port, on the ship and into our cabins—my back began to ache just watching the processional. Our baggage had swelled with the addition of my mother's and brother's belongings; they had joined for the excursion. We had twelve heavy pieces altogether, and I kept paying for their passage. I consoled myself with the metaphor that this process was a lot like psychotherapy—paying someone to assist carrying your baggage.

The heat had barely faded from my wallet when I found us crowded once again into a small space, this time aboard a seaworthy vessel. My ammunition considerably diminished, I waited for departure, a new and sloshing adventure to a land where poverty was a way of life. Somehow, I understood the irony of paying to join the poverty.

Though my cell phone remained impotent on the high seas and the TV didn't work, the voyage had plenty of pomp and circumstance. Dinners were formal and dressy occasions, and I forgot for hours at a time how far I was from take-out pizza.

During dinner on the first night, the ship began to undulate. We veterans of California earthquakes welcomed a hint of home, although this sensation was different and certainly more prolonged. One of us, however, took the heaves seriously. My son, Neal, developed that head-hung-low look of a dog just before it vomits.

I took advantage of this moment to solicit his receptiveness to TFT. Figuring that the thought of Callahan Techniques usually elicits his revulsion, I wondered if his present nausea would mask it. He must have been in a sorry state, because this time he welcomed the overture. The ship was tipping, and we were tapping. A few holons later, he was composed enough to rejoin our dinner. Digestive and cognitive dissonance yielded to reassurances and rationalizations that his seasickness was just a "temporary thing."

I Wanna Be Over This…

We docked in Nassau the next morning under the teeming patter of sudden rain and impetuous caprice of tropical weather. The storm abated as we gobbled breakfast and made our tourist plans for the day. I was okay with most any activity, as long as it didn't involve packing, unpacking, schlepping, or eating. In addition to porters, I was also tipping the scales heavily. Something had to give, and, believe me, I was tired of it.

We decided on boarding a glass-bottom boat and watching colorful fish, as we glided to a primitive island for a day of play and fantasy. The ever-energetic Bahamian guides entertained us with informative descriptions in their stereotypic lilting and seductive islander accents. With regularity, they reminded us that we were on vacation and should drink more alcohol. For some reason, it seemed different than the interval beer commercials on sportscasts.

"Ya' mon! Ya're on vacation, so have a good time! Drink triple, see double, and act single. Ya' mon!"

Now, I don't like to drink during the day, and it was fortunate for the sake of an opportunity that awaited: parasailing. I'd always wanted to try parasailing, and the locals had boats launching game tourists into the gorgeous Caribbean sky.

The boatman strapped me into the rig as my bachelor brother sat on the gunwale, cracking jokes that I tried hard to laugh at.

"Even if something happens, Mark, you've already had male children. They're on shore, so the Steinberg name will live on."

"Never mind your jump shot—you've always wanted to sky high enough to dunk; this is your chance."

I was ready to go. "Lissenup, mon," the boatman yammered above my thumping heart. "Keepya hands away from dese." He touched the nautical clasps that fastened my harness to the rope. "Das d'only ting keepin' ya from fallin' away, mon."

Before I could reconsider, I was aloft, a rigidly ascending ballast drifting rapidly away from the speedboat that seemed propelled by my brother's animated but fading cheers.

I held on for dear life, the one time in it I could remember *not* wanting to release tension. My hands gripped the straps tightly. I concentrated on relaxing. Suddenly, in terror, I noticed my fingers resting on the clasps. No, mon! I jerked my hands back reflexively, as if recoiling from a horrible creature. The harness wobbled and yawed, and I could view the sprawling ocean without looking down. In panic, I crept my hands carefully down the straps to regain my grip. Stopping short of the clasps left my elbows bent and my forearms unnaturally tensed. Performing the nine-gamut was out of the question. Whirling my eyes produced other problems. I could hum "Happy Birthday" and hope I reached another one.

I decided to focus on enjoying the ride. *Yes, you can can, Yes, you can, Callahan can, Yes he can can, Allah can…*

I want to be over this ocean.
I will be over this ocean.
I am over this ocean.
Holy cow! I'm 300 feet over this ocean!

Suspended between heaven and earth, I noticed an island with some houses on it. I recognized it as the island that the tour guide had pointed out as Eddie Murphy's Caribbean abode. I thought of Woody Allen's routine about facing the Ku Klux Klan. All of a sudden, his whole life flashed before him—but it was the wrong life!

Now, the movie life of Eddie Murphy played through me. I was an adventurer, performing his own stunt in the starring role while the camera rolled below. (Never mind that the camera was manned by my brother, and the video subject to God-knows-what postproduction editing.)

Heh, heh, heh!

Bon Voyage

The big ship steamed its return toward the Florida coast. I welcomed the embrace of cellular airspace, and ordinary messages soothed my disenfranchised hiatus from the workaday world. *Please enter your password.* Ya' mon!

Please show us your passport. The custom was Customs, and we stood on line to "clear" Customs, as if it were some sort of toxin. Actually, the reverse was the case, as Customs was looking to detect anything it considered toxic contraband.

Each time the line moved in its interminable crawl, we had to inch twelve-plus bags forward. Tipping the stewards had landed our gear at the dock, and now it was up to me. *What's up, doc?* Certainly not my posture. The only thing I was smuggling was a backache and a nasty attitude. This was becoming torture.

We must have looked hopelessly suburban, for some Customs officials recognized our plight and led us to the front of the line. Wistfully, I remembered the times I looked threatening enough to warrant a strip search. Now I was benign in the spine, a middle-aged wallet-bearer and benefactor of the service industry. The airport was two miles away, but by now, I measured distances in dollars per bag. My mind flashed on a restaurant in San Jose that had a jar at the cash register sporting the sign, "Tipping is not a city in China."

My wife, children, and I whiled away several hours as we waited for our flight from Fort Lauderdale to Atlanta. The time passed quicker than anticipated, and, already, gelling memories packaged our vacation into reminiscences that glowed in a softer light than when actually experienced.

In talking about the cruise, Neal admitted grudgingly that the Callahan Techniques Thought Field Therapy was good for some things—i.e., seasickness—but that the claims should not be exaggerated. I wasn't sure whether this was his way of opening the door to further exploration of TFT or a sequestering of the treatment to rare occasions and infrequent problems; we would not likely board a ship any time soon. I knew enough to just nod and listen.

Our flight to Atlanta was uneventful. At Hartsfield International Airport, I would part ways with my family. They would continue on to San Jose, and I would stay over in Atlanta, where I was scheduled to appear on television the next morning. The interesting part, of course, was what would happen with our baggage. By now, you can glean that this had become an obsession.

(Science question: What are the rings around Saturn made of? Answer: Mostly lost airline luggage.)

We had already separated our belongings into assigned suitcases, of sorts. This was only approximate. Since I had a very large suitcase, I had absorbed some dirty laundry and one of my wife's dresses, which hung along with my suits. It was quite temporary. I would be happy and relieved if we arrived in San Jose in pieces, as long as we had all of them, even if it was on more than one flight. I fretted about managing the several pieces of luggage remaining with me, realizing that my unpaid porters were casting off into the sky westward with their mother. In a moment of dramatic reverie, I fancied myself as Humphrey Bogart in Casablanca.

"Here'sh to you, shweetheart," as I handed my wife her carry-on. There were no propellers, no cigarettes, no fedoras... only brief hugs and kisses, and they trudged off to concourse B. (You don't see porters or luggage in Bogart flicks anyway, I contented myself.) In this uxorious mood, I watched them disappear into the melding crowd, wishing them well and missing them already.

I looked forward to returning to San Jose. I eagerly longed to move out of suitcases and back into my closet.

Out of the Closet

From Hartsfield Airport, I journeyed by taxi through a light rain gracing the springtime Georgian landscape. My destination was the new Embassy Suites in downtown Atlanta where, the next morning, I would appear as a guest on the NBC television show *Peachtree Morning.* My topic was (what else?) Voice Technology and Thought Field Therapy, and I zealously anticipated beaming out the wonderful message to the greater South.

The Embassy Suites is a spanking new hotel adjacent to the CNN Center in downtown Ted Turner (I mean, Atlanta). Its lobby boasts a satellite television studio, from which WXIA Channel 11 broadcasts *Peachtree Morning.* This would be a piece of cake (or should I say, peach pie?), staying at the hotel and taking the elevator to work to make my TV appearance. I was tired, hungry, and excited as I checked into the hotel.

Despite all my tipping, the baggage transfers had their inevitable impact. Upon settling into my suite, I discovered that my suit was quite wrinkled. This would not make a favorable impression on camera. I solicited the help of the concierge, whose felicitations amply reassured me that most any reasonable guest request would be honored. The only problem was that it was about 7:00 p.m., and commercial establishments that could press my suit were already closed. To my amazement, the concierge volunteered to iron my suit herself. Indeed, this was service, and I felt relieved and honored.

A knock on the door announced the concierge's arrival to collect my attire. I ushered her in and, with due propriety, bade her wait while I quickly retrieved the garment. She looked ill at ease, and I found this unusual. Surely, as a concierge, she had to deal regularly with male business visitors. I handed her my suit and thanked her profusely, making some inane chatter about wrinkles and professing my motto of "dress for success!"

The concierge backed out the door with a weak smile and a promise of quick return of my suit. As I turned around after seeing her out, I realized with embarrassment the source of her reticence. Directly in view from the front door was a closet bearing my hanging and open suitcase. At the fore of the clothing was my wife's dress, posturing in pastel and prim incongruity. I flushed just looking at it. As if pulled by magnet, my gaze then shifted to the adjacent sofa, where a Raggedy Ann doll named Rosie smiled stupidly in blatant exhibition. I was preparing for the TV show where I would demonstrate "Ring Around the Rosie" to illustrate the principle of electrical and energy flow among people. (This doll was special; when an unbroken circle of human hands included the doll's hands, she sang "Ring Around the Rosie.") The doll just sat there, a dead giveaway that I was no ordinary redneck.

The confused concierge had already heard me talk of eliminating negative feelings in minutes by gentle tapping. We had had a brief conversation about the intuitive and subtle nature of energy healing. I had blasphemed wrinkles with my "dress for success!" proclamation. Realizing that she was taken aback by the dress in the closet and the doll on the couch, I felt suddenly impelled to tell her, "Really, you must have misinterpreted…you see, we had all this baggage and my wife left me in Atlanta; she took the kids back to San Jose with most of our things, but left me this dress…I'm going to be on TV, right here in the hotel, tomorrow…no, really, will you watch? I promise, I won't wrinkle the suit, if you'll just believe me and watch…"

Alas, the concierge had left with my suit and whatever thoughts the experience had generated for her. It was time for dinner and trust that I would get my suit back and enough rest to appear fresh in the morning.

Time to Heal

It was getting late. Luckily, the hotel had a good restaurant. Although I was in no position to be fussy, this was a pleasant and unexpected fortune. I was seated at a table and given a menu bearing rich and overly appetizing temptations. I could easily get carried away.

I put down the menu and began tapping myself with an addiction algorithm, hoping to thwart temptation and minimize my dinner order. To my surprise, a waiter approached my table, smiled, and bellowed, "It's 8:40, sir." Lacking any explanation for his announcement, I continued with my algorithm.

The waiter approached again. "It's 8:42, sir." Gee, the staff certainly was attentive. Now, I was almost ready to order, and, hopefully the meal service would be prompt as well. As I was tapping on my collarbone, the waiter hurried over, expressing his intended devotion.

"I'm ready to take your order, sir, I know you want service. It's not necessary to keep pointing at yourself."

Pointing at myself? Goodness, he saw me tapping on my collarbone and perceived some egocentric signal commanding him to wait on me! And the time announcements—that was a response to my tapping on the gamut spot. He thought I was gesturing to my wrist to ask the time!

This southern hospitality was something else!

I finished my delicious meal without further departures from normalcy. The tapping had inadvertently produced great service, so I was obliged to part with yet another big tip.

I was glad they didn't see me roll my eyes (would the maître d'hôtel have appeared at tableside?), hear me hum "Happy Birthday" (would this have signaled an impromptu cake?) or do the collarbone breathing (this would probably have invoked paramedics with oxygen).

Upstairs in my room, my suit had been hung in the closet, looking perfect. I glanced at Rosie, who didn't say a word. We would hold hands the next day on live TV. This night, we had no contact, and I slept quite peacefully by myself.

Over the Airwaves—with Image

In the morning, I awoke crisp and refreshed. I strolled down to the lobby in my nicely pressed suit, feeling in top form and eager to get on with the show. I looked for the concierge, but she had not come on duty as yet.

The show was pleasant. I enjoyed the opportunity to meet and talk with one of the other guests, the well-known veteran TV journalist Linda Ellerbee. She is an empathic woman whose battle with and survival of cancer has drawn a huge and loving following. She recounted her postrecovery activities, which included authorship of some compelling children's books. Her fragile, careful movements and quiet strength were inspiring, and she exuded a masterful, experienced stage presence. I felt sorry for the audience for having to watch me next.

However, I enthusiastically greeted Atlanta and surroundings with the gospel of energy healing. In the recesses of my awareness, I know that the world is full of millions of parallel affairs—but, for the life of me, I cannot believe that anyone truly has anything more important to behold than the miraculous and pervasive betterment provided by TFT. So, beam me up and out there, Scottie, and shine the lights on my traveling partner, Rosie!

The program went well. The host was prepared and asked good questions. The pressure of media appearance and the condensation of precious time forces explanations into short and simple "punchy" sound bites—which, for someone with my background and education, is probably a good thing. Still, you never know the full measure of how it comes across. I would later get phone calls inquiring about "what kin' o' voodoo you done to dat li'l chile," referring to the "Ring Around the Rosie" demonstration. Apparently, the close-up camera shots were very convincing.

Witch docta you talkin' 'bout?

Da one on Peachtree Mornin', fool.

In television performance, the saving grace about feedback is the understanding that viewers may have grabbed a snack or visited the bathroom in the middle of your presentation. Thus, their ignorance or misinterpretation becomes excusable. And you have the tape to review, criticize, and rebut.

In everyday life, though, your audience constantly departs without notification. The lights are on, they are in their seats, but few are listening carefully. It is sobering to realize how one presents and is perceived. At least my suit looked good. I could hardly wait to find the concierge and reclaim some sense of manhood and credibility.

The concierge was watching, indeed, and she was generous with her praise and congratulations. I boosted her image by bragging to the staff about her saving the day with ironing. I appreciated her going the extra mile, and she would get a big tip. (Why not? She was deserving, and I was getting very experienced at tipping.) Unbeknown to me at that moment, she would be instrumental at subduing the next trauma in my path.

Time arrived for my trek back to Hartsfield Airport. The concierge proudly took charge of my departure, regaling my checkout with personal supervision. She called a limo, escorted me to checkout, and had my bags portered and loaded behind my back. This VIP service actually backfired, because at the airport terminal I discovered I was missing a suitcase! Frantically calling the hotel, I tried to locate the concierge who was my last best hope to erase this incipient horror as my flight time relentlessly neared.

Rosie was in that suitcase! Surely, the staff would understand, and, besides, how could a suitcase disappear? "That's right," I clamored to the voice from the hotel front desk, "I was the guy on TV that morning who could get rid of any negative feelings by phone." Now I was on the phone, and very challenged by my own negative feelings, which were quickly maturing from anxiety into hostility.

The concierge was a doll who palled Rosie by comparison. She delivered (literally) by sending the limo driver racing back to the airport with my suitcase (it was discovered up in my room—blithely ignored by myself and the porter!).

In retrospect, the big tip I gave her wasn't enough. Neither was the profuse tapping I was doing at the airport. Catching my flight was going to be a very close call. As I hobbled across this immense airport, tugging at my carry-ons, my cell phone rang. I answered with apprehension, fearing further notice of an amnestic aftermath from the Embarrassing Suites in Atlanta.

It was a patient of mine, calling for Voice Technology treatment. Barely containing my frustration, I told him that I was at the Atlanta airport and could not treat him at the moment. Despite his anxiety, he "thoroughly understood," and I promised to be available after my flight. After hanging up, I felt abashed and realized that I must have sounded exasperated. Not what patients need...there are disadvantages to being human. I muddled over God's sense of humor and the humility that poor modeling brings.

Airport Insecurity

Glancing at the airline departure screen and quickly at my watch, I knew I had to hustle. I hoofed it to the security checkpoint where, to my disgust, the lines were at least twenty people deep. I felt that flash of helplessness and resentment that accompanies the futility of challenging something bigger than oneself. There was nothing to do but go along to get along. Airport personnel are quite reptilian: they have absolutely no sense of humor. This is not my type of place.

So I did what I often do when there is no discernible escape—I tapped into fantasy. What if this *could* be my type of place? I imagined setting up Voice Technology booths in place of the metal detectors.

Please, empty your meridians, put your toxins on the conveyor belt, step through the perturbation detector, and say, "I want to be over these delays."

Wouldn't that be great? There would be no more airport insecurity, anger, air rage, stress, fear, or loathing.

Step up to the VT booth and clear yourself of perturbations. No phobias allowed on board. Travel much lighter without perturbations. Tap along, thank you, next...

The line had moved rather quickly, and I was passing through the metal detector. *Beam me up, Scottie, hopefully in a ship.*

This crisis behind me, I dashed for the gate. What a long way to go—God! I had to board a subway and traverse endless walkways and escalators.

Do you know the way to San Jose?

I huffed along, wondering if I'd make it on time. *Yes, you can, can, yes you can...*

With Dionne Warwick and the Pointer Sisters crooning in the back of my head, I reached the gate and boarded my flight.

Over the Airwaves—with Baggage

I found my seat in the rear of the plane, a window seat beside a huge man planted in the middle seat and a small woman in the aisle seat of that row. They both stood to let me in, yet the tiny aisle space made my entrance like a scene from *The Three Stooges.*

"Scuse me."

"Sure."

"Pardon me."

"Why, soitainly."

I sat down and almost immediately realized that I had a bag in my lap and my computer in the overhead bin. I decided to leave it that way, not wanting to generate any further fuss. At least I had a book to read.

"How ya doin'? Name's Rich. This here's my wife, Marlene."

As he gestured, I introduced myself.

"Marlene, honey, say hello to da man."

Marlene obliged, and we settled back to pass the time. The quarters were very tight. Rich was huge, seemingly too big for the seat. His arms and elbows rested against mine; there was nowhere for either of us to tuck our appendages. No stranger to girth myself, I visualized us as adults squatting and squirming in kindergarten chairs. Unfortunately, airplanes are like that, and this one was full to capacity.

The curving contour of the cabin where the window graced my head made me feel more cramped. I had stuff on my lap and my feet could extend only as far as the briefcase under the seat. The seatbelt nested against my midsection, and Rich's very adjacent body was like an extra harness. Man, I was anchored! I wasn't going anywhere, and I realized with a stab of mounting alarm that I had to endure this discomfort for over four hours. Parasailing now seemed like freedom.

I wanted to tap, but didn't even have enough room to move my arms. Trapped! How was I going to survive this Houdini-like fix for four hours?

Yes, you can can, Yes, you can, Allah can can, Yes he can, If you can't, Callahan can, Yes he can can, Allah can…

Resigning myself to enduring the trip, I slumped as far down as I could and gazed out the window. The plane was banking away from the South, and I could feel the gravitational force pressing my head against the fuselage. I thought of San Jose, of schlepping my bags yet one more time, of forking over more money because I had rubber arms and too much stuff. As I looked down upon the lighted landscape below, the aircraft turned and canted, and I knew that I had developed a new anxiety—fear of tipping. I decided to call this *costrophobia,* and I chuckled lightly, drifting off to sleep.

Rich Dip or Rich Chips

When I awoke, the thrum of the jet engines reminded me immediately of my environs. Peculiarly, I felt comfortable except for the nagging reminder in my bladder. Despite the hassle of rousing Rich and his wife, I had to pee.

Though it carried the heavy anticipation of moving day, I ultimately notified Rich, and we all lumbered to a vertical position. I saw them standing in the aisle, either with confidence in my quick excursion or because the effort of sitting down again required preparation. Seeing me waiting on line at the lavatory prompted them to sit. Within minutes, the whole ritual repeated, as I returned to sit down.

I settled back in and opened my book.

"Stephen King, eh?" Rich was in a garrulous mood. "You like Stephen King?"

No, I hate him. I just read his garbage to get myself good and angry so I can be obnoxious to busybodies. "Yes, as a matter of fact, I do like Stephen King," I replied politely. "His writing makes *me* feel normal." I thought this might give Rich caution, but it didn't make a dent.

"I don't really like Stephen King. Actually, I don't really unnerstan' his stuff," Rich offered thoughtfully.

I kept my face in the pages, but Rich was not to be deterred.

"You live in San Jose?"

"Yes, I do."

After a pause: "I'm from Georgia…actually, nevah been outta Georgia, 'cept for de military…ain't dat right, Marlene?" She nodded inaudibly. "We goin' to San Jose for a marketing convention." With that, he held up a binder bearing the name of some multilevel company unfamiliar to me.

"You like it dere?" he continued.

"Yes, Silicon Valley is a very nice place."

"Now, tell me sumpin'," Rich continued with a burst of second wind, "how can dey make all dat money just from *silicone?*" His emphasis startled me. "I mean, dey have dat much demand for breast implants?"

I breathed deeply, knowing I had more journey time left beside this large, well-intentioned bumpkin.

"Rich," I drawled in slow and measured pride, "you'd be surprised. We gotta lot of fi-i-ine looking women out here. Right smart women, too. Good at business. Sharp. Know what they want. Lotta money. Valley does a lotta swe-e-ell business."

This seemed to resonate with Rich. "Well, it's just amazin', das what. All dat money from gel!"

"They're in the chips, Rich. They're in the chips!"

Across America

The engines whined steadily beneath my floating mind, as I absently watched America pass below. All the tipping and tapping over thousands of miles had formed a rhythm that enhanced my lyrical excursion across colloquial boundaries of geography, culture, customs, and personal experience.

My reverie harkened to the pristine Bahamian waters, and the following song played softly:

We sail on the Sloop Nine G
Practicing TFT
Around Nassau Island we shall have fun
I wanna be a one
Oh, won't you let me reach one (oh, yeah)
I feel so worked up
I wanna be a one.

We let this treatment set sail
When other efforts have failed.
I know that my anxiety keeps me at home.
And I want to roam,
Oh, won't you please let me roam (oh, yeah)
You sound so broke up
It must be my cell phone.

We sail on the Sloop Nine G
With Voice Technology
No matter how weird it gets, we're right near a phone
The phobia's gone
Smooth sailing's gone on
With TFT we're at one no matter how the wind's blown.

In this quiet moment of reflection, airborne and defiant of gravity, trapped, buckled, and dispossessed of humor, I contemplated how life can weigh us down with baggage, both material and psychological. And how we can tip and tap our way out. For burdens, God gives shoulders—and collarbones.

1996
Written in response and satirical review of my children's embarrassment over me.

DR. CHUCKLE AND MYSTIFIED

A Cutup Develops a Split Personality

The inevitable has happened: My son has decided that I am embarrassing to him. Imagine! Me!!?! The psychologist/father who has spent decades developing and refining tastes, eclecticism, humor, and a predilection for really cool things, as well as making it my business to understand what children detest about their parents…It's my *job* to be hip! (Is it okay to use that word?)

I figured this would happen, but I am surprised at the quick onset; my son, Neal, is only nine. Perhaps every victim bargains with similar plaintive innocence: "So soon? Why me? Is it my time yet?"

The symptoms are neither suspicious nor subtle, so I am spared the futility of pretending. In his anxious appeal, Neal blurts the directions that devastate my self-image. He tells me how to behave at the karate club party. "Don't talk to anyone, Dad. I don't want you to embarrass me. And, most of all, *PLEASE do not tell any jokes.*"

I am speechless and mystified, a sudden and depersonalized split from my identity as the infamous Dr. Chuckle, the veteran paternalistic, puckish prankster. I look in the mirror and greet the welcome hybrid of Santa Claus and Robin Williams. My son's vision does not reflect this jolly and benevolent appraisal.

Neal beseeches me with a contorted expression of filial respect and the pain of his wresting humiliation. It is agonizing for him to confront me. He is caught in that warp of development between the imminent polite skills of socially correct reproof and the raw certainty of his discomfort with my behavior. The pressure reminds me of stomach cramps.

"Da-aa-d!" he bellows, "I hate it when you joke around and talk to other people. It makes me embarrassed."

"What would you like me to do?" I reply indulgently, figuring that my calmness will both humor him and hide my growing mortification. After all, this is ridiculous; surely, my son does not expect me to be a mute chauffeur, detached in the formality of my role and bashfully deferent to the social cadence of children. In the face of my seeming consideration, Neal will realize his egocentric folly and will verbalize his appreciation for my wit and charm. "I should just stand there, smile, and not say anything?"

This logical invective seems to provoke him. "Dad...," he begins in tight-lipped disapproval, slightly shaking his head in a pretentious correction. "Don't say anything, don't *smile,* just *be* there, but don't talk to anybody. You embarrass me, don't you get it?"

The knell has sounded, and I am nearly deafened by its impact. My son is placated only by my promise of restraint, and I grant him this as I withdraw into fantasy. With all the boldness and beauty of a turtle, I yank my ego inside and fold my personality into protection. I am Dr. Chuckle—benevolent, receptive, spontaneous, funny, understanding, and matured to an immunity from rebellious offspring. I worked terribly hard to develop this way, as can plainly be verified by comparing me with *my* parents. I could/would never be like them! They were not even my *real* parents—they *couldn't* be! (Remember that one?) Same deal here. My real children would appreciate me. They would recognize the vigilance with which I avoided becoming a jerk, committing myself to the sacrifices that would improve me to the status of a father worth taking pride in and having around. Part altruistically and part vengefully, I carved and molded my personality away from the queasy memories of my father's interactions. It sickened me to hear his repeated jokes and to watch his animated expectations of laughter and attention. It was all I could do to refrain from jumping at him and screaming, "You've told that one eight times before!" Instead, I sat there and tried to force the laughter, telling myself that diluting the audience's disdain was a suitable sublimation of my disgust.

Having this precedent, I grew with a fail-safe guidance toward becoming humorous. I would sidestep boorishness with the aplomb of a running back. Truly funny, yet taken seriously, that's what I would be—and so evolved Dr. Chuckle—intellect and respectability, with a punch line.

Now Dr. Chuckle is mystified. My personality is split by Neal's maturation through the stages of his identity. During his earlier childhood, I was his security and strength, his bastion against a world too big, indecipherable, and threatening. The fountain of my knowledge cascaded into his bottomless admiration. In the middle years, his developmental tasks would revolve around mastery and the growing exploration of his independence and competence. It is coming time for Neal's personhood to assert itself; my role develops into part-time sparring partner for the training and tempering of his identity. Competition exists so Neal can defeat and reject me. The glimmers of pubertal chaos are too soon, too real. No applause for Dr. Chuckle. I know the process well, yet I am entrenched and mystified. It is high time for Neal to experiment with the varieties of pushing me away. The Jekyll-and-Hyde iterations of identity development pass through the generations. My son doesn't want me around for the world to see on the outside what he feels and fears lives within him. He is right, of course, though it is still training camp for the vigorous sport of adolescence. As the season unfolds, there will be cheers, adrenaline, and perhaps injury, as biology and environment vie for championship.

Exasperation and perspiration may later ensue. The games begin with a plea, a scoff, some put-downs, and the shielding psychology of one-upmanship and talking trash. Thankfully, we are not yet at that stage. I have time to prepare for the incipient horror of Neal's rejection of my dress and appearance. No man's ties survive the cultural attack of his son's coming of age. In my closet, a neckwear collection hangs without defense against the passage of time. I peer into the future, skittishly sketching his mockery of my cravats.

For now, a proud developmental task is at hand. Neal's first necktie has been purchased, and he anxiously awaits my instruction, so he can present himself with fashion at the upcoming party. We have a minor skirmish over his insistence on practicing with a polo shirt.

"You can't wear a tie with that kind of collar!" My sense of taste is offended. Pompously, I fret that heritable dishevelment has skipped only my generation.

"Why not, Dad?" he pouts with surly insistence.

"Because it looks ridiculous!" Oh, boy. Dr. Chuckle is generously scattering the coffin nails now. In a few years, Bozo will look more fashionable than Dr. Chuckle.

"Okay, okay." Neal capitulates, and we fumble and struggle to coordinate minds and hands in a knot over his new shirt. This act is symbolic, touching, and farcical: the father, the collar, the cloth, the laying on of hands, the confession of his immaturity. As if to etch our struggle of wills in dexterous contrast, we confront my right-handedness with his left-handedness. My automatic habits are a conundrum as I look at the world through Neal's eyes. I laugh once again through tears of mystification.

"What's so funny?" he snorts indignantly, but with a contagious amusement.

"Never mind, you look great. You'll get the hang of it." I pat him approvingly, and I watch as he gingerly pulls at the tie and marvels as the knot rises to his neck.

With this temporary reprieve, I am valued again. His tie is loose, but I am choked up. I can tie knots in his tie, but he knots my stomach and throat. At the party, he will bear no sign proclaiming, "My dad helped me tie this tie (and taught me so many other things)!" What is available to see is that he is my son, a proud announcement he does not want me to make.

"Thanks, Dad," as he scampers off.

I nod. "You're welcome," I say to the air.

As I arrive home from work one evening following such encounters, Neal greets me solicitously. He runs barefoot toward my car, eager in his purpose and oblivious to the cold driveway.

"Dad, there's something I've got to show you!" In the clamor of reentry to the family abode, he leads me to two long branches straddling each other amid fishing wire.

"I made fishing poles and we went fishing for crawdads!" An impromptu display of his gear ensues, and I follow my practiced discipline of easing into the house and out of my business attire while fielding the excitement of the day. Going to the bathroom could wait—my son, no longer estranged by embarrassment over me, shares his exuberance. We both enjoy this familiar transition into the roles that have often worked so well. Neal and I would share eagerly for awhile in a barter where tacit territory is understood: he offers a recounting of the day's events and anxieties, while I, in turn, listen without judgment, censure, or invasive inquiry. I play my part, and remind myself that these are the good old times I will remember.

"Really? How did you do that? I mean, where did you get the idea for fishing poles?"

"I just did…I found the branches and then we cut them down, and Mom gave me the fishing wire…Dad, you should've seen how the crawdads went after the bait—they really like hot dogs."

"How do you know they really like hot dogs? Did they hang around for mustard?" Dr. Chuckle is back.

Early the next morning, we review the crawdad fishing over dip'n egg (sunnyside egg with a bagel). The sunrise peers over the mountain through the window and falls across the table in slats of sharp effulgence alternating with shadows. The yolk of Neal's egg glows; fresh sunlight stripes his hair with early brilliance. Breakfast platitudes develop into deeper discussion.

"The fishing poles are okay… (mouth full of bagel, dryness… takes some time to masticate the thoughts and bread)…but it didn't turn out the way I wanted."

"What do you mean?"

"I mean the fishing poles didn't come out the way I pictured; they're different. Lots of times things don't turn out the way I picture them in my brain—I mean, when I try to do them, they come out different. It's frustrating."

"You know, that's something I experience, too. For many people, there is a *big* difference between what they think about, say, or want to do and what actually gets done. You're not the only one."

Neal looks at me quizzically, with genuine interest and reflection.

"Part of growing is learning to bridge the gap between what you have in mind, the way the world seems to you, and what you can get across to other people—so that they see and experience the same things that you do. Part of living is also accepting that there *are* differences, sometimes major differences, between what you intend to happen and what actually occurs."

"Is it that way for you, Dad? Do you make stuff that turns out different from the way it's supposed to be?"

"Yeah, Neal…even my jokes." (Dr. Chuckle has to chuckle at this.) "I guess that many times I come across way different than what I mean to…and I know that I can embarrass you and make you feel funny and worked up and annoyed."

My son is studying me. This performance will be written into his philosophy, I sense jitteringly.

"Just like your fishing poles came out different than what you pictured when you started to make them, my humor and attitude and the things I say can have a different effect than what I mean or want. It makes me mystified."

"What's *mystified*?"

"It's like a part of Dad that's a different personality. One part of me is in charge, confident, knowing from practice and experience how things will turn out. That part of me jokes, plays with people, turns on the lovable charm, acts automatically. But there is another side of me that gets confused when the things I try to do turn out otherwise than what I had in mind—when people react against me, or what I thought would happen doesn't—then I get puzzled, mystified.

"O-o-oh," Neal coos in that beguilingly precocious tone he has. "So, *mystified* is what you are when I don't like the way you act as a parent!"

Right.

Or, when I don't like the way you behave as a child. We've both got a lot of growing up to do. And it may not turn out the way we had in mind (chuckle).

DR. CHUCKLE AND MYSTIFIED, PART TWO

Sown in Stitches, Grown to Heal

"I don't deserve to live; I wanna die…I'm just gonna take a gun to my head!"

This plaintive bellow echoed from my son, sitting next to me in the car, across legions of advice I'd given to parents over the years when their children appeared suicidal. I knew it was a yelp of severe angst, the flair of a perturbed state, and not to be magnified beyond the expression of a person absorbed in making himself miserable.

I felt calm within myself, working moderately and successfully at not being provoked. But I was in the paradoxical pain of knowing my son's quandary and being rebuked and pummeled in the face of the obvious solutions I generously extended to him. Excited and out of control, he ascribed his dilemma in every conceivable manner to the conspiratorial events and people around him. I was the bad guy—me, Dr. Chuckle—the prankster sent to torment him. In his state, his soul was conned, so he would not be consoled!

Life teaches us to defend ourselves against the intermittent onslaught of insults, affronts, fears, and provocations that parade under the banner of anxiety. We develop coping skills, learn techniques, and assume veneers that become our roles, our personalities, and sometimes even our careers (Dr. Chuckle, for example).

The nature of upset is fiction. Its story line appears real, as if the environment unfolds events, feelings, and experience independent of the characters. The *response-ability* of being actor, observer, and author at once is usually beyond us. So our coping attempts often include subplots of victim, aggressor, and stage foil. Some of us abandon the production altogether—we put the book down, walk out of the play, withdraw from others, and leave the work incomplete.

Some folks blame the devil for these painful lies. Good fiction, after all, must be believable, and the devil is the master of deception. He makes us believe what is not true. He also uses humor with its many well-honed blunt and sharp-edged varieties. The devil has quite a repertoire of humor, as most will admit, though his humor consists of weapons rather than tools. Recoiling from the horror of a sly infliction, we realize the value of beating the devil at his own game. So the jokes must be quick, and witty, and carefully aimed, and ever ready to joust the devil where he lurks. Don the shield of funny self-protection and watch it work in mirthful ways. The devil hates to be exposed; he disappears from light. The light of humor brings Dr. Chuckle alive, and with him come the merry angels of raillery, parody, caricature, ridicule, banter, mimicry, impersonation, pretense, buffoonery, fantasy, and many puns. The humor must be funny without being hurtful, and there's the rub. For the devil's humor wounds, and in this hurtfulness, blinds us to the drama's falsity.

Accepting life on its own terms and responding with the lightness of jest empowers us to see truth, accept reality, and engage seriously with respect for life's rules. The devil hates to be topped, and especially in good spirits. When the joke is "on us," it is coming from "out there," outside of ourselves. We are mocked by life's penetrating intrusion. When we make the jokes, we make light (in the abstract literal sense), and we create a new perspective and see the reality of which we can take hold. On this stage, Dr. Chuckle makes his entrance.

"Son," I began, "I have a story to tell you." Neal rolled his eyes and inhaled slowly and purposefully, the breath of gathered tense resignation; it was his acknowledgment of my incipient lecture.

"I went out to get a haircut the other Saturday. When I arrived for my five-thirty appointment, the hairdresser was still working on someone. Though mildly disappointed at the delay, I sat down quietly and waited my turn, which surely would come in several minutes. I thought about the propane tank in my car, which I needed to fill to barbecue the dinner that you and the family were waiting for me to cook; I reproved myself for not stopping at the gas station before the tardy hairdresser, and also for being rushed and not allowing a few extra minutes to fill the tank early.

"As I sat waiting a longer time, I became impatient, and my thoughts turned from guilt over delaying the family dinner to righteous indignation about being kept waiting. With my eyes aimed at a magazine, I could feel my self-piteous anger directed at the hairdresser. I felt twisted by an embarrassed concern that she would somehow sense my bruised ill will and a rage that she seemed neither to notice my impatient waiting nor to apologize for the delay. After twenty-two minutes she glanced at me and said, 'Just a few more minutes, I'll be with you; this lady has a lot of hair.'

"And a lot of nerve, the both of you! I was quietly fuming and incensed. I let out a sigh, casting an aggressive glance at my watch. *Ten minutes later,* she beckoned me briskly into the chair. During this time, I was plotting how to vent my displeasure. Now, mind you, my motives were tempered by the fact that I respected and liked this hairdresser a lot, and she had been cutting my hair for years. But I had these pent-up feelings, my family was waiting for dinner, everything was late, and I'd come for her to cut my hair, not my pride.

"I decided to tell her politely that the next time she would be running more than a few minutes late, I would really appreciate her letting me know that as soon as I walked in the door, so I could accomplish whatever errands were pressing on my efficiently busy schedule. In the adult gamesmanship of etiquette, that would be enough to reveal my wrath under the guise of assertive communication. I knew I had to do this, and I waited for an opportune moment. Her daughters were hanging around, so I couldn't risk embarrassing her. As I counted the minutes that she did not apologize fawningly for the delay, I seethed. Twenty minutes into my haircut, she had talked about her recent vacation (which I envied), and it was evident that the vacation was not restful for her. She prattled on to people in the hair salon, kept a watchful eye on her daughters, and answered the phone. Her scissors dangled above my head for long pauses, as my family withered with hunger at home. I noticed how tired she looked, how busy she was, and I remembered my appraisal of her tendency to stretch herself to accommodate many people's needs and demands. I also noted that she accommodated my request for an appointment on the same day—as was our pattern over the years. These thoughts were inconsistent with my recent frustration; I began to feel sheepish. Yes, I *am* busy, but also self-important and imposing.

"Into my reverie the hairdresser shook her head and tossed this lament: 'That lady had lots of hair. I been cutting her hair since a *quarter to five*, just cutting!' Seventy-five minutes of shearing, and I missed over half the show. And our hairdresser usually starts at seven thirty on Saturday mornings.

"'Her six-year-old son is *so* cute, but her ten-year-old is kind of retarded. You know, very slow.'

"What? Who? Oh, the selfish, hairy customer preceding me. Who was slow? I felt slow. Snapping back to the present, I decided to forgo my assertive communication and to concentrate on my haircut, which was turning out very nicely. The phone rang again, and the hairdresser turned her attention away from me. My mind wandered into an attractive place filled with thoughts of pride and fortune: I had accomplished much today, the shopping, the haircut, the exercise, the time with my family. I would soon go home and cook and eat good food. There was another weekend day ahead. The hairdresser turned back to me and snipped (with scissors, of course). I noticed the time she was spending with me, and I felt her care for me. She had been caring for me for years. How had this hairy delay stressed her, and what kind of breach might she have surmised in our relationship? I decided to let it go. The happy thoughts returned with my complacency. Perhaps the recent loss of hair let fresh air into my head and evicted some stale thoughts. I walked out of the salon mystified at the change in me over the past hour. It was not the first time."

Dr. Chuckle emerged from this anecdote into the pondering quiet of Neal's gaze.

1995
Written in satirical humor after waiting for dinner in Chevy's Mexican restaurant.

THE DERRIÈRE DIMENSION

Bottomless Energy in a World of Arrears

"Name?" As the hostess jotted our heritage on the list, she lilted affectatiously, "Party of four?" One child's eyes bugged, and his body stiffened to its full four feet, six inches. "Party? Gosh, Dad, I though we were just going out to dinner!" Already, there were early bird signals that this would feel like a long event.

"How long is the wait?" I ventured.

"About fifteen to twenty minutes," the hostess responded matter-of-factly.

Nimbly, I ran this response through my mental formula, calculating caloric deprivation for at least fifty minutes and seating at a relatively brisk thirty-five. I decided there was ample time to practice my routine.

"How heavy is the length?" I inquired with poker-faced sobriety.

"You know, how long is the wait, how heavy is the length?" I smiled carefully.

The hostess parried my smile with her vacuous imitation of service-industry camaraderie. I realized immediately that I would be denied the satisfaction of mirth at whatever later time my pun seeped beneath her cortical umbrella.

Rebounding within the safety of her profession, the hostess asked condescendingly, "Would you care for some appetizers or drinks?"

"No thanks," I demurred. "I'm watching my height." Still, no applause. My children studied this bombing with dazed admiration, while my wife pretended not to notice. (Were my wife and the hostess conspiring to make me keep my day job?) "You see," I continued, "alcohol makes me feel too tall..."

Now the hostess regarded me with experienced disdain, the kind usually reserved for patrons about to be expelled from the bar. The only problem was, I was sober and yet to part with money in their crowded establishment.

"...so I'll just order a polite."

"Excuse me, sir?"

"*Po*lite, you know, like a Bud lite, only without the beer—you just bring me a glass of water, and I'll drink it, pretending politely that it fills me up while I'm actually waiting to fill up on real food, and you politely pretend to either get my jokes or not, and we'll both politely tolerate each other until my family and I can eat." I meant only to be playful, but this hostess knew how to conceal amusement.

"Your table will be ready in just a few minutes," she lied.

"Which one is ours?" I peered emphatically into the dining room beyond.

The faintest trace of engagement streaked her expression. "Sir, I meant that an empty table would be coming up soon."

"Gee, I'm amazed. I fully expected that we would walk to our table."

She met my snicker with facetious reluctance, so I graciously receded for intermission. I silently praised myself for providing entertainment. More truthfully, it has become a way to contain my restlessness in the world of adult situations that are boring, protracted, and contain precious little that is interesting to do. Adulthood wants you to wait and be still. Childhood knows this is difficult and stupid. I vacillate between the two in...the Derrière Dimension.

The Derrière Dimension is the zone of existence dividing those who prefer life in sedentary positions from those who have ants in their pants. Across the spectrum of life's activities and events, this dimension essentially sorts people into categories of perception, propensity, and population. Once understood, the Derrière Dimension handily accounts for much of the conflict and angst generated by those sitting (or standing) on either side of this invisible yet highly noticeable barrier.

Most people start out in life instinctually with the Dimension's restless side, and there are familiar biological and developmental reasons for this. Children must grow, strengthen, explore, and learn. It takes curiosity, play, energy, and activity to achieve the physical and mental skills needed for survival. Nature's energy donation to younger people seems to accompany its own time requirements for neurological maturation. This is small comfort to those with a larger share of Derrière in the sedentary zone who know cerebrally that energy can neither be destroyed nor created—only siphoned mercilessly from the larger tanks with less fuel to the brimming dynamos who would waste it in capricious movement for its own sake.

Even superficial observation yields a behavioral awareness of the differences among people at the levels of physical size, coordination, and movement. The Derrière Dimension, however, goes deeper and wider. At its core is a spiritual warfare waged incessantly between the guardians of energy and entropy conservation and those predisposed to seek stimulation and action. Like other spiritual battles, those in the Derrière Dimension are engaged on many stages of daily life; however, the scripts and props are often given too much credence and taken far too literally. Only the actors are truly consequential, as they play out their roles in the Derrière Dimension.

Dinner theater was far from the minds of the restaurant staff in our midst. We were restless and hungry and making our presence felt. Even I began bouncing from my chair to the hostess table in search of a commitment to assuage my appetite.

"We'll seat you soon, sir, if you'll just sit down." This illogic backed me slowly away. The polite water cocktail was beginning to take effect; I slurred my words as I attempted to chaperone the kids. "Shut down…I mean, sit up…I mean, sit down and…"

I was beginning to detect accents from the Berlitz secretions in my stomach when I heard our name. After rounding us up, the hostess strode aloofly in front of us to our table with a purpose and speed that reminded me of unpleasant childhood horseback rides; during these frightening excursions, the lead horse paced unrelentingly and without awareness or sympathy for the captive riders who tottered and lurched on the nags following like railroad cars.

Swooning with giddiness (and hunger pangs), we stopped short to the quick announcement of our leader: "Pat, your waitperson, will be here to take your order. Enjoy your dinner." And a second later, our hostperson fairly galloped away, leaving me speechlessly wondering about the gender of waitperson Pat.

My socially graced family was already sitting and had begun the ravenous restaurant ritual of seated stalking—manual pacing with the dinner napkins, frenetic silverware rearranging, and neck-stretching attempts at waitperson sighting. I brought my own derrière down for a chair landing just as Pat arrived.

"Hi, I'm Pat, and I'll be your waitperson this evening. May I tell you about our specials? We have…"

"Hi, Pat, this is my family, and we're pretty special! We'll be your diners and tippersons this evening, and, for the next hour or so, we hope to be your main source of income. Tell us, what do you plan to do with the money you're making off us?"

"We-e-ell," stammered the surprised Pat, "I *am* planning on college in the fall." He tapped his pencil nervously against his order pad, since he had no food or drink to spill or scatter before us. My derrière had settled comfortably, and we were both just warming up. I continued, "How many courses were you planning on taking?" I paused before emphasizing, "Our local university has a five-course semester special. I hear that, with certain mainstream courses, the research is very fresh."

My children had used this exchange as a backdrop against which to develop their silverware sideshow. The acrobatic forks had taken unfortunate tumbles beneath the table, so, suddenly, I was dependent on our audience, Pat.

"That's okay, sir, I'll get you new silverware. Are you ready to order, or would you like a few more minutes?"

My wife, who had been studying the menu with the absorption of a bettor scouring the racetrack program, suddenly sprang to life. "We'd like to order food that doesn't take a long time to prepare. The children are very hungry."

Sly, tactful, honest…these moments reminded me of her precious, practical skills! Despite her cogent communication to the waiter, my wife is masterful at the art of indirection. Rather than deny or deceive, she practices sleight of mind, focusing unsuspecting attention spans on previously unnoticed details, causing them to levitate obsessively in narrow awareness. Like a soothing cocktail, her manner steals upon the gullibly animated, deftly distracting troubles away. She is a dedicated, unpretentious professional who shuns the limelight in favor of daily performances in the circus of child rearing.

Pat excused himself with the speed of a wide receiver; after a sprightly buttonhook behind some adjacent tables, he returned with new silverware. *Thanks for the ammunition, Pat. How 'bout a target? We're starving!!*

He took our orders as my children prepared to go *en garde* with fresh dinner tools. Now, coveting a basket of bread, they expanded their repertoire. I was contemplating the boring aspects of that adult convention called *waiting for dinner* when, to my mortification, the children rocketed through the Derrière Dimension again. The event was table hockey, as the children fired rapid slap shots with their knives. A wad of bread-puck ricocheted into my lap; the younger player—not to be denied—reflexively reached with his knife into my lap. I parried him with my forearm, realizing that I risked more than a face-off. He retreated and studied me in anticipation of reproof.

"Don't you know that hockey is played on *ice*?" I demanded, rebuking this interference as well as the silent sweat on my brow.

"Sorry, Dad," he mumbled. But penitence was shattered almost immediately, as he winced into defense against his brother's knife swipe sending an ice cube skittering across the table.

By this time, my stomach was grumbling unabashedly, and my bladder begged for relief. I had reached the stage where water addiction mollifies the hostility generated by slow service. Restraint from this nervous attraction to my water glass was no longer an option. I was becoming more agitated, hungry, and bloated by the minute. There was so much motion around me, and it all seemed frivolous. Waiters bustled to no avail for my hunger. The children were doing laps around the table. Suddenly, the hostess sashayed into view, bearing all the friendliness of a neon No Vacancy sign. I stopped her abruptly.

"Can you tell me what crime I've been charged with?" I queried with mock innocence. She faltered momentarily, as my punch line hit squarely. "For the last half hour, we've been isolated and fed only bread and water!" Our eyes locked and our wills danced briefly in this twinkling of absurdity. Shuffling away, she countered, "Your dinners should be here any second. I saw them being prepared in the kitchen; the cooks are finishing them right now." Whereupon, the administrative gazelle pranced unfettered to her perch in the dining room jungle. *How does she get away with it?* I ruminated despairingly. *How can she shield herself from ravenous diners with only hostess-speak?*

My boys were prowling more aggressively. The breadbasket lay pillaged, its linen undergarment flailed open in sloppy surrender.

My wife made her move. "Boys, it's only about twenty minutes until dessert. Whoever can sit quietly for the next five minutes will get an extra bite of *my* dessert." A valiant effort, but nature proceeded undeterred.

"Dad, I have to go to the bathroom!"

An excuse for the Derrière Dimension to assert its influence—this time, I welcomed it, the chance to transition to a mobile frame of reference in the quest for structuring randomness and containing chaos. Besides, I really needed to go to the bathroom, too.

The path, though certain, had inviting distractions.

"Dad, can we go inside the kitchen?"

"No."

"*Please!*"

"No, you can*not* go in the kitchen!"

"*Why* not?"

"It's dangerous...people are hurrying around, there are knives and hot plates and ovens...and, besides, the kitchen has a job to do, and there's a lot of pressure, demands, food all over, and people running around...it's no place for kids."

"Sounds like a perfect place for kids," my younger one piped.

"It's not," I countered.

Perceptibly attuned, my younger son asked, "Dad, why are they so nervous in the kitchen?"

"They're working very hard so that the customers can relax."

Once again, the paradox of the Derrière Dimension has surfaced! Frenetic behind-the-scene kitchen smolderings hurtled hustling disarrayed waitpersons into sharp contrast with their sedentary customers. As both patron and parent, I was reminded of the poignant proverb that the world appears very different depending upon whether you are the hawk or the mouse.

The chase was on—I played both mouse and hawk, alternating between discomforts. I trailed my children as they scampered toward the restrooms, ostensibly supervising their exodus from the boredom of dining. Yet I, too, scurried aside and scuttled under the bustling restaurateurs bearing down upon me in predatory posture with their talons extended under scalding trays.

As the kids and I weaved through the aisles dodging waitpeople, I flashed on a familiar memory: *watch the hips; he ain't goin' nowhere without his hips.* In my youthful athletic days, when prodigious advice from coaches watered my thirst for competition, this maxim saved me from flummoxing many plays. The genetic dice rolled me out well under six feet, so I learned to play defense. In the shuffle of chicanery, ambivalence, and crossover fake moves, I followed hips and rear ends closely and developed the persistence of flypaper. In my youth, I was active—a swaggering, swift hyperbole of intention. Yet my understanding of the Derrière Dimension was just nascent.

In college, the Derrière Dimension had new lessons for me. I learned the psychological principle of displacement activity (e.g., the sudden urgent need to engage in pressing tasks, such as cleaning my oven the night before final exams). And I met Joe…at the athletic club. He was lost somewhere in middle age with the illusion that his overweight sagging body could match him equitably against men sporting half his years. Joe's balding pate sweated faithfully in the gym and on the racquetball court. While I feared for his health, Joe crouched in fun. He didn't run much, and jumping only went on around him, but Joe knew the rules. He was savvy and tenacious. On the basketball court, he set picks that would bruise; on the racquetball court, he was a Copernican nightmare. He shined at the center of stars constellating and burning out around him. Joe would plant himself in the middle of the court and hit the ball artfully at his favorite spots along four walls. I ran and bounced and sneaker-squeaked inches short of Joe's anchored body. Almost every play I banged into walls with the grace of an untied balloon, propelling and caroming aimlessly to a quick, deflated depletion. When I wasn't wide-eyed with adrenaline for an impending crash, I watched Joe's hips. They barely moved. Joe knew one dance step well: the pivot. I never scored more than five points to Joe's twenty-one-point victories. In his orbit, I glimpsed the prophecies of the Derrière Dimension across the ages.

Joe was older, fatter, and wiser. He may have lacked the excitement of feeling the wind rush through his hair (what hair?), but he knew where he was and sensed the location of others. He could compensate, and it served him well and joyously. Time has warped my energy and derrière; it's enough to be in one place at a time. Life is lived looking forward, but understood looking backward. The Derrière Dimension has taught me also to use mirrors. The reflections can be wise, but sometimes confusing.

In the right lighting, the wisdom of sages pierces through the Derrière Dimension. Carl Jung, the eminent psychoanalyst, knew about the Derrière Dimension when he categorized personality archetypes nearly a century ago. Jung characterized with vivid dimensionality the temperaments behind the scenes of human activities, needs, and preferences. He portrayed one-dimensional aspect of personality as the tendency to be active and extroverted and a counterbalancing tendency toward passivity and reflection. Jung's work was refined by William Marston in the 1920s and John Geier in the 1970s. Marston defined a matrix in which behavioral types were combinations of active and passive tendencies, and expectations were combinations of favorable and unfavorable outlooks. Geier adapted this matrix to practical applications of coping skills and environmental modifications. Although these eminent scholars did not specifically mention the Derrière Dimension, it is certain that they knew the Dimension well, and that it prominently influenced their work. These scholars explained personality and behavior in lowest common denominator terms: the restless, the quick-acting, the impatient, the impulsive, the need for variety and stimulation...pitted perennially against the staid and steady, the consistent, the familiar, the need for security and slow (if any) change.

In view of the Dimension's complexities and the differences among people, our universe can be gracefully accommodating. After all, except for the first few years of life, we all use the same size toilet seat, *n'est-ce pas*?

Après relief, we have settled back down to finish the rummaging at our table. The bathroom break was a welcome diversion, but I knew we were well past intermission and nearing the end of this prandial show. I discerned this perceptibly from my wife's manner. Although she did not pace, her disquietude became apparent. It was almost time to go; the afterglow of digestion would be brief. Peristalsis has rarely slowed our children. The Derrière Dimension holds daily wonders.

My kids are terrific, I marveled. A shuddering thought accompanied my prideful glow: this is the *alphanumeric* generation, a mutant cultural deviation affecting all socioeconomic classes, English, science, and even homeschoolers. This is the first generation in the evolution of man to use keyboards as principal weapons. Whereas we hitchhiked with our thumbs, our youth hit the highway with more than one finger. The modem is the main vehicle of the runaway. Gone are the days of bawdy rebellion; here is the era of baud rate rebellion. Generation gap is now signaled by disconnection from the network.

Yet for all their technological rocketry, my kids represent the generation that thinks cereal grows in colorful boxes, money grows in parents' clothes, paper and plastic are the state's two indigenous trees, and recycling means going for *another* bicycle ride. The changes we think of as modern are simply fashion statements on the timeless stage of the Derrière Dimension.

Waitperson Pat returned for what he hoped would be a final bow. Although his temporary desertion caused indignation, his return brought a surprising embarrassment. At our table, dessert had decomposed into a swirl of psychedelic sugar stains that my children attacked with primitive slurping swallows. I felt as though *Wild Kingdom* had come to film our dinner. At any moment, Marlin Perkins could have appeared with the check.

"Can I get you anything else?"

"Yes, Pat," I retorted, determined to instill the good work habits he would need to succeed in college. "We'd like to take home the leftovers—in biodegradable containers, of course. I'm teaching the children about conservation of energy and resources."

Pat absconded in a fluid and skittish motion.

"And thanks for the attentive service," I tossed after him.

Surveying the remains of our strafed meal, I gulped the last of my drink and nodded toward my family with a languid, dysphasic smile. "If youth but aged, if would but could," I murmured complacently. Contemplating this description of life's order, I tilted my glass upward and waited for the last rivulets to meander tongueward. Through the convex glass window seat, I peered around the generational distortions and caught my children's quizzical stares.

Nothing would diminish my lip-smacking, savoring toast to the differences in energy, temperament, and movement that characterize the Derrière Dimension. *Bottoms up!*

2003
Written many years after realizing I am not a very good musician.

DOMESTIC VIOLINS

I'Stradivarius Instruments of Family Discord

The clarion call has sounded for the relief of a spreading, pernicious, and discordant trend in domestic harmony. There is a crisis in the abuse of euphonics, our social fabric threatened by the proliferation of seemingly innocuous romantic musicals. Sirens blare within the erstwhile melodious orchestra of family relationships, and this is nowhere more blatantly evident than in the painful shrieks of domestic violins.

The mournful, musical melodrama of domestic violins occurred in my family; my childhood was marred by this tragedy. Hopefully, this story will encourage other sufferers to come forward. In keeping with the family patterns that perpetuate such difficulties, my clan history must be revealed.

Until the turn of this century, my family generations were from Eastern Europe. Poverty and discrimination reigned, undoubtedly giving rise to such stress reducers as fantasies of immigration and upward mobility and the yearning for musical expression. The poverty and stress continued in New York, where my mother and father grew up in separately strange households, preparing themselves unknowingly for the crescendo of discord in which I would later solo. My father's family was apparently *de rigeur* with regard to musical development. That side of the family had scant musical talent, and there is no documentation of efforts in that regard. They listened and enjoyed the tunes devised by others, passively contributing occasional royalties, and steering clear of police and emergency rooms by mollifying their anger under the big band harmonies of the day. This was no small accomplishment, considering the cramped apartments, open windows, and humid ethnic venting so common on the Lower East Side of Manhattan. My father's family thought themselves pillars of the Jewish community, respected for their earnest professional work and pioneering efforts in the development of "elevator music" popularity. My father and his father were dentists. Life was predictable, one could sleep safely on a park bench, and moods were regulated by popular and dance music. (Bipolar disorder was then thought of as a problem of acoustics.)

My mother's Brooklyn upbringing was somewhat different. Pennies were always at a premium, and the tenor of the household pierced stridently argumentative. Grandma's dream seemed coming true until my mother broke her wrist and could no longer continue the violin lessons eked out by the sweat of the matron. Alas, those precious discretionary pennies dwindled, and when my mother's wrist healed, her opportunities for musical advancement had vanished. The genetic imperative would have to wait another generation.

Aside from the sporadic spankings, frequent frustration, and constant screaming, my childhood was uneventful until I began seeing a psychiatrist in my teens. The traumas then unfolded like a torrent of rainstorms, washing away my makeshift defenses and cascading me with memories of unwillingness and embarrassment.

I was about ten when the family violins reenacted. It began innocently enough with my mother's suggestion that I take violin lessons because my "obvious genius and talent should be given a chance to blossom in many directions." Like so many victims, I succumbed to the flattery and charm of a loved one. Her stories of pathos about her own aborted career inspired me with guilt and determination. This was a family mission, and I was the identified musician.

Oh, how I tried! With valiant persistence, I mixed small amounts of practice with volumes of avoidance. I stared daily down the convergent strings along the neck of the wooden beast I wanted to smash. In the harsh light, those beady pimples of the études glared at me defiantly, taunting me with complexities of emotion I hadn't the discipline or maturity to master. I wanted to reach back in time and strangle Mozart. Instead, I remained helpless and incompetent in the face of my short and stern German violin teacher who punished me with weekly regularity.

"Dumkopf!" he'd bellow in disgust, with the accompanying thrust of his palm into the end of my violin, causing my neck to reverberate in pain and the rest of me in shame. Herr Steinberg was seldom pleased. This severe man had two things noticeably in common with me—his last name and his height. As my headaches subsided, I would wonder if namesake musical proficiency came with the associated costs of stunted growth and sadism. Herr Steinberg was a meticulous, attentive, and consistent teacher. Every mistake elicited a slight blow to the violin (along with its conductive anatomical result) and an insult about my performance and general suitability as a student.

Domestic violins had begun its toll. I wore turtleneck sweaters to hide the bruises on my neck and collarbone. In secret, I cracked my knuckles obsessively, hoping to loosen the cramping and attain flexibility in my fingers. I drowned my sorrows with quarts of Pepsi to wash down the aspirin and replace the tears I shed listening to the maudlin strings of the Percy Faith Orchestra. Eventually, I became a rosin abuser. With addictive persistence, I rubbed and varnished my bow to unnecessary sleekness. It was partly nervous habit and partly desperate development of *something* in my repertoire of violin playing that I could do without revealing my ineptitude. I prayed that the rosin-coated bow would glide across the violin bridge smoothly enough to eliminate the creaking/shrieking/whining that characterized my playing and my punishment.

I brushed and coated and swathed the bow with rosin until the deep grooves in the amber wax caused it to thin and to break. When my parents requested a new rosin bar from Herr Steinberg, the secret was out. I could contain no longer my wrath, my oppression, my neck aches, my incompetence with this elusive instrument, and my resentment at having a teacher of my height and my name who didn't understand me.

Herr Steinberg said his piece, too. How frustrating it had become for him to work with undisciplined American students! The lack of regimentation and compliance pervading these families! It is no wonder, then, that despite the grueling efforts of European masters such as himself, there would likely be few worthy violinists native to this soil!

Despite his shortcomings, history bears him out. We idolize Itzhak Perlman and Yehudi Menuhin, and we marvel at the developing brilliance of Asian violinists. We are stuck with the embarrassment of domestic violins. Even as we revere the contributions of foreign protégés, discord and lack of harmony shatter the peace of so many American families.

What is to be done about this terrible problem? A number of solutions have been proposed. As usual, advocates loudly proclaim education as the answer. This platitude continues to *sound* good; however, domestic violins grows, even as levels of education rise. Paradoxically, budgets for music education are being cut. The movement toward greater education would appear, then, to progress in a minor key. A grace note: there is an expanding effort to educate children away from domestic violins by means of the Suzuki method of violin instruction. Although the more refined and foreign cultural influences are commendable, it remains to be seen whether the Suzuki denizens will treat their loved ones to sweeter harmonies or will propagate the American tradition of violins to its shattering consequences.

A militant constituency is demanding punishment for the first offense. Our society is becoming less tolerant of deviant behavior, and more exposure greets the public ear. The concealments of past generations are emerging under scrutiny and criticism. This has its value. Social scientists have affirmed that families model bad behaviors as well as good ones. I can attest to this from my own sordid experience. My youthful fiddling was enjoined by my grandmother, perhaps from her recollection of her failure to provide for my mother's musical development. Grandma habitually would pick up my violin and try to play—always the same song—"Hatikvah," the Jewish national anthem. Under a master's bow, this dirge could evoke enough sorrow to make *Schindler's List* appear as comedy. There are no figures of speech to describe the agony of Grandma's repeated renditions. At the time, I thought that perhaps washing her mouth out with rosin would be appropriate. This fantasy effected only minimal distraction from her torturing performances. It is another matter, however, to imagine that today Grandma could be incarcerated for her musical behavior. And since she was born in another country and played only one song, a foreign anthem, I'm not sure whether this would be seen as actual domestic violins…

We have too few shelters to accommodate all those who try their hands at domestic violins. Far too many of us are imbalanced, unstable, impulsive, uncoordinated, insensitive, or just plain tone deaf. Incarceration is not the answer. There are multitudes who practice what they screech. Earplugs won't do it. Perhaps diversion programs would help; we could encourage the more aggressive repeat performers to take up the drums. The stage has already been set by the rising popularity of rap music. (Contrary to popular beliefs amplified through media hype, rock 'n' roll, hip-hop, and rap music have not increased the use of domestic violins. In counterpoint, the renewed interest in classical music has contributed to the practice of domestic violins. Classical music is serious, provocative, and deeply emotional; it stimulates primitive instincts and plays upon heartstrings.)

What then? Perhaps an old-fashioned solution applies—the use of beautiful "music to soothe the savage beast," as the saying goes. We need fewer tariffs, more global recognition for performers, and an influx of recorded artists on imported labels. World-renowned orchestral music, serious strings, and the works of long-dead composers could be piped into public buildings and commercial enterprises. This would make the reduction in domestic violins a community effort.

In the meantime, rehabilitated offenders like myself are left to tinkle aimlessly and harmlessly on synthesizers with automatic bass clef chords, programmed songs, and factory-reduced volumes. I make no attempts to improvise or cause sounds to arise from acoustical stringed instruments (my family would report this to the authorities). Occasionally I sneak a little jazz listening, but, for the most part, there is harmony in my home.

The cupboards have been cleared of all Percy Faith, 1001 Strings, and even Mantovani albums. Temptation to engage in domestic violins has been greatly diminished. Lawrence Welk is not welcome in our home.

There is a moral to this tragic saga: don't fiddle around with domestic violins—you can damage major, minor, and spinal c(h)ords. Remember that it takes more than playing with words to (M)ache (m)usic.

1997
Written the night before my first knee surgery and during my first marriage.

SEX-CHANGE OPERATIONS

Provocative Undressing and Bandage Practices

I want to talk about sex. Doing it is preferable, but that is impractical now, since I've just had knee surgery and my positioning is limited. My temporary disability has occasioned, however, new discoveries and adventures in intimacy with my wife who, alas, also has just had surgery.

A new and unexpected episode in middle age has brought us closer than I thought physically possible (given the medical circumstances). Even better is the renewed sense of indulgence and sharing as we grope for pleasure in a frenetic interdependent imbalance. At this tender time, when a two-point toilet seat landing seems a great accomplishment, I am experiencing plateaus of conjugal sharing never hinted at by the *Kama Sutra* or the excesses of previous biology and physiology courses.

Lest the reader be taunted by verbal foreplay, I will come straight to the point: Twenty years of sexual devotion to my wife, Barbara, hardly prepared me for the novelty of doing it while medically impaired. The challenge therein relegates conquest secondary to performance and gives rise to the truism that "desire is the mother of intention."

Four years after the battle scars of breast cancer, my wife was bluntly surprised by a suspicious mammogram, necessitating a biopsy and further assaulting an already wounded breast. Fortunately, the results proved healthy and normal this time, but not, however, without surgical intrusion leaving tenderness, swelling, and a *kabash* on normal activity. I, in turn, have been limping along at the effects of torn meniscal cartilage, supporting my family with a lot more certainty than my own weight or sense of buoyancy. Barbara and I have noticed the impact of impaired kneeling on activities other than prayer. And breasts, though normally sensitive, become much more shy after encounters with the surgeon's tools.

Physicians don't usually talk about sex under these circumstances. As patients, we are so concerned about the prospects of healing and returning to our normal activities that we never get to discussing with our doctors the process of healing and engaging in our normal activities.

Whether it is a fling back at youth, the normal throes of desire, or our determined attempts to salvage pleasure in the gritty face of middle-age insults, Barbara and I bucked the twinges of pain and elevated our bandaged conditions to the ritual of careful undressing. These erogenous adventures have given new meaning to the concept of blood flow.

The merely physical endeavors cannot describe the levels of intimacy we experienced when we compared tissue samples. I assure you: this is a piercing level of familiarity. It is a whole new experience to discover your lover at a cellular level. It is not the path we would have chosen but for the symptoms that required lab reports. Exposed to such scrutiny, my wife and I appreciate each other beyond the physical degradation we were led to confront. That Barbara and I had a magnetic attraction could hardly prognosticate the moments we would review MRI reports. There is a peculiar voyeurism in watching my wife's breasts palpated by the surgeon. Although we trust him, we both want out of there. Instead, the show progresses, and I watch detailed pictures on the fluorescent screen. With unexpressed irony, I observe this situation where I can publicly stare at a woman's breasts (my wife's) in male company (the doctor) with encouragement (in the name of medicine). I can look, but not touch. I am not turned on, but I am rather electrified by the passion and caring I feel for my wife. In tactile powerlessness, I reach feebly and stroke the X-ray, searching for the strands of fascination in my wife's tissues that are the cause of such fuss.

A nurturing affectionate mood sweeps over me in waves as I regard my wife and our memories swimming through my glands. It is my body vulnerable here, even as she houses the nerve endings. I think of our myriad passionate moments, and I realize how connected we are through commitment. Separate orgasms have blended over time and repetition into one organism, a spiritual relationship that nourishes two bodies. At times, we nourish and nurture each other in unexpected ways. Discussing and comparing our pain medications is one of the more eccentric twists in our present closeness.

Evenings with drugs, needles, and risky outcomes were absent from our innocent attraction. Barbara and I had a typical courtship that included movies, concerts, restaurants, graduate studies, and time spent grooming and admiring each other's appearance and abilities. We offered the obligatory good impressions upon each other's families, never paying the least mind to the genetic factors they bestowed. We married with the naïve belief that our parents were simply guests at our wedding and observers of our union. The concept of children served as a rationale for our parents' slow learning tendencies, and we never considered early in our relationship that sacrifice would produce wisdom and gratification or that passion would evolve with wrinkles, cellulite, and accommodation of injuries and family vulnerabilities.

In the earlier years, sex was all that we drove it to be, except difficult—which posed it in sharp contrast to many other areas of life that were strenuous beyond suitable reward. We sought each other frequently in fervor and ecstasy; we excused mutual faults and hid resentments beneath newly acquired carpets and appliances, so we could rejuvenate covertly from an oppressive commercial world. Sex happened quickly, but love took its time.

The blessing of children brought new perspectives on time and privacy. It also taught us much about ownership and stewardship of one another's bodies. The demands of parenthood and the routines of security slowly anesthetized desire. Spontaneity became once again a difficult spelling word, and obligation tended to stretch itself beyond abdomens. Over the years, life's surprises harnessed inroads to novelty, but none so abrupt and arresting as our middle-age medical crises. By this time, we were stuck on each other, as well as with each other. As soon as the terror of disease doom subsided, we wondered secretly and covetously about the resurgence of FUN. I looked at my wife, whose innumerable expressions are mapped in my midbrain, and knew intuitively that the soothing lubricant would be accommodation. We would have to vary our repertoire again. While anticipating excitement, I feared a groin pull.

Medical treatment, especially elective surgery, has that "Last Supper" effect. I hobbled to bed with Barbara, going for broke while we each defended our tender parts. It was a memorable game, despite the injuries. Part of what made it so good was knowing that my wife would not hurt me beyond the bruises and insults I'd already sustained—and that she knew my previous playing abilities and seasonal averages.

My turn under the lights arrived, and I mulled compulsively over the quality sleep I hoped my doctors had the night before. With my usual aplomb, I told at least ten jokes, hoping to have the OR staff in stitches (no pun in ten did). The anesthesiologist quaffed me with his elixir, smothering me in overstated humor, and suggesting, as his sedation encroached, that I could have the "pinking shear designer second circumcision" at no extra charge. With a captive audience, this guy was a knockout. I slipped from consciousness with a vision of this religious ritual, wondering if it would result in the Second Coming…

Après surgery, Barbara ministers to me while nursing her own healing wounds. We are an experiment in recovery. My leg is in such pain that I am without energy to hypothesize pleasure. My wife is so nice to me, and so vitally alluring. Her most attractive feature right now is that she can walk. The achievement of climbing stairs must precede the prospect of climbing each other. I aspire to ascend again the physical heights of buildings and pleasure.

It is said that time heals all wounds—but what about sex? Aha, we are mature and responsible adults; we can stimulate and pleasure each other without the need for isopropyl alcohol. We use ice at opportune moments. Engorgement and swelling come naturally. Analgesics and pain ensure heavy breathing. We are equipped and somewhat eager. Veterans of the "mile-high" club hold no prestige above our delight—we are pioneers of the "passed out, but coming to" club of sexual interest. We are creative and devoted to each other. Our lust is revived by the knowledge that if illness required one of us to finish the other's sentences, each would undoubtedly know what to say.

We've enjoyed rare moments when rapture was speechless (except for the surgeon's narration). Perhaps the climax of our mature affection occurred (dare I reveal) while watching an arousing physical video featuring my very private parts. The theme involved cartilage and excited nerve endings. I always suspected that a loose tag of tissue distinguished me—and here it was being shorn on camera! Had this film been properly titled, it would be called *The Throbbing Meniscus.* This viewing had both of us on the edge of our bed. It was a very tender moment, but I could only relive and relieve it with Percocet.

Although it was filmed under antiseptic conditions, Barbara and I treasure my knee surgery as our one-and-only dirty video. This compellingly personal, deeper-than-naked penetration reminds us how fragile and important we are to each other. The phrase "I need you" now carries additional meaning. And new meaning is what it's all about.

It may be a bit kinky to eroticize surgery, but we find that meaning and humor and love abound. Our experience is reminiscent of the patient who responds to the Rorschach cards with a parade of sexual images. When the psychologist comments about this, the patient says, "But Doc, you're the one showing me the dirty pictures!"

My sex life with Barbara is so satisfying because we really know each other inside and out.

1990
Commentary on what goes on in families.

EVOLUTION OF NAGGING

Have you heard these lately?

Talking to you is like talking to a wall! I'm not talking just to hear the sound of my own voice. How many times must I tell you? Do you think I enjoy this? Mom, pleeease!!

The Problem

Everybody hates nagging! We avoid people who nag, and we scurry from self-recriminations and guilt over exhibiting this dreaded behavior ourselves. Ironically, the negative reputation of nagging is undeserved. This is because nagging has survival value. Just as food nourishes and fortifies our bodies, nagging nurtures and strengthens our abilities to cope. The problem is that our modern society has flooded us with nagging, just as it has glutted most of us with more food than we need. Given this inundation, we tend to lose perspective. For example, many dieters think food is the enemy. This, of course, is ridiculous. Food is necessary and pleasurable; it is the indulgence in too much and the wrong kind of food that gives eating a bad name. So it is with nagging, an activity whose fundamental value in building ego strength, interpersonal skills, and neurological endurance has long been overlooked. Nagging has evolved to facilitate the primary human survival tasks of socialization, learning, and self-protection.

Socialization

As a socialization technique, nagging is matchless. Nagging continues to be the most popular and effective method of convincing someone else that you are right, that he doesn't know what he's talking about, and that only the vigilant expression of your opinion will save him from the error of his ways. The altruistic benefit of nagging has the additional merit of inflating the nag's ego, thus reinforcing the sense of belonging. This samaritan practice originated and still flourishes in the family, that bastion of security in which socially acceptable behaviors and their variations are endlessly rehearsed.

In the days before TV (please refer to curricular American history textbooks), nagging was the basic form of family communication. (It was much more effective then, since it could amplify to head-splitting crescendos without the deflating, distracting, and narcotizing saturation of TV.) Family communication is facilitated by familiarity, an element conducive to nagging. In psychologically normal individuals, nagging requires a measure of familiarity; thus, nagging in a relationship signifies that the nag is capable of intimacy, perhaps to excess.

Learning

Besides socialization, nagging plays a critical role in education. Fortunately, this important aspect of child development is ideally implemented by our schools, thereby complementing the effects of family life. Charged with the task of fostering learning, educators extensively rely on nagging to avail and intensify learning opportunities. Despite euphemisms like "guided practice" and "reinforced feedback," good teaching basically consists of presenting information in an environment where students can be relentlessly nagged and coerced until they remember it. Since learning is a function of repetition, nagging ranks high on the list of effective teaching techniques.

By definition, nagging *is* repetition. People learn through repetition. People buy because of repetition. For generations, merchants and governments have incorporated elements of nagging into profitable trade and nationalism. However, modern advertising has overly commercialized nagging. Electronic media have removed the subtle "human element" from salesmanship, the original art form of nagging. Actually, the decline of this art form has reached a nadir with the advent of computerized telenagging (see below).

Self-Protection

Nagging is instrumental in developing endurance and ego-protective defenses. Building a resistance to constant carping helps people ward off life's noxious impingements. Unfortunately, too much TV hinders this process. Nagging and TV have opposite effects on the nervous system. TV is a temporary anxiety suppressor and analgesic whose insidious effects appear months and years later. Alternatively, nagging is an anxiety inducer. While producing virtually immediate unpleasant reactions, nagging relentlessly builds an endurance and imperviousness to most types of intrusive stimuli. The process strengthens immunity such that, after years of aversive nagging, most of life's difficulties are readily ignored or tolerated.

Criticisms of nagging as "manipulative conditioning" or "negative modeling" overlook the survival value of nagging as assertiveness training. Nagging's bad reputation can hide an important psychological function it serves: maintaining interpersonal distance, a necessity for avoiding the hurt and disillusionment that lead to depression.

The Solution

The power of nagging is that it seems overwhelming, pervasive, and unending; it simply wears us down. It throws us into self-pity or impulsive escape. However, a prudent understanding of nagging's merit, as well as its overextensions and illogicality, will ease its adverse effects. Identifying nagging by "type" is one way of reducing the stress that often results in self-pity, escape, or violence. Refer to the following guide:

Prompting (intellectual and scientific nagging)—this jargon refers to providing cues or "arranging the environment" so that a subject will give the desired response. Used on living creatures ranging from rats to humans, prompting is a theoretical excuse to nag. When I took psychology and education courses in college twenty years ago, "prompting" was nagging, and it's still nagging today.

Expressive nagging—a generic form of nagging, usually perceived by the nag as being overly reasonable and indulging.

Dominagging—this industrial strength variation is mostly practiced by people who delight in exerting dominance (very popular among managers and administrators; also traditional in ethnic parenting).

Editorial nagging—this is a truly persistent and annoying habit in which the nag verbalizes a running commentary on all events in life. This form of nagging originated with the philosopher Barkeley, who postulated that phenomena exist only when someone perceives them. This philosophy is even less romantic today.

Teaching—this prevalent and exalted form of nagging is fundamental in all walks of life. Professional technique and theory notwithstanding, getting someone to learn new behaviors justifies the means. Along with parenting and salesmanship, teaching probably makes the most valuable use of nagging.

Neganagging—all forms of whimpering and complaining fit in this category. Neganagging can be aggressive ("You'll never amount to anything!") or passive ("What did I do to deserve this?"). The key feature in identifying this type is the presence of large amounts of disgust.

Culture glue (bonding)—imparts a sense of individuality and belonging through adherence to particular family, peer, religious, or community norms; it uses guilt incisively. Imagine how you would feel if you missed that gathering!

Nagatising—refers to the variety of advertisements that bombard us regularly. Although it is frequently not consciously noticed, nagatising works. Check your bank statement.

Telenagging—incorporating all forms of electronic intrusion, this was popularized through "Reach out and touch (push) someone" commercials; telenagging stretches from family phone calls to unsolicited robocall offers by a computer.

Meshugganosis—this serious condition (identified by Dr. Jonathan Greene of Los Angeles) affects the erstwhile normal person's ability to monitor how many times he has said something, despite intense feedback from others. It involves perceptual dysfunction in which mindless repetition (e.g., jokes, health advice, opinions) is perceived by the meshugga as original insight.

With this basic background in the evolution and character of nagging, you are ready for some practical examples. (This exercise is much more effective without medicine.) Try to identify the following by type, and think how you would respond in your own life:

"Talking to you is like talking to a wall!" (Actually, it would be more accurate to say "talking through a wall," since usually the people who hear the nag are in the next room or next apartment.)

"I'm not talking just to hear the sound of my own voice." Correct—in addition to bellowing the sound of his voice, the nag is probably raising his blood pressure, creating tension, irritating his throat, and annoying innocent bystanders.

"How many times must I tell you?" This apparently innocent Zen question probably has a specific numerical answer—and requires interminable patience to discover it.

"Do you think I enjoy this?" Absolutely.

"Mom, pleeease!!" Aren't polite children wonderful?

By now, you should hold a different attitude about nagging. If this isn't enough to convince you, please accept the sobering fact that the only known cure for nagging is to have grandchildren. (The cure is twofold: Firstly, since grandchildren by definition have less history of nagging than older family members, they are more gullible and less inclined to interpret nagging as nagging. Secondly, research has shown that grandparents' nagging is significantly inhibited by recognition of their own nagging traits in their children as parents.)

If you are not a grandparent, the best thing is to acknowledge the contribution of nagging to your personality and well-being. You can reap the benefits of nagging without being a victim. By discovering the roles that nagging plays in your daily life, you can take control of this powerful motivator.

Indeed, there is much more to write on this topic—but I'm being nagged to finish this article for publication.

As a tool for expression, nagging is unparalleled. The primitive icons chiseled by cavemen leave little doubt about humankind's distinguishing commitment to impressing its view upon others. The colonization and conquest of many frontiers undoubtedly followed years of persistent agitation.

Delving into the psychology of nagging requires the consideration of three primary theoretical orientations: behaviorism, psychoanalysis, and social learning theory. Behaviorists would explain that, in the nagging paradigm, the child has conditioned the parent to say something fourteen times before the child will attend or comply. Psychoanalysts would interpret that the nagging parent compulsively replays a guilty identification with a parent who nagged him. Social learning theorists would claim that people learn to nag by imitating influential models. However, these viewpoints fail to explain the multitude of situations in which nagging occurs without apparent provocation (e.g., the adult nags the child who has already satisfactorily done what he was asked) or role modeling (e.g., the child nags his parents for a procession of toys while omniscient grandparents smugly and silently watch).

Moreover, the traditional psychological views overlook the value of nagging in building ego strength, interpersonal skills, and neurological endurance. It seems that nagging has purpose and origin quite different from its traditional stereotype.

In the days before TV (please refer to curricular American history textbooks), nagging was the basic form of family communication. It was much more effective then, since it could build to head-splitting crescendos without the deflating, distracting, and narcotizing inundation of TV. Nagging and TV have opposite effects on the nervous system. TV is a temporary anxiety suppressor and analgesic whose insidious effects appear months and years later. Alternatively, nagging is an anxiety inducer. While producing virtually immediate unpleasant reactions, nagging relentlessly builds an endurance and imperviousness to most types of intrusive stimuli. The process strengthens immunity such that, after years of aversive nagging, most of life's difficulties are readily absorbed and tolerated.

Nagging assists people in warding off life's noxious impingements. Though it is frequently explained as a manipulative conditioning, nagging is actually crystallized purposeful behavior, fortified with the discipline of practice: the original assertive behavior! Although it may appear as modeled negative social behavior, such interpretation masks the true social function of nagging: maintaining interpersonal distance, a critical element in avoiding the hurt and disillusionment that lead to depression. Paradoxically, then, nagging is an important part of growth, skills development, and adaptive socialization. Fortunately, such a critical aspect of child development is ideally implemented in our cultural family life and curricular education.

Nagging is instrumental in developing endurance and ego-protective defenses. Building a resistance to constant carping helps people rebuff life's offensive intrusions. Unfortunately, too much TV hinders this process.

Another troubling defense against the effects of nagging is the recent prevalence of inexpensive headphones and tape decks. These ubiquitous items extend the repertoires of children in tuning out adult nagging in so many environments. Freud would attribute this indulgence to an ego defensive narcissistic regression—but, then, Freud never listened to Whitney Houston or New Kids on the Block.

In psychologically normal individuals, nagging requires a degree of familiarity in the relationship. Thus, it is a sign that the nag is capable of intimacy (perhaps to excess). In his treatise on attachment theory, psychologist John Bowlby popularized the concept of human bonding—but then, Bowlby wrote before Crazy Glue was around.

By definition, nagging is repetition. People learn through repetition. People buy because of repetition. Commercial advertising has perfected nagging. Electronic media have removed the subtle "human element" from salesmanship, the original art form of nagging. Actually, the decline of this art form has reached a nadir with the advent of computerized telenagging.

While observing our four-year-old son watching an inane sequence of commercials on Saturday morning TV, my wife and I engaged in a discussion about nagging. Actually, this intellectual exercise served to defuse the anxiety created by our child's nagging: "I want this...Mommy, could you buy me this toy...Daddy, I want that...Mommy, Daddy!"

I excused myself to my office to better concentrate and reflect on the subject of nagging. (Lest the astute reader interpret my action as a cowardly escape, I should mention that I had performed my low-probability behavior of housecleaning, and was therefore free to engage in my high-probability behavior of daydreaming. My family has trained me well!)

1994
A specialty diagnosis.

A PENSION DEFICIT DISORDER

A National Epidemic

As we plunge headlong into the next century, scientists and economists alert us to a controversial disturbance affecting more Americans than ever before imagined. The problem is known as a pension deficit disorder, and it is apparently reaching epidemic proportions. This handicapping condition (which afflicts millions) smolders like a fire in the walls, just at a time when more and more Americans are looking to the government for assistance. Left untreated, this disorder could leave millions without adequate resources and abilities to cope with the increasing demands and complexity of our society.

The root cause of a pension deficit disorder is not specifically known; some think that it is environmental, the product of a culture oriented toward immediate gratification—seek pleasure now, pay (if there's anything left) later. Others see the problem as inherited from our nation's capitalist foundation (thus, a pension deficit disorder is sometimes associated with Tocqueville's syndrome). There are those who maintain that the problem results from an imbalance of economic transmitters. Still others believe that the condition results from a systemic cause—a malfunctioning fiduciary gland, frontal office damage, or a staff infection.

Despite the disagreement regarding etiology, most professionals and an increasing number of lay people are beginning to recognize the collection of symptoms by which it is characterized. A pension deficit disorder is identified by the following hallmark signs:

- Poor self-regulation of the governing body
- Excessive risk-taking
- Poor planning / lack of follow-through
- Lack of concern for consequences
- Tendency to downplay problems and view them as belonging to "someone else"
- Lack of compulsiveness about money
- Deficits in organization of the organization
- Tendency to misplace or lose valuables
- Authority problems / rebellious attitude / disrespect for rules
- Sudden or progressive loss of interest
- Lack of accountability or responsibility
- Deficient executive control of the working body
- Inconsistent memory
- Poor attention to details
- Inability to concentrate assets

In addition to the classic symptoms, the individual with a pension deficit disorder often has problems with anger and, thus, usually operates in the red. So far, two subtypes have been classified:

1) A pension deficit, solitary type with poor residuals

2) A pension deficit with helpless activity

Invariably beginning in childhood, the diagnosis of a pension deficit is frequently not made until well into adulthood when compensation deteriorates. Tragically, this condition often coincides with a lifetime of travail, leading to little to show for all the exertion. Understandably, those with a pension deficit are prone to associated hardships such as depression, depletion, and destitution. The cardinal symptom of a pension deficit is the failure to derive benefits from experience. These people are often without a clue as to what happened. They often have unrealistic appraisals of their assets and liabilities.

Interestingly, two distinct personality types have been linked to the development of a pension deficit. The solitary type can be identified early. As a child, this person is easily recognized by an independence of spirit and nonconformist attitudes and behavior. Usually flaunting self-will and a predilection for autonomy and originality, this individual is seriously at risk for job dissatisfaction, especially while working for someone else. He is likely to find fault with inefficient bureaucracies and to venture out on his own in the marketplace. Undaunted by conservative rebukes or fear of failure, such a person may actually start his own business without the protection of a retirement plan. Self-willed, restless, risk-taking business owners without adequate savings comprise the majority of the subgroup of adults with a pension deficit disorder, solitary type.

A pension deficit with helpless activity is a more pervasive and perhaps more debilitating condition. This disorder is most often suffered by the personality type that places great faith in authority, only to be taken advantage of in the long run. During childhood, these people typically follow the program "going along to get along." Often they are preoccupied with security, sometimes to the extent of developing irrational beliefs that a "parent" organization will take good care of them. Eventually, a pension deficit overtakes them in later years, leaving confusion, poverty, and bitter distrust.

Controversy stirs the debate over what to do about a pension deficit. Some believe that the preferred treatment for a pension deficit is socializing medicine. Critics of this approach point out that while medicine may be increasingly needed by those with a pension deficit, they are also (by nature of the disorder) less able to afford it. Additionally, they note that medicine may provide temporary and palliative relief for a complex problem with social and behavioral ramifications.

Proponents of behavior modification have taken their cues from labor unions by capitalizing on collective bargaining procedures. Pension deficits have been traditional trump cards and bargaining chips in labor negotiations for years; likewise, the problem of a pension can be used as an incentive in behavior modification. Setting goals, adding interest, accumulating funds, building savings—these can all be part of a token economy. Penalties for early withdrawal may further limit impulsivity.

Scientists have basically reached consensus that a pension deficit virtually always involves nervous transactions. Something is wrong at the top, and the malfunction usually implicates nervy firings at the head of the system. Faulty executive control is both at the top and the bottom of these deficits, and researchers increasingly look to self-regulation as a solution that is far more effective and economical than government intervention. Toward this effort, training with biofeedback has shown itself an effective precursor to the radical treatment of polygraph control (dubbed "lie-o-feedback"), a method that has produced startling results with numerous high-functioning, top-level executives with such longstanding deficits in organizational integrity.

For a pension deficit with helpless activity, training in self-awareness, behavior management, and accounting have proven fruitful. In several groundbreaking studies, psychologists have successfully trained sufferers to transfer their skills of keeping track of the wrongs of others to keeping accounting ledgers. When asked for a statement regarding such intervention, three subjects produced balance sheets (rather than the pretreatment verbal abuse). Researchers are encouraged by this trend toward balance and stability.

Financial planning is a vital component in ameliorating a pension deficit. Remedial subsidies dwindle as victims of this disorder experience constant needs for stimulating infusions and arousal of resources. One proposed solution is to cure a pension deficit through a public offering of group assets. However, this is considered risky, as public offerings by those with a pension deficit have typically been unstable, and they tend to decompensate in groups.

Educational approaches seem to portend the most widespread and potentially encompassing need. Because of students running amok in our schools, many teachers are leaving the profession prematurely. Consequently, our educational institutions are singularly disadvantaged by the prevalence of a pension deficit disorder. Experts demand that something be done to save our children's trust (funds). As the twenty-first century approaches, leaders from allied fields clamor for a more profitable investment in the future. Perhaps no group puts it more plainly and succinctly than the nation's teachers:

Please, pay a pension!

1997
Travels across America as a teenager blend with neuropsychological acumen and common sense later in life.

PEACHES AND EGGS

During college, I spent some time among the Oglala Sioux Indians in South Dakota. I remember a very provocative discussion in which a tribe member described cultural and racial differences in rather stark terms.

"White man," he said, "is like a peach: soft, fuzzy, and inviting on the outside, but deep inside there is a hard pit. Indian is like an egg: hard shell on the outside to protect, but inside is delicious goodness and life-giving yolk."

While this analysis may have dubious racial accuracy, it does provide a useful, very simplified model for understanding types of personality responses and differing coping aspects within ourselves. It has practical applications in the healing arts and sciences.

From years of engaging in therapy with clients, I have learned that some people protect themselves by remaining impervious. Their chief coping mechanism is a bland shell, inside of which they hide a delicate and underdeveloped self. These individuals are the eggs. Some of them will lie dormant, yet many yearn to emerge and grow under the right conditions.

Therapy with these individuals requires high dosages of nurturance and support. Their egg-like characteristics seek and attract mothering, protection, reassurance, and encouragement. The process of healing involves consistent reinforcement of behaviors akin to "spreading of wings" until they are confident that they can engender successful outcomes and weather unpredictable storms. Egg-like people often have a fractured self-image, along with a sense of incompleteness or abandonment. Although very sensitive, they can remain barren and inert to the environment for relatively long periods, concealing in isolation their rich nourishing potential and embryonic aliveness. These folks are essentially uncooked or unhatched, with only a thin and seamless veneer to cover their vulnerability. Therapeutic healing involves bringing them out of their shells, displaying the richness to environmental flourishing. Part of this process is the building of resistance, the girding up to reduce vulnerability and withstand imposition and impact. Metaphorically, some egg-like people need to become more hard-boiled to survive.

An ordinary yet interesting experiment reveals the inner status of an egg—spinning. An uncooked egg will not spin. This is because the soft and tender yolk rocks to and fro in response to the centripetal force, thereby shifting weight unevenly and preventing the egg from sustaining momentum. The yolk is yielding, but unsuited to environmental pummeling. A hard-boiled egg, however, will spin. Egg-people, it might be said, need girding up and inner fortitude to roll (or spin) with life's punches.

Peaches bruise easily, and the people who present like peaches will show their hurts quite readily. They are easily offended yet often more resistant than the surface blemishes reveal. As peaches are more attractive and yielding on the outside than toward the center, so it seems that peachy people offer inviting charms and juicy characteristics. They seek attention, and their very being summons tactile exposure. Their surface warmth is easily compromised by sensitivity and offense in response to surroundings deemed inhospitable. Peach-people suffer righteous indignation all too regularly, as they are jostled in life's basket of experiences. Their fey expectations must be carefully countered by the realistic medley of community experience.

Although eggs and peaches are each exquisitely sensitive, they must be treated differently—as foods and, metaphorically, as distinct cultures of individuals engaged in healing processes. Egg and peach characteristics shape differing contexts for understanding, interactions, and treatment protocols. These contexts manifest in particular methods for connecting with their experiences, reframing their perceptions and cognizance, and modifying their cognitions and moods.

Successful healing with peach-people and egg-people resonates with their rhythms of spirit, their lifestyle, communication, thinking and personality patterns, and their vulnerabilities and habits of central nervous system response.

The metaphorical essences of peaches and eggs are known intuitively to sensitive healers through many guises of perception and practice. As we understand ourselves, we gravitate toward and discover varieties of experience that resonate with our dispositions and needs. These experiences occur at levels of behavior and preference and within interpersonal, cognitive, emotive, fantasy, diet, biochemistry, and neurologic interactions.

Because we are creatures of habit, we tend to self-reinforce and recall mental states that are familiar to us. These states include consciousness levels, moods, perceptual habits, and preferences. Our brains tend to regenerate and continue our familiar patterns, even when some of them are uncomfortable or dysfunctional. This happens because our brains recognize repeated events (such as mental or physiological states) as reference points for "home base" or normality with regard to previous functioning. The brain associates what it has done previously with survival (since, after all, it has survived). Like computer system software, it boots up to new events with the previous user settings (in this analogy, "user settings" are those familiar states employed to cope with the demands of living). Under stress, our brains "search" for the system settings most compatible with the present demands. The probability, however, remains high on selecting states most familiar and frequently used. This repetition and reinforcement tends to produce responses and experiences that shape and establish conditions of personality and coping effectiveness.

Thus, peach-people can approach life with the steely reserve of pitted centeredness, hardened against the many bruises of life, accommodating and sensitive on the surface, but impenetrable at the core. Despite seeming self-contained and confident, they are frequently overreactive. Such individuals are wound tight and dense inside, and they may be vulnerable to incidental contact as threatening, insulting, or wounding. Though fuzzy and alluring to the outside, the peach-person is often detached from core experiences and usually unaware of hard resistance at the center of being.

The eggs among us roll gingerly along the angles and elevations of immediate environments, inclining resignedly to the forces of gravity, always hedging and protecting against the potentially fatal blow. The egg lives in a nascent mind-set—maturing, developing, not quite actualizing inner life with outward manifestation. Eggs need catalysis and arousal to create the conditions for flourishing.

In retiring the anthropomorphic status of peaches and eggs, it is notable that, though the brains of peach-people and egg-people are made of the same stuff, they function differently in some aspects. Not surprisingly, variations in treatment protocols and programming can bring each of these lovely creations to states of harmony, healing, balance, and better survival.

Appropriate healing methods can also be programmed through technologically assisted modalities in tune with the leanings and homeostatic needs of peaches and eggs. One very effective example is EEG neurofeedback. Using this technique, both peach- and egg-people can be brought into balance with regard to nervous system excesses or deficiencies through the training of brainwaves. As the technique is practiced, the internal states it induces become more familiar to the brain and are retained as relatively permanent and useful learning.

In undertaking EEG treatment with people of differing constitutions and orientations, it is vital to appreciate their individual central nervous system response patterns, habits, character, and vulnerabilities. The characteristics of peaches and eggs are helpful guidelines in apprehending what is necessary for homeostasis and for setting treatment parameters accordingly.

Our brains have tremendous functional plasticity. This means that learning and new behaviors can occur through many different channels of circuitry, that new "programs" can run on the same hardware once it has been tuned, and that "system software" (self-regulatory and self-awareness states) can be upgraded and modified. EEG neurofeedback catalyzes this process by practicing the brain in operating system states that correlate with differing levels of arousal and hemispheric communication. As this technique is practiced, the brain tends to become both more flexible in shifting to a state functional and appropriate for a particular situation and more likely to recognize as its "normal" setting a range of arousal levels suitable to the relief of previous symptoms that the brain thought "belonged" with it old settings. It is as if the brain learns that it lives at a new address; the incoming mail of experience is delivered to a different place, the vantage points and perspectives have changed, and the needed repairs at the old address are no longer pressing.

Par for its course, the brain carries on from its new perspective, embellishing and reinforcing in its inimitable manner—elaborating on what it has been shown.

According to the mind-body system, the brain needs certain operatives to achieve the balance and regulation (homeostasis) necessary for the alleviation of distress, relief of symptoms, and the propagation of continuous healing. Peach and egg attributes provide telling clues about the required parameters for success.

Clinical treatment with EEG neurofeedback involves matching training protocols with cortical sites (areas of the brain) based on an analysis and interpretation of client functioning, history, symptoms, and desired outcomes. The neurosciences have mapped out the structures and functions of the brain's components. This knowledge has been amplified through the vast number of clinical trials administered by practitioners. For example, we know that auditory and visual stimuli are processed through the parietal lobes and that symbolic and linear information is typically processed in the left hemisphere, while visuospatial, gestalt, "intuitive," and emotional material are more heavily processed in the right hemisphere. The application of this knowledge with treatment success is heavily influenced by knowledge of client characteristics, which may be integrated with the prescription of effective treatment protocols.

Since people with peach characteristics tend to be overwrought, heavily defended, and less in touch with visceral inner experience, we typically treat them with EEG neurofeedback protocols that are in the lower midfrequency ranges and are applied to the right hemisphere. The gradual effect is a softening of "pitlike" rigidity, a relaxing and loosening up, and a release of the obsessive determinations and concoctions about threats from the environment. It is a beautiful process to behold as anger subsides, sentience emanates, and intelligence is evoked with the flavor of compassion.

For the fragile, underdeveloped, underaroused egg-folk, we generally apply a high-frequency protocol targeting areas of the left hemisphere. This treatment tends to brighten the brain, sharpening perceptual faculties and elevating mood. High-frequency left parietal neurofeedback stimulates thinking and mental coherence; it helps many people connect thoughts with spoken words. It catalyzes courage, assertiveness, and expressiveness. The developing sense of strength and mental organization seems to help egg-people come out of their shells. It is encouraging!

Coping with environmental stressors and internal imbalances necessitates an alertness to changing conditions. The processes of monitoring and adjusting are the hallmarks of well-regulated people and effective healing techniques. In behavioral science, the matching of interventions with client types is known as aptitude-treatment interaction. Generations of mythologists and scientists have expounded upon observable personality types and temperamental daemons. To an extent, humans need to categorize the world in order to fit comfortably into it. With little surprise, then, do we behold the blending of scientific technology, nature, the healing arts, and living metaphors with the wisdom of change.

The Oglala Sioux wisdom reflects the mask of appearances more than the immutability of nature. As species develop, they vary. Identities change, and the process of adaptation always involves discovery. It is not unusual to find peaches and eggs intermingled in the same basket atop any given set of shoulders.

Sometimes I am like the uncooked egg—fragile, needing protection, sensitive, not wanting to be spun around. There are also many moments when I feel the peach pit deep within me, that core of impenetrable resentment steeled against intrusion, impervious to nature, existing only to implant and reproduce my being under favorable conditions. That is the state impelling me to sow the seeds of growth in the lives of others.

1994
Ode to the necessity of having computer IT support. This is how it was in the old days.

PAGE BOY, PAGE BOY, GIVE ME A RING

Look! Up in the sky…it's a bird…it's a plane…it's a cellular satellite!

Listen! In the next room…it's the doorbell…it's the phone… it's…PAGE BOY!!

Page Boy, Page Boy
Give me a ring.
Answer my call,
Service you bring.

Where you inhabit
Mystery enshrouds.
Surface when needed,
A genie endowed.

Finish your task,
Then disappear.
Home base independent,
Yet digitally near.

Page Boy, Page Boy
Ever efficient,
Leaving impressions
That you're omniscient.

Page Boy, Page Boy
Give me a ring.
Betrothed dedication
To fix anything.

I don't know where he lives. He must sleep somewhere; perhaps he has a toothbrush, even a desk phone. He seems normal enough and, indeed, has exalted the societal virtues of promptness and service to impeccable levels. Yet he operates within the specter of officelessness, and I am haunted by this ephemeral business mode. Oh, he is no mere mortal with a mortgage and a service delivery truck. He is...PAGE BOY! Independent courier of on-site service. A human boomerang of my touch-tone intent, Page Boy returns my dialed distress within moments. Sometimes cleverly disguised as a corporate employee, he moonlights as the Beeped Crusader, materializing in my office or home to repair, construct, service, and support. Plumbing, wiring, or troubleshooting the microlevels of my computer anxieties, he is there when I need him—and that is increasingly often!

A return call from Page Boy soothes with the familiar voice reaching out from anywhere on the planet—or, more literally, above it. (I am reminded of those DHL delivery commercials, where the vans have wings.) Many times Page Boy has talked me down from solo anxiety flights and helped me avert computer crashes and serious work injury. When he cannot be there in person, Page Boy rescues me via cable or satellite. Usually, he tinkers beside me, a visual spectacle of patient mastery, vanquishing my helplessness in a complex universe of gadgetry and manual labor. He inspects and jury-rigs. Watching him work provides a complete lesson in concentration, purpose, intensity, and capitalism. My mounting adulation is interrupted by the sound of his heart beep—his pager discreetly announces another need. I know he must soon vaporize to another call. I admire his hustle, and I fantasize about the valor and freedom of on-site travails, a lone independent contractor battling the villains of a universe winding down.

Page Boy's personal attention is impressive. He is busy, no doubt, for, across America, VCRs blink "12:00" tauntingly (complicated by daylight savings time, which causes them to blink "11:00"). Electronic dalliance is one of his many talents. Like most superheroes, Page Boy wears many disguises. He is a handyman, a masseur, a plumber, a trainer. Available by private code, the touch of the # key mobilizes him to respond. He marks a new page in the history of service and enterprise. Neither catalog nor store, Page Boy brings intimate and immediate mindfulness to isolated, busy, and needy technophobes. For the people of my generation who have been psychologically traumatized by trusting and allowing six to eight weeks for delivery from Battle Creek, Michigan, Page Boy's prompt responses baptize a rebirth of commercial faith.

This seeming mutation in standard business practices has caught the attention of economists and scientists, who have tried to analyze this phenomenon at the cellular level. However, cellular communications seem to be only partially involved. The legend of this super phone hero is rooted in the inexpensive paging device. Like a modern John Wayne, Page Boy shoots from the hip.

There is widespread mystique and gratitude regarding this digital intervention and the innovative blend of technology and human assistance—in response to a local phone call. Despite the expanding range of pagers, decentralization and local control figure prominently in the upsurge of Page Boy as role model. This has been underscored by the media.

Recently, on late night television, David Letterman hosted a rabbi and a priest discussing the impact of modern technology on spiritual access. The priest displayed his cellular phone, enthusiastically describing how it put him easily in touch with parishioners and the Vatican. The priest wryly alluded to privileged clerical conference-calling among the clergy, the Vatican, and (!!!the digitally dialable Deity!!!). Suitably impressed, the rabbi asked if he could try such a call on the priest's phone. Handing him the phone, the priest invited the rabbi to participate, regretfully noting the exorbitant charges in airtime. The priest apologetically lamented the excessive cost of this technology, asking the rabbi, in turn, how he managed. The rabbi asked to use Letterman's phone, saying he would demonstrate a call for spiritual response. Somewhat disconcerted, Letterman balked. "Don't worry," the rabbi reassured him. "I have a direct line; it's a local call."

Before a speechless Letterman, the rabbi punched in some numbers. Seconds later, Letterman's phone rang. "Hello, this is Page Boy."

2002
After this was published in a local newspaper, I received calls requesting treatment for this condition.

THE SERIOUS PROBLEM OF DYSGRAFFITIA

If you know someone with learning problems, you may be familiar with the terms dyslexia, dyscalculia, and dysgraphia. These labels describe respective disorders in which a person has great difficulty in reading or spelling (dyslexia), impairment in basic arithmetical computations (dyscalculia), or dysfunction in writing (dysgraphia).

As controversial as these disorders are, there is a much more serious and widespread condition (largely unrecognized and untreated) that afflicts millions of people: *dysgraffitia.*

Whereas dyslexia affects the ability to decipher written symbols and dysgraphia hampers the production of writing, dysgraffitia is a malfunction in the ability to *see the handwriting on the wall*; people with dysgraffitia have extreme difficulty in relating to consequences, a kind of deficiency in profiting from experience. Dysgraffitia does not necessarily involve deficits in logical thinking, but rather describes problems in the sensible application of what one already knows. It is a dysfunction in the ability to understand and learn from natural consequences. Sometimes known as the "ostrich syndrome," progressive forms of dysgraffitia lead some individuals to totally disregard the reality around them.

It is a serious problem because it affects most of us at some point in our lives, where we habitually attend to the urgent while neglecting the important. It influences the way we parent and teach children; it influences the patterns by which children develop critical living and learning habits, including discernment and critical thinking skills.

The term itself, *dysgraffitia,* has a fascinating multicultural origin: the prefix *dys-* (from Greek) means bad or difficult; *graffito* (from which we get graffiti) is Italian for scribble or inscription on a wall; and, of course, graffiti originated as a New World adaptation of Old World tradition in the underground melting pot of New York City—writing on the walls of subways.

In fact, dysgraffitia has surfaced in the many experiences of people in New York who become so absorbed in deciphering the subway graffiti that they get lost, get mugged, miss appointments, etc. (This even happened to me many years ago: While trying to figure out the esoteric meaning of TAKI 183, I missed both my train and an important test at school.) Chronic cases of dysgraffitia have been documented in which responsible citizens actually clean up graffiti, thus demonstrating severe inability to profit from experience and relate to the natural consequence that graffiti will insidiously reappear.

Though examples of dysgraffitia vary with regional differences, experienced diagnosticians are sensitive to the strains of terrible judgment that often pervade this disorder. Recent California incidents highlight some rampant cases of dysgraffitic behavior:

- A Morgan Hill man trained a pit bull to fight and guard his suburban marijuana crop; the dog mauled and killed a neighboring toddler.
- Oakland city officials proposed plunging the city $600 million in debt to bring back the Raiders football team (without a public vote on the issue).
- The Oakland school system issued regular payroll checks to staff who had not worked there in two years.
- Hank Gathers, basketball star of Loyola Marymount University, collapsed from a cardiac disorder while playing basketball, yet he continued to play (against doctors' orders) until, within weeks, he died from this condition on the basketball court.

- The superintendent of San Jose Unified School District bought full-page *San Jose Mercury News* ads to tell the teachers' union and the community that the district didn't have enough money to settle the strike.

Some of the more advanced forms of this disorder appear in the life patterns of people who habitually behave as though they can live indefinitely on resources and talents they were given, rather than on the sacrifices and work expected of them. In many instances, this can be traced back to childhood experiences in which individuals rarely did homework but relied on their native ability or the efforts of others.

A common symptom of dysgraffitia is the abundance of specious insight, usually resulting in the concoction of creative excuses (the degree of creativity is correlated with both intelligence and the progressiveness of the disorder). This symptom reflects a cognitive process in which consequences are interpreted to fit the victim's abridged view of reality. Such a compensating mechanism allows dysgraffitics to function without the requirement of proper balance between consistency and compromise. Not without its merits, an occasional side effect of dysgraffitia is the honing of this excuse-making tendency into a career asset, usually in politics or comedy.

The dysgraffitic tendency to avoid or misinterpret the handwriting on the wall seems to afflict individuals at all levels of society. However, people most at risk for its paradoxical devastation are those who work in government or private industry and those who have a history of violent or sexual misconduct, substance abuse, or bankruptcy. Among the most severe cases of occupationally related dysgraffitia reported are those of people working in public policymaking jobs, savings and loan organizations, the lumber and mining industries, and companies producing toxic wastes. However, ambitious dysgraffitics from many walks in life have risen to prominence. Some examples are Richard Nixon, Ivan Boesky, Jim Bakker, Ferdinand and Imelda Marcos, and Leona Helmsley, to name a few.

Dysgraffitia is becoming more recognized for several reasons. In part, current trends have made foolish behavior more stylish, or at least acceptable. Additionally, pressure from special interest groups and the media have reduced stigma and increased exposure relating to various conditions and afflictions. However, dysgraffitia has been thrown into the public limelight in large measure because of its specific inability to deal with environmental issues. To the dysgraffitic, Earth Day is as meaningless as Air Day or Water Day. (Indeed, one optimist thought that Earth Day was a proposed ballot measure to add an additional day to the week so there would be more time to get things done.) This tendency to think in egocentric terms plus the marked deficits in relating to consequences and profiting from experiences are the hallmarks that deter dysgraffitics from relating effectively to environmental issues.

For example, conceptualizing the half-life of plutonium is particularly difficult for the dysgraffitic (who tends to be very practical and oriented to the present and immediate gratification). The dysgraffitic has enough trouble coping with balloon mortgage payments. Another frustration experienced by dysgraffitics is the inconvenience of having to request water in restaurants, and then asking the waiter to remove the fancy printed placard (explaining drought conditions) to make room for the water glass. Conceptualizing time often puts the dysgraffitic in a disadvantaged and embarrassing position—as in the case where one restaurant patron asked the manager for a sentence and statement of charges; in response to the manager's quizzical reaction, the diner complained that he had been there for an hour on a ration of bread and water.

Obese dysgraffitics cannot understand why their doctors order them to drink at least two quarts of water per day, while public officials ask that they flush their toilets less frequently. Students who are taught in science classes that matter and energy can be neither destroyed nor created are most perplexed by the admonition to conserve energy, especially on hot days (these students tend to conserve energy by ignoring homework, thus extending the scope of dysgraffitia in everyday life).

Perhaps you recognize some symptoms of dysgraffitia in people close to you, and you wonder how this serious problem continues unaddressed. I'll share some clues. As a lifelong student of human development, I observe the acorns of childhood grow into the oaks of maturity. Such relationships thicken with the passing of time, yet their roots are grounded in the teaching of consequences. If we want our children to see the handwriting on the wall, to live purposefully, and to learn from experience, we must teach them how to expect and accept consequences. Effective learning takes time, consistency, and practice. Variety may be the spice of life, but unpredictability is the heartburn.

As for the confirmed and inveterate victims of dysgraffitia, there is hope in the willingness to change. However, change is difficult. The only person who really likes change is a wet baby. Those who struggle with the obvious might remember this—if you keep doing what you're doing, you'll probably get more of what you've already got.

For those who heed admonition, here are the warning signs of dysgraffitia:

- Spending more on your divorce than you spent on your family.
- Ignoring your bills.
- Rash behavior or persistent itchiness to cause bruises.
- Inordinate amount of time scrutinizing the meaning of markings, fissures and irregularities in sidewalks, streets, buildings, and neighborhood structures (earthquake victims and professionals excepted).
- Avoiding dietary fiber.
- Eating late at night and waking up in the morning feeling that way *again.*
- Blurriness of vision when reviewing your budget or bank statement.
- Thinking of the IRS in abstract terms.

- Struggling over your child's homework.
- Practicing assertive behavior with your neighbor's pit bull.
- Believing your children won't try any tricks that you didn't as a child.
- Having tendencies toward reversals in physical symptoms (e.g., your feet smell and your nose runs) or redundancies in self-image (e.g., striving to be an upstanding and downsitting citizen).

If you have any of these warning symptoms, you may be eligible for assistance.

1993
I sent this to Dr. Jarvik. In gratuitous good spirit, he sent me a signed photo of his Jarvik heart—now there's a man with a good heart!

THE JARVIK STOMACH

WARNING: NOT FDA APPROVED

There's a revolutionary new medical device that has escaped public awareness until very recently: the Jarvik Stomach. This artificial organ was invented by the same Dr. Jarvik who popularized the artificial heart. It is revolutionary both in its design and function and in its implications for nutritional and dietary habits.

The Jarvik Stomach (JS-1) is an implant device that essentially filters out for excretion those foods a person has eaten but does not want metabolized through the digestive system and bloodstream. (Think of it as a digestive "morning-after" pill.) Here's how it works:

The device is implanted through ingestion—it is packaged as a dried, compacted, foamlike ball. Immediately after it is swallowed, the JS-1 begins to expand in the recipient's original stomach. This process is facilitated by natural digestive juices; additionally, a chemical drink swallowed immediately following ingestion of the stomach allows the JS-1 to bind to the lining of the natural stomach. The Jarvik Stomach is made of a semipermeable organic material implanted with computer chips. Initially, the doctor programs these chips to align the stomach properly, adjust osmotic flow, and manipulate the binding of secure connections with the esophagus and intestines. This is done without surgery and is usually performed on an outpatient basis.

Once installed, the Jarvik Stomach is owner-programmable. Using a portable home computer, the "patient" controls which foods are to be digested and absorbed and which foods are to pass through excretion directly from the stomach. Thus, the Jarvik Stomach permits the owner to eat foods of any composition and quantity without experiencing the immediate effects of food allergies or sensitivities and the long-term effects of caloric and fat surplus.

To protect against abuse by the gourmand and junk-food eater alike, the Jarvik Stomach requires weekly monitoring of dietary intake (although maintenance three times weekly is recommended). Using an electrode attached to the home computer, the JS-1 owner affixes the electrode to the skin at the top of the stomach, just below the solar plexus. The computer tabulates the components of food intake during the preceding daily or weekly interval, and evaluates the amount and proportion of essential nutrients ingested. Using this information (and programming based on medical and health-conditioning input), the computer displays and prints the nutritional requirements needed, along with a list of recommended foods to achieve the desired nutritional balance and objectives. The JS-1 computer automatically programs the Jarvik Stomach to allow absorption and metabolism of the selected foods. All the owner has to do is remember to eat them. (Dr. Jarvik promises that future software versions will accommodate updated information on the latest nutritional discoveries.)

Well, this Jarvik Stomach is really a dream come true for the legion of frustrated dieters, gourmands, and individuals prone to disease through genetic predisposition, dietary abuse, ignorance, or incorrigible gluttony. Besides making life much more pleasurable for the orally oriented, the Jarvik Stomach ushers in a new era of medical care, health management, and individual self-control. The Jarvik Stomach makes "power to the people" a visceral reality.

Why, then, hasn't this radical invention reached the public? The answer lies in the conflicts of interests aroused by the potential of the JS-1. Behind the scenes, a commercial civil war is imminent. As you can imagine, the Jarvik Stomach has aroused scathing antagonism from powerful giants in the food industry. The most intense pressure has been from manufacturers of diet and health foods, most notably the makers of substitute sweeteners and fake fat. In a rather unusual coalition, environmentalists and the health-food counterculture have sided with the establishment makers of diet and processed imitation foods—each of these factions fears that the Jarvik Stomach will lead to increased proliferation of high-calorie, high-fat, high-junk-and-waste-container foods. (Incidentally, on this last remark, a provocative irony has accompanied the patent process of the Jarvik Stomach: the first commercially available JS-1 models will be marketed under the name Waiste Container.)

The Jarvik Stomach has profoundly divided the food conglomerates, whose overriding united objective is to get us to eat more. Heralding the JS-1 and fighting opposition by the weight-loss and health industries are the food purveyors who provide what we really want to eat. The restaurant and catering industries are elated by the Jarvik Stomach, and many small businesses have contributed to the mounting legal costs of going public with this product. Of course, the most substantial donations have been offered by McDonald's, the American Beef and Dairy Councils, and Baskin-Robbins, to name a few.

Radical in design and momentous in its implications, the Jarvik Stomach has already spawned controversy and surprising alliances among self-interest groups, and it has stimulated an odd admixture of ethical and philosophical posturing. Diverse groups are becoming united against an invention that lets people eat what they want with impunity. Businesses promoting weight-loss products and programs are quite threatened by the Jarvik Stomach, as are companies who manufacture sports and fitness equipment (not to mention athletic clubs). Equally concerned are the pharmaceutical companies deriving hefty profits from antacids and similar elixirs—the JS-1 eliminates the need for them, as it selectively excretes irritants, thus relegating overindulgence to a subjective mental state.

Aerobics instructors, however, may encounter new limitations in their work (if they have work) as they try to convince acolytes of the benefits of exercise. Without the motivating visible symptoms, people are less likely to put out effort to change their ways. The Jarvik Stomach presents this obstacle to another group of coaching professionals not ordinarily grouped with aerobics instructors and other gym rats: behavior therapists. These are the folks whose professional lives are devoted to changing behavior, and they are very concerned about the impact of the Jarvik Stomach on impulse control. The most staunch behaviorists (the Thin-Skinners) maintain that eating is a learned behavior and that meals should be carefully scheduled.

Psychoanalysts, on the other hand, do not seem defensive about this new product. After all, physical food is (in their view) only a symbol, a substitute for other needs left unmet in early childhood. For the analysts, eating is merely an anxiety-reducer, and the Jarvik Stomach appears to have little bearing on their patients' early childhoods and the main source of the analysts' income: their patients' guilt.

The guilt phenomenon is pivotal for religious leaders, as they evaluate and adjust to the Jarvik Stomach. If temperance and moderation are replaced by "eat it if it feels good" practices, efforts to instill spiritual growth and self-restraint could be undermined. After the advent of easy birth control, it is doubtful that the religious community could stomach another technological blow to its gut-level appeal for moral self-control. Alternatively, religious leaders are practical people who are sensitive to their dependence upon ritual and ceremony in spreading their messages. This involves ethnic and cultural traditions of intensely heavy feasting—which could be facilitated and expanded with a preponderance of Jarvik Stomachs among followers. For some, it is not easy to take a stand on this issue.

Loyalties are mixed among medical professionals' reactions to the Jarvik Stomach. Doctors are involved in most people's births, deaths, and traumas in between. Some physicians are preventatively inclined, and others prefer cleanup medicine. Orientation and practice specialty probably determine doctors' individual reactions. As a relevant corollary, the Jarvik Stomach will present a dilemma to health insurers. Will they gamble on lower costs through prevention? Or will they adhere to the short-term bottom line practice of excluding the Jarvik Stomach as experimental, cosmetic, or not medically necessary?

The new frontiers of medical and technological advances will affect all of us. As the introduction of the Jarvik Stomach invariably ripples through various segments of society, it is difficult to predict all the beneficiaries and those adversely impacted. Clearly, this is a major new direction for bioelectronic engineering. First they put computers in our workplaces, next in our homes, and ultimately in our bodies. To quote a famous marketing slogan, the JS-1 will be the stomach "for the rest of us." Anticipating their potential profits, some venture capitalists have code-named the JS-1 the "upset stomach" of the future market.

The old saying "the way to a man's heart is through his stomach" has been revamped by the pioneering work of Dr. Jarvik. For him, the way to the stomach was through the invention of the artificial heart. Indeed, the indefatigable Dr. Jarvik has not been idle. Psychoanalysts may especially take note of his most recent miraculous invention: the Jarvik Memory. This trailblazing invention was covertly sponsored by our former president, Ronald Reagan, one of the first volunteer subjects. Development of the Jarvik Memory has been dormant in the wake of our country's political and economic struggles. Let us hope that research funding for this valuable innovation will not be forgotten.

1997
Written decades after graduating from drugs to news shows.

LET'S DO A LINE

WARNING: FOR MATURE READERS ONLY

Although sex is still a big attraction, my wife and I draw the line far short of recreational drugs for hedonistic pleasure. That is why, when one of us says, "Let's do a line," the partner knows this refers to *Frontline* or *Dateline* on TV. I am hopelessly codependent in the newsmagazine addiction. Fortunately, the supply is plentiful. We have an underground connection—the cable company—that feeds our habit almost daily through its lines.

We are prisoners of media gossip, slaves to the rush of the inside scoop. We crave the exposé, and we snort with pleasure at the contortions of the deceitful and greedy as they squirm in the glare of investigative journalism. Line by line, we get sucked in, until we are no longer satisfied by the half-minute hits of evening news. Tolerance has built, and we've turned hard-core, needing an hour minimum nightly, yet craving the time-released documentary—*60 Minutes* is no longer enough. Rooney tunes are for the unenlightened.

News attraction appears to be biologically based. Like hair color and density, its progression advances with age. Youth bore energy for making waves, rather than tuning into them; callow youth paid scant attention to the headlines. In middle age, however, my biological clock is better attuned to the broadcast channels. Public television may not have commercials, but commercial television sure has the public! As in other matters of behavior and style, men and women often have different preferences. I like the PBS specials, whereas my wife prefers the commercial opportunities to talk about things. When we can't agree, the lines are drawn on news taste, and we feed our habits in different rooms. I am luckily married to someone who respects my muted passion for political scandal and who shares my worship of the timely tidbit. We accept the growths of opinion that accompany our aging and hope they are benign. We are hooked on pleasure fueled by fast images, juxtaposed times, and quick words.

The parade of images unfolds, injected into consciousness by faceless editor-lords who manipulate our sentiments. The opiate of the people takes effect, and I am plastered to my seat, a couch poppy. I succumb, staring bleary eyed in a den of televised iniquity, until the fix reaches a crescendo and my nose for news is aroused by the incensed burning of issues. So much of it is pulp, just milk sugar cut for the masses. If McLuhan were alive, he would insist that mediocrity is the meth-age. I often wonder if I am up to speed.

If there is profit in this venture, it cannily escapes the consumer. However, the junk news epidemic is insidious, pernicious. The father of this addiction was none other than Walter *Cronk*ite. Today, we feed our heads with Hugh *Down*s and *Stone* Phillips, and it is easy to *Kop*pel line with Ted on *Nightline*. The comedic component has its roots in Jack *Benny*.

How did this addiction form? It started out innocently enough: childhood filled with "anchors" of theatrical pretense—Mister Rogers, Soupy Sales, "Officer" Joe Bolton—who moderated dramatizations, thus readying an audience for the future features of visual journalism. The comedic control of the Three Stooges, Abbott and Costello, the Marx brothers, and the Honeymooners brought the seductive satisfaction of belly laughter, while preparing us for a spacey future ("to the *moon,* Alice") and conditioning a skepticism about the nature of people ("I wouldn't belong to a club that would have someone like me as a member"). Oh yes, hindsight shows that the groundwork was laid well before cable snaked underneath.

Delivered through clear thick tubes, such elementary black-and-white pleasure hooked us individually and collectively with thousands of deliciously memorable lines. The seeds of media addiction were sown and prophesied in generations past: shows like *Dragnet* foreshadowed the Internet. Before the World Wide Web there was Jack Webb, originator of the famous line, "Just the *fax*, Ma'am."

Throughout history, secular satisfaction has been maintained by the delicate balance between stimulation and excitement and the restful inhibition of the vegetative vicarious state. Into this theory of drive-by reduction the modern media has plugged its multiple lines. The hits are verbal, visual, and voluble. Seduction seems complete, as my wife and I solicit good lines. It can take over one's life. One week, we tried an experiment. We turned off the TV and spoke to each other only in venerable movie lines. My wife was charmed with the surrogate security of characters from the foreign flicks we saw in college. I acted and imitated, but felt estranged, a surreal voyager on Planet Hollywood. I yearned for the earthiness of current affairs I could gape at and do nothing about.

The sedation of viewing is offset by suggestive titillation—sometimes by blatant revelation, but often by couched innuendo. Along these lines, the entertainment industry has circulated its influence through the veins of most Americans.

The tabloid shows offer splash to highlight much routine that is otherwise dreary. Against the background of these shows, a minor difference of opinion can turn dramatic. Certain moods and events can even precipitate tabloid sex. This occurrence, however, is infrequent, since timing is everything, and the tabloid shows usually air too early. We tend to let excitement build until *Primetime.*

I often engage in fantasy. Sharing one episode with my wife during an evening interlude, I pondered the possibilities made available by satellite TV. Owing to her practicality, my wife questioned the value of expanding our horizons in that manner. I replied that besides the addition of viewing choices, a satellite dish would have aesthetic value. Her interest was piqued. "Yes," I continued with romantic mystique, "I could come home with eager anticipation, grab you and the programming guide, and exclaim gleefully, 'Wow, you are some dish!'"

Recovery from such induced reverie is a difficult road. I've been tempted to go cold turkey, cut the cord, or at least not pay my cable bill. But the TV would get fuzzy, and I would then need a fix; I would once again have to rely on my local *dealer.* There is no escape. Furthermore, the condition appears to be familial. My children will watch the *snow* while listening to scrambled stations. We are tenant farmers in the vast entertainment industry empire, channel surfers among the fickle waves of popular culture, reaching frantically, repetitively, compulsively for meaning and gratification through the lines of media communication.

Perhaps the entertainment industry could issue a rebate in the form of apologist "lines." Contrition would be obviated by the airing of appropriate shows:

PRESS

"*Mainline* investigates an exposé of one-liners and double entendres. Who are the people behind these *pun*ch lines? Are they *con* artists or simply *pro*lific geniuses? Is Hollywood once again responsible for the corruption of straight lines into more violent punch lines? And what about the music industry? Are current artists given a bad rap while Cole Porter is dripped into the mainstream?"

(Segue…)

PRESS

I get no kick from sham pa-a-a-i-in
Rubbing alcohol doesn't soothe me at all
So tell me why should it be true
That I crave the lines done with you?

Some get a kick from cocaine
I'm sure that if I took even one sniff
That would bore me terrifically too.
But I love the lines done with you.

PRESS

"And, now, on *Frightline*, a fascinating story of psychological intrigue, a scary look into the inner workings of a deviate mind—we cover the strange departure of a middle-age doctor from a successful professional practice to devote increasingly obsessive amounts of time to satire and social commentary. Some people are disconcerted by his free associations. Others are shocked that he charges for them. At the outset, however, we warn you that this feature story may be utterly without socially redeeming value…"

Frankly, my dear, I don't give a…

1995
Written in praise and love for my old Doberman, Diamond, as she approached her final days.

MY DOG

My dog is an old dog—thirteen years, in fact. She may embark on a permanent vacation soon, although that is another matter. Right now, she is a happy companion, sweet as ever of temperament and interested, as always, in the affairs of animals and people. She would chase the cat if she could, but she must settle for plaintive barks through the patio glass door. Beyond this transparent barrier, the cat meows and stalks and taunts by just being feline.

Years ago, the patio partition did not obstruct with its present authority. The dog saw a squirrel and leaped off the couch right through the glass door. She didn't catch the squirrel (does a dog ever?), but was nevertheless a very lucky torpedo. She stood on the other side of this fractured reality, shimmering back through the sunlight with shards of glass and trickles of blood adorning her curious expression. That was just one of the miraculous times she was spared.

Though the cats have always escaped, my dog has undoubtedly usurped some of their "lives." She has been hit by a car, stolen and recovered in another city, poisoned, and stricken with cancer. This is her latest pariah, along with muscle atrophy and the inevitable arthritis. She also has enormous cysts, ballooning her body as if she were pregnant with an "elephant" pup. People stop me on the street to ask what's wrong with her, and they shake their heads in wonder and pity.

I don't really notice these things, and I am repeatedly surprised when they are pointed out. I see the same dog everyone else does physically, but I regard her differently. This is the very creature whose Olympic sprightliness I've captured on videotape as she cavorted through fields assaulting sprinkler heads. I never watch the videotapes, not shying from wistfulness or lamentation, but because I prefer to see my dog as she is in the present.

Friends and visitors note her imperfections, her odd growths and labored gait, the way her feet turn in, and how she struggles to climb the stairs. Sometimes, she falls down on walks and needs assistance getting up. I help her automatically, waiting momentarily to see if she is imploring or merely resting, as I wonder about the impending likelihood that I may have to carry ninety pounds of Doberman in my arms up the hill.

For all their pathos, sympathetic onlookers imply that I am burdened with an old and terminal dog. I don't feel burdened, and my dog appears to enjoy life continuously, having adapted her schedule to include more leisure than she has already relished throughout our years. I have adapted gradually and imperceptibly to my aging dog. We no longer run together, she cannot sit in my lap anymore, I must be far gentler with her, and sleeping with her in my bed is out of the question. Her occasional accidents are maddening, and she is driving me into an unintended relationship with the carpet cleaner.

Our habits have changed, though we are still attached. My dog and I honor our commitments to each other, and the relationship seems free from resentment. She settles for less attention, as I am busier. She knows I will be there until her finale, and I pay her increasing bills without balking.

She is only a dog, and not my first. I could trade her in under the complete social approval of all who have beheld her infirmities. It is an alien notion, not due to guilt, but because of the unanticipated, blossoming rewards I derive from my old dog. Besides loving her for herself, I treasure the part of me that she reflects: my ability to adapt, cope with, and enjoy what *is.* I accept my dog and mundanely choose to enjoy her in the present. This highlights a side of myself at which I am truly amazed and pleased. I don't mourn the imperfections or even perceive them as such. I feel no need to trade in, no remorse at spending before the new model arrived, no haggling with the decision to fix or replace. Rather, I assume the familiar comforts, responsibilities, and burnished memories that greet me daily in the expectant gaze of my old dog.

These compensations transcend the call of novelty and the uncertainty of relentless change. My dog favors me in many ways. In her frailty, I become unexpectedly satisfied and fulfilled in growing old-fashioned and reliable. Faithfulness and habit are the virtues my dog knows best. I am proud of the way we learned this together.

1995
With respect to revered and powerful institutions…

MICROFIRM

In a recent development certain to shake up the computer industry and financial markets, Microsoft Chairman Bill Gates announced the merger of his company with the Internal Revenue Service.

The merger comes after years of apparent failure by the IRS to develop computer systems effective enough to collect the estimated billions it is owed by taxpayers. The merger is expected to be mutually beneficial in many ways. The IRS hopes to emerge from its administrative quagmire, to streamline efficiency, and to collect moneys owed. Gates has demonstrated, in recent years, his desire to move into the enormous market of financial transactions.

Concurrent with the merger, Microsoft will unveil several new products: ProAudit, Communicationist, and two new operating systems, Telescope and Microscope. The new operating systems will replace the popular Windows and will contain key features that support both ProAudit and Communicationist. In conjunction with the IRS, Microsoft has developed operating systems that integrate spreadsheets, accounting packages, communication software, and income and payroll taxes. Upon any attempts by users to purchase goods, make online transactions, or enter data, ProAudit and Microscope will automatically determine whether such transactions are within the legitimate budget of the user. These calculations will be based on individual databases of past tax records, maintained within each user's computer, and accessed (via the Communicationist and Telescope software) by the IRS. The new system is expected to streamline tax filing and recordkeeping, and to provide a safety net for consumers against cheating or overspending. Gates and the IRS are also expected to announce modifications of access to the Internet. Indeed, the name may be changed to the Interevnet.

Regarding name changes, Mr. Gates has announced that Microsoft will become Microfirm when the merger is finalized. When questioned about the selection of the name, Gates alluded to internal company programming code, in which the name Microfirm translates to "little hard ball."

On the subject of translation, Gates has taken umbrage at IBM for its recent commercials portraying people of other nationalities jabbering in foreign languages about solutions using IBM. Gates thinks the portrayal of these populations and their IBM software usage as "friendly" is deceptive. In accord with the IRS, Gates has, therefore, announced plans to drop development of user-friendly software interfaces. Centralization and frank practices will characterize the new merger, Gates promised.

(It was reported that Bosnian Serbs, in response to the series of recent "Eastern Bloc" IBM commercials and the Gates announcement, have begun buying up all available Macintosh computers.)

Gates has said that he is delighted with the new merger agreement, as it allows him to fuse professional ambition with civic contribution and economic growth. The new system software is set to ship by the first of the year. A sophisticated feature of the integrated package is the automatic shutdown—users who have not filed accurate taxes on or before each April 15 will be unable to boot up their computers until payments are sent to Microfirm. Beta tests now under way could provide the development of a prototype in which payroll and income tax accounts are filed online through Microfirm, which would then make deductions and disburse funds to the IRS. The linchpin for this prototype is said to be the Communicationist software.

Prior to the rollout of the new gem program, Communicationist, Gates has announced a gala media party event. Chairman Gates will preside over the Communicationist party, and it is rumored that the party may be communicated online.

On a personal note, Gates is enjoying the fruits of his success by building a huge mansion. The estate development is supervised by architect Saint William, and the project is code-named after the grand entrance to the property: the Squirrelly Gates.

Although it is well known that passage to heaven can't be earned or purchased, it appears that Bill Gates has appropriated the next best thing.

1998
Reflections on the short end of doctor-patient relationships.

PATIENTS, PLEASE…

Little in the Way of Understanding

There is the story about the elderly man who went to the doctor because of his scoliosis, which was increasingly causing him to stoop over. Indeed, this progressive condition had shortened his height by two inches. The reception room was packed, and the poor man had been waiting over an hour to see the physician. He mentioned this to the receptionist, and was told, "Sir, will you please be a little patient?" Whereupon he responded, "That's exactly the problem I'm here for!"

My problem, as a patient, is different. Although I *am* short on height (and sometimes on patience), I've sought medical help for my snoring. I'm about to be treated with somnoplasty, a procedure in which the tissue of the palate is reduced through radio waves. In this instance, I am the patient. However, I am also a doctor. I am physically pretty healthy, and, as I exchange roles, I am about to face some challenges regarding my mental perspective. Being a psychologist, this experience tests my integrity.

They say that doctors make the worst patients. Perhaps that is because, as a stereotype, doctors are driven, decisive, and have little patience. Then there is the issue of need for control. The questions and doubts of patients can easily be interpreted (unwittingly or consciously) as threats to the doctor's control and image as authority. Let's not forget our own doubts and questions. The cases that did not go well shadow the background of our experiences. Despite what some may think, each of us knows that *other* doctors are human. Humans make mistakes. Mistakes are understandable, and people are forgivable. When my body, health, and wholeness are at stake, however, my tissue and trust are not easily for giving. It's up close and personal. Doctor as patient is anachronistic. In this drama of role exchange, faith is tested where the big dilemma lurks: How much should the doctor disclose to the patient, and how should the patient's questions, doubts, and anxieties be handled?

It is the doctor's responsibility to diagnose the patient's condition, determine treatment appropriateness, and explain to the patient the risks, benefits, and options. The desired outcome is an informed conscious decision by the patient. The patient's concerns, independence, understanding, and power of veto must be honored. This process becomes complicated by several factors. The doctor specializes in relieving distressing conditions, such as the patient presents; his experience and fruition contribute to convincing and reassuring patients of the likelihood of successful treatment. Despite their concerns or doubts (expressed or not), patients *expect* to be convinced and reassured. When a person cannot relieve his own symptoms, he is not in control. Quite simply, to trust that relief is achievable, he must yield control. Since each of us wants to be sovereign, this deferment of control creates a natural and unavoidable tension.

Additionally, the doctor and the patient may hold different views of positive outcomes. From the doctor's perspective, treatment is most often an appropriate and helpful intervention with a statistically high probability of relieving symptoms. To the symptomatic patient, the doctor's promise may signal more. Under the burden of distress, patients may imagine that the treatment under discussion will erase a variety of problems somehow connected with the condition being treated. Opportunities for fantasies, misrepresentations, and disappointments abound. In the professional and confidential relationship between doctor and patient, disclosures and leadership, uncertainties and expectations weave a fabric of dependence where integrity and confusion often collide.

I am familiar with this quandary, both as a doctor and as a patient. As a doctor, I field all kinds of inquiries from current and prospective patients. The questions and concerns range from what I consider typical and reasonable to those that seem provocative or preposterous. Typical appropriate questions include:

- How does the treatment work, how long does it take, and how long does it last?
- How much does it cost, and will my insurance cover it?
- If this treatment is so good, why aren't more people doing it?
- What is the success rate generally?
- How do we know what my chances of success are?
- What can I expect in the way of improvement, and how would you define success in my case?
- Will this treatment interfere with anything else I am doing, and what discomforts might there be?
- Are there any known dangers or disadvantages?

Challenging questions and attitudes include:

- I know that this treatment is controversial and has a lot of critics, but...
  (Are you expecting me to answer unnamed critics and defend against the assumption that the treatment is controversial because of naysayers?)
- Why does it cost so much?
- Send me some research to prove the validity of your treatment.
- My doctor doesn't believe in this treatment.
  (So why are you telling me this? Do you want me to convince you that your doctor is wrong? If you believe your doctor, why are you asking me? If you don't believe your doctor on this matter, why involve him as a credible source?)
- There are so many conflicting opinions, I'm just so confused.

(This is either a consumer choice issue, in which case you're on your own, or it is a condition requiring treatment, which, in turn, requires your trust in my ability to bring you out of confusion.)

- If only I knew it would work, I wouldn't hesitate.
  (Meaning, if it weren't costly, you wouldn't hesitate. On what basis is this treatment different in that regard from any of life's other uncertainties?)
- Treatment is so time-consuming.
  (And your problem isn't?)
- Sounds too good to be true; there must be a flaw.
  (Are you asking me to validate your negative, pessimistic attitude, agree with you about your doubts, admit that I am a charlatan, and close my practice?)
- If my insurance would cover it, I would do it.
  (This usually comes at the tail end of a host of other challenges and requests for proof of success.)

The objections listed above are usually pretreatment excuses or skepticism. They can be more readily dismissed or countered than the concerns and perceptions of patients who undergo treatment. In the tenuous balance between educating and convincing patients of treatment benefits and restraint from overselling treatment, the doctor must anticipate and interpret each patient's expectations, as well as the occurrences of elevated standards that correlate with improvement.

The phenomenon of changing standards is aptly described in the *tooth, shoe, lump* anecdote: A man with an extremely painful toothache calls the dentist. Although the dentist is overbooked, the man is told to come in on an emergency basis. In his near delirium, the man gets dressed and dons a pair of old shoes that are too tight. He manages to drive to the dentist's office, where the only empty chair in the packed reception room has a lump in the seat caused by a protruding spring. Hardly noticing, the man sits in this chair. Although his head is throbbing, the agony from the toothache has subsided slightly due to his previous ingestion of painkilling medicine.

Now the man notices the discomfort in his feet, as the tight shoes are pinching him and limiting circulation. Baffled that he could have donned such an ill-fitting old pair of shoes, the man slips them off. The relief is profound, and the man sits in alleviated exhaustion, waiting for the dentist. As he waits, he becomes impatient and distraught by the uncomfortable chair. Keenly aware of the protruding spring, his attention shifts away from the toothache to focus on this immediate annoyance.

And so goes the relentless shift in preoccupations to (hopefully) ever higher levels of demand and expectation in our adaptive survival.

When my severely torn meniscus was diagnosed, I was relieved to discover a medical reality for the pain in my knee. This allowed me to concentrate on the knee pain without distraction from the mental anguish of worrying if I was overreacting. After surgery, I was grateful to walk again, but soon I was livid that the surgeon's prognosis that I would run in eight weeks was dashed. My standards had certainly changed. Along with physiological differences, I had altered some memories of physical conditioning that had limited and debilitated my running over a long period of time prior to the torn knee cartilage.

For many patients, the doctor appears as the responsible harbinger when life is not so rosy at the next level, and continuing challenges surface. It is tempting to blame the healing professional when the knee or the tooth is fixed, but the lump in the rear end or throat leaves a taste or impression of disappointment.

In my own practice, patients bring years of behavioral baggage in for overhaul. At the outset of treatment, their conditions are largely disabling. Few people seek changes in their own character—they simply want mitigate the disadvantages in the package of their lifestyles, habits, and relationships. Yet many will seem disenchanted by the limitations of the improvement that they readily acknowledge as a result of intervention. It is curious that patients frequently acknowledge gains but tend to minimize or discount improvements as they focus on the next challenge. The ability to do such shifting is *clearly* a function of the patient's release from distress, although this is not always apparent to him. Interestingly, as the patient loses distress, his sense of reference about that distress also diminishes. Major hurdles become less significant in retrospect—such is the nature of emotions. They exist only in the "present," whose timelessness can extend indefinitely through encapsulated trauma. When the trauma is released, the person can access the memory, but not the disturbing emotion or powerlessness associated with it. It is like the difference between bleeding and watching a video of bleeding. It takes the mind some time to catch up with such quantum transformation, and most of us are parsimonious in comprehension and stingy in endorsement of the heroics we have just observed when this transformation occurs.

It is typical for patients to acknowledge treatment success, yet they remain curiously skeptical or diffident regarding new endeavors. This failure to generalize and correctly attribute is oddly at odds with treatment efficacy and patient awareness.

Getting better often includes getting more realistic and skilled in the nature and nitty-gritty of compromise—and that is *the* challenge for most of us.

As I think of my patients, I am reminded of the boy whose top-achieving parents placed (in my opinion) excessive demands on this ten-year-old. Enrolled in a rigorous private school and nationally competitive athletics, this attention-deficit child could not begin to please his parents, one of whom screamed and berated him constantly. He languished under frustration, and he modeled his father's explosive outbursts. Nevertheless, with treatment his school performance improved from Cs and Ds to As. He paid better attention, began to make friends, and started to act his age rather than resort to the baby-like behaviors that had alienated people. Yet his mother bemoaned her disappointment that his outbursts (against only his parents) continued sporadically. (Without the parents getting help, is it any wonder?)

Another patient improved his reading scores by three grade levels in six months; however, his mother lamented that the adolescent's problem of sleeping late on school mornings remained. Alas, she was unable to confiscate his car keys for fear of his reprisal against her.

After two months of treatment, a depressed and contentious adolescent with a long history of rebellion and academic failure became, in her mother's words, "a pleasure to live with." However, this high-schooler was still failing because she had never learned how to study but had made a career out of avoidance. Her school staff had done little in the way of recognizing, much less remediating the problem.

What about the patients who improve marginally? At what levels are subtle gains deemed significant or worthy? Is it easy for their families to downplay intervention and chalk up improvement to maturation? (One thing we know is that maturation heightens the probability and prevalence of snoring. Most people believe maturation is a good thing. I believe that if the somnoplasty works, my doctor will get a lot of referrals.)

When treatments work, they are often very specific. Expectations are always at work, and they tend to be generally encompassing.

I hoped that the somnoplasty would help my wife sleep better, and that most of her other annoyances and complaints about me would silence along with my snoring. In my confabulated anticipation, I supposed that I would also lose fifteen pounds. Weight loss, I heard, reduces snoring...This is the way the mind works...patients, patience, please!

I visited my ear, nose, and throat doctor for a postsurgery checkup. He is satisfied with the tissue healing. (This is surely a sign of my aging—when I ask my parents how they are feeling, the answer is usually, "I saw the doctor, and he's satisfied." *Yes, but how are* **you** *feeling?*) We discussed my wife's status, which I reported dutifully, since I had just examined her the previous day. She said that on a one to ten scale where I had snored consistently at a ten before treatment, now I was at an eight about 40 to 50 percent of the nights; the rest of the time, I was at a three or lower. (This last part was relatively silent for her and music to my ears.) How, then, to assess the impact of improvement?

When is it fitting to take what we get and to work with the clay we are given? When do we stretch for the sky is the limit? Who is accountable to what degree? And where is discretion the best response?

Modern life on the cutting edge can be so complicated.

In Southeast Asia, there is a primitive tribe called the Semai. They have a distinguishing ritual featuring the "birth hammock." In this culture, when a woman is in labor, she goes off quietly in the privacy of the bushes to bear her child. At the same time, her husband writhes in a "birth hammock," where he simulates labor pains and gets sympathy and attention from the clan.

This tradition holds great appeal for me, I must admit: role-playing heroics drawing attention, sympathy, nurturance, and popularity. The right stuff for treating a substitute patient. (I wonder how the Semai deal with snoring—does the man go sleep in the bushes while they mutilate the woman?)

It's too early to tell whether the somnoplasty has worked on me—it takes about six weeks after the procedure to assess the results. Meanwhile, my sleep is restful as ever, and I have the additional benefit of "birth hammock" status. I am nursing a sore palate, and my family considers me brave, though loud. I sleep peacefully and blissfully unconcerned with my undulating uvula, knowing that my wife has received the very best treatment. This is even more remarkable since the doctor and my wife have never met.

I dream of my surgeon gently rocking my wife to sleep in a birth hammock. She is pregnant, and we can hear the baby snoring. The doctor is writing something in the chart. He looks up pensively as he taps the pencil on the chart. The tapping grows louder and becomes annoying. I awaken to my wife's tapping me and reminding me to stop snoring.

Although human nature has basically not changed, medical technology has given birth to a new era of possibilities and changes in human functioning. Let's hope that both the expectations and the results (uvula excepted) don't come up short.

1993
When my children were learning to communicate.

GRAMMAR CAMP

That's it…my wife and I have had enough bad language! We're sending our kids to summer grammar camp. The experts expound that language development is gradual and that grammatical competence is acquired through experience; yet I have rather quickly acquired a teeth-grinding headache from my children's grammar. Barbara and I want an idyllic reprieve between the cuteness of their present expressions and the impending horrors of teenspeak.

Neal and Jeremy are basically good kids. However, their verbal behavior causes irregularity and tense confusion in our household. May I share some glaring examples?

"Dad, Neal breaked the window."

"That's not yours, it's mines!"

"Have you saw this new thing on TV? They telled about something that we didn't already buyed it, Dad. I just heared it again before."

"I'm sorry I fighted with Jeremy. I did what you said, I thinked about behaving, but it gived me a headache."

"My stomach gots fat and it hurted me. When I lay down, it's okay, but when I lay up, it's still hurted. It's more good now, but I still don't feel so better."

"The gooder player goed first and the badder player goed second."

"This is not very fun; I'm boring."

"When we goed to the store, Jeremy was lost, but he catched up with me and Mom."

"Neal sayed bad words."

"When is it the weekend yet?"

(crying) “Neal hit me and I was unhappy…”

My retort: “No, son, you say, ‘I am unhappy.’ I mean you are unhappy now, right? I mean, why are you so unhappy, son?”

According to my younger son, most of our grammatical corrections are “totally bogus.” He is at a tender age where incongruous witticisms seem smart rather than sassy, an age where “sticks and stones may break my bones, but words don’t mean as much as grown-ups get excited about.” Alternatively, his father grew up in New York, where every resident carries a sharp tongue in self-defense. If the pen is mightier than the sword, then the tongue is atomically capable. This is particularly volatile in the “nucular” family. Roosevelt’s motto, “Speak softly, and carry a big stick,” recycled for me as “Speak rapidly, and carry a big vocabulary.”

A classical education introduced me to the Whorfian hypothesis, and I’ve become enamored of this philosophy. The Whorfian hypothesis is derived from the work of Benjamin Whorf, a brilliant linguist, who theorized that human thought is both formed and limited by language. It states that meaningful thought occurs only within the boundaries generated by internal language development.

I’m afraid my children think that the Whorfian hypothesis is a gnarly surfboard move close to the Santa Cruz boardwalk—is this the result of pier influence?

I’m at my wits’ end. I look at my wife and think, *Hey dude, where doed we goed wrong?*

Fortunately for my family, when the children’s communications make the present tense, the solution (we hope) may be Grammar Camp. Among the hordes of camping experiences fund-raising for our children’s future, we may have found the ultimate deal. Even the ad was captivating:

Are your children responsible for their action words?
Is your family *linguistically correct?*

At **Grammar Camp**, we teach verbal responsibility!

Your children will communicate as never before after a summer at

GRAMMAR CAMP

Dedicated to the preposition of what grammar is good for

Charter member - GARBLE (Grammatical Association for the Reduction of Bad Language Expression)

As we read the promotional literature, Barbara and I became more impressed. The syllabus looked outstanding. Among the courses were:

- Subject-verb agreement and conflict resolution
- To conjugate or not to conjugate: safe sentence structure in the 1990s
- Taking responsibility for your action words
- How to use gerunds
- The wisdom of Webster
- Vocabulottery
- The role of past participles in US history
- Emphasis without whining

Equally important, the staff appeared to have superb credentials. Grammar Camp attracts professionals from several disciplines. These are accomplished individuals who want to make a difference in the lives of children and English teachers, as well as in the preservation of our language. (The camp was founded with a grant from George Bernard Shore, a descendant of the famous George Bernard Shaw, who loathed English spelling inconsistencies, and who studied under Benjamin Whorf.) Of course there are speech and language specialists and English teachers (who double as lifeguards). There are several psychologists experienced in modification techniques, towing their arsenals of rehabilitative adjectives and adverbs. There are graphics professionals and resident artists to help in the diagramming of sentences. Perhaps the most innovative staffing feature is the use of comedian-tutors to address the need for low camper-teacher ratio. Grammar Camp assigns one comedian to tutor two students in the belief that this is the optimal arrangement for learning the double entendre, a pinnacle of language mastery. This unique approach depends heavily on the professionalism and ego-strength of the comedians, many of whom are not known for their versatility with clean language or ability to perform well for such small audiences. Grammar Camp hires only qualified comedians—individuals who can write long-winded essays (shaggy-dog stories in print) and who have other sources of income.

The camp's head counselors are all attorneys. By virtue of their professional training, these counselors are quite at home with verbal confusion. Masterful with language, sequence, timing, and tense, they can artistically obfuscate what happened, when it happened, and what people say about it. We feel our kids will benefit from exposure to such mature sophistry.

The mainstay of Grammar Camp's effectiveness lies in its administrative authority and its constitutional foundation. This institution is exemplary in its discipline. Following the creed *we mean what we say, and we're mean when we say it,* the chief administrators are magistrates with a flair for poetic justice. These sagacious judges know how to structure a sentence and make offenders do time right. They are merciful in distinguishing between misthemeaning crimes and capitalization offenses. Their nonsectarian approach to verbal violations teaches values by imposing a sin-tax on grammatical errors. When the director of Grammar Camp was asked how he felt about punishing poor expression, this man of few misplaced words said, "Just fine." (It is rumored that he ghost-wrote the camp song "Let the Predicate Fit the Time.")

The literature advertises periodic seminars by celebrities. This summer, a special guest visitor will be Judge Wapner from *The People's Court.* He will bring with him a set of spare apostrophes to distribute judiciously. The highlight of Judge Wapner's visit will be the Mute Court, in which he will arbitrate cases argued only in writing by young adversaries.

Transcripts from previous Mute Court cases have reflected the judge's practical wisdom in settling youthful disputes. The following is typical:

Prosecution:
"He gave him the joystick along with that other one who trashed the game and then wouldn't admit that he did it, even when everyone their saw them with his own two eyes."

Defense:
"It ain't true, and you're making it up, ain't that true, 'cause you're afraid that if someone found out the truth, so's he would make you look bad, badder than you already look when you told that lie about your mother giving your brother worms for lunch and telling him it was whole wheat spaghetti until he barfed all over the..."

Fortunately, Judge Wapner is very experienced, so this should be a piece of cake for him. For the older kids, Wapner will conduct a seminar in metaphorical and poetic justice. I suspect our children will benefit from their exposure to such advanced mental gymnastics.

Not all is work in Grammar Camp. For recreation, baseball is a favorite pastime. As a side benefit, the staff has also found baseball particularly useful for prepositional instruction. Children need to learn verbal directions. "Two on and two out, with the outfield shifted toward right and the infield in..." Naturally, some quirky baseball phrases should be translated (e.g., "Following Manager Tug Crotchety's advice to 'hit it where they ain't,' he really creamed that pitch, and that ball is going, going, gone!"). I do hope, however, that the staff will explain why my son "flied out" instead of flew out or "home runned"—at least we won't say he "striked" out. Fortunately, the great Lawrence "Yogi" Berra, famous catcher of fast ones, will be there to provide insight and instruction on baseball and verbal expression.

Grammar Camp provides many exciting and stimulating adventures. Perhaps the most eagerly awaited activity, however, is the Olympic field trip event, Raging Proverbs. After a summer of instruction and practice with the twisting and turning of phrases, this exercise pits campers against the simultaneous challenges of grammar and gravity. At the site (Raging Waters drains the chutes in sponsorship of Grammar Camp's mission), teams ascend to the top of assigned chutes. Each team member is given a placard containing a piece of a jumbled proverb.

Members must then configure themselves into a discernible and familiar proverb before sliding down the chute. There are time constrictions (according to ability level and handicap); and, of course, campers must configure themselves without dropping words (or themselves) off the elevated platform. This event requires tremendous cooperation, communication, and expressive agility. Although the competition is friendly, its gravity is evident as contestants slide down the chute, preparing their placards for the photo finish.

Previous favorites among the judges were:

—wise to rise early and to bed a wealthy man early and makes healthy

—lose not or it's how you counts that it's whether you win, play the game

—lose or it's how you win that counts, it's not whether you play the game

—he who bests, lasts—laugh laugh

—and with you alone, the world laugh laughs and you cry cry

—well well that's all ends

Although my children are looking forward to the experience, their anticipation also harbors uncertainty about our motives. "Dad, why do we have to work so hard learning language skills during the summer?"

"Because even Shakespeare worked very hard before he knew he was going to be Shakespeare."

Touché, dude.

Postscript from My Own Childhood

Grammar was somewhat confusing for me, as I grew up in a bilingual environment. My parents spoke Yiddish at home. Black English was spoken at the finer Bronx schools I attended. Occasionally, my parents attempted to introduce culture by injecting a little French into their conversation:

Voulez-vous do your homework, you les miserables?

Please, have merci.

I've had beaucoup of both of you.

Mettez le homework, you bête.

You bet.

Zultsdt, mitt-in-der-ritten in draärderein…which means, "May you gargle with nonkosher drain cleaner in the middle of hell."

My mother's behavior would never be tolerated in today's ghetto: typical of her invective (while yelling out of the tenement window) "If you don't come home now, I'll murder you," or the more metaphorical, "You'll be the death of me."

You're eating my heart out…Mangez mon couer, s'il vous plaît, bâtard.

French was out…I always admired the British way of speaking, but since my father was a dentist, I had just about enough of watching stiff upper lips.

1993
Like parents, like children…(but don't tell them)

OVERWEIGHT, BUT MODELING ANYWAY

Our Words Are Worth a Thousand Pictures

Over dinner at a restaurant of my parents' choice, we had an argument that reminded me of my teenage years. In the manner of rehashing old patterns, it was a replay; but this recapitulation had a significant generational twist: my children were present. We were visiting Grandma and Grandpa, and, for several days, the arguments and irritations had been mounting.

There was nothing special about this visit in the formal sense that characterizes scrapbooks, calendar events, tragedies, or recognized milestones that warrant the gathering of relatives. Just a time to be with loved ones, to celebrate how much the children have grown, to enjoy the bad humor and good health that still prevailed in our family. And to complain and argue, a set of skills carefully honed over generations and transmitted and practiced ever so thoroughly. Mine is a clan of lawyers and comedians, most of whom eventually manage to get day jobs.

The nascent teenage years dawning on my crop of Steinbergs brought weeds of rebellion to shroud the nourishment of the future. I sat at the table with my two sons, Jeremy (eleven) and Neal (thirteen), who were temporarily quiet and mollified by their dinners but conscious (all of us) of the interplay between my parents and me. I supposed that watching one's parent argue with *his* parent is the closest approximation to seeing one's parent as a child. My oldest, Neal, had been battling with Grandpa for two days, reliving the combat with which I was so familiar. It was painful to watch my son's paltry attempts to portray himself as grown-up and my father's embarrassing descent into puerile competition with a child.

Despite the psychodynamics and restimulations, I did not feel like a child. I had come to visit simply to *be* with my folks, to swim in their conflicts, nod along with their prejudices, lament the injustices propagated against senior citizens by Nature and politicians, and let them dote on their grandchildren. Similar to the mysteries children project about the adult affairs they're not yet privy to, I wonder, in middle age, about the satisfaction of grandparents as they watch their children struggle with parenting. With winks and nods and gloating smiles, the elders are getting even. They refer to this process as "the chickens coming home to roost." I allow them this pleasure, partly out of deference and mostly out of wonder. All the toys my money can buy cannot purchase this secret wisdom that only unfolds after years of walking the walk. I have to raise my children to the point where they can raise their children in order for me to get a glimmer of this special satisfaction. Despite my multiple joys of fathering, this process is almost unbearable—the effort to balance nurturing, supervision, decision making, and observation; the impossibility of picturing my children as independent adults; the waiting; the ambivalence of letting go; the uncertainty of an empty nest. This seems yet another of Nature's inscrutable tricks to teach patience and to keep man in his place and time.

When I was a child, I talked like a child, I thought like a child, I reasoned like a child (1 Corinthians 13:11)...I wondered about the mysteries that adults carried on behind closed doors. I fantasized about sex. I vigilantly watched adult expressions and carefully searched their countenances and activities for any disclosure of information about the secret codes of adulthood. It was like standing on a long line at an amusement park ride—the eager, dusty, endless wait, punctuated by a periodic outflow of giddy patrons disembarking from their orgasmic ride.

When I became a man, I put childish ways behind me (1 Corinthians 13:11)...Caught between the guardianship of my children's peering advances and the speculations about geriatrics, I still fantasize about sex. Only now, it is with marvel that I contemplate what sex may be after fifty or sixty years of it (and with the same person!).

I am at an age of hard work, where reflection is a precious luxury. My thirteen-year-old has reminded me of his cheeky definition of middle age: it's when you stop growing at both ends and grow in the middle. I can stomach my son's biting witticisms, for his quest is maturity and the recognition of its attainment. His jocularity is a bit tentative, as if testing the limits of respect with each foray. I have learned to live without respect, although I now attract plenty. A prophet is without honor in his homeland, except when that homeland is heaven. Life's denigration has, thankfully, made me humble rather than bitter; so, I accrue respect like interest on a hefty account.

Mostly, I shut up and smile. I've learned to let people express and expend themselves without my having to get involved in unwinnable fights or join marathon sessions in the processing of anxiety. This style has served me well, and I wore it implacably during our turbulent visit.

Now, however, I had something to say. With some time and rehearsal, I had worked up the energy to voice my concerns with the intent of modeling for my children. When I was younger, more impulsive, and full of myself, it was easy and natural to spout forth with my imposing and verbose opinions. It was hard to shut up. Now, self-restraint is the default, and I must mobilize the energy to interject when my contribution is imminent, lest I choose the path of least resistance and check out of the conversation and relationship.

I had been vexed by my mother's communication over the past two days, and I wanted to speak about it. I felt she had been deceptive about her own motives, and when I challenged her, she covered up with exaggeration and denial.

We had visited a flea market and shopped separately. I bought a picture, which the seller wrapped and taped in brown paper. As we unloaded our purchases back at my parents' condo, I intentionally left the picture in the trunk of the car. When my mother questioned this, I replied that there was no need to bring the picture inside, since it was wrapped and ready to travel home with me. She then told me that the sun would shine on it and ruin it. "But Mom," I pleaded incredulously, "the picture is *wrapped and in the trunk.* How could the sun shine on it?" My mother then mumbled something about pastels deteriorating, and how it would be nice for her to see the picture anyway.

"Mom," I said reprovingly, "the picture is *not* pastels, and if you want to see the picture, then simply say so, straight out."

"No," she demurred, "I was only looking out for your interests. I don't need to see the picture."

"Oh, come on!" I objected. "You want to see the picture!" Impassive silence on her part. "Okay, I'll take your word for it. We'll take the picture in the house but we won't unwrap it." I could almost savor myself pouting, but I wasn't the type. This felt wrong. It was like a Seinfeld skit, but without the applause and laughter. Actually, despite the ridiculous dialogue, there was nothing funny about it. Phony pretense notwithstanding, it was all too real. The scorching sun was sickening the already sour grapes. My mother and I stood arguing like silly, obstinate children. In my righteousness, I pursued truth and honor. In her innocence, my mother sidestepped the attack. There we stood, two overweight models, strutting impetuously in the sweltering tropical sun, as the boys endured this sweating pomposity.

With this flustering scene in mind, I wanted to model for the kids how to hold someone accountable without hitting below the belt—that is, without using emotions to batter or manipulate and without making the *person* wrong. It would be good for my children to witness direct communication with I-messages and limit-setting, unadorned or impeded by familial affect and old emotional patterns competing for the lead.

Unfortunately, my mother's defensiveness made the lesson hard to discern. She was not enrolled in my School of Straight Talk.

"Mom, I'm bothered by the way you communicated about the picture I bought at the flea market."

"What?" Imploring, beseeching look, her ready response to my opening gambit. What could Mother have possibly done wrong? Mothers don't hurt their children.

"I felt that your comment about the danger of leaving the picture in the trunk was deceptive. I believe you wanted to look at the picture, and that's why you wanted me to bring it in the house."

"Nuuh-oow!" Head shaking and chewing. Was she caught off guard and quickening her swallow in reflexive guilt, or was this just for spectacular effect? "I was being honest—I really wanted to protect your picture. I didn't care whether you showed it to me."

"Now, Mom, I don't believe that. I'm not looking to make you or your motives wrong. I just wish you would be straightforward. It discredits you when you lie."

At this point, my father had swallowed enough food to join the argument. "Would your mother lie to you? If she says she just wanted to help you, that's what it was. Whatsa matter with you? You don't trust your own mother?"

They have an interesting relationship, my parents. They claw at each other truculently and hammer home their grievances with invective. But let anyone else dare impugn or malign either of them, and they defend each other vehemently. With friends like these, you don't fear enemies.

Can you imagine? Marauding their own flesh and blood! It was time to take the gloves off (too hot in Florida, anyway). I could only hope that my children would identify with that pinching sensation and not tune in to my growing immaturity.

To Mom: "This is typical of you, and you know we all despise your penchant for little white lies."

Mom, imperiously: "I resent that. I don't hurt anyone. Who beside you, Mr. Holier-than-thou-I'm-gonna-analyze-you, do I bother with my so-called *communication indiscretions*?"

"Look around, Mom." Whereupon, I insolently named family members. The kids were squirming in high gear.

Dad: "Your mother is so good-hearted; people don't appreciate her."

Mom: "They appreciate the rewards they get from my *little white lies.*" Facetious irony.

One, two, left, right…the pummeling setup for the knockout blow.

Dad: "Er, Dr. Freud, finish your dinner."

I wasn't going down easily. "Dad, do you mean to tell me you are not bothered by Mom's constant little white lies? How could you deny this?"

Alas, the conspiracy was progressing—silent, methodical chewing. Icy, wounded stares. This conversation shambled to lessening avail. Furthermore, the food was cooling, and the children's attention was turning to restless indifference. The No Sale sign was posting on this demonstration. I had played my part well, ensuring that neither generation nor geography would truly interfere with the family communication patterns I had learned so well as a youngster. How heartfelt to get reacquainted.

I had originally planned to visit so I could spend time with my father. He's getting on in years, and it's hard for him to travel. My mother overshadows him during telephone conversations, and he is not one to initiate a call just to chat.

The cramped household made it awkward for my father and me to fall naturally into private conversation. He is now too sedentary for walks. Still, we managed one customary tête-à-tête. I don't think my dad has told me much new in twenty years, though I strain to listen respectfully to the familiar but difficult lectures of wisdom. As we age, I react less to the unsolicited advice, and he shortens it. (This contrasts noticeably with his interactions with the grandchildren, which accelerate and feed off their captious cycles.)

"So, what's new, son? How's business?"

To defy monotony, I was determined to share something new with my father, to reveal a part of myself as a token of intimacy. It took more effort than I expected. Since we were talking about my professional adventures in helping people cope, I decided to apprise him of one of life's important secrets I had learned well. After all, this is the way we relate, this is what we share. He no longer orders me around, and he has shirked the erstwhile pastime of communally criticizing Mom. What could remain besides the gifts of survival advice? He contributed, as usual, the predictable financial and health counsel. I was about to share one of my very few nuggets. I hoped he would comprehend it.

"I've discovered over and over again the beneficence of separating emotion from thinking, and then integrating feeling back again. It's not just a matter of self-discipline or self-control; it's knowing how the mind works and how to work with it. This is so important because it governs practically all interaction with yourself, your activities, and with other people. Dispelling negative emotion and blending positive emotion with purposeful thinking is a potent key to productivity and happiness.

"I make a living from showing others how to do this. Moreover, it makes living much more pleasant and worthwhile." I was ready to continue with my pitch about self-soothing as a fundamental and vital skill for survival and how the self-management of emotion and anxiety interweaves with coping. Though sounding academic and plumed, this message was intended earnestly for my father, who was good at being by himself, but not so successful at self-soothing.

This might have developed toward an interesting discussion (or at least an excuse for talking until the usual confusion encroached), but we were interrupted by some yelling outside the room. Within a minute, my mother burst in, and our conversation was mercifully over.

Dad and I communicated like the two mythological sisters battling over an orange. One wanted the pulp for juice, and the other wanted the rind for baking. Instead of compromising, each to her own needs, they ended up killing each other. We have been more fortunate, ostensibly, to return to our corners over the years, simply scratching our heads.

Our conflicts left limited room for physical or mental respite. We were falling over each other in efforts to retreat and reunite. The condo was quite small, though our egos stretched beyond limits. Throughout the traumatic accommodations each of us made, Mom was there to smooth ruffled feathers and cuddle the children in a way that made them feel it was all worth it. This is a grandmotherly trick, and my mother is an experienced magician. She's so good, we could enjoy being hoodwinked. She reeks of protection and enthusiasm; under her umbrella, the weather seems perfect or irrelevant.

I slept as much as I could, quartered, nonetheless, in the room where Mom and the kids vied for the computer and watched TV. The atmosphere could have been titled *Air Conditioner Named Desire*, for my father kept the thermostat at a crisp eighty-two degrees. I retired to the squawking and fussing of night owls; I awakened to the harsh jabbering of CNN. Dad made it his business to know the latest in world events—and he made it our business, too. The children awoke to chiding about their laziness, interspersed with news and stock market reports. This was a bed-and-breakfast they would not forget.

Our confined proximity favored the probability of collision, and this occurred in the form of property damage. Neal led off by breaking a glass Coke bottle. A day later, I contributed by knocking over a porcelain vase. Dad, batting cleanup (though Mom did the actual cleanup), splattered a jar of salad dressing hours later in the apparent clumsy competition. Talk about modeling! This was a cross between the Three Stooges and War of the Roses. Neal played a scorekeeper of sorts. It was probably his way of defusing anxiety to announce the errors of each player. With some backhanded praise he kept reminding his audience that Jeremy was without fouls. It was no jinx, since Jeremy remained aloof from such blunders. As expected, the broken items shattered the fragile peace we were struggling to maintain. The salad dressing did it. All bets were off, as the blaming and yelling resumed. We were back to family business as usual, with tension the ritual and self-soothing an apostasy.

We had to get away from the crowded delirium of the house. I invited eleven-year-old (almost) Jeremy to accompany me on my walk. He accepted, and I knew it wasn't for the sake of exercise. About a mile into our excursion, I risked steering the conversation around to Jeremy's reaction to the dinner argument.

"Well," he began, "I know this sounds kinda sick, but…I liked to see Grandma and Grandpa defeated." Silent deliberation, then, "I mean, it's not that I want them to take offense or anything, but they should know that they were wrong, and it's nice to see you win an argument."

This was said genuinely with rife emotion, but without any trace of anger or vindictiveness. It surprised me. Jeremy's communication was more about justice than pride or resentment. He simply saw that domination and authoritarianism were wrong and he knew that they hurt.

"I appreciate your support, Jeremy, and I especially value your courage in expressing yourself. I really mean that"—quick tap on the shoulder and arm hug—"but I wasn't trying to win any argument. I just wanted to let Grandma know how I felt, and to do it in a straight and direct way. Hopefully, you can practice doing this, too."

Jeremy seemed emboldened by my candor, though he took a different tack.

"Dad, I wish grown-ups would understand that kids calm down by playing video games and being on the computer. It's a great way to relax; I just go into my room by myself and play, and it totally relaxes me."

This tyrannical computer wizard who elicits my admiration and delight was scoring more than a pitch for his territory and habits (woe to those who try to unglue Jeremy from his competitive and intense involvement with computer activities!). He was defending his recourse, his coping outlet under the stress of grandparents. Jeremy's Internet tutelage of Grandma was bartered for hours of monopolizing her computer. We were in tight quarters, and he couldn't retreat in isolation at the expense of others. Self-soothing was at a premium.

"I do understand, son, and I think it's a good thing to have ways to calm yourself down. But the calming should be in service to other activities and interactions, not an end in itself."

"Huh? Whaddya mean, Dad?"

"It's like this, Jeremy. Let's compare your calming down on the computer to a battery recharging. The purpose of recharging is so that the battery can be effective for its various uses. If the battery needs to recharge each time it faces some demand, then it will spend most of its time regaining its strength but not functioning very well as a battery. Similarly, what you do to calm down should replenish your ability to interact with people, not substitute for it. When a kid spends so much time playing video games to calm down, even though it may work, it becomes an escape—like the battery whose main life is sitting in the recharger."

After a thoughtful pause, "I get it, Dad."

I had hit my stride, both in walking and abstracting. "And besides, Jeremy…there's always the danger that an overcharged battery might catch fire. Too much gaming makes some kids…"

"Da-aad!"

In the end, my modeling transpired in unrehearsed pose. The visit was difficult, and I participated in the dysfunction. Indeed, I produced this episode of *Pall in the Family*, for I suggested and organized the trip. I came, I saw, I argued...I forgave.

I simply wanted to *be* with them. I was willing to dive into the seditious Sea of Steinberg and be swept away by a wave or stung by jellyfish. This was my intention and my freely given gift. I wanted to share it with my children and encourage whatever fun and benefit they could derive in the circumstances. In retrospect, my willingness was rewarded, for I made my peace with hardship and double-minded love. We each did the best we could, and I came away okay with it. I tried to model logic, equanimity, and selective assertive expression. The script was clear, but no one wanted to follow it. Instead, I had only acceptance to show and forgiveness to offer.

There was a heaviness in the air that deeply saturated the Florida humidity. The best we did left gaps and left us wondering whether it was good enough. The modeling was less than graceful, but it would have to suffice for my children to learn and copy. They will know how to carry themselves without running away, how to eat what is served without sacrificing taste. Hopefully, they glimpsed the diplomacy of negotiating boundaries without destroying citizens. When it comes to emotions and vulnerability, they may well discover treasures from navigating the tempests of ambivalence. I wanted to be a swashbuckling captain, but I may only be an obscure lighthouse. In the long run, this may quietly help my children find their way.

I reminded myself that the purpose of my leadership is to make them independent. We want desperately to be needed, yet to grow less needy.

It was time to go. Our baggage sat defiantly blocking traverse along the narrow path to the door. The suitcases clumped in silent chorus, as if to mock us with a parting stanza from the crowded weekend opera: all of us, tripping over each other on a stage too small, the tragedy of each a hero in his own play.

My father sat dejectedly as I bent over to kiss him good-bye. "Thanks for having us, Dad. I'll miss you."

"We'll see about that," he whispered. With my face next to his, I could hear tears welling up through his sinuses.

As if to gild our journey with special effects, weather and flight delays disrupted our return home. There were lightning storms in Atlanta severe enough to start fires. The updates from our captain were not encouraging. After two hours sitting in our first plane at the gate in Florida, we took off amid tremulous confidence and uneven skies.

On the way to Atlanta, bolts of lightning set off Neal's anxiety, which he expressed through rapid-fire questions about weather science and aviation.

"Dad, can the lightning come all the way through to our seats? Will the wings conduct it? Should I not touch a soda can?"

"It's okay, son, the lightning can't get through to us," I reassured him with the aplomb of someone who specialized in little white lightning lies. Fortunately, my prediction held up, and we landed in Atlanta with only jangled nerves and schedules. We missed our connecting flight, of course, and waited on lines for more hours. Eventually, we boarded a flight for San Francisco and landed only fifty miles from our intended destination of San Jose. Not far off, really, for a journey of three thousand miles. We got home at 3:00 a.m., however, and that was California time. The clock inside me was cuckoo.

I got enough sleep to arise to Mom's second phone message. This adventure stretched her beyond the call of normal duty for worrying.

Mom was so miffed by the indignities her loved ones endured on the return trip that within two hours of hearing about our travail, she had wangled $1,100 in compensation from the airline. To the best of my knowledge, she did this without once mentioning the sun beating down upon the plane, where my picture lay vulnerable during those extra hours on the tarmac—honest. The airline was probably grateful to have flown unscathed through those treacherous areas where little white lightning lies. So were we.

1994
A summary of genetic wisdom.

VALUABLE LESSONS MY PARENTS TAUGHT ME(OR REINFORCED)

condensed from *The Steinberg Survival Guide*

1. Be smart, but don't be a wise guy. (It's nice to be smart—but be nice!)

2. The best exercise is the push-away: do it at the dinner table and against overindulgence and sin.

3. Avoiding fools and foolishness stimulates agility and alertness.

4. In traffic and other dangerous competitive avenues—if it's a tie, you lose.

5. Don't smoke, go easy on alcohol, no drugs without labels, and don't fool around with women (other than your wife). Don't fool around with men at all.

6. Among the best pleasures in life: good food, good sex, hot showers, good books, affectionate grooming, and comfortable furniture.

7. Save for a rainy day, and you'll probably have fewer of them.

8. You can't dance at too many weddings.

9. When in crowds, guard your pockets; when guarding on defense in sports, pick the other guy's pocket.

10. To do any good, the dentist has to be in somebody's face—and, yes, there is sometimes pain.

11. Man plans, God laughs: keep planning, man, but learn to appreciate God's sense of humor.

12. Invest in your future.

13. Work for your money, but let your money work for you.

14. When in doubt, forgive.

15. Humor nourishes the coping cells; digest new jokes regularly.

16. Nothing comes from nothing.

17. Do what *they* (the experts, the wise people, and those in authority) say; it will reduce the pain in your future.

18. Be honest, live cleanly, listen to your conscience, pray, enjoy life—it passes quickly.

19. Children grow up, and parents grow old.

20. Opinions come easily on a full stomach.

21. Justice on Earth is relative: what's good for the goose is good for the gander.

22. How you make your bed, that's how you'll sleep. If you're tired enough, you'll sleep anywhere.

23. Rich or poor, it's good to have money.

24. Men understand three basics: food, sex, and money. Women understand a lot more, but men are usually busy with the three basics.

25. When buying, look for bargains; when selling, discount the deal, not yourself.

26. Heaven and Earth are two different shows.

27. Grandparents know what researchers try to prove.

28. The lesson of Humpty Dumpty is still relevant.

29. Small children, small problems; big children, big problems.

30. What people can think up for themselves, their own worst enemies couldn't wish upon them.

31. If you do more of what you're doing, you'll get more of what you've got.

32. Step lightly around the flowers—someday, you, too, will be pushing up daisies.

33. Get to the bottom line!

1992
Documentation on gender habits and the technological aspects of relationships.

HOW REMOTE IS YOUR FAMILY?

A recent story on ABC's *20/20* featured the behavior of people using TV remote controls. The gist of the story was this: males and females differ significantly with regard to their use of the remote control, and males tend to covet the instrument, using it to frequently change channels and "hunt" among televised programs. The story further suggested that male behavior with remote controls is a modern version of some instinctual, predatory, "hunting" behavior; presumably, the remote device substitutes for the hoary weapons that men traditionally used to protect and provide for their families.

Whatever the merit of this interesting theory, it is likely that, regardless of who changes the channels, two points are valid:

1. The family certainly needs protection from the bombardment of inane, offensive, and commercial trivia televised.

2. Vigilant and consistent "hunting" is required to provide the family with entertainment and information having nourishing or socially redeeming value.

Male Remoteness and the Self

With respect to the theoretical comparison of remote controls and male predatory behavior, I find self-examination to be disarming. Although I have never owned any weapons (except for shooting paper clips with rubber bands when I was a kid), currently I am overrun by these remote control weapons. At last count, I own (between home and office) nineteen remote devices—not including cordless input devices for computer equipment (five of those). Admittedly, I am an audiovisual enthusiast—but a macho predator? Perhaps I should have my testosterone (or at least my battery alkaline levels) checked. Wait—before you call me the Infrared Ranger or claim that I am damaging the ozone, let me explain:

I am as much victim as hunter with this new technology. Taking this issue in hand (which commander am I holding, please?), I proclaim my resistance to this electronic oppression, and I seek a new definition of the male role. As Henny Youngman would say (if he were doing new material), "Take my remote, please!"

The behavioral science news features have not covered an important corollary to the remote control behavior issue: this daunting electronic technology paradoxically offers opportunities to revitalize male chivalry. In our home, I practice charity and deference. To my wife and children, I say gallantly, "Of course you can have the remote; here..." Underpinning this gracious attitude, however, are some selfish and cowardly truths:

- I cannot operate the thing correctly anyway.
- In frustration, I will probably hurt my fingers and perhaps yield to the temptation to yell rhythmically in impolite language.
- Given my repeated failure as a hunter to bring into our home broadcast material worthy of consumption, I might as well fall asleep in front of whatever is on the tube—thus, I can greet the new day well rested for "hunting" in the civilization of real people.

Have you noticed how surreptitiously complicated this technology has become? I remember my immigrant grandmother peering suspiciously at an old black-and-white

TV and finally exclaiming, "Wonderful! But how did they get those people to squeeze inside such a tiny box?"

One of my remotes has more buttons than the lobby of the apartment building in which I grew up. In that building, the buttons were labeled: Jacobs, Finkelstein, etc. At least when you pressed a button, you knew what would happen. (There were four basic responses: 1) Nothing 2) "Who is it?" 3) "Yeah, whaddya want?" and 4) "Go away or I'll call the police!")

Insecurity grips me as I clutch the remote, half expecting that the response to my finger pressure will be "Go away, or I'll call the cable company!" My remotes have buttons labeled: Status, CS, PIC, and many other intriguing and mysterious features. These devices also have doors that slide and swing open (yes, I have broken the doors while trying to slide the swinger and swing the slider). Inside the doors are a host of buttons for inflicting exotic long distance effects on the telecast prey. Although I am mystified by these functions, I have learned through trials and errors that if the doors are not completely closed, the outside buttons actually activate the inside buttons. These "smart" remotes are so incredibly stupid that they cannot sense I have broken their flimsy door hinges and am clumsily trying to press the outside buttons! My most consistent shot with this weapon produces visual static and the on-screen display "00" along with a volume surge and an air-raid sound, notifying all occupants in the house that the cautious male hunter has again protected his family with a domestic civil defense drill.

A Handful of Hunters

The inventors of these new generation remotes must have lived in the kind of apartment buildings I did. This is obvious, because only people who have stood before a panel of doorbell buttons labeled R. Jacobs, S. M. Jacobs, D. Finkelstein, L. Finkelstein, etc. would invent remote devices with offspring whose buttons access the same family. This is not a joke. Two of my remotes arrived at our house with "mini-remotes"—those credit-card-sized relatives so cozily suited to catalyzing family feuds. Now, the male predator role has been undermined by these guerilla assistants. These dual remotes are really "duel" remotes. A wise head-of-household monitors what the children watch by whatever crafty means are necessary. Sometimes, domination through trickery is the last resort. My children and I have spent delightful moments dueling with remotes to the point where no one in the room could possibly follow the TV show.

This exciting home teaching experience has instilled in my children an unerring sense of timing and the mathematical foundation that only working with manipulatives can provide. They know, to the millisecond, how long it takes to turn the TV sets on and off. The long-term effects of this infrared warfare on their development is yet to be determined.

Another fascinating feature of remote controls is their influence on cause-and-effect thinking and perceptions of reality. This is particularly interesting if you anticipate learning how to operate units with different brand names. Some manufacturers create their little weapons such that you must press the ubiquitous ENTER button to make happen what you spent the previous five minutes programming—within very few seconds. This feature was commercialized by engineers who remember trying to get into apartment buildings where the residents "buzzed" people in after the prospective entrant pressed the apartment button on the panel that was invariably located thirty-five feet from the locked lobby door. Where were remotes then, hah?! I'm sure these hapless not-yet-engineers wondered. And truly, they have achieved revenge. Other manufacturers' brands make their remotes implement the change as soon as a suitable combination of buttons is pressed—which can be frustrating if you're hurrying to watch the channel "02" news. A third type of remote requires pressure on the EXECUTE button—which is, of course, exactly what you feel like doing with this weapon once you determine that there is no ENTER button.

Some among you may pompously think, at this point, he should read the manuals and learn how to work the darn things. Aha! Why is it that each new automatic device I get makes me increasingly dependent on its corresponding "manual"? Alas, such is the strenuous paradox of modern life! New and improved threats to the male ego, which thrives on delusions of independence and intelligence. Remember, we are dealing with new versions of stereotyped behavior, and that includes the ordinarily sexist division of labor. My wife collects and reads manuals. I grow hair and fire stray infrared beams. Around the house, I am dubbed "Hide-the-batteries." Unfortunately, this moniker has been extended to local electronics stores, because whenever "Hide-the-batteries" Steinberg tries to get a salesperson to explain how the remote works, the darn thing "has no batteries. I'm sorry, sir…"

Dysfunctional Detachment

Besides their influence on logical thinking, remote controls tamper with perceptual accuracy. This hallmark of reality seems to have fallen by the engineering wayside. For example, look at PIC (picture-in-picture)—if you can figure out how to access it. This feature allows you to watch two channels simultaneously. In psychology, when a person sees two different realities occurring simultaneously, we call it schizophrenia. Sony, however, calls it progress. One of my sets can display (with the push of correct buttons) thirty-six miniaturized channels at once—this is fascinating! I'm not sure of its entertainment value, but I can certainly appreciate its application in training air-traffic controllers and, perhaps, in the experimental inducement of attention-deficit disorder.

As though these burgeoning deviations weren't enough, the technology spawning remote controls has revealed another subtly prevalent handicap, one from which I suffer increasingly: *decadigislexia*—more literally, "ten meaningless fingers." This progressive condition is manifest through repetitive, purposeless button pressing that accelerates over time. Although it is not yet clear whether this digital restlessness leads to degenerative arthritis, many of the more severe cases have been linked to individuals having satellites or cable television. It is hypothesized that these finger responses eventually become involuntary; however, this is difficult to verify since people with this behavior routinely justify their button pressing as "consciously choosing" selections.

Remote Possibilities

Despite these hardships, I am still struggling to learn this remote multimania. The technology of fusing realities simply strikes a resonant chord in my personality(ies). My eventual goal is to have two shows communicate with each other on the same TV. Just imagine the possible permutations. We could arrange a political debate: say, Dan Quayle and Murphy Brown, live, right on your own screen. In the interim, I'll settle for a camera sequence of a quarterback throwing a long pass that ends up (through the miracle of picture-in-picture) sailing through the net of a basketball hoop. Those Nike commercials have the right idea.

Although technology relentlessly advances, its ultimate acceptance depends on the ability of people to personalize their relationship with its products. Just as people name their pets and project all kinds of human qualities on them, perhaps the answer lies in developing more intimate remote relationships (pardon the contradiction in terms). My family uses this approach. We refer to the remote control device as the *schmitzschig*. This word means "thing" in Yiddish; *schmitzschig* is also the neo-Freudian term for "potent thing."

Muted Meaning

Here is an example of remote communication in the Steinberg home: It is nighttime, and the children are asleep. I am sitting in the family room, staring in stupefaction at images on the TV, the *schmitzschig* dangling limply in my hand. My wife, Barbara, sits beside me.

Barbara (sweetly):
"Honey, could you flip the *schmitzschig*?"

Mark:
"Sure."

PRESS (Presses CHD+ and the news appears, with the reporter talking loudly in front of blaring sirens)

Barbara (appealing loudly):
"Could you turn it down? I'd like to tell you something…"

Mark:
"Yeah, go ahead."

PRESS (fumbles with fingers, mistakenly pressing VOL+ and turning the sound uncomfortably high)

Barbara (vaguely threatening):
"Would you mute that thing, please!"

(Notice the inadvertent lapse into English vernacular, referring to the "thing.")

Mark (finally stumbling across the MUTE button): PRESS
"Honey, I'm sorry, I couldn't hear what you said."

Barbara:
"I wanted to tell you, today the kids were…"
PRESS
(Mark accidentally hits the MUTE button again)

Newscaster:
"…in Oakland…" PRESS

Mark:
"In Oakland?!! PRESS "I thought you went to the local library…"
PRESS

Barbara:
"We did—you're so silly when you're absorbed in…"
PRESS

Newscaster:
"…SPORTS…next…" PRESS
(commercial break)

Mark (nonchalantly acting as though he has control of the MUTE button): PRESS
"So…honey, continue about you and the kids."

Barbara:
"We were in the library, and the kids were…"
PRESS

Sportscaster:
"…thrown out for unsportsmanlike conduct…" PRESS

Mark (excitedly):
"I just cannot believe that kind of behavior!"

Barbara (trying stoically to communicate):
"How was work today?"
PRESS

Newscaster:
"…epidemic…" PRESS

Barbara:
“That bad, huh?”

Mark:
“What?” PRESS

Newscaster:
“…shows no signs of recovery…” PRESS

Barbara:
“Sounds bad…”

Mark:
“No, really…did I tell you what happened today?” PRESS

Newscaster:
“…economic downturn…” PRESS

Barbara (irritated):
“Mark, this is distracting. I simply asked how work was today, and whether…”
PRESS

Weatherman:
“…there’s a chance of fog lifting…” PRESS

Barbara (coyly):
“Can I please hold the *schmitzschig*?”

Mark:
“Okay, honey, but let’s go to bed; we can watch there.”
PRESS

As my grandmother would ask, “How did they manage to get all that command, communication, and control into one little *schmitzschig*?”

II
ESSAYS AND ARTICLES

2014

THE MOST BEAUTIFUL MUSIC YOU CAN MAKE

Occasionally, something new seems to surface, standing out among the ordinary and repetitious: an interesting gadget, a novel idea, a helpful device or invention, a lovely literary, artistic, or musical expression. Mostly, though, what looks new initially turns out to be a retread or recapitulation of what has been before. This is not necessarily a disappointment, but a reiteration of patterns that nature has woven into the fabric of life, the world around and within us, and our perceptions of reality. Not that things never change—surely, they do—but it is the manifestation of nature that we recognize and repeat familiar patterns of biological processes, behaviors, and preferences.

This is evident in our habits and also in the unfolding of art, music, creative endeavors, and, most strikingly, in the experiences of emotions and relationships. If "something new under the sun" does occur, it is weathered and reflected by our perceptions of the familiar, the assimilation and integration of new experiences into what we already know. A new event must somehow make sense and gel with what we have already understood. This is necessary for problem-solving and survival, and it is also true for aesthetic pleasure, moral rectitude, and conscience and integrity.

For example, consider the myriad ways that foods, music, and artistic creations can be combined. While tastes differ, any appreciation of something "good" or "special" or "new" is a recognizable spinoff of something previously experienced. The new version or creation contains elements of the old presented or combined with fresh or innovative flair. A recurrent theme is not the same old thing when presented with variations that suggest originality.

In music, the notes are finite, but the combinations and sounds and the permutations of styles and timing continue to push the envelope of exploration. What makes us *like* a piece of music is its sensory effect on us and the recognition of its themes and elements and attachment of them to familiar harmonies, melodies, and rhythms in our experience. We gravitate toward and seek to repeat something that is familiar and that satisfies.

So it is also with emotions and human interactions and relationships. We become used to hosting certain emotions; often the behavior of others elicits the feelings most familiar to us, and yet we tend to see circumstances and others as causing these feelings. We develop patterns of interaction and relationships that fulfill and confirm our needs and beliefs, patterns that form our character and react to the character of others. Circumstances are the content of our lives, and they become embedded in the context of character and world view. They are like lyrics and melody, harmony and timing. The music may be somber or uplifting; yet its inexhaustible variations are crafted from limited elements into themes with repeated practice and presentation.

We learn to identify what is pleasing to our ears and the rhythms that make us want to dance or cringe. We use labels and categories to help us find and express what we like and avoid what is unpleasant. So it is, too, with sensing and listening to people.

Recently, a patient related to me the constant hardships of living with a family member. According to my patient, his sibling was regularly cranky and demanding. Listening to the details of my patient's complaints (not for the first time), I formed a picture of his sibling as an irritable person with a flawed personality marred by entitlement and self-pity issues.

Though I had never talked to his sibling, I understood my patient's needs and outlook, his frustrations, desires, talents, and limitations. I was familiar with his lyrics and rhythms: a sad country song, it seemed. In response, I tried to validate his longsuffering responsibility, to praise his devotion without enjoining or reinforcing any justification for resenting or criticizing his sibling.

One day, after lamenting his sibling's recent offenses, he said something unexpected and remarkable. Almost as an afterthought, he remarked, "It's strange—even though she's very difficult, I have sympathy for her."

This thought seemed to surprise him. Though he wasn't asking for validation, I sensed an opportunity to expand upon his sensitive emotional offering. I said, "Thanks for sharing your feelings about (name). I appreciate your sensitivity and what may come as a surprising discovery in your experience. There is a name for what you've just shared. But before I tell you what it is, I want to tell you a story from my own experience:

"As a young adolescent, I loved music and wanted to play an instrument. But I balked at instruction and discipline. Formal violin lessons were a misery for me, and my teachers undoubtedly suffered with me through their attempted tutelage. Still, I had music running through my head, and I wanted to express it through my fingers. In a gymnasium/auditorium where I practiced basketball, there was an old piano. During my rest breaks from basketball, I'd tinkle the piano keys; quickly, I could emulate melodies of the popular songs I heard on radio. This was exciting to me, and soon I could expand and augment my melodies by spreading my fingers into chords that sounded harmonious. Though I was simply playing by ear, this provided me with great satisfaction. I could copy what I heard and be an active part of the music. What I played resembled what I listened to on the radio.

"Soon thereafter, I persuaded my mother to rent a piano and furnish a piano teacher. During my first lessons, I demonstrated for the teacher what I had learned on my own.

As I played each chord and melody from my limited repertoire, he nodded and commented with descriptions of what I was playing: *'That's an A major chord... and a D major seventh.'* *'C major, D minor, A minor seventh—very nice!'* This amazed me—there were *actual names* for what I was doing. Moreover, one chord related to another in a conceptual, as well as musically aesthetic, manner. My teacher was introducing me to music theory, using my life experience as a basis to escort me to newer levels of understanding and expression!

"I learned from this profound lesson that there are labels that signify categories of common experience—and that these labels can help us recognize and identify the nature and belongingness of what we see, hear, and feel.

"I tell you this story as a prelude to helping you recognize and generalize the feeling you've just shared with me about your difficult sibling. You have expressed and are experiencing feelings of *compassion*—this, despite your sibling's offensive and demanding behaviors. When this happens, you are in harmony with God's music, his sympathetic, understanding, and forgiving nature. It resonates well, doesn't it?

"Contrast this with your familiar and discordant negative ruminations about how badly life has treated you and how difficult you've had it. There is a label for that music, too: it's called *self-pity.* And it has its own surrounding theory that rankles and attracts more of the same."

My patient regarded me thoughtfully as he absorbed the categories and labels I'd appended to his feelings and experiences. I was hopeful that he could continue to recognize and reinforce his feelings of sympathy and compassion to lift him from the discordant doldrums of self-pity to more prevalent opportunities to feel and offer compassion and sacrifice.

There are many types of music, of course. From finite notes, rhythms, and instruments, we can produce and experience magnificent sweet sounds and harmonies, stirring or relaxing rhythms, and cacophonies of restless disturbance. We tend to recognize and recapitulate the imprints of preference and experience with which we are most familiar. Life presents them to us with discernible themes and multiple variations. Like our tastes and choices in music, our categorizations of and practiced responses to people and events develop and confirm our character and worthiness. Whatever your gifts, whatever your tastes—I believe that the most beautiful music a person can make is the music of compassion and self-sacrifice. Such music is always pleasant and inspirational to the ears of humans and God.

I don't play much piano these days; my hands are arthritic, and my musical prowess has diminished from its former limited development. But when I act on the opportunity to identify the melodies and rhythms of repetitious patterns in the lives of my fellow humans, to point out and label the pleasant chords of compassion and the melody of selfless love and sacrifice, I hear echoes of resonance, and I know that there are angels playing the most beautiful music in heaven.

1990
A succinct summary regarding the essentials of a popular platitude.

STRAIGHT TALK ABOUT SELF-ESTEEM

Recently, a parent called my office to inquire whether we offer classes on self-esteem. Although I've heard such requests regularly over the years, this particular call further motivated me to express some thoughts on a topic ascending in popularity to the heights of commercial cliché. After all, aren't good parents concerned about their children's self-esteem?

Understanding this concern, the idea of classes on self-esteem nonetheless seems rather peculiar to me—rather like holding classes on love, happiness, success, growth, or patience. Certainly, these concepts are vital, and formal instruction can address the development of skills and characteristics associated with them. Self-esteem, however, (like love, happiness, etc.) is a process: an internal, subjective experience that accompanies each person's activities and perceptions of daily living. Like the development of character, self-esteem is a continuous process that cannot be confined or defined by the limits of instructional objectives, classroom content, or certificates.

The popular view of self-esteem is nebulous: most people champion its value, think it is important to build self-esteem, relate negative behaviors to poor self-esteem, feel sorry for those with self-esteem problems, or even use the term as an explanation for inadequate performance. But what is self-esteem?

Self-esteem is the value with which we regard the various aspects of ourselves. It is not the same as self-confidence. A teacher may be supremely confident in her ability to teach math, but may also suffer from poor self-esteem. A spelling champion is confident with words, and a bully is confident in dominance; yet each of these people may hold himself in low regard, despite high confidence in a particular level of functioning.

Although it is a concept, self-esteem does differ from self-concept. The ideas we have about ourselves form our self-concepts. The values we place on those ideas constitute self-esteem. Each of us has ideas and beliefs that structure our identity, character, and essential qualities and that distinguish us as distinct and separate from all others. Self-esteem reflects the honor with which we regard our reputations and ideas about ourselves.

As a consciousness, self-esteem derives from the subjective interpretation of two questions concurrently:

1. What am I good *at*?
2. What am I good *for*?

Self-esteem comprises answers to both questions, which we may examine in relation to our survival needs of significance and security.

What am I good at?

Learning to survive independently requires a host of functional and integrated skills. Growing up involves the labor of practicing skills, applying them to satisfy needs and wants, and carving out areas of specialty in which we can perform well. Discovering what we are good at shapes and fortifies our ideas about who we are, thus molding our sense of significance by establishing niches of competence and contribution. Security is reinforced by the confidence that what we do is valuable—therefore, we are valued, needed, and desired.

The exercise of mastery and competence at producing and performing is inseparable from our images of ourselves. We depend upon others for feedback about how well we accomplish tasks, show strengths and compensate for weaknesses. Through honing and recognizing skills of achievement, adaptation, accommodation, and adjustment of expectations, we determine what we are good at.

What am I good for?

Our society allows adults to freely ask each other the question, "What do you do (for a living)?" This social convention permits us to describe what we are good at. The more sensitive and private question, "What are you good for?" is usually restricted to a therapeutic milieu, spiritual/religious discussion, or philosophic inquiry. (Here's a way to glean someone's answer to the "What am I good for?" aspect of self-esteem: following the person's answer to "What do you do?" ask, "Why?")

We enter the world completely dependent on others to care for us and about us. This requires unconditional love—a willingness to indulge that is unfettered by expectations of reciprocity. Humans are created with this capacity; it is exercised in relationships and is heralded by the recognition of human value and dignity. Eventually, we learn about conditional love, approval, and rewards, which are contingent upon performance and other criteria. We never lose that profound need for unconditional validation of our worthiness—to be loved, accepted, and treasured as individuals, irrespective of skills, performance, personality, limitations, or burdens.

When we are loved unconditionally, we are secure. Where we are wanted, valued, and cared for, we feel we belong. A self that is honored and regarded so highly by others is surely significant!

Life's perplexity and challenges are often overwhelming. It is tempting to inflate egotistical significance through climbing on top of others. The powermonger and put-down artist mistakenly try to build their significance through denigrating the well-being of others. As well, the pleasures of immediate gratification belie a false and temporary sense of security, yielding quickly to impulse, addiction, and deflated worthiness.

Building self-esteem is a lifelong process, a kind of equity balance for the soul. It supersedes educational cheerleading, media hoopla, political movements, and curricular confinement. We can't take legitimate classes on self-esteem. We can, however, teach and demonstrate to children (and adults) how to develop skills-based competence. We can recognize their virtues, treasure their relationship with us, and treat them as worthy. We can identify and provide for their needs, and show them how to meet the needs of others. We can reinforce the value of accountability in an environment of unconditional love. In daily manifestations of our inner selves, we can proclaim significance and security as we build our own and others' self-esteem.

1995
A perspective on the “space” for forgiveness.

TIME TO FORGIVE

As our children bustled and played noisily upstairs, my wife remarked with amazement how quickly they “forgot” their arguments and fighting with each other in favor of cooperative play. Incredulous, she noted Jeremy’s “forgiveness” of Neal’s insults so readily in the wake of present glee. Why, just a short time ago, they were at each other’s throat.

Her comment about forgiveness and time struck a resonant chord, harmonious with my observation: children *are* quick to forgive—and they function seemingly without the sense of time that orders and binds adult experience.

I wondered: Is the relationship between time and forgiveness deeper, more profound, more accessible than the linear, sequential adage, “Time heals all wounds”? Could forgiveness be realized by the three-dimensional timelessness so characteristic of childhood? Can the development and exercise of visuospatial awareness heighten the ability or propensity to forgive? Conversely, can the practice of forgiveness foster the development of cognitive skills?

My knowledge of brain organization and cognitive functions leads me to examine the possible correlation between visual and spatial development and the tendency to forgive easily. Despite its spiritual foundation and the commitment that forgiveness requires, people vary in their abilities to “let go” and bear no grudges, to let bygones be bygones. Such release implies the capacity to relate to time in a nonlinear context. To forgive is to abandon the sequential causality/origin/basis of wrongs perceived and their ensuing consequences.

Forgiveness breaches linearity and challenges the serial nature of experiences. To harbor forgiveness, one must suspend the hypothetico-deductive (if-then) reasoning that serves so reliably in the practical world. This requires capacious flexibility in dealing with time.

Linear convergent thinking depends upon time. The mental process of "narrowing down" to presumable conclusions uses cause and effect in a time-bound manner. However, when we forgive, we dismiss the order of facts in favor of outcomes eerily void of evidence trails.

My observations of people who forgive easily suggest that tendencies toward amnesty relate to the predilection for living in the present. The less bound we are to logical linearity, the less fettered we become with restraints and rationalizations about our feelings. Forgiveness allows the clock to reset, and people who favor organizing information three-dimensionally are prone to be rather flexible with memory and more selective about recalling past data that would interfere with present expedience.

Children generally live in very three-dimensional, present-focused realities. Forgiveness seems natural for them; perhaps this is a function of their developmental limitations in accessing symbolic, sequentially stored memories.

To forgive is to dismiss from grievance. This process requires selective attention to particular stimulus aspects of a person, situation, or emotional experience. Its accomplishment depends on a person's ability to mentally arrange and order circumstances in a way that discharges the negative emotional loading of events.

The rearranging of mental events is a cognitive function that carries great survival value. Normal human development spawns these abilities progressively, and we observe their results in the age-related achievements of growing children: the gradual deferral of immediate gratification to anticipatory pleasure (which depends on internal manipulation of time sense), the adjustments to varying schedules, the experience of loss, and the recognition of familiar objects and concepts in different forms—these fundamental survival skills accrue from our abilities to assimilate new experiences and integrate them with our existing models of how the world works. To make sense of changing circumstances, we must constantly assess new information and modify perceptions. The mapping and remapping of experience revolves around saliency, or what the mind believes to be important in a particular string or field of events.

The "act" of forgiveness is literally a behavior whereby the forgiving person manipulates saliency. Saliency is a function of time, space, order, and symbolic representation. In our accumulating multisensory record of experience, each of us programs determinant features according to the way our thinking patterns establish saliency. The inclination and ability to manipulate saliency in order to forgive constitute a talent that seems highly related to mental flexibility.

The composition of this talent changes as mental development occurs. In childhood, it is natural to live in the present. Forgiving is unfeigned, as the act of "letting go" is pervasive to puerile cognition. Maturation brings abilities to abstract and the consolidation of preferential thinking styles. Some people encode reality in verbal/linguistic terms, while others become predominantly spatial and visual. Time is held differently by those two domains.

Forgiveness is basic to the reality of the moment. It is neither a stochastic reflection of periodic weakness nor a concession to wishful thinking. Rather, it is the inherent or honed ability to master time in a manifest transaction. To forgive is to pardon; though not to imply forgetting, forgiveness adduces the context, "as though it didn't happen." It may be that those who forgive more readily have greater cognitive fluidity with space and time.

The development and exercise of visuospatial thinking changes with maturation. The "timeless" childhood consciousness yields to the influences of symbolic learning as it integrates with organizational and proprioceptive skills. As we accumulate experiences, we file and order them in a sequential manner, such that antecedents and consequences form cause-and-effect patterns; we rely on these patterns for survival, retrieving information about what worked in the past. The ability to view life from varying perspectives becomes constrained by the grounding in time that serves survival tactics so well. Yet survival also depends heavily on flexibility, adaptation, and, in essence, the alteration of perceptual saliency.

Children's penchant for forgiveness may be related as much to visuospatial immaturity as it is to a state of innocence. The challenge, then, is to integrate visuospatial flexibility with convergent/sequential skills while retaining the ability to let "timelessness" predominate. Practicing forgiveness may help our cerebral (as well as spiritual) development. We have much to learn from (as well as teach) children.

If we regard forgiving as an act of mastering time in our worldly lives, then we simultaneously vanquish the relentless advance of aging and play by the rules of the eternal.

2011
Your child is always your child, even hopefully "grown up."

YOUR ADULT CHILD IS NOT AN OXYMORON

For those unfamiliar with the word "oxymoron," it means an expression with contradictory words—for example, "jumbo shrimp." The words are oddly paradoxical, yet the pairing exists and even makes sense (though not semantically). Thus, your adult child is not an oxymoron. He or she is still your child but has grown (or aged, at least) to the status of adult. Your offspring—imagine! Who knew, in those days of diapering, whimpering, and reassuring that your child would turn out this way?

Yet the adult is still a child, not only through blood or attachment, but because he or she still depends on you. Many young adults still rely on their parents financially, especially in these economic times. Many more need guidance and emotional support, even when they bristle at receiving it. Some adult children rely heavily on parents to help raise their own young children.

Your role as a parent of an adult child changes dramatically as he or she emerges into young adulthood and what should be independence. You must facilitate the transition by many small acts of encouragement and limit-setting so that your child learns that he or she can and must make it on his or her own. This involves gradually becoming more self-sufficient in the basic areas of financial self-support, emotional maturity, worldly skills and experience, and the sense of humility and understanding that life does not *owe* him or her anything.

Some children fledge rather easily and some cause and endure drama or tragic setbacks. Due to disabilities, accidents, unforeseen events, or developmental problems, many children achieve only marginal independence, or they falter and remain needy of parental support through many years of adulthood.

In the process of "launching" your child to healthy independence, you must navigate the uncertain terrain of what is good for your child along with what is good for you, all tempered by changing and constraining circumstances. This process is long and trying because all parents have mixed feelings about children separating from them. On one side are feelings (and thoughts) of impatience, frustration, resentment, etc. regarding the adult child's slowness or failure to fend for himself or herself—the sense of entitlement that is projected when the child asks, expects, and takes for granted that the parent will indefinitely provide. On the other side are thoughts and feelings of worry, guilt, and an overriding love, protection, and responsibility to the child so that he or she will not drown or flounder. This ambivalence can be wrenching.

The dilemma of weaning your adult child evokes no easy answers. There are times, realistically, when it's appropriate, if at all possible, to support your adult child in many ways—even though it costs you financially and emotionally. Above all, you have a responsibility to yourself and your family to provide leadership and maturity so that everyone involved can become as self-sufficient and contributing as possible.

Toward this goal, I offer some insights gleaned from cumulative and collective knowledge about human development.

1. **Expect and reinforce attitudes and behaviors that give you a reward for parenting (honor, joy, fulfillment, satisfaction).**

   I have long maintained that it is the duty of all children to yield to their parents the continual experience of being *rewarded* for parenting. This concept may be compared to honor and respect, but it is actually a bit different. While honor and respect are the ideals and the Jewish notion of "nachas" (translating roughly to joy from your children's behavior and achievements) is also desirable, being rewarded for parenting means that you find the long-term course of parenting *fulfilling*, regardless of your child's accomplishments and misadventures and the mistakes each of you makes.

This is a two-way street. You must have that objective in mind as your right and expectation, and your child must be indoctrinated with that expectation and responsibility. Raising a child is demanding and expensive, and the counterbalance is your well-deserved reward of fulfillment—to which you are entitled even if your parenting is imperfect and your child departs from expectations.

2. **Let your child make and learn from his or her own mistakes.**

Parents are advised to let children learn from their mistakes throughout childhood, starting from an early age. The delicate balance between encouragement and the challenge of learning from failure evolves into a style of parenting shaped by your beliefs, knowledge, and skills. Younger children, of course, require more intervention, teaching, and monitoring. As children grow, they become progressively required to rebound from mishaps and stand on their own feet. Lack of parental involvement (either actual or perceived) can lead to feelings of neglect or abandonment. Overprotection carries its own downsides of potential helplessness or ineptitude.

By the time your child has grown up, the die is cast—not on his or her inevitable adult fate—but on the habits of indulgence you have practiced over decades. Sometimes these habits are incompatible with family economics or the healthy independence and separation that should normally occur when a child reaches adulthood. Though your adult child may be ill equipped to navigate or survive the complexities of adult living, your efforts should steer toward urging and allowing your child to make adult decisions and abide by the consequences.

Occasionally, a bailout is needed. However, rescuing your adult child from persistent mistakes usually results in repetition of the maladaptive behavior, as well as resentment by both generations.

As a wise friend often says, "The hungry dog makes the best hunter."

3. **Work toward being a friend to your child.**

   Parents are warned not to be "buddies" to their kids. This separation of identity is naturally crucial. When your child is growing up, he or she transitions through many stages. The desire for a parent to be "hip" or "with it" must be tempered by the resounding leadership of adult authority, responsibility and, hopefully, wisdom. As the parent, you must establish and maintain boundaries, however much you may want to be liked and revered by your youngster.

   Being a friend to your child operates on a different plane than being popular or informed and conversant with trends. What is truly important is to develop a relationship of trust and respect, so that when your child reaches adulthood, he or she will come to you for advice and to share confidences. Such intimacy and trust is a profound blessing for you and your child. It will enable and empower your child to take the risks appropriate to successful independence. It will also provide a haven of experience and judgment to draw upon in order to evaluate and make adjustments. The friendship between you and your adult child cannot blossom from authoritarian or harsh upbringing, nor can it flourish in an atmosphere of permissive avoidance of setting limits.

Don't you want your child to come back to you for caution and advice when he or she is old enough to make independent (though not always prudent) decisions? The seeds of this blossom are planted early in family life and are nourished and watered by intermittent allowances of choices by your child, followed by an evaluation of behavior and learning about consequences.

In their quest for autonomy, often welded to stubborn rebellion, children may not listen or heed. Of course, they need correction and sanctions. But you will be gratified by developing a relationship with your children where open lines of communication eventually lead to *their* requests for guidance, even when they are old enough to act on their own.

It could be an inquiry about worldly commerce, such as getting a car fixed or purchasing insurance; or it might be an imploration to assist with the grandchildren. Interactions like these between you and your adult child will change the generational dynamics and provide you with a rich and rewarding perspective on your impact upon raising children.

4. **Meet your own needs through relationships and activities apart from your child.**

It is natural for parents to want their children to have a "good life." To most parents, this means achievement (matching or exceeding the parents' own), financial sufficiency and stability, and similar values. Many parents unwittingly succumb to living vicariously through their children's accomplishments; this can take the form of involvement in the child's sports or extracurricular activities or through an emphatic pressure on achieving high grades and getting into the "right" school. Though such involvement can motivate children and play a vital role in their development and lifelong values, parents need to recognize when to back away. When parental involvement continues inappropriately, it becomes a substitute for the parent's own lack of satisfaction and/or the stunted ability to let children go.

Effective parenting requires good modeling. Therefore, parents should have their own relationships and activities that provide involvement and reward apart from their children. Not only is this good for the child to observe during development—it makes the transition of letting go easier on both parent and child. Age, physical status, and life responsibilities all differentiate the interests and activities of parents and grown up children. This is as it should be. Don't fall into the trap of resenting your children for being involved in their own lives. Calling and visiting may be enough, especially if you are busy with your own satisfactions.

5. **Recognize and accept the changing and diminishing role of your job as a parent.**

Whether your adult child is succeeding in the world in an age-appropriate, socially approved manner or is expressing an "inner child" playing video games in your spare room, your relationship must change as you and your child grow older. On a biological level, you have done your job by reproducing and/or nurturing your child to adult mammalian status—food, clothing, shelter, and medical care are the basics. On a social level, you have tried your best to educate, inculcate, and impart the skills and experience your child needs to make it independently. The result is not guaranteed. On an emotional and spiritual level, you owe it to your

> child, yourself, and the rest of your family to evolve with the grace and wisdom that aging brings.
>
> There is an old saying: "The only love that should grow asunder is that between parent and child." It means that the normal and expected bonds between parent and child naturally mature and change as the child makes his or her way.
>
> You will always love your child, whether he or she brings honor or disappointment. Your child will most likely outlive you and, in many cases, take care of you as you age. Difficult to think about, isn't it? Yet this is the reality that soberly guides us in appreciating the big picture. In that broad view, your child will always be your child, however old he or she grows. And you will, in this life, always be older and steps ahead in experience. God made it so.

It is also natural to wonder and worry about how your child will fare when you are no longer able to assist or provide. When children function marginally as adults, their parents fear about their survival and well-being. The truth is: you can only do so much. As your child matures into his or her own life, your role changes from supervisor to observer and recipient. Learning to recognize, participate, and yield in this process is neither formally taught nor generationally transmitted in this culture. Discovering how this is done can be liberating and rewarding.

Remember my earlier statement about how you deserve to be rewarded for the hard work of parenting? You can give this to yourself, regardless of how well your child is doing as an adult. Despite any pragmatic entanglements you may still have in your adult child's life, he or she still needs you to developmentally let go and declare that the child is his or her own person.

There is another saying (from Texas, I believe): "You ain't a man until your daddy says you're man." It goes for women, too.

When will you make that declaration?

2014
Explanation of a critical concept in the psychological underpinnings of self-sabotage.

PSYCHOLOGICAL REVERSAL REVISITED

After many decades of practicing psychology, I have thankfully found reliable ways to improve people's lives. I also apply these principles and methods to myself and have been able to greatly improve my health, well-being, productivity, and relationships. Since most people have too much frustration and not enough time, I want to reveal a basic principle and practical solution that will help you overcome obstacles that may have hindered you for years. The principle is called *psychological reversal.* When you understand it and practice strategically correcting it (which takes seconds), you will release shackles and frustrations that have impeded your progress in specific and, perhaps, varied areas in your life.

Of all the theories and techniques I have learned and practiced, psychological reversal is the most significant gateway to overcoming bad habits, psychological and physical symptoms, "stuckness," and motivational dysfunction. Later in this article, you will learn how to identify and correct psychological reversal. First, though, it's important for you to gain some understanding.

Explanations for the psychological underpinnings of behavior are legion. Traditional psychodynamic (e.g., Freudian) theories focus on subconscious primal instincts that blend with early childhood experiences to govern behavior in ways that the conscious mind masks. On the other side of the spectrum, behaviorists believe that most behavior is determined by previous conditioning that forms habits that increase the probability of certain behaviors.

Neuropsychology and neurophysiology explain behavior in terms of physiological reactions of the brain and nervous system. I have been trained in all of these disciplines and, over forty years, have observed and considered the relative contributions and influences of these theories in practical terms. That is, I have watched how patients (and friends and family) respond, and I have evaluated the methods of influencing motivation, changing habits, and relieving many conditions of distress.

Getting Results

As a results-oriented person and a professional partial to math and probability (having taught statistics in graduate schools), I tend to analyze problems and form solutions based on the most productive and economical interventions derived from evidence and experience. In statistics, there are methods of analyzing large amounts of data that determine which variables account for the largest part of the observed results (e.g., factor analysis and principal components analysis).

For example, decades of educational research have found that class size (number of students per class) is one of the greatest factors in determining educational outcomes. In another example, certain sports depend upon size, strength, and agility as primary factors that characterize the emergence of superstars. In a different domain, verbal skills are a principal factor in successful sales, teaching, and broadcasting.

In other words, factoring out the most potent and statistically relevant determinants of outcomes yields the biggest "bang for the buck."

Psychologists also seek the most efficient and influential methods for helping people change behavior and eliminate distressing emotions and counterproductive habits. For many decades, I have utilized different methods and meticulously observed and measured the factors that are most relevant to progress and healthy functioning. Though there are a number of factors that heavily influence outcomes (and I am partial to neurophysiological and behavioral modes), there is one factor I've found to be particularly important in determining success in treatment and general positive behavior change: it is known as *psychological reversal.*

What Is Psychological Reversal?

A psychological reversal exists when a person claims he desires to achieve a specific goal, but his actions and major motivation, as well as his results, appear to be contrary to his professed goal. The person may appear to be striving to achieve (in the *specifically reversed* area), but he will significantly or subtly sabotage the effort.

Psychological reversal occurs naturally and in all people at different times and to varying degrees. When you make "dumb mistakes," do something that is against your known better interests, persistently avoid and procrastinate, or repeatedly fail to resolve or overcome obstacles, chances are that you are impeded by psychological reversal.

Signs you may be psychologically reversed include:

1. A problem persists despite repeated efforts to overcome it.
2. You engage in self-sabotaging behaviors (doing things against your desired goals or best interests).
3. A problem or symptom that was successfully treated recurs.
4. You feel unwell or experience a recurrence of symptoms after eating a particular food.
5. You habitually engage in negative thinking.
6. You engage in avoidance.
7. You struggle with addictions.
8. You suffer from a persistent illness.

It is very common for people to become frustrated, confused, and even sanctimonious in the face of behavior that opposes common sense or stated intentions. The phenomenon of self-sabotage often carries connotations of character weakness or deception. It is tempting to conclude, "If you *really wanted to* succeed (e.g., lose weight, stop drinking, get healthy, finish a project, etc.), you would—therefore, you must not really want to!"

Sadly, this outlook is inaccurate as well as hurtful. There can be many reasons for not succeeding, but it is rarely for lack of wanting and trying. Setting aside real-world conditions beyond your control, you can focus and improve your own power and success by understanding correcting psychological reversal.

Though psychological reversal *is* a form of self-sabotage, it *is not* a subconscious "death wish" or an attempt to subvert or deny something you think you don't deserve. Rather, *psychological reversal is a state or condition in which polarity is reversed.* This is a very difficult concept for many people to understand. The mention of "energy flow" in the context of psychological constructs elicits skepticism and dismissiveness by traditionalists and those who are uncomfortable with intangibles. Yet psychological reversal itself is measurable and correctable, as are its effects on behavior, thoughts, and feelings.

Psychological reversal can affect attitudes, behavior, perceptions, and judgment. The brain and nervous system have organizational patterns and references for orientation—mapping points, essentially. Psychological reversal is kind of neural disorganization in which reference points and orientation are scrambled, resulting in blockages to the energy flow along neural pathways. To conceptualize this, think of driving from San Francisco to Los Angeles by *going north from San Francisco.* Obviously, this is an inefficient way since Los Angeles is *south* of San Francisco. However, if you are reversed about this, you may think (and insist) you are traveling south when you are actually heading north and away from your destination. So, psychological reversal creates a glitch in the body-mind navigational system.

The following pictures give an idea of how reversal affects perception and, indeed, one's outlook on reality:

REVERSED

NONREVERSED

Testing and Fixing Psychological Reversal

Psychological reversal can be tested when a person is attuned to a thought field. A field is an invisible, intangible structure in space that has an effect upon matter. A *thought field* is defined as a connection between cognitive awareness and emotions that generates a field that may contain perturbations. For example, for a phobic person, the thought of getting on an airplane or confronting an insect may generate an intense negative reaction. In such situations, we say that the thought generates a field that contains perturbations (disturbances) responsible for the negative emotions.

Testing for psychological reversal can be done in many ways. Because body and neural polarity generates holographically, it is measurable through multiple physiological responses. Muscle test strength and weakness, heart rate and variability, blood pressure, respiration rate, GSR (galvanic skin response), visual acuity, and voice projection all can reveal reversals.

After so many years of identifying and correcting psychological reversal, I can often detect it in a client's manner, facial expression, attitude, or verbal content. One obvious clue to reversal is outright hostility, negativism, sarcasm, or hopelessness. Some people are much more subtle than others. Repeated failure for no obvious reason is frequently a sign of reversal.

The preferred and most efficient way to test psychological reversal is through the voice. Nature encodes both the sources of distress and their solutions within our bodies and minds. Because of nature's recapitulation and signaling system, the human voice indicates with precision the causes of emotional and physical disturbance and can be used in tandem with Thought Field Therapy to eliminate the source and symptoms in minutes. Psychological reversals can be detected through the voice in seconds, and the appropriate corrections can be applied through self-administration of tapping repeatedly on specific meridians while attuned to the thought field in the problem.

Psychological reversal is associated with several meridians in the body, most often the small intestine alarm point. Initial reversals can be corrected or cleared by tapping at least fifteen times on the terminus of the meridian, most easily on the side of either hand in between the wrist and the tiny finger. It is critical to focus on the thought field that precedes and indicates a reversed state. Vocalizing the problem helps to focus the mind on the reversed thought field.

For example, if you find yourself opening the refrigerator to find (or replace) the stapler, you are reversed with regard to this issue. To fix the reversal, say out loud, "I want to be over this problem," and then tap fifteen times on the side of either hand in between the wrist and the tiny finger. There are multiple levels of reversals and specific ways to correct them by attuning the thought field and tapping in sequence on meridian termination points such as various hand and finger points and the philtrum under the nose.

For starters, try thinking of a problem that plagues you, as you say out loud, "I want to be over this problem." Then, tap on the side of your hand between the wrist and the tiny finger. Though it may sound silly and simplistic, this is an important first step in correcting any reversal that may be associated with a blockage for a particular problem that has kept you stuck. It is important to remember that fixing a reversal is not a panacea, nor does it cure any problem other than the reversal itself. It makes it *possible* for treatment to contribute to cure. It appears to be a necessary precondition for effective cure or achievement in any area.

After fixing reversals in a timely manner appropriate to their associated thought fields, proper treatment effectively eliminates symptoms such as negative emotions, cravings, compulsive thoughts, and habits. Fixing the reversals in sequence is a necessary precursor to success, but there are additional treatment steps involved.

During treatment procedures, advanced levels of reversals are revealed after the initial ones are corrected and as treatment progresses. Voice Technology is so efficient in the process that hundreds of corrections and perturbations may be dispatched within minutes by phone. This procedure has resulted in the elimination of symptoms at least 95 percent of the time over decades of experience and thousands of treatments.

For the layperson, becoming aware of psychological reversal and practicing the simple techniques outlined in my book, *Living Intact: Challenge and Choice in Tough Times,* can prove extremely helpful in clearing the path to quicker and more effective progress toward one's goals.

Most people need professional guidance in making significant progress that has thwarted them for awhile. However, you may find that by practicing the techniques in my book and by habitually fixing your own reversals whenever you find yourself engaging in counterproductive thoughts or behaviors, you are surprisingly able to get over negative feelings and accomplish things more effectively.

Recurring Psychological Reversals

Reversals may have to be corrected repeatedly in order for progress to continue or to reestablish gains previously attained. Certain people are more prone to reversals, and, with some conditions (e.g., addictions, chronic illnesses), recurring reversals are a common and expected occurrence (and—most importantly—successfully treatable).

An analogy might be helpful for understanding recurring reversals: suppose you have a bicycle with a flat tire. You must fix the flat in order to ride the bicycle and go forward. Now, suppose you fix the flat and then ride through a field with thorns and broken glass. You are likely to puncture the tire, resulting in another flat. So you repair the flat and then ride off in the same field and again flatten the tire. Frustrating and disillusioning, of course, but you are not intentionally trying to puncture your tire. You just may not know that there are sharp objects hidden in your path. When you discover the truth (i.e., the cause of your recurring flats), you provide correction (again fixing the tire) and subsequently avoid the cause of the recurrence.

Here's the analogy: In the pursuit of your goal, you may encounter obstacles that put you in a state of reversal (the flat tire). Until you fix the reversal, you are pretty much stuck. After fixing the reversal, you can then proceed efficiently. However, if you run into reversals again, you will have to fix them in order to reasonably continue forward. If you cannot detect the cause of the reversals (what is repeatedly giving you the flat tire), you will likely thwart your own efforts to reach your goal.

Notice two important points in this example:

1. In the original problem, the tire must be fixed before progress can occur. That is to say, a psychological problem must be treated and relieved in an appropriate manner before the potential of recurrence may be addressed.
2. The bicyclist is not intending to self-sabotage by riding through thorns and broken glass. He simply doesn't know that that these influences are what is reversing him! Similarly, people with persistent frustrations and problems are not "shooting themselves in the foot" on purpose. They are simply in a state of reversal whose undetected cause continues to surreptitiously block progress.

Impact of Psychological Reversals

An interesting fact about psychological reversal is that it can be specialized, affecting only certain areas of one's life, or less commonly, it can be massive and affect most areas of one's life in a negative way. The incidence of massive reversal is higher in people who have struggled with severe addictions or other psychological problems for a long time.

The will, or control over oneself, is definitely limited in a reversed state. The choices available are restricted to negative choices: one's thoughts and ideas tend to have a negative slant. In a severe state of psychological reversal, there will be strong resistance very often against doing the recommended procedures, treatments, or lifestyle changes that would aid in relieving the affliction or symptoms.

The phenomenon of psychological reversal is measurable; its effects are predictable, regular, and scientifically lawful. If a person is in a state of psychological reversal, he is unable to respond favorably to an otherwise effective treatment. If the reversal is corrected, he will then respond to an effective treatment.

The incidence of psychological reversal varies from problem to problem. For example, anxiety and phobic problems have a reversal incidence of about 40 to 50 percent. That is, about one-half of all phobic problems are blocked from getting better or completely better. Some may get partially better and then not improve any further. When the treatment for psychological reversal was discovered, the success rate for treating phobias and anxiety immediately increased dramatically. Most of the phobias that were previously untreatable became treatable after the simple and fast correction for psychological reversal was administered.

The incidence of psychological reversal is higher among addicts than for any other group. In fact, virtually all addicts suffer from some psychological reversal that blocks them from getting better. This is the primary reason why addictions are the most difficult to treat and why so many addicts relapse, even after they seem to be getting better.

Toxins and Reversals

Toxins are substances that cause a psychological reversal and may block or reverse the effects of successful treatment. Typically, many foods, toiletries, aromas, and supplements act as toxins for a percentage of people. For many people, the sustained positive effects of treatments and better health require the identification of and abstention from toxins. Toxins can be identified through muscle testing, but they are most easily and accurately identified through Voice Technology.

The recurrence of urges or any problem once successfully treated is usually due to an *individual energy toxin.* Toxins are a critically important issue for many people and especially for those enmeshed in addictive cycles. Toxins often induce psychological reversal, which has the effect of "undoing" or reversing a previously successful treatment and also of interfering or blocking the progress of an incipient treatment. Aside from its impact upon Voice Technology (VT) and Thought Field Therapy (TFT) treatments, the effect of psychological reversal is also a major factor in many other treatment protocols and can undermine desired goal-oriented motivational states.

Summary

Psychological reversal occurs naturally and in all people at different times and to varying degrees. A state of psychological reversal creates self-sabotage on specific and general areas of one's life. This can affect thoughts, feelings, behaviors, attitudes, achievements, and physical health. Psychological reversal can be corrected by attuning the thought field associated with the reversal and tapping in sequence on meridian termination points such as various hand and finger points and the philtrum under the nose (see *Living Intact: Challenge and Choice in Tough Times*).

Different levels of embedded reversals appear after initial reversals are corrected. Recurring reversals that undo treatment successes or block progress may be attributable to toxins that should be identified and subsequently avoided.

Even the novice layperson can learn to correct psychological reversals in order to facilitate success and progress in previously impeded areas of life.

2014
Spiritual gifts and natural reasons.

NOT FOR THAT REASON

As time passes, the beauty of some things fades, while the beauty of others increases. Flowers bloom and wither, material things tarnish, pulchritude ages and wrinkles. Nothing tangible lasts forever, and we must adjust to change, including the change in value we attach to what we desire and cherish.

There is a beauty that has increased profoundly for me over the years: that is the marvel and appreciation of the different gifts that God gives to different people. The more I know myself, the more profound is my wonder and admiration for capacities and talents of others. When I was younger and less secure, my limitations were things to be denied, hidden, and resented. I competed and pretended to have the talents of others. As I often fell short of the mark, I wandered into a thicket of self-absorption and envy. *Why can't I be like so-and-so? Why aren't I taller, thinner, etc.?* Along with this frustration and resentment, I became dismissive of other people's gifts and prideful about my own. *My talents are better and more useful than theirs.* Not surprisingly, this attitude led to isolation and loneliness.

Under the grace of God's leadership, I have come to increasingly appreciate and enjoy the diverse attributes and abilities of others. Through life experiences and my professional skills in the assessment of abilities, I savor how one person can build or repair machines, while another can paint and another can sew. For me, it is no longer the idolization of star performers, but rather the commonplace distribution of diversity that captures my adulation. Moreover, I am increasingly aware of and comfortable with my dependence on teamwork and the abilities of others to get things done in my life. Where would I be without the specialists, both menial and professional, whom I turn to for mundane solutions, care and service, labor and guidance? Could I build roads and bridges, fix my own teeth, bring crops from afar, design computers, or even have the patience and know-how to tend the bedridden?

No, I have been given a small set of gifts that I have learned to hone and value and offer to others. Fortunately, these gifts prove useful; they are more so when I blend them with the work and proclivities of others. For we are interconnected in a grand design that paradoxically highlights and humbles the unique gifts apportioned to individuals.

Scripture speaks of individual gifts and combined utility by using analogies of the physical body and community. This is beautifully described by the apostle Paul in 1 Corinthians 12:

> *Just as the body, though one, has many parts, but all of its many parts form one body, so it is with Christ. For we were all baptized with one Spirit so as to form one body—whether Jew or Gentiles, slave or free—and we were all given the one spirit to drink. Even so the body is not made up of one part but of many.*
>
> *Now if the foot should say, "because I am not a hand, I do not belong to the body," it would not for that reason stop being a part of the body. And if the ear should say, "Because I am not an eye, I do not belong to the body, it would not for that reason stop being a part of the body. If the whole body were an eye, where would the sense of hearing be? If the whole body were an ear, where would the sense of smell be? But in fact God has placed the parts in the body, every one of them, just as he wanted them to be. If they were all one part, where would the body be? As it is, there are many parts, but one body.*

> *The eye cannot say to the hand, "I don't need you!" And the head cannot say to the feet, "I don't need you!" On the contrary, those parts of the body that seem to be weaker are indispensable, and the parts we think are less honorable we treat with special honor. And the parts that are unpresentable are treated with special modesty, while our presentable parts need no special treatment. But God has put the body together, giving greater honor to the parts that lacked it, so that there should be no division in the body, but that its parts should have equal concern for each other. If one part suffers, every part suffers with it; if one part is honored, every part rejoices with it.* 1 Corinthians 12:12–26.

I have read this passage many times. Yet recently, I was struck by one phrase: *not for that reason…, it would not for that reason stop being a part of the body.*

Suddenly, I had an epiphany, an "aha" moment! I was reminded, tangentially, of a notable Winston Churchill quote: "Men occasionally stumble over the truth, but most of them pick themselves up and hurry off as if nothing has happened." I had just stumbled over the impact of the phrase, *not for that reason.*

The idea is this: The body is composed of interrelated and necessary parts. Should one part disassociate or declare itself not part of the body, it would *not for that reason* stop being a part of the body, necessary and unique, as God has designed and apportioned.

The analogy is straightforward and obvious, but the implications are extensive and profound. Just as the foot cannot secede from the body because it is not a hand and the eye cannot say to the hand, "I don't need you," a person cannot disassociate himself from others because he feels disconnected from them or that he is superior or inferior to them. In other words, we are all part of and responsible for each other, regardless of our position or perceived importance in a hierarchy.

The person who says, "Because I am not smart enough or good enough, I do not belong," would *not for that reason* stop belonging. One part of the body (i.e., a person or group of people) cannot say to another "I don't need you!"

Let the message from 1 Corinthians 12 echo in your mind and heart:

> *God has placed the parts in the body, every one of them, just as he wanted them to be. If they were all one part, where would the body be? As it is, there are many parts, but one body... On the contrary, those parts of the body that seem to be weaker are indispensable, and the parts we think are less honorable we treat with special honor. And the parts that are unpresentable are treated with special modesty, while our presentable parts need no special treatment. But God has put the body together, giving greater honor to the parts that lacked it, so that there should be no division in the body, but that its parts should have equal concern for each other. If one part suffers, every part suffers with it; if one part is honored, every part rejoices with it.*

This is fantastic news for those who feel depressed, alienated, inferior, and so forth. This biblical truth means that you *are valuable and do belong*, regardless of your self-estimation or the judgment of others. If you have an opinion about yourself in relation to others that makes you conclude that you are not worthy enough or do not belong, you would *not for that reason* be less worthy or cease to belong.

Furthermore, the body (the human body and by, extension, the church and other communities) bears a corporate responsibility to care for and honor all parts of the body belonging to it. Additionally, certain members deserve special honor and special treatment due to their weakness and presentability.

In reality, we cannot withdraw from connectedness based upon perceptions and feelings. Conversely, we cannot dismiss or abandon the value of others, *not for that reason.* The key concepts are belonging, protection, interdependence, security, and responsibility. The implications of scripture are clear, profound, and joyous.

1. Belonging

Regardless of who you are, where you are in life, how much or how little you have, how healthy or sick or young or old you are, you belong here, and you belong to others. If you think others do not care or have wronged you, *not for that reason* would you stop mattering or belonging to others—family, friends, community, even passersby who notice and interact with you. You may have experienced trauma and feelings of hopelessness, abandonment, and/or despair. But *not for that reason* would you cease to belong and to matter. You are part of the body.

2. Value

Not only do you matter, but your uniqueness counts—your gifts, problems, weaknesses, and special circumstances. God created you and he has a place for you, although you may not like or appreciate it for a given time. You have a special role to play, and you are included in the suffering, joy, struggling, service, and ups and downs that are a part of every life. You are precious to God, and you have value in the eyes of others. Look around. Find who loves you, needs you, and how they notice and care about you. If you have doubts, *not for that reason* would you lack immense value.

3. **Needing others**

As the eye needs the hand and the head needs the foot, so, too, do you need others and they need you. People are often hard to deal with, and they can be cruel and dismissive. But God designed the parts of the body to work together:

> *...there should be no division in the body, but that its parts should have equal concern for each other. If one part suffers, every part suffers with it; if one part is honored, every part rejoices with it.*

There are times when certain parts don't work or are absent. But *not for that reason* is the need for and dependence upon other parts diminished. It is this need that reminds us of belonging and value.

4. Responsibility (not dismissiveness)

For these reasons, we bear a shared responsibility to work together and seek each other's welfare. You may be intact and feel self-sufficient. Wonderful! But *not for that reason* would you be relieved of your duty to others. You may be without resources or attributes you desire, and it may be heartbreaking! But *not for that reason* are you exempt from serving others or receiving grace and service. You are not alone, and you are neither excluded nor exclusive.

5. Care and protection

Finally, no matter where you are, no matter what your circumstances or deeds, you are entitled to care and protection, *according to God's word.* To realize and fulfill this blessing, however, you must accept what God says and act upon it. Pragmatically, it's a two-way street: others value and do for you, and you value and do for others. God's divine roadmap is a two-way street: he reaches out to us as the initiator, and we must respond by following the path toward him. Interestingly, it is by following God's roadmap that we are led to others, and by traveling with others, we draw closer to God.

God has overcome the world. You may feel overwhelmed, but *not for that reason* are you isolated or without the love, protection, care, and belonging that God has designed and proclaimed for those who will claim them.

From the intimate, personal stirrings and anxieties within each of us to the complex social and global interactions that conflict and challenge us—we must remember and act upon the interconnectedness and responsibility of the body. God does not let us forget or act alone.

FULFILLING THOSE TWO COMMANDMENTS

Daily life is filled with struggles and frustrations. Along with obligations and responsibilities come the realities of fatigue, imperfection, and continuing demands. It's as if people, the environment, and one's own body cry out discordantly, "What have you done for me lately?"

Thankfully, life's difficulties are mitigated by rewards and intermittent joys that fuel motivation and persistence. Periods of satisfaction and well-being are achievable. There are good things to look forward to and enjoy. However, most of us are preoccupied with the efforts and worries prompted by constant demands. Crouching in the shadows of the "need-and-do" merry-go-round are the specters of *shoulds, oughts, what-ifs, if-onlys* and the ubiquitous criticisms that diminish peace and happiness.

When time and energy allow the focus of soul-searching, the important questions surface: *What really matters with regard to purpose and duty? What is expected of me and to whom am I obligated? How shall I act?*

Many (like me) turn to the Bible for answers to these questions. The foundations of contemporary laws and rules in society are based upon biblical principles, including the Ten Commandments. Even so, the complexity and interpretation of commands can be overwhelming. When tested and confronted with a request for priority and ultimate importance, Jesus was very clear in his simplified answer:

> *Love the Lord your God with all your heart and with all your soul and with all your mind. This is the first and greatest commandment. And the second is like it: "Love your neighbor as yourself." All the Law and the Prophets hang on these two commandments.* Matthew 22:37–40.

Jesus provides clarity, a shortcut, and a tall order. How, then, can these commandments be practically fulfilled?

For me, it is a daily commitment, bound by challenges and blessings. Loving God with all my being involves knowing who he is and who I am in relation to him. I know I am given to this life for two purposes: *to reflect and express my creator and to love and care for other people.*

These purposes manifest in my life by the exercise of my gifts and character and by my work and commitment in taking care of others. I am a caretaker—that's what I do. As a family man, I protect, provide for, and guide my wife and children. As a professional, I deliver services to care for and heal patients. My tools include experience, biblical wisdom, professional skills, and compassion. I also realize that God has given me special gifts that I work on honing and using to express who God is and what he means to me. As a child of God, I accept his grace, forgiveness, and direction. Hopefully, this is reflected in my writing, my projects and creative endeavors, and in my service and sacrifice for others.

Loving others and treating them as I would want to be treated involves more than service and sacrifice. There are many kinds of service and sacrifice, and their varieties are not always specified uniformly for every individual. What is required of me is to take care of people. This I do with great commitment, joy, and alacrity.

Since I am a doctor and a family leader, my caretaking is proscribed by role-related responsibilities. However, I recognize that others also take care of people in many different roles and capacities. When I observe my wife's constant care for her aged and infirm mother, I want to jump up and cheer, as if for a home team winning the championship. There are no athletic heroics, no crowds, no hometown fervor—just the mundane and fabulous commitment and constancy of love and caretaking. By this I am awed.

When I shop at the market, eat at a restaurant, or get my car fixed, there are people who take care of me. When I call customer service, there are people who help me. They may not have fancy titles or extraordinary skills, and their services may not heal maladies. They are simply doing their jobs: exchanging their services and products for my money while they earn their money. But they do provide care for others—including me—nonetheless. And when they do it well, with concern, care, and attentiveness, they are honoring God and fulfilling that second commandment.

Jesus claims the first and greatest commandment is to love the Lord your God with all your heart and with all your soul and with all your mind. So how does that relate to the second greatest commandment: to love your neighbor as yourself? To love your neighbor as yourself, you must see yourself in him—as him. I am blessed by God's forgiveness, instruction, constant presence, and leadership in experiencing how to love and forgive others by virtue of how God treats me; thus, I copy and reflect (as best I can) how God treats me by translating that into how I relate to others.

When I find this duty difficult (often), God is there to help me. When I make mistakes, God may reprove me, but he accepts my repentance and he forgives me. When I don't know what to do or how to cope, God eventually provides light and guidance. He may do this through inner stirrings, through consequences, or through unexpected appearances of people and circumstances.

I'm grateful that Jesus simplified the manner of fulfilling requirements and pleasing God. As I go on in life, I see that by adhering to the two greatest commandments, I gravitate toward and learn how to abide by other commandments and requirements. Realizing how much God loves me as he loves others is both humbling and strengthening. It empowers me to consider others, to care for them with commitment and compassion, and to realize and rid myself of selfishness on a routine basis. It is a way of life that requires effort and awareness and that provides great rewards and satisfaction. It binds me to my creator and to the world and communities he has created.

2014
Basics for calmness and productivity with others.

DON'T ASK, DON'T YELL—JUST TASK AND TELL

It is a common and vexing problem that children often don't listen or do what they are told. Actually, the problem is not limited to children: spouses, parents, friends, coworkers, vendors, and peers are frequently the perpetrators of forgetfulness, disobedience, or mindless underperformance. It is a frustration that all of us have experienced. For some, this underpins the daily battle to get things done and becomes the bane and strain of relationships.

The knee-jerk response to repeated underperformance is remonstration: an arpeggio of criticism ranging from reminding and disparagement to scolding and a crescendo of intense raised voices and yelling. Unfortunately, this natural and seemingly justifiable, automatic response is counterproductive and gradually intensifies the habit or "dance" of nagging, arguing, and resentment. It reflects the age-old truth that "if you keep doing more of what you're doing, you're gonna get more of what you've already got."

Most people recognize this; but the problem is what to do otherwise and how to do it to obtain a different and better result. When things don't go right or when people seem unmotivated, willful, or defiant, it is tempting to become provoked and critical, and to overreact or nag. It is easy to succumb to the justifications and rationalizations that threats and reason will evoke a positive change in behavior from those who avoid or underperform.

When the mismatch between your remonstrations and subsequent satisfactory responses becomes obvious, you are ready to do something better. You can turn bad habits into better performance by employing some simple techniques that will save you time, energy, and frustration. I've coined an epithet to summarize the process:

Don't ask, don't yell—just task and tell.

I'll explain how this works; but first, let's review the behavioral paradigm that determines how habits (both favorable and unfavorable) form and increase the likelihood that you will "get more of what you've already got."

Reinforcement Rules

There is a basic principle by which people learn and form habits. It is called *reinforcement.* This is a process that occurs for everyone throughout life, a part of nature that helps us form associations among events, know what to expect, and perform efficiently and automatically without having to evaluate every situation. *Reinforcement* occurs (or has occurred) when a consequence follows a response, is associated with that response, and results in a strengthening of the response in frequency, intensity, or duration. In other words, *reinforcement is what makes behaviors more likely to happen again.*

This seems more sensible and interpretable when you observe people working for "rewards" and forming adaptive habits based on getting something desirable for their efforts. Of course this happens regularly, especially in regard to sanguine relationships and functional habits. But it is only part of the big picture of reinforcement. Just as gravity, fire, friction, and other natural forces can work for you or against you, so can reinforcement. It is an equal opportunity, nondiscriminating force—meaning that reinforcement strengthens undesirable behaviors as well as desirable ones.

It is problematic that reinforcement strengthens undesirable behaviors, too, often in a manner that seems counterintuitive. Classic examples of this are the many ways that people get attention by misbehaving. The psychological insight that they are misbehaving *to* gain attention may or may not be true. What is clearly the case is that misbehavior in its many forms (defiance, aggression, avoidance, forgetfulness, etc.) *does* get negative attention, whether it is purposeful, conscious, or inadvertent. The result is the same: an undesirable behavior becomes stronger and more probable.

Thus, a vicious cycle of reinforcement becomes a trap ensnaring people in faulty behavior, rapid and critical censure of the behavior, and a relentless strengthening of the probability that more of the same will occur. For example, a child misbehaves (talks disrespectfully, refuses or ignores directions), the parent nags or yells (because "if I don't stay on top of him, nothing gets done!"), the child seems to respond ("Okay, okay," and may hurry to comply *at that time*), everyone is frustrated, and the cycle repeats itself over and over again. What is actually happening through this repetition is that the child is reinforcing the parent's tendency to remind and yell, and the parent is reinforcing the child's habit of waiting to be reminded or yelled at as a cue to perform.

It is a pattern that most people find familiar and frustrating. Let's invoke a practical and simple method to escape this trap: *don't ask, don't yell—just task and tell.*

1. Don't ask

In the face of bad behavior, typically repeated despite many warnings and "consequences," a natural response is to confront the offender with questions about why he did or didn't do something. When Johnny has yet again made a mess, failed to do or turn in his work, disrespected someone, or dawdled in his own world while you wait for him to comply, your frustration and impatience compound, your nervous system accelerates, and you try to cool yourself and modulate your temper by asking confronting questions:

"Why didn't you do your homework?"

"Why did you hit your sister? Don't you know that's wrong?"

"How can you live in such a messy room?"

"Didn't you hear me tell you to stop playing on the computer?"

Although such questions seem instinctive and appropriate to the child's defiance or noncompliance, they are actually rather foolish questions. No offense meant, reader; we all err this way, but they are, indeed, inappropriate questions that almost always lead away from the result you want.

Think about this: What is the child supposed to say to this third-degree interrogation? He resorted to his usual behavior that displeases you (not necessarily to displease you, but because of his habit of doing what he wants and his becoming used to having his actions heavily reinforced). You are confronting him and asking for a justification for behavior you have already judged unjustifiable! When pressed for an answer, the child will look for a way to escape the spotlight and pressure. Answers like "I forgot," or "Sorry" will likely vex you further and heighten the inquisition.

"What do you mean, you forgot? Haven't I told you a hundred times?" (Yes, of course you have!)

By questioning the child in this way—putting him in the spot with accusations dressed as questions—you're ensuring that he will give you answers that are unsatisfactory and even infuriating. However, the questions are setting the child up for more shame and anxiety. Unwittingly, parents can hammer this home even further by challenging the child's answers.

"*Sorry?* How can you say you're sorry when you've done this over and over again?"

"Am I supposed to accept your excuses?"

You're getting the point that such interactions devolve into more avoidance, frustration, lying to avoid censure, resentment, and *reinforcement (despite its unpleasantness) that the scenario will happen again.*

It's not what you want, but this is the usual result of asking people why they did something you don't like. They weren't thinking at the time what you would want them to think, they don't have answers that will satisfy you, and they just want to get away from the pressure.

Indeed, are there any satisfactory answers to the mindless questions you're asking as you vent your frustration? The questions are usually seething and inappropriate. Don't do it this way.

2. Don't yell

Yelling, nagging, and invective questioning form an unpleasant, yet forceful method of delivering reinforcement, or strengthening, of the very behaviors you are trying to discourage. As described earlier, yelling is not only stressful and ineffective, it backfires into repeating and fortifying the cycle. When you raise your voice or yell, you are reinforcing your own tendency to repeat, remind, and yell, and you are reinforcing the child's habit of waiting to be repeatedly reminded or yelled at as a cue to perform.

People generally don't yell because they are mean or blind to its deleterious effects. They do so because they are frustrated, triggered by the reinforcement "dance" of prior conditioning, excited emotionally, and aroused physiologically. Afterward, they justify their behavior with disclaimers that, despite downside of yelling, it's the only way to get compliance.

This, however, is far from true. Let's examine alternate effective ways of eliciting compliance, forming better habits, and reinforcing calmness and cooperative spirit.

3. Just task

What you say is important, as is the way you say it. The old adage "Say what you mean and mean what you say" is relevant. When you want someone to do something, you must communicate that message in language that is simple, direct, clear, and unadorned by extraneous or conflicting messages. Unfortunately, many people unknowingly complicate and confuse their messages with criticisms and side comments that obfuscate the action to be taken.

We interpret and respond to messages with our conscious and subconscious minds. When the information is conflicting or ambiguous, we may ignore it or respond in ways that misinterpret the intention. And the mind acutely processes the semantics of messages that help interpret and comply with what is said. Without taking this into account, we can subvert our objectives by delivering mixed or confusing messages that leave our audience unsure of what to do and unmotivated to follow through.

For example, when a child has failed to comply or follow through, parents (in utter frustration) may deliver a message such as, "How many times do I have to tell you? You're irresponsible, and you'll never get anywhere by this kind of forgetfulness. Now turn off the computer and do your homework before I give you a consequence you'll never forget!"

Think about the content of this message, as well as the emotional impact. *"How many times do I have to tell you?"* Is your child really supposed to answer that? If so, the answer would probably be, *"Too many, just like you usually do."* Calling him irresponsible and forgetful reinforces his negative self-image and reputation, and it does nothing to shape the adaptive response you want, which is compliance and follow-through. Telling him to "*turn off the computer and do your homework before I give you a consequence you'll never forget!*" literally tells him that after he complies, you will deliver some unknown and awful punishment. The net effect is to intimidate the child into immediate and apparent submission. But this is not effective or enduring.

Instead, *just task*: state your request in simple language, unadorned with criticism or superfluous comments. For instance: "John, please quit any and all games and entertainment *now*. Begin your homework within ninety seconds. If you need to use the computer to do your homework, make sure that homework assignments are the *only* items on your screen or browser. I will check on you in two minutes to see that you are complying. Go ahead."

Simple, to the point, unfettered with emotion or side criticisms. This allows his mind to focus better.

Here's another example of an ineffective tirade: "I can't believe you forgot your materials again! Is this what you call maturity? I don't know what I'm gonna do with you. You seem to never learn. Now find out from the Internet (or friend) what your assignment is. You are so forgetful and irresponsible!"

Instead, just task with clear and simple directions: "You forgot your homework and materials. Okay, you still have to make efforts to find out what your homework is and to do as much of it as you can. Look on the school web page that shows your homework. Also, show me your last three assignments in this class. Name two students in your class who you think know the homework assignments. Write down their names. If you don't know their phone numbers, you're going to find them out the next school day and report their phone numbers to me, so you won't be stuck like this again. And please e-mail your teacher and request a description of the due assignment. Show me when you've finished these items. I expect you to show me within thirty minutes."

Another example: Instead of, "Your room is a disaster. Clean it up," you might try it this way:

"I'm giving you twenty minutes to clean up your room. Please do the following: Pick up all clothes off the floor. No clothing is to be touching the floor except two pairs of shoes. Put dirty clothing into the laundry basket. Put your clean clothes on hooks or in drawers. Put items you are unsure of on your bed and we'll go through them when you have cleaned up everything else. All papers you need should be in folders or drawers. All other papers should be thrown away, including wrappers and leftover items. When I inspect in twenty minutes, anything lying around where it's not supposed to be will be taken away."

Such instructions are explicit and communicate specific actions and standards. Tasking your child in this manner doesn't assure that he will follow through, but it does heighten the probability of compliance. Speaking directly and simply with specific parameters will enable your child to focus on what he needs to do, rather than on his previous failures and your disappointment in him.

As you practice this proactive direction, you will be more concise and clear, as well as less frustrated and nagging.

The next step after *tasking* is *telling*—that is, evaluating performance and reinforcing accountability.

4. And tell

Venting frustration, disappointment, and negative criticism is poisonous to your relationships and it is inimical to getting people to step up and improve their performance. An effective alternative (or, perhaps, antidote) is the habit of reinforcing accountability by describing outcomes and evaluating their adequacy in a timely and objective manner.

Specifically, get in the habit of responding to your child's performance or lack of it by simply reporting on the observations and facts. So, for example, if your child ignores your directions or has not followed through on responsibilities, state your observations as if you were a reporter or announcer.

"John, I told you to turn off the computer and begin your homework twenty minutes ago. I notice you are still playing games and have not started your homework."

"I told you that you could not play on the iPad for the rest of the day, and you are complaining and challenging my decision."

"When I asked you about your homework, you claimed that you don't have any today. Then you told me you don't have the materials to study for the next test. I know from past experience that you get homework almost every day and that you should be planning and putting in study time five days a week in addition to assignments due the next day. So your answer is not appropriate to your responsibilities, and I'm holding you accountable for that."

"I notice again that when I ask you if you have completed your homework and prepared your backpack for school, you told me you will get to it. I didn't ask you about your intentions or plans. I asked you if you finished these tasks. Did you or did you not finish them?" (Pause) "I take that as 'No, I've not done what I was supposed to do and agreed to do.'"

"When I ask you to stop jumping around and to finish your meal, you say, 'Okay, okay!' However, you continue to get up from the table and run around instead of eating your food."

This objectivity will focus both you and your child on the reality of his accomplishment or lack thereof instead of becoming sidetracked and emotional about the habitual poor performance. It is not, by itself, a complete modification of the desired behavior, but it is a proper component of focus and direction, and it will steer you away from the nagging and complaining that typically substitutes for evaluation of performance and reassignment of the task.

Your discrete commentaries on what actually happens may also include your feelings and a challenge to your child. However, you must be careful to present your experience as a time-bound event and not as a piling on of disparagement about your child's abilities and character.

For example, you could say, "When you ignore my directions or answer me in that way, I think and feel several things: I feel frustrated and disrespected, and I am tempted to criticize you and be disappointed in you. This is about my reaction, not about your behavior. So I have a problem, and I'd like your opinion. Do you think my feelings about your lack of follow-through are out of line? If you were me, what would you do in this situation?"

Your child will be *very surprised* by this approach and may not have much or anything useful to say. However, it will get him to think because this approach is solicitous and nonthreatening. Also, it is a good way to communicate that you have uncertainties and sensitivities and that you are open to his feelings and point of view.

The task-and-tell strategy is a reliable and productive habit that you can practice to describe and focus upon what did or didn't get done, how you think and feel about it, and to highlight your child's excuses and avoidance behaviors—all without yelling, nagging, disparaging, or becoming so emotionally reactive that you focus on the argument and frustration rather than the incomplete task.

Ultimately, there needs to be consequences for avoidance or unacceptable behavior that exert a corrective effect on motivation and follow-through. This is where task-and-tell can lead to administering *response costs,* which are impositions of what your child has to pay or do for his excuses, avoidance, or misbehavior.

Turn Excuses into Work

Rather than argue with your child about his "reasons" or excuses, you can attach a *cost* to his habitual offering of such responses. Response costs are most effective when they are proximal to the offense—that is, administered quickly after the unacceptable behavior—and involve some palpable sacrifice. They are, in a sense, like parking tickets. The message is *"I can't stop you from parking here when I'm not looking, but I can make you pay a price that will likely discourage you from doing this again."*

Taking away possessions and privileges—a traditional strategy that parents use but often find ineffectual, especially with intransigent children—is less effective in curbing transgressions than attaching an immediate and unpleasant cost to such behaviors. Costs that the child must pay quickly and by some action tend to work much better than confiscating favorite possessions. If you take away his gaming privileges, he will resent you and passively acclimate. However, turning his excuses or misbehavior into an immediate labor requirement is a sacrifice that will make an impressionable and lasting impact.

You could impose a consequence for forgetfulness or disrespect that involves some menial work that you can monitor without much effort. "John, that excuse will cost you ten minutes of washing the dishes. Begin now." (See, you are tasking.)

"But I didn't mean it. Besides, the dishes are clean."

"John, that's another excuse, which will cost you an additional ten minutes of washing the dishes. You must now wash dishes for twenty minutes. I will find some dishes for you to rewash. Every time you make a complaint or excuse or stop washing for more than sixty seconds, it will cost you another ten minutes of washing."

Tasking and telling can become a productive habit and save you effort and aggravation. Turn your complainant's excuses into work by attaching response costs. You can invent many different effective costs. The idea is to be immediate and reinforce the association between the misbehavior and the mandated payment. It's not mean, it's just fair—according to the rules you institute.

Instead of following the ingrained but unproductive habit of mindlessly ranting and reminding, practice the strategies described above to restore calmness, control, and productive outcomes to your relationships and the accountability of those around you.

Don't ask, don't yell—just task and tell.

2013

EVERY PARENT'S UNFINISHED JOB

It seems that once you become a parent, your job is never finished. Children are often a joy, routinely a challenge, and always a lot of work. First, there is the constant attention required to meet every need of the helpless infant and then the hovering supervision of the toddler and early childhood years. As your child grows, there is safety to ensure, noses to wipe, lessons to teach and schoolwork to review, trips and playdates, sports and music, limits to set, hobbies to venture, friends to approve, privileges to entrust.

The maturation process unfolds, revealing who your child is becoming and providing clues and uncertainty about how you're doing as a parent. Every child is different, and no amount of experience as a parent or professional fully prepares you for what is in store.

As your child matures through the stages of growing up and becoming more independent, there are lessons you try to teach repeatedly and thematically. Among the most fundamental of these are the following:

1. I can't protect you indefinitely.
2. You have to find your own way.
3. Other people matter, too.
4. As you get older, your perspective will change.
5. Know your strengths and limitations, including a fluid awareness of your emotional and thinking patterns.
6. Your beliefs, attitudes, and selfishness will influence how you filter your perceptions and the actions of others.

7. Learn how to test your desires and will against reality and the ways of the world that conflict with what you want.

Inevitably, you release your child into the world to fend for himself. Truly, you repeat this act of faith many times. You wait with ambivalence, and weather the pride and anxiety as you watch the achievements, mistakes, and growing pains that follow you and your child as you both age, with you always leading the way.

As necessary and when you can, you intervene. You contribute money (always welcomed), advice (sometimes tolerated), and emotional support and presence. Whether it seems necessary or futile, you worry. Despite being reassured or chided against worrying, you cannot help but worry for your child's well-being.

From the moment you met, your child needs you, and you delight in many aspects of that need. Though it turns wearisome, you and your child will argue and contest about his or her need for you and the extent to which you are welcomed or tolerated in his or her affairs. It is the nature of parenthood that your heart is meddlesome. It is a job never quite finished: this burden of providing what you can, investing in the outcome, waiting for results, and wondering what you did. Even when your child is gone—grown, independent, married, estranged, or perhaps missing or deceased—you will always be the one who came first but tried to put your child ahead of you.

One of the most important life skills your child must learn is the self-awareness and self-regulation of emotional states. We must know our own bodies and minds, from the most basic functions of filling ourselves with food and water to emptying ourselves of unnecessary waste. This is true also of feelings and the ever-shifting balance of emotional and neurological states: those events that provide us with information and sensations about our degree of satiety, whether we feel threatened or safe, and whether we can relax or must gear up for action. We are "hardwired" this way for survival, and from our earliest moments, we discover and practice this balance through the bonding with a mother figure who provides primary nurturance and security. Whether or not this early bonding goes well (sometimes babies are difficult, or mothers are stressed or absent), the process of sensing and regulating one's internal affairs continues throughout life and assumes more sophisticated disguises in the veneers of personality, cultural mores, and social and business customs and expectations. You have to hold some volatile feelings in check, express your desires and frustrations in acceptable ways, read and interpret the messages of others, and somehow manage all of this for decades without overly taxing or exceeding the capacity of your organs to help you deal with all that life throws at you.

Every parent and child engages this process routinely and repeatedly throughout the rigors of family relationships: "I want this. Can I have this?" and "Don't do that! You must do *this*." It is how people learn to relate, act safely and productively, and manage life's demands and rewards. It is acted out and practiced over bedtimes, getting dressed and ready, homework, eating, tantrums and aggression, possessiveness, respect and compliance, and many other activities that happen in families. We all learn to cope, but many do not do it successfully, thereby collecting traumatic scars and habits that detract from physical, emotional, and social wellness.

Every parent knows the challenge of managing his or her own stress levels and reactions when a child is acting up or unreasonably. We also know that children are modeling from us, and that they learn lessons and have side effects we wish we could divest from their experiences.

The job of teaching your child to manage the inner life of feelings and states remains unfinished because we are all lifelong learners and practitioners of how to enjoy and control ourselves. You give your child an intense and protracted head start, but children grow up and must manage themselves independently. You hope to get them going in the right direction.

There are many techniques for fostering this development, some natural and seat-of-the-pants, and others fancy or therapeutic. I am reminded of the ethnic comedy stand-up routine about the use of "time-out" in certain strict families: "After my father would whup me, he'd give me 'time-out' to pick up my teeth."

Not all were disciplined into fear and submission. I remember how my father used to communicate feelings, often through the use of physical metaphors. We had in our small kitchen a shelf on the wall above the kitchen table. The shelf supported an ancient transistor AM radio that doused my father with news. Hanging from the shelf under the radio was a toy plastic "doghouse"—a small replica with four plastic dogs hanging on hooks beside it. My father had labeled the four dogs with adhesive tape bearing our individual names: Dad, Mom, my brother, and me. Though my father took the lead, there was an unwritten rule that each of us could place his own dog or another family dog in the doghouse. This symbolic representation was powerful: it could be a statement of depression, despair, illness, or victimization, as in my father's frequent self-description, "I'm in the doghouse today." (My father was often depressed throughout his life.) Or it could be an intended aggression or perhaps sympathy and validation, as when one of us placed someone else's dog in the doghouse. This could mean, "I'm mad at you, so get away from me and stay there!" Or maybe, "You look sad and hurt. I recognize this, so take some time to lick your wounds and heal. I won't keep bothering you."

The doghouse plaque was barely three-dimensional. Each dog had his own hook, but the doghouse had only one hook. It was deep enough to allow two dogs. I don't know if the manufacturer was working out any "issues," but the way my family used the doghouse, a maximum of two people could have recognizable emotional constraints at any one time. The doghouse was only so big. Was this a metaphor for the emotional competition in my family, the jockeying for pity, solace, or recognition? Perhaps my memory is stained and my family members would take none of this seriously. I do know that my father's game we played provided an outlet and taught me the rudiments of nonverbal expression in a family that had difficulty expressing emotion intelligently and accepting its varied and intense manifestations in others.

Unfinished as it was, my parents handed over this job of emotional awareness, regulation, and expression to me. I practice a lifetime of getting better at it and helping others to do so, too. It is a very important job whose value cannot be measured or compromised by a lack of completion.

The old plastic doghouse is long gone. We have modern-day tools including many gadgets and graphics to materialize and express ideas. It is a love affair between art and science. To foster self-awareness and emotional interpretation and expression, I use "emotion meters" (see below). These are renditions of applause meters that register degrees of intensity in decibel levels. Of course, there are many such meters, such as those in Radio Shack and the sophisticated instruments used by scientists. The ones I use are makeshift, though extremely sensitive. You assess the level of satiety, intensity, and arousal in yourself and others. Parents and children can use it adeptly and satisfactorily. It is a simple and useful tool for an important and unfinished job. There's something quite satisfying and powerful about identifying and expressing feelings in yourself and those important to you. Play with the meters and have a good time!

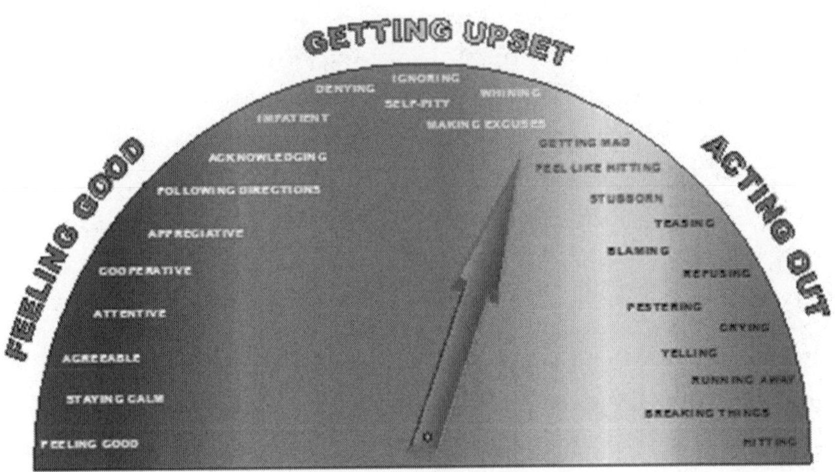

CHILD EMOTION METER

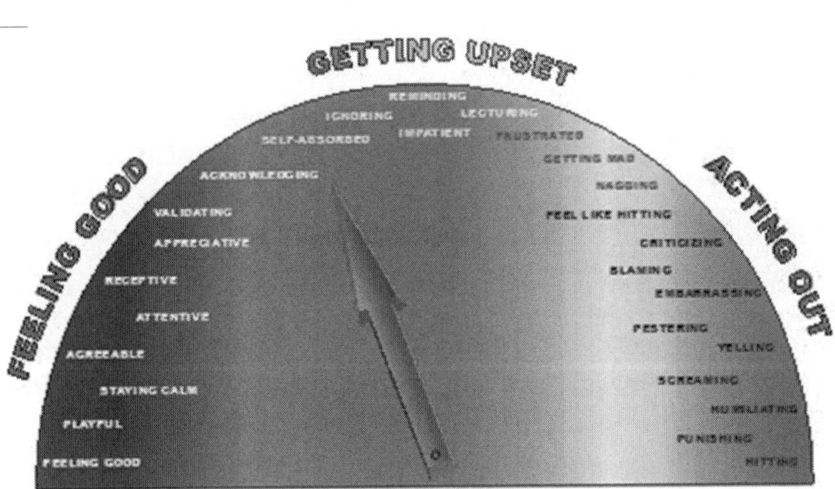

ADULT EMOTION METER

2013
Getting to the bottom of disputes.

A RECTAL DYSFUNCTION

The question must be asked: *Am I an ass?*

Every man asks himself this question, less from self-doubt or insecurity and more from reality testing in response to his partner's allegations and insults. We have all had people disparage us, call us names (usually featuring the less esteeming aspect of body parts), and ascribe to us the likes of some sort of waste or uselessness. I'm referring to those intimate ones who love us and who have shared with us at the deepest levels.

Still, a man knows what it's like to be a warrior to the world and yet faulty in the eyes of his family. For most men—and I include yours truly—the arbiter of *ass*ignations is the wife. To not be a prophet in your hometown is one thing, but to bring home a profit and be unappreciated is quite another.

Calling someone you love an ass requires a high degree of audacity. Firstly, it is an aggressive and offensive act. Emboldened by the negative emotions (disgust, anger, disappointment, impatience, etc.) that sponsor such an overture, the person venting the *ass*ault takes the risk of stepping out of loving character or, perhaps worse, reinforcing the less savory parts of her own character. Secondly, a cost associated with hurling the ass epithet is a backlash or reciprocation in hostility or at least defensiveness. Perhaps you can call a spade a spade, but the downside of citing an ass is a striking loss of diplomacy and intimacy.

Why is this so common? I take assumptive liberties, here, but I'm confident that readers will identify with and relate to this unseemly convention. Traditional psychological insight might explain this tendency as a manifestation of feeling safe enough in a relationship to reveal latent hostility and aggression. (*Latent?*) The idea is that if you are secure enough in the relationship, you can express negative stuff without fear of rejection or abandonment; namely, you can call an ass what he is without getting your own kicked. However, I find this theory lacking on two counts: first, its reliance on the intangible suppositions of psychological security and safety; and second, its lack of account for what I see as the real and tangible basis for hurling insults as body part labels. That is, holding people accountable. There's the rub (without benefit of toilet paper).

When you hold someone accountable, there is bound to be backlash. Accountability is a large and complicated domain in the annals of human interactions. I posit a theory that most people survive overwhelm and dysfunction in their relationships by employing a strategy that easily entices others with similar anxieties: *you don't call me on my nonsense, and I won't call you on yours.* This tacit agreement on the burial of accountability serves to avert conflict and embarrassment, albeit at the expense of corrupting integrity and truth. It is not limited to families, of course, but the intimate and prolonged patterns in family relationships easily highlight what may be described as *a rectal dysfunction.*

It goes like this: He (the king of his castle) questions an expense, finds fault with the housekeeping, or complains about some personal habit or idiosyncrasy in his beloved partner. She (the queen bee) must defend her prerogatives by making him pay for illustrating a quirk or asking for justification. She becomes defensive, perhaps territorial or haughty, and hurls the A-word. The hive has been invaded by a demand for accountability, and all the bees become agitated *wannabes.*

There are many scenarios of perceived attacks and threats. She questions his whereabouts or comments on some habits of demands, behavior, or hygiene. The cardinal rule of the secret game is violated and blowback ensues.

You don't call me on my nonsense, and I won't call you on yours—remember? Well, apparently not in this instance. The stops have been pulled out, and you have disrupted my peace and pretense. You have snatched the bottom card that collapses the deck of confabulated integrity. You are asking for justification, evidence, rationale, even truth. If you claim that the emperor is not wearing clothes, then you are the ass that's showing—no longer an emperor in anyone's imagination.

We are conflicted because we have dual commitments: one, to protect, edify, and cherish our loved ones; and, two, to petition for relief of grievances by holding others accountable for their actions and consequences. Each of us will only go so far in cleaning up the messes others make before calling attention to the inequities.

In the light of your own very obvious foibles, calling attention to needs, grievances, hypocrisies, and accountability shows a stubborn devotion to reality that earns you the classification of assification. You know what I'm saying: assert your position, and this act will challenge the integrity and flexibility of the most mature and loving cohorts. No ifs, ands, or butts—just yours.

Unfortunately, there is no defined solution to this problem. When you are called an ass, even if you are right, the matter always has two sides. Blowing the whistle by holding someone at close range accountable may result in that person hearing the sound of your flatulence.

1995

THE PILL

Tantrum Contraception and Attention Deficit Population Control

An Oral Tradition

Several decades ago the "pill" (oral contraceptives) revolutionized sexual behavior in a significant population segment. Its impact reached across realms of opportunity, interpersonal relationships, responsibility, self-control, medical health, and moral and spiritual underpinnings. In the 1990s the new "pill" (medication for attention deficit) is fomenting another revolution, causing upheaval, controversy, and profound individual and social consequences. The parallels between these pharmaceutical solutions deserve examination. To the extent that history tempers expectations and risks of social and biological experiments, such examination might limit personal tragedy, avert the curtailment of freedom, and promote individual and social responsibility.

The "pill" of the last generation was oral contraception. This remedy for the "chemical imbalance" making women susceptible to unwanted pregnancy changed the behavior of users and the expectations of people around them. The pill remedy did not change the condition of susceptibility. Freedom was illusory, pleasure was temporary, and many paid heavily for the wager with nature. The panacea of symptom relief and crisis avoidance frequently had hidden costs: accidents (despite the pill's relative efficacy), sexually transmitted diseases, broken hearts and broken relationships, guilt and manipulation, and unwanted medical side effects. In the aftermath of the sexual revolution launched by the pill, we must rebuild our understanding of sex with an appreciation of self-governance.

Human sexual behavior involves complex repertoires including factors of physiology, genetics, culture, social conditioning, maturation, age, values, motivation, attitudes, etc. Sexual episodes may or may not result in conception (although the link is almost universally causal). Because of the ramifications of pregnancy, however, it becomes easy and tempting to simplify sex around the issue of pregnancy. Enter the pill. Instead of sex causing pregnancy, the opposite becomes seemingly true: pregnancy (specifically, the avoidance of it) causes sex. In this departure from logic (a habit of many enlightened people), the variance of sex (a statistical term representing the degree of difference measured in observed behavior) is largely accounted for by the pill—that is, since pregnancy is such a controlling variable affecting sexual behavior, the contraceptive pill becomes the single greatest factor determining the occurrence of sex. The absurdity of this example is obvious only when the scope of sexuality is broadened beyond the narrow issue of biochemical science.

Similarly, attention deficit involves complex interactions of physiology, genetics, environment, learning, maturation, age, values, motivation, attitudes, etc. Attention waxes and wanes constantly. Its irregularity in those with ADD causes disruption and embarrassment that may be likened to the habitual occurrence of unwanted pregnancy. Just as teenage pregnancies can divert bright futures, so can ADD sidetrack and limit the learning and achievement of otherwise capable individuals. When the solution is a pill, the analogy is clear: oral contraception of dysfunctional behavior is the determining pivot defining constellations of behaviors whose cause and effect have other gravitational forces.

With pregnancy as the overriding determinant, the pill seems necessary, even as it aborts a truer holistic view of sex. With disruptiveness, tantrums, hyperactivity, and the like, Ritalin looms inevitably, even as it treats the hemorrhage with a daily supply of Band-Aids.

Contraceptive Comparisons

This exposition on contraceptives may lead some readers to wonder whether I hold ancient, sexist views that oppress women. Be at peace, for I do not disfavor birth control. When used appropriately, contraceptive methods are a blessing that can enrich intimacy and help couples develop a better environment in which to have children. (Indeed, oral contraceptives have other medical uses besides contraception.) I am not a purist who would hold out against the miracle of antibiotics or other medications that effectively cure diseases.

Am I against the use of medication to treat ADD or associated disorders? No, I am not. Ritalin and other medicines have turned lives around. However, the use of drugs in isolation to treat multifaceted problems bears more similarity to substance dependence than it does to Hippocratic medical practice.

The dispensation of birth control pills to pubescent girls has stirred controversy. Even those who favor this approach would find it deplorable to leave adolescents to fend for themselves with only pills for protection. Sex can be powerful, confusing, overwhelming, traumatic, seductive, even habit-forming. Dealing only with the biological reproduction aspect surely deprives our children. Young people need to learn about living, not just creating life.

The distribution of attention control pills deals strictly with the physiological aspects of motor response and arousal. Picture a locked thermostat on a timer, with the key in the Ritalin vial. Each dosage is a manual adjustment of the thermostat timer. The patient, however, may have windows wide open or a fire burning out of control. He needs more flexibility and greater resources than afforded by the locked thermostat.

Daily functioning persistently requires us to regulate the "temperatures" of arousal, attention, cognition, emotion, and conduct. Freedom is limited by the degree of dependence on external controls to continue this process. Just as people learn to balance on a bicycle, handle strong emotions, rest when tired, avoid certain foods, and suppress biological urges, each of us can and must learn to self-regulate our internal environments. For some, like ADD sufferers, the terrain is a rocky mountainside, and balancing the bicycle is much more difficult. Artificial supports can be crucial in assisting the learning process. As the topography changes with human development, some adjustment in balance and concentration is necessary. As one acclimates to the turf, the process becomes smoother and more automatic. Training wheels, like medicine, can only assist but never solely accomplish this process.

Meditations on Medications

What about the claim alleged by the "pseudo-scientific-minded" that afflicted individuals cannot control this biochemical imbalance, thus justifying medication as the only humane and effective answer? The problem with this view lies not in its accuracy, but in its narrowness. The "cannot control" part cloaks irresponsibility and authoritarianism in the guise of enlightened compassion. Relieving symptoms at the cost of the flexible and independent self is an unnecessary tax. As previously stated, medication used judiciously can be a life-changing intervention. Whether or not medication is used, we must exercise care and wisdom in the treatment and development of self-control. Couldn't the "cannot control this biochemical imbalance" rationale be applied to the sexual urges of teenagers (or people of other ages, for that matter)? The urgency, intensity, and consequences of poorly managed sexuality would therefore be controlled strictly through forced chemical intervention. What measures are we willing to invoke to coerce conformity and prevent uninhibited departures from convention?

An Arousing Philosophy

Beyond the trumpeting of "safe sex," this decade should resonate with echoes of "safe focus" and calls for attention to learning as a method of developing lasting self-regulation.

Like it or not, dysfunctional sufferers bear the burden of discovering themselves in the truest and most practical sense of developing identities. They are reminded at virtually every turn in life of their differences and difficulties accommodating the routine tasks, frustrations, and impingements that the "well-adjusted" folks hardly seem to notice. The obese person, the epileptic, the diabetic—here are common examples of people who struggle painfully with metabolic regulatory functions that most of us take for granted. They must adapt, integrate, adjust, cope, and develop healthy attitudes and lifestyles against odds they would not have chosen. Medication may help, but it's just a beginning. Those afflicted with disregulation may discover a silver lining in their troubles. Symptoms, danger, and threat drive the development of more autonomous self-management. Vulnerabilities often serve as the vehicles for the learning that makes life work better.

For this philosophy to have value, it must be fueled by practicality. There is a saying: *The society that exalts its philosophers and eschews its plumbers will have both bad philosophy and bad plumbing.*

The practice of medicating solely and routinely on the pretext of nonvolitional imbalance parades as scientific pragmatism, although it is more realistically a bad philosophy. The logical tenets of this philosophy are as follows:

1. There is something wrong with the patient that he cannot fix himself.
2. Experience has shown that medication produces positive changes.
3. The cure or solution is to find the right medication.
4. The benefits of the right medication outweigh the disadvantages.

Let us examine the practicality of these points:

1a. There is something wrong with the patient that he cannot fix himself.

This assumption, of course, wrests control from the individual. Under the guise of medical treatment, the patient becomes a passive recipient of chemical and prescriptive control. Whatever control he had is diminished by the treatment that bases its effectiveness on the patient's powerlessness.

A frightening corollary to this assumption is that the judgment of disability is usurped entirely from the person being treated. Disability is "proved" by the continuation of behavior disliked by adults in circumstances where other behavior is desired. Children who are misplaced in curricula ill-suited for their needs or development are frequently medicated in response to the expeditious adult conclusion that the children cannot fix it themselves. Seldom is any analysis done to determine the environmental and developmental factors that maintain undesirable behaviors and to differentiate them from true neurological dysfunction.

2a. Experience has shown that medication produces positive changes. Experience has shown that medication often produces *striking* changes in a significant percentage of the treated population. The valence of these changes frequently depends upon the eye of the beholder and the context in which the beholding occurs. While parents and teachers may observe a reduction in difficult behaviors, the child may experience a benign neglect or a variety of physiological discomforts.

When the assessment of positive effects rests exclusively in the convenience of parental or teacher relief, danger proliferates systematically. The "positive" effects of medications are so highly esteemed that diagnosis is determined by treatment. The methodology is "let's try him on this medication, and if he responds well, we will know that he has ADD."

By extension, we are back in the province of prescribing birth control to adolescents to determine what their sexual behavior is really like. Though foolhardy and unscientific, this treatment philosophy and practice prevail.

3a. The cure or solution is to find the right medication.
This is more complicated than it sounds. Even though the selection of drugs generally accepted for treating ADD, depression, and compulsive disorders is rather limited, finding the right medication and the optimal dosage is time-consuming, imprecise, and often fraught with side effects. Unlike learning paradigms (in which people quickly adapt by recognizing task demands, identifying rewards, and respecting limits through properly set consequences), medication must be fitted to the individual. Since the patient lacks (by previous medical assumptions) reasonable awareness and responses to internal states, he must (by consistent definition) have this done by a supervising physician.

Medications are typically prescribed according to these guidelines:

- Physician familiarity and experience with particular drugs
- Patient (or parent or teacher) symptoms and complaints (sometimes any will suffice)
- Patient body weight (and sometimes age)
- Previous medications tried for the problem
- Contraindications, if any

Rarely are medicines titrated (dosages adjusted) using data from psychometric measures extremely sensitive to the very symptoms for which the medication is prescribed. Attention, for example, can be measured in milliseconds of response time, impulsivity, and variability. This is done using sophisticated neuropsychological tests (many of which take less time and cost about the same as routine medical lab tests). However, this information is scarcely sought and routinely disregarded in those cases where the information is provided. The doctor typically writes a prescription and advises the patient or family to call in and report on how things are going. Effectiveness is judged upon how little trouble the patient causes or experiences subjectively. Although the tools are readily available, the patient's internal experience is neither measured nor heard.

Finding the "right" medication is usually a tricky balance between a strong enough dosage to induce the desired effects and a dosage (or medication) whose side effects are tolerable. This often leads to experimenting and locating through trial-and-error the dosage or combinations of medications and dosages that work. Although most of the medications typically prescribed are deemed "reasonably" safe by themselves, medications are increasingly used in combinations for which there is only very recent clinical experience and little, if any, research.

Experimentation and diligence notwithstanding, a substantial segment of the symptomatic population still does not respond well to any psychotropic medications.

4a. The benefits of the right medication outweigh the disadvantages. The technical problems of finding effective medications for individuals are significant. So far, this discussion has not addressed the issue of side effects; for many people, side effects are intolerable, while for others they become a habituated annoyance. Then there is the enigma of tolerance. Dosages that are effective to begin with do not remain that way. Over time, increased dosages are needed to maintain the desired effects. As dosage levels increase, adverse side effects can become a major problem.

Although I treat many people with ADD, depression, and a variety of dysfunctional conditions, I do not prescribe medication. I do, however, get to watch the process, hear the complaints, field the frustrations, and notice the successes and failures. My observation has been that successful medication treatment (that is, where medication plays its adjunct role effectively without causing undue side effects and without substituting for appropriate interventions) takes time simply to establish. Stabilization generally takes about two to four months with children and about one to three months with adults. Even when it works, it's not so quick or simple.

There may be benefits, but there are clearly disadvantages. Medicating someone is like filling the proverbial leaky tire. The effect is always wearing off or leaking out, thus requiring constant replenishment and monitoring. The peak effect of Ritalin, for example, lasts about 90 to 120 minutes, after which a rebound effect often makes the user crankier and less attentive than before medication.

Technical problems aside, the biggest disadvantage of psychotropic medications may occur in those situations where users respond remarkably well. Such positive responses carry the danger of "omissibility"—what is not being done because the palliative effects of drugs make it easy to do little else.

Balancing the Future

In my practice as a clinical neuropsychologist, counselor, and educator, I have seen too many cases of children's development embezzled by medication. When hyperactivity subsides and conduct and concentration improve, adults feel little motivation to provide youngsters with the structure, training, education, and coaching they need. Time and again I have witnessed children with horrible histories receive medication as their only treatment. When these individuals emerge through puberty, the hyperactivity usually abates, even in the absence of medication. Also missing are the self-controls, prudent judgment, self-worth, and reflective, consequential, and critical thinking skills that never properly developed because no one noticed they were not growing. Mostly, these kids were noticed for misbehaving and disinhibition. When medication suffocated these symptoms, the kids were thought to be okay. Since nobody kept track of their cognitive processes, self-esteem, coping skills, or rebound from early failure, they were never afforded the chances to imbue the stepping-stones and practice mechanisms for survival that the unafflicted take for granted. These individuals were busy "acting out" or "acting in" their formidable problems with self-regulation; they seldom practiced and refined the subtleties of social nuance, negotiation, dealing with ambiguity and ambivalence, and edifying living habits. They spent their formative years depending on others to regulate their thermostats—this was provided for them through chemistry and punishment.

How tragic it is to overlook such critical development when effective tools are available and affordable. We can teach self-control skills, and we can empower people (even toddlers!) to self-regulate appropriately. In so doing, we can eliminate symptoms without causing side effects. The technology has existed for years, and it constantly improves. Why keep refilling the leaky tire when it can be made to keep its air?

EEG Biofeedback—the "UnPill"

EEG biofeedback is a viable and effective method for teaching people to self-regulate. This is a technique in which people are taught (by means of real-time computer feedback) how to produce more of the brainwaves associated with desired behaviors—such as concentration, attentional focus, relaxation, cooperative behavior, and reduction in irritability, pain, and sleep disturbance.

The remarkable quality of this technique is that the results are so obviously generalizable; this is because the procedure teaches people specifically to modify brainwave activity—it addresses no specific symptom, yet it has profound effects on a wide variety of symptoms.

This is because EEG biofeedback very efficiently modifies the control mechanisms responsible for producing and maintaining the symptoms. The struggles and inconsistencies people have with learning, paying attention, controlling moods, pain, and alertness are largely caused by irregularities in the way the brain self-regulates its "housekeeping" and higher-order functions. EEG biofeedback is a way of teaching the brain to produce more waves in the bandwidths associated with better self-regulation.

EEG biofeedback is a training regimen in which the client reinforces himself—often one thousand times or more during a thirty-minute session! It is a relatively pure learning paradigm with no punishment, negative reinforcement, or emotional content. It does not require talking. The client's brain cortex information is simply displayed in a way that allows him to change it, earn rewards, and see and hear the results of his efforts, moment by moment.

My colleagues and I have used EEG biofeedback successfully (in over ninety thousand sessions) with a variety of symptoms and conditions. Many of our clients are taking medications, some will not, and others have quit or reduced dosages because of biofeedback. One key to the success of this treatment, I believe, is that it requires the client to participate. Although it is self-healing and not conscious, it is an *active* process. Thus, the improvements are lasting because the individual has engineered it himself—such is the nature of learning! Moreover, this self-monitoring, self-rewarding, self-regulating technique lays the foundation for successful behavioral training and modification in the larger environment. Biofeedback will not do it all, but it is tremendously helpful, particularly for those individuals whose internal monitoring systems (thermostats) falter. Learning better self-regulation relieves symptoms *and* paves the way for rebuilding a fractured self through a variety of interventions. These might include counseling, coaching, specialized teaching, environmental modifications, and a number of targeted "mentoring" strategies that would complement and integrate the neurophysiological gains.

Perspective

Treatment becomes as much about rebuilding an entire sense of self as about medication and behavioral management. The anguish of ADD and other self-regulatory disorders carry histories of failure, confusion, and unhappiness usually resulting in deep-rooted pain and low self-esteem.

According to Drs. Edward Hallowell and John Ratey (who coauthored *Driven to Distraction* and *Answers to Distraction*), "The most overlooked mistake in the treatment of ADD is thinking that medication can do it all, particularly when the child gets a good response to, say Ritalin." These medical experts insist that "medication is not the whole treatment for ADD. Never was. Never will be. Most adults with ADD have been searching their whole lives, knowing something was wrong, but being unable to identify the cause of their distress. This very issue is what can make treatment more difficult."

Often the diagnosis provides such relief from the pangs of unfulfilled longing that ADD sufferers cling to their identification as a shield against the former agony of functioning as an annoying collection of symptoms. Although the protection of the new identity is understandable, this too can serve the destructive ulterior purpose of maintaining the imbalances (in emphases, preoccupations, and priorities) so characteristic of this disorder. Balance is a learned and dynamic process. It cannot be managed with chemicals as though it were a swimming pool.

Life is not always balanced. For some, the disequilibrium is daunting, the responsibility of self-management too overwhelming. The promise of a magic cure finds many easy targets. Our pill-popping culture has become lax in marksmanship. On the frontier of innovations, this could result in casualties.

Eventually, they will invent a pill for dyslexia—a drug specifically targeting the auditory-visual centers of the brain believed critical in the processing of symbols. I anticipate this within my lifetime, and I await with eagerness the advent of such a pill. The shame and struggle of dyslexics will end, as will the need to teach reading, math, literature, and writing. Better chemistry will alleviate the inefficiency of instruction and the tedious process of learning. Many teachers will lose employment, yet this will be productive. It will reduce the educational budget, much of which is spent ineffectually. Fortunately, legions of erstwhile educators will find lucrative employment in the burgeoning pharmaceutical industry.

2013

SCREWED OR UNGLUED: HOLDING FAST THROUGH ADVERSITY

So many of the conversations I have with patients seem to repeat the frustrations they have about changing things: other people, circumstances, even themselves. I hear about people and from people who come unglued by adverse situations. The reports of these happenings are composites of people assimilating and integrating their interactions, often in a state of overwhelm. They are partly venting, partly rationalizing, and partly seeking validation and support for the impropriety and stress of life's intrusions. Sometimes the teller is even remorseful about coming unglued or overreacting—but even this self-recrimination is almost always accompanied by an appeal for pity, comfort, and acknowledgment of the legitimacy of overreacting and umbrage.

Surely, we all want support and understanding. We want to connect with people who feel our pain and offer solace. The truth is, however, that overreactions and taking offense are maladaptive. Such reactions debilitate our nervous systems and countervail the spiritual blessings of the One who oversees everything. Adversity is a routine part of life. Dealing sanely with it is necessary for health, adaptive functioning, and productive and rewarding relationships.

Holding fast through adversity is not a matter of repressing feelings, stoically "manning up," or avoiding conflict. Rather, it is a set of skills and attitudes that can be learned and practiced. Coping effectively with adversity builds character and perseverance, but you need to confront and understand certain fundamentals in this process. We live in a universe that often doesn't give you what you want and when you want it. Most people can intellectually accept this truism, but when things don't go your way, it's easy to be led by pride, a sense of entitlement, and the negative emotions that can so easily sway you from self-control and the better paths of interpretation and response.

Several factors shape and reinforce the tendency to overreact. First, most of us have a propensity to be selfish, and we tend to act in accordance with what seems to support our own self-preservation. Although this is vital for self-care, protection, and the acquisitions necessary for survival, self-interest can easily morph into an overblown sense of importance and entitlement. It is easy to believe that life *owes* us.

Second, our culture reinforces self-orientation and egotistical self-aggrandizement. We are fed commercial inducement to indulge our impulses and desires for gratification. The "me-first" culture ratifies that we deserve what we want and that we must be strong, fierce, and first, or the dog-eat-dog world will prey upon us. Aggression and defense are taught and touted as elite methods and values.

Third, most people have developed highly overaroused and sensitized nervous systems. This sets the stage for easy provocation and dramatically excessive responses to the challenges and annoyances that routinely ensue from life's demands. We all have genetic vulnerabilities that can make us overly impressionable to the intrusions and affronts we face. This is why we feel threatened, become ill, and even succumb. Whereas we truly need defenses against what will harm us, the great preponderance of our defense mechanisms is targeted to protect us against perceived threats—and this is what revs up the brain and nervous system into a constant state of vigilance that makes it seem like the world is out to get us. Living this way is unhealthy and illusory. It is perpetuated by the nervous system's addiction to fight-or-flight adrenaline, social reinforcement for winning and showing power, and the basic human instinct to justify self-importance and entitlement.

To some extent, we all have a subterranean context of "poor me, I don't deserve this, I'll show them!" This selfish and reactive side can emerge when we are depleted, traumatized, blindsided, frustrated, taken advantage of, or simply overwhelmed. The mind springs to action in response to neuronal and hormonal alarms, and we rationalize the need for battle. This is not assertiveness or conscientious demand for accountability. This is the nervous system run amok in desperate protection against a perceived threat to integrity. It is what leads to coming unglued. And it can become a devastating habit. Here are some tips for dealing with situations when things just don't go your way:

1. **Don't be surprised. Expect hardship, trials, and people not behaving as you would like.**
   Becoming miffed or upset is a habit. So is taking things in stride. This process begins with the receipt of bad news or the observation that things are not going well. Expecting the worst can be self-defeating, but accepting unpleasant events is an adaptive mind-set in adjusting to reality. You will be often tested, sometimes victimized, and intermittently affronted by the unfolding of events and behaviors that are not to your liking. If you take for granted that this is the nature of things, you will be much less frequently blindsided or enticed into volatile or irritable reactions. Your subconscious and your spirit will be prepared to weather discomfort and adversity as another routine function, inconvenient though it may be. Thus, you will handle it better than you would if your initial response were an overreaction.

   I remember vividly a time I reviewed a telephone bill as I scanned my mail in front of a colleague. "WHAT?" I exclaimed petulantly. "AGAIN?" I was reacting to something in the bill I didn't like. "Yes, Mark," said my colleague in mock patronage, "the phone bill comes every month." Indeed, he was "on the mark." Though I was reacting to a specific annoyance, his comment broadened the perspective to the habitual reactive surprise I had attached to a routine burden.

Don't be surprised when people displease or blame you, even when they are just being themselves (objectionably, as the case may be). You may not quite embrace the situation, but omitting the surprise/indignation factor raises the probability that you will respond with dignity and efficacy.

2. **Identify your negative emotions in your reactions.**
   Self-awareness is key to controlling your feelings before they get the better of you. Learn to observe yourself with the objectivity of a baseball umpire. As the pitches arrive, call balls and strikes without taking sides. Recognize the "heat," the curveballs, and the pitches in the dirt for what they are. When you accept the call, you will be better prepared to adjust your play.

   Recognizing and identifying emotions are not just a labeling exercise, a cathartic end in itself, as many well-meaning guides would practice. They are a prelude to taking conscious and assertive action in planning and executing more meaningful, organized, and effective responses.

3. **Use cognition and reason to establish whether your negative emotions that are embedded in the reactions are *necessary or useful.***
   If you are angry about something, ask yourself if the angry feelings are *necessary*. This question may seem ridiculous when you are worked up, but it serves as a meditational tool to counteract the adrenaline. Our mind narratives always invent justifications for wrath

("The lousy so-and-so did this; can you believe it?") and vindication. However, is anger—though instinctive—really *necessary*? I challenge you to provide evidence that truly supports utility instead of the self-serving rationale and rationalizations in which it usually masquerades.

The next question to ask yourself is whether the anger—whatever the circumstantial justification—is *useful* in putting you in a better position to deal with the particular issue. Again, the question seems silly if you are in the context of obligatory neuronal and social response. ("Of course I'm angry…who wouldn't be?") But the proposition of *utility* transfers your energy to the mode of consequences and their *functional* link to planned and purposeful action and control.

I am not advocating logic and reason as a means of reframing distressing emotions so they don't bother you as much. I am suggesting that logical thinking can engage your capacity for evaluation and planning so that the *habit of negative emotional reaction* does not become self-sustaining. If you analyze and decide that negative emotions are neither inevitable nor helpful, then you are ready to employ tools to successfully rid yourself of these hindrances.

4. **Eliminate your negative emotions.**
   There are many ways to calm down and/or shake the shackles of distress. I have found that in the grip of turmoil or obsessive preoccupation with potentially explosive issues, many techniques for gathering composure yield limited value. The technique I recommend that yields rapid and reliable positive results is Thought Field Therapy. This is a systematic tapping procedure that you can apply to yourself and that will eliminate your negative emotions consistently in a matter of minutes.

In its various formats and incarnations, this method has been validated by many thousands of people, and it is effective for any and all negative emotions. You can teach yourself these techniques by following the procedures outlined in my book, *Living Intact: Challenge and Choice in Tough Times.*

The simple and methodical sequence of identifying your impeding emotions, questioning their inevitability and utility, and implementing a quick intervention to free yourself from their detracting effects will clear the path for you to deliberately conceive and carry out a more organized and appropriate response to your quandary.

5. **Plan your responses, and execute your plan.**
   As the saying goes, *plan your work and work your plan.* Once you are no longer responding to strangling emotions, you are better able to figure out a way to achieve what you want and can achieve under the presenting circumstances and constraints. You may be able to make inroads against an injustice, or you may have to settle for airing your grievance diplomatically and holding the other party accountable, whether or not you get relief.

   Sometimes you can right wrongs, and in many situations it is challenging just to assert your rights. The more you take things in stride and accrue experience with a level head, the more wisdom, discernment, and discretion you will develop for dealing with the next wave of adversity and challenges.

   Even though you can't always change someone else's habits or keep the cookie from crumbling, you can definitely exert more control over your own behavior and how you will deal with the broken pieces.

6. **Assess how well you did and what you might change next time in a similar situation.**
   Taking charge of your habits in weathering adversity is progressive. Your intact emotions and developing powers of objective observation and analysis will help you make small and significant adjustments to how you respond and what emotional attachments you want to preserve and integrate in similar situations. Handling adversity requires learning from experience, and that implies assessing the situation and making adjustments. This is intelligence in its purest form.

7. **Reinforce yourself for small steps in reacting more adaptively and strategically.**
   By noticing minor positive changes in the ways you respond to adversity, you will program and train yourself to be a person who increasingly weathers hardships astutely and who maintains an integrity and identity that are not significantly altered or perturbed by things not going your way. You will hold together through the petty annoyances and storms that invariably come your way. Little by little, step-by-step, you will build more flexibility and a more sanguine and adaptive repertoire of answers to the confounding questions, challenges, and intimidations you face.

   When you get less angry, impulsive, sarcastic, or inclined to complaints, do pat yourself on the back for such small steps, which are truly major accomplishments on a journey toward building your ultimate disposition and moral fiber.

When something arouses your desire to respond negatively or a "hot button" instigates your "need" for correction or restitution (in attitude or action), consider your response to the adversity. Pause and ask yourself if you are exercising choice and flexibility, or whether you are being programmed and controlled by uncomfortable emotions and habits masquerading as justifications. Circumstances are the above-water icebergs of reality, and they warrant awareness and navigation, though only a portion of their mass and potential impact may be visible.

Circumstances trigger feelings and behavior patterns that trick us into believing that events and people *make* us react in certain ways. It is not the circumstance or the provocation that forces the response, but the perceptions, emotions, and habits that influence the response. *Circumstances rarely outlast habits. Consequences usually outlast feelings.* A trying circumstance will pass sooner than your practiced and habitual responses to the challenging circumstance usually change. We all tend to use the same tools repeatedly because we are accustomed to them. Feelings, too, are transient, even though they may recur, often unwelcomed. But behaviors acted out in response to emotional provocation tend to result in consequences that have enduring ramifications, long after the feelings have subsided. The repetition of response patterns and feelings are what constitute the habits that determine how you handle adversity.

When you feel victimized (screwed) and become negatively reactive (unglued), you are reinforcing a character of resentment and powerlessness. Life gives us plenty of adversity as practice to develop perseverance, hope, and compassion. We are not owed a prerogative on fairness. Choose to hold fast through adversity by exercising the principles and skills that make you the benevolent commander of your responses.

2004

VIDEO GAMES ARE OCEANS APART

Video games have become a staple in the American sensory and entertainment diet. The interactive animated electronic screen prevails over games and entertainment the way word processing software has essentially replaced typewriters. If video games are the fast food of the mind, then there is mounting evidence that we are filling minds with unhealthy junk and supersizing the delivery to boot. In contrast to other pariahs of the modern age, video game phenomena are largely skewed toward the younger population, particularly children and adolescents.

It is estimated that a staggering 92 percent of young people tune into the virtual worlds of electronic entertainment purveyed on computers, arcades, and electronic gaming devices. In 2003, computer and video game sales generated a whopping $16.9 billion! Amid the hoopla of retail frenzy and controversy about video games, it mostly escapes the professional and lay communities alike that there are video games specifically designed and proven to reduce the risks often associated with and attributed to the video genre. Aside form aesthetic or thematic appeal, video games are not restricted to a single stratum commercial wave that engulfs and drowns its players in a tsunami of mindless capitulation.

There are video games that teach the mind to think, to focus, and to function more flexibly and grow toward greater capacity for learning and self-regulation. This trend unfortunately can become submerged in the tides of digital sensuality swelling from an opposite direction. An anecdote from my college years hints at the paradox of confusing or substituting entities with apparently superficial similarities:

During my graduate studies in the 1970s, I had an erudite professor, well known for his academic work and publications in the field of measurement. Dr. Paul Lohnes was a swarthy and eloquent Irish mentor whose passions waxed redolent of the New England seashore. Lohnes told the story of the time he was encouraged to accept a professorship at Stanford University. He was tempted by the opportunity; as he stood out on the veranda of a Stanford colleague's home, basking in the magnificent view of the mountains and the gentle California air, wooed by the invitation to join a prestigious faculty, Lohnes wistfully declined.

"I dunno," Lohnes pined, "Stanford is wonderful and all, but it's just too far from the ocean."

His colleague rallied with rebuttal: "Well, Paul, you don't have to live in Palo Alto. Lots of people make the commute from around Santa Cruz, where you're right by the ocean. Or you could live..."

"No, no, no," Lohnes interrupted. "Not that ocean—*The* ocean!"

Perspective looms significantly over interpretation, and the frame of reference makes a difference. In the world of video game effects on brain functioning, different types of games are indeed oceans apart. It behooves consumers, parents, educators, and other professionals to survey the software landscape with an eye toward the geography of behavior and the topography of brainwaves while surfing the digital age.

The miniaturization and sophistication of digital electronics has done more than create virtual worlds. Whereas my grandmother used to marvel at black-and-white television, questioning how they got the little people inside those small boxes, now the mature generations warn us against the evils of computer addiction, the escalation of copycat violence and insensitivity, and the dissipation of real relationships in trade for gaming escapades and instant messaging.

Professionals and the consumer public tend to regard video games as entertainment run amok, a dark side of technology indulging and reinforcing a cavalcade of fringe and mainstream young minds as prey to the spell of make-believe lives. The method of quieting Johnny on those long car rides is the invidious electronic companion that will crowd out the reality of homework, chores, sports, and relationships, and it eventually may extrude upon the steering wheel itself as Johnny eventually sits behind it as he drives in traffic. Indeed, potentially a deal with the Devil himself.

There is, however, a flip side to *Mutant Forces of the Avenger*, *Bloody Vampire Sequel*, or whatever is currently selling at the outlets. More than a silver lining in the clouds, the video games that productively train minds (using operant conditioning of brainwaves) are perhaps the most effective direct use of technology's creative and productive purposes. As an analog, we can cite the dubious programming on commercial TV to justify disparaging video culture, or we can exalt the same technology that allows us to benefit from microsurgeries, to control astronomical instruments from millions of miles distant, or to review the action of a sports event, crime, or undersea adventure. And yes, we can not only take pictures of the brain, but we can transform those pictures in virtually real time so that children can watch them as characters of their own brain activity, which they can modify to improve their brains, their behavior, and their lives.

This type of video game playing is done in conjunction with training the EEG. Known as EEG biofeedback, EEG neurofeedback, or just simply biofeedback or neurofeedback, these games train and condition brainwaves while children operate them remotely by sending electrical signals from their scalps. In these games, the operation, the brain involvement, and the aftereffects are quite different from the entertainment genre.

The differences between video games as entertainment and video games as brain training are summarized as follows:

Entrainment versus operant conditioning for flexibility

Arcade-style and role-playing commercial video games generally have the effect upon the brain known as *entrainment.* This means that the stimulus (the game) essentially recruits brain circuits into a pattern that matches the electrical rhythms of the stimulus. Quite literally, the brain of a player really involved in the video game begins to tune to the electrical frequencies generated by the game. It becomes habit-forming and, in many instances, is quite pleasurable to the player. This "programming" is not peculiar to video games, but it plays a role in other activities we consider harmless or even useful. For instance, when you find yourself moving to the beat of a familiar song, it is because you are entrained to the frequencies generated by the music—that is, your brain is syncing up to an external frequency.

High sensory stimulation versus sensory modulation

The big draws in commercial video games are realistic graphics and high sensory stimulation. This "realism" may temporarily satisfy the ubiquitous addictive cravings for stimulation; unfortunately, their energy consumption of computer processing power and programming genius does not translate into lasting concentration or edification of the game players. Instead, this attraction leads to more addictive craving for such stimulation (which may be good for the computer game business, but is not so healthy for consumers).

By contrast, neurofeedback games use interesting, yet rather basic graphics and sounds to promote *sensory modulation*—the awareness and control of subtle changes and differences in *state,* the arousal level of the mind and body that reflects attention, alertness, perception, and mood. With regard to the state of boredom and need for stimulation or entertainment, commercial video games tend to offer a fleeting fix for the craving, whereas neurofeedback games actually fix the insatiable need or craving. Learning to control and modulate inner state has profound positive impact upon one's ability to adjust to circumstances and to levels of stimulation that may not be optimal (such as "boring" schoolwork).

Punishment (direct and vicarious modeling) versus shaping

A major concern about computer gaming is the amount and realism of violence that permeate most games. The pundits claim that this is surely setting bad examples (at the least) and more than likely tied to directly to increases in aggression and its expression in real life. The argument against video violence is that it desensitizes players to violence and suffering and that it both models aggressive punishment and provides encouragement (in the form of game points and victories) for such console behavior. In other words, the whole idea in playing many of these games is to punish your opponent. In so doing, you hone skills and demonstrate mastery, all the while discarding empathy as a relevant emotion. After all, it's just a game, right?

In neurofeedback games, there is neither violence nor punishment. Game characters and objects do not get hurt, killed, or eliminated. Game success is simply represented by adduced points, faster movement, and particular displays of sounds and graphics. Better brain activity is rewarded in combination with consistency and sustained performance in a process known as *shaping*. Irrelevant or undesirable response patterns are simply ignored (or unrewarded). Although superficially simple, both the programming and the effects on human behavior with these games are far more complex and adaptive than that of typical commercial games, wherein faulty moves result in punishment or game termination.

In order to behave correctly and effectively, people must respond to challenges more flexibly and constructively than by shooting them down or destroying them. When poor or wrong responses are punished, people tend to become, anxious, aggressive, inhibited, or helpless.

Thus, engaging with a video game that only rewards appropriate moves but does not penalize inappropriate ones has a vastly different effect on brain capacity, stability, and motivation.

Competitive win-lose versus self-paced self-regulation

Generically, video games carry the objective of winning—defeating either one or several opponents or the computer itself. In neurofeedback, there is no "winning" in the traditional sense (or losing, either). Success derives from "observing" the game, thereby practicing increasing control over one's brain activity.

Imaginary experience and pseudo-control versus real body experience and self-control

People enjoy fantasy and escape. Without question, the computer age has progressively heightened and variegated the types of such entertainment and the opportunities for its distribution. Fantasy is a useful tool in stress reduction, play, and human psychological development. Like other palliatives and escapes, imaginary experience can substitute for the necessary (and rewarding) realities of actual experiences. Though not limited to the domain of video games, the temptations to overindulge in imaginary life increase with our use of technology.

Neurofeedback training promotes the exact opposite of escape. Ironically, changing brain state exerts its relieving effects whether it happens through diminution or augmentation of present conditions of reality! Whereas the phantasmagoric possibilities that commercial games materialize through simulation provide entertainment and respite, the necessary cost is suspension of reality. Conversely, neurofeedback creates this effect by immersion and reinforcement of the *present*—a state of brain awareness so often muddied by inadequate neuronal regulation that transport to proper regulation causes people to feel rested and recharged.

Training vigilant high-adrenaline emotional state (stress) versus training relaxation responses to challenge

As discussed above, people become conditioned to high-alert internal states. After a while, the nervous system recognizes such stressed states as frames of reference for "normal" and seeks and relies upon adrenaline rushes to maintain these states. This habit is deleterious to the body and deceptive to the mind.

Commercial video games capitalize on this addictive need in much the same way as junk food purveyors cater to our yen for sugar and fat cravings. The cycle feeds and escalates itself.

Neurofeedback, on the other hand, develops a different cycle. By playing games that reinforce only health-promoting and adaptive responses to challenges, children and adults can easily train themselves to relax and focus while finding and producing the most effective and appropriate responses to the situational demands.

Addictive tolerance effects versus generalizable enduring effects

A significant problem with many things that feel good is that, over time, you need more of them to induce the accustomed effect. Pleasurable and salutary benefits aside, actions and substances must often be intensified to obtain desired outcome. Whether gaming or medicating, jolting or relaxing, habit usually breeds tolerance (acclimatization that results in the need for increased amounts to get the previous effect). Thus, players anticipate and may require heightened levels of intensity, speed, violence, realism, or whatever achieves the "wow" threshold.

With neurofeedback, people tend to develop greater sensitivity to their brain states, thus achieving more exquisite control over the cadence of the game. It becomes more enjoyable when you do it better, so novelty yields to self-challenges and self-observations about consistency and mastery. The actual neurological effects are correspondingly different, too. Whereas games that rely on stimulation and novelty for player fulfillment build in their own satiation and obsolescence (paving the way for the next generation of stronger dosage), neurofeedback makes the brain more balanced and normalized in terms of sensitivity and perception. Because both the effects and the game-playing itself deal in the currency of brain state and arousal level, the practice of neurofeedback play generalizes enduringly beyond removal from the game situation. This, too, explains the ubiquitous reduction in dosage need for both prescribed and recreational substances to induce the desired effects.

The digital age is most certainly pressing upon us with its logarithmic presence and its permanence. Video gaming is here, and we had better accommodate the landscape of its variety with suitable vehicles and keen understanding of its neural topography. Whether you are preoccupied with the dangers of terrain or just interested in brain reactions and entertainment, it is wise to recognize that video games are indeed oceans apart.

2008
Getting to the bottom of disputes.

TWO LIES AND THE TRUTHS THAT BELIE THEM

Among the disparate experiences that make people think they are different, there are two deceptions surprisingly common enough in human affairs to unite us and provide comfort and connection. These are lies that filter through the complex variations and peculiarities that comprise family culture and dysfunction.

These two lies—which usually begin with well-intentioned parental efforts—become reinforced and internalized as we grow up and find confirmation of what we believe about ourselves. The lies are:

1. You are special.
2. Nothing you can do is good enough.

You are special—This is a theme, repeated in love and nurturing, usually from one parent. It is the redundant mantra mothers often intone that builds the bond of protection, connection, and trust with a child.

My mother frequently told me how special I was, and I, of course, believed her. After all, mothers don't lie (about important things). To whit, my mother's repetitive observations also reflected her good judgment. Being special, I thought—consciously or otherwise—that I should receive special treatment. Thus, I developed an attitude of entitlement, the expectation that I should be treated well and considered ahead of others. Over time, the manifestations of this mindset ranged from impatience at having to wait (for anything) to righteous indignation at the slightest suggestion that someone else's point of view should prevail.

My special status was its own gift, substituting for intimacy and frequently justifying the isolation and emptiness I felt when faced with the conclusion that others simply couldn't handle the brusque inequities and their own place in the hierarchy that my perceptions divined. Being special also entailed unusual honors that logically accompany privilege: feelings of separation and burden of being envied. Ironically, only those who were special and those who recognized these privileges could appreciate this plain truth.

You might be among the select elite who are fortunate enough to appreciate this. Perhaps you are one of the chosen few, serendipitously encountering this discovery that you, ahead of others, can acknowledge. If so, you can relate to the onus of rarity that taxes your gifts with the pangs of being misunderstood. Perhaps we are kindred souls, and the empathy I have honed to an art that should have more deserving recipients finds you sharing the lonesome indignity of being treated as... *average!*

Nothing you can do is good enough—This is the plaintive cry of the weary, dutiful, and ultimately unappreciated sufferer. Such denizens have long ago dropped any hopes and notions that hard work, forbearance, and persistence will result in the justice of recognition and compensation for efforts. Too much rejection and criticism have reinforced the realism that effaces the remnants of faith, dignity, and self-confidence.

I had ideas about my creativity, motivations, and the fortunate genius that would translate my efforts into practical rewards. However, these inspirations passed for years through the gauntlet of my father's ubiquitous evaluations. Sadly, the dirge-like process eroded my esteem and the erstwhile desire to please and satisfy. Though other people didn't look or sound like my father, apparently his furtive campaign of opinions had prevailed to the point of influence where nobody worthwhile was going to endorse mine.

As you may surmise, the problem is that the standards of others are unreasonable. Herculean efforts and the patience of Job cannot satisfy the demands and whimsy of those who require my allegiance—and I am good, but not yet legendary. Furthermore, sensibility demands that unrequited exertion be tempered eventually and that commitment and motivation be tailored appropriately to accommodate negligible results and the due conservation of energy. A person is given a limited amount of resources, and this includes only one ego.

Few detractions can decrease motivation like a person who cannot be satisfied. When it dawns upon you that nothing you can do is good enough, the tendency to try decreases, but the tendency to internalize fault does not. Blaming the other person for unattainable standards and grudging acknowledgment only masks the hurt and guilt caused by knowing your insufficiency. The lie that *nothing you can do is good enough* has a subtext that it is also your fault.

An epitome of this phenomenon occurred to me when I landed a publishing contract for my first book. After signing with a major publisher offering a handsome advance, I proudly told my father about this achievement. His perfunctory congratulation was eclipsed by a quick admonishment and reference to Rudy Giuliani, the former New York mayor who had just signed a $2 million book deal at the height of his popularity after 9/11. Dad thought I could do better, and he held out Giuliani as an example. With the bar lifted ever so much higher, I could no longer jump to my father's provocations. Rationally, I knew this was ridiculous and insensitive of him. Emotionally, however, I believed it was my fault that I could never do enough to satisfy him.

Living out the details of these two fundamental lies affects character. In my case, being special—yet never doing well enough—resulted in the development of hobbies that sustain me. Among these are:

- *Collecting injustices*—the satisfying, though pungent, process of reviewing, refining, and extending the list of resentments, grievances, and notations of those who have failed to heed my special status. In my more reflective moods, I know that this is a major symptom of my diagnosis of Righteous Indignation.

- *Worrying about things that are not going to happen*—this goes beyond prudent caution or sensible preparation. This hobby (which seems, subjectively, more like an obligation) is an outgrowth of *not being good enough* to prevent bad things from happening. It is the fantasy world of control freak wannabes.

- *Planning to do insignificant tasks and feeling guilty and obsessed with them*—the to-do lists of those *who are special* carry an urgency preemptive of relaxation and the habit of putting other people first. The importance of organizing my records, replacing lights or fixing gadgets, generating music playlists, ordering items, complaining to the utility companies or other organizations who overlooked the value of having me as a customer, filing papers, cleaning the garage, checking my gas mileage, etc. underestimates the amount of attention it requires to remember them, much less to do them. Their existence (albeit, mostly in my mind) provides confirmation that nothing I can do is good enough—which should be humbling, yet, strangely, is not.

Decades of living disabused my acceptance of these two lies, as told, and also eroded my compulsive (and largely subconscious) need to act out the false beliefs. The disappointments suffered and growth sustained eventually showed me that I was like other people in more ways than I was different and that my determination and competencies could prevail consistently enough to warrant genuine appreciation and recognition that remained credible even to me. A handsome interaction arose from the double defeat of being special and not being good enough: The better I felt about myself and proved to be, the less need I had to assert special privilege.

Ingrained habits die hard, though, even the habit of blaming those believed to have instilled the bad habits! My old nature pulls me, at times, toward narcissistic self-pity, self-righteous justification, and idolatrous absorption in solipsistic preoccupations.

Fortunately, I have a new nature, one that lifts me from the ashes of hopelessness and defeat and allows me to see and reinterpret truth and falsehood—what's actually so in a world of fragmented light, shifting shadows, and the confusion of lies that belie the truth.

If you are truly special (which I trust, since you are reading this), then you will appreciate the real truth about the lies that may have taken you captive, too.

***You are special*—the TRUTH**—The fact is that you and I *are* special, but not in the self-centered way that we fancy. We are special because God created each of us. Out of all the permutations and possibilities in nature, we exist. Each of us is unique, yet we share many commonalities as humans and inhabitants of a universe that God claims as his own. Each of us is a created being, a reflection of the Creator who says that each of us is special. He gives each of us particular gifts and hardships, and He knows what is in store for us. He is *always* there to guide and support us, and His promises to care and provide supersede any fear, anxiety, self-pity, or doubt about our importance as individuals.

Our special status confers value in distinction, individuality, and relevance, but not in superiority. The lie about special status is that it bequeaths privilege in pride and hierarchy. This lie requires constant verification through social deference. The truth about special status is that it doesn't require circumstantial confirmation. Surely, we all appreciate recognition and honor, acknowledgment and inclusion. The need for preferential treatment, however, is a type of bondage, an enslavement to the caprice and opinions of others. The truth about being special—that in God's view, you are indeed very special and precious—is tremendously liberating. When you have the security of belonging to God and reveling in your importance to Him, the need for preferential treatment wanes and the locus of identity shifts from recognition and deference by others to recognition of and deference to God.

***Nothing you can do is good enough*—the TRUTH**—In your own power, you will ultimately fall short. Though you may possess great talent and resources, self-sufficiency is basically a developmental principle that becomes saddled with grandiose expectations, illusory values, and achievements that lose satisfaction. If you are fortunate as well as special, you will experience your limitations and brokenness as gifts, allowing you to realize that good and competent and well-meaning are not enough: there will always be dissatisfaction, unmet needs and expectations, circumstances that cannot be mastered, and people who cannot be pleased.

This reality can become twisted into the lie of self-criticism, fault and blame, and the consequent inability to please and serve. This is the lie construed from the comments and intimations of others. It is strengthened by the combination of dependence upon external approval and recognition (even worship) and the prideful crediting of self as the generator of creation and resources.

As you wonder whether you are—or can be—good enough, consider the evidence aside from your own and others' evaluations of your efforts: God has made payment for all your debts and faults. All He asks is that you acknowledge this profound gift, the ultimate donation made in your name and in the names of others who accept it.

Needing God and other people (who are also gifted and special) is the legacy of human connectedness. You may be good enough to reach goals, attain positions, and overcome obstacles. Your skills may be applauded, and that is excellent and deserving testimony to your efforts and gifts. At the end of the day, however, you are no better or worse to God than those with lesser glitter or competence. The greatest lesson in equality is that it is not possible to buy or perform one's way into what truly matters.

God is the teacher of this lesson, along with the corollary that, although nothing you can do is good enough, *you are* good enough and what you do with God's strength will suffice.

Some people will recognize this truth and some will believe in the lies. How do I know this? Because God says so. That's what makes me special and good enough.

BEST FRIENDS FOREVER

Playdates with God

When my wife and I were courting, we talked about ourselves, what each of us wanted from a relationship, about children and parents, what friendship means, and about marriage. I promised to be faithful, but confided that I was already heavily involved in two other relationships: my betrothal to God and my involvement in my work. I let it be known that my commitments were to God, family, and work, in that order.

I had long ago come out of the (prayer) closet about my relationship with Jesus and my lifestyle. Fortunately and necessarily, my wife felt the same way. We became best friends. In my book, *Staying Madly in Love With Your Spouse: Guide to a Happier Marriage*, I discuss many facets of intimate relationships, including parents, children, and spouses. The last chapter is entitled "Best Friends Forever." Having a best friend (or series of them) is a sweet and penultimate experience of intimacy, a bonding that makes life so much more worthwhile and rewarding.

Best friends share trust, affection, rock-solid companionship, and fascinating life experiences. Best friends learn to be selective and to discriminate between people they can depend on and people with whom they have less exclusive relationships. Developing friendships and having a best friend emerge from the ranks of these friendships rates among the most treasured joys in this life. Not that "best" friendships are without strife, jealousy, competition, and insecurity. Nonetheless, the emotional roller coaster that often comes with attachment is worth it.

Best friends love to spend time together. From childhood forward, we copy what we like, see, and experience, and we practice on the people we know. Socialization takes lots of practice and is fueled by the desire to exchange love and affection, establish competence and worthiness, and be truly known and accepted. These days, social arrangements for children are often called playdates. In my childhood, this term was not used. Had the word been around, it would have been no more a part of our actual lives than "quiche" or "cappuccino." Still, we had friends, best friends, social groups and pecking orders. Our "playdates" were not known as such, but kids gravitated toward those they liked and wanted to be around. Of course, there were in crowds and outcasts.

When I was growing up in the Bronx, the in crowd was called the "gang," though that word did not have the same connotation and activities it does today—we lacked violence (in addition to quiche and cappuccino). One's rank and status in the gang was determined mostly by athletic prowess and devotion to sports, verbal skills, one's age, and how protective or laissez-fair one's parents were. Weirdness to a certain degree was tolerated, but it factored in well behind the other social measures.

I remember a boy named Jeffrey who was a big kid and kind of an awkward klutz. He was an outsider. There was nothing overly wrong with him—he just didn't quite fit in. In those days and in that environment, kids often appealed for companionship and activities by standing outside the window of a friend's apartment and calling up for the friend to "come down." Jeffrey often stood outside windows, looking forlorn and calling and waiting for someone to come down and play. I remember one cold winter day, staring at him alone in the cold outside and beneath my third-floor window. My mother came over and noticed. "Poor Jeffrey," she said, "he probably has a lousy home life, just wants to get away from his parents, and doesn't have anywhere to go." As my mother looked over my shoulder at lonely Jeffrey, I silently turned crimson with rage and confusion. *No, Mom, I'm the one with a lousy home life. I'd like to be out there with Jeffrey, and if you weren't so overprotective, I could go down and play. He may be a little strange, but I'd rather be outside with him than cooped up here with you and your watchfulness and opinions.*

Decades later, my life and professional experiences have convinced me that all families are dysfunctional to certain degrees. I also know that we desperately need friends, best friends, and that we wade through competition and pecking orders to establish identities and worthiness. We drag parts of the dysfunction with us, hoping that very little of it shows and, especially, that our best friends won't care about those parts of us.

Back in the Bronx, I played high school basketball for the Bronx High School of Science. I wore a team jacket, a status symbol of the green and gold. It was a mixed blessing: I felt proud, but some people ridiculed me. To some, I probably looked like a prideful yokel, a short white kid in a borrowed leisure suit, prematurely playing the role of a "wild and crazy guy" Yortzig brother character of future *Saturday Night Live* shows. Perhaps some were envious. There were always tough guys waiting to beat up the vulnerable. I managed to escape physical assault, but I was often called names, especially the ones considered slurs against gay people today. I didn't have any best friends on the team. It was all about winning, impressing the coach, and competing for playing time. The subway rides to games at inner-city high schools in the South Bronx, Harlem, and Bedford-Stuyvesant were fraught with apprehension. Wearing my jacket into these hostile environments was scary. These were tests of survival, not playdates.

And yet God was watching over me, preparing me through trials to seek and value true and rewarding friendship. God anticipated the time in later years I would seek him, recognizing and welcoming his presence and playdates.

Just the other day, I had a great playdate with God. This one included my friend John, a brother for over twenty years. John is my barber and has also been my realtor. He is a fellow Christian and a true friend. He's very outspoken and opinionated. He has enough guts and drive to be successful and also conspicuous flaws that make him vulnerable. I love John's integrity and dedication and also the way he "gets it" about people's tendency to feel entitled. John has wonderful sayings. I especially like this one:

"I'd like to buy you for what you're *really* worth and sell you for what you *think* you're worth."

As you might imagine, John can rub people the wrong way. On this recent encounter, he lamented again that he turned some people off and away by talking about Jesus. As he cut my hair, he said, "But, *Jesus*, how can you *not* talk about Jesus when you know him?"

Amen!

For me, the tentative days of worrying about what people will think if I express my faith are long gone. Thank God! My testimony tends to reflect role modeling and talking about my own growth rather than preaching. I try to be supportive, strong, and compassionate, hoping that people will feel this love and ask how I can be this way. Then I can explain my friendship with God and how I want to give others what God gives me. Yet I know that many people do and will reject my message. Not everyone will like me, but I've learned to accept that. In seeking acceptance, it is tempting and seductive to seek human adulation, but such pursuit can be burdensome and even become idolatry. The habit of coveting diminishes joy.

I treasure my playdates with God, and they are usually better when others join. On this same day when God made his presence available to me, God was also with me in Starbucks. I noticed a flyer on the bulletin board announcing "The Self-Love Diet: The Only Diet That Works." I thought to myself: *The Only Diet That Works…REALLY?* And then I envisioned a flyer saying *Jesus: The Only Way to Get to Heaven.* Someone else might look skeptically at such an announcement, just as I had judged the diet flyer. After all, don't we all think we're right? That we can discern the one and only way?

It's not *my* way that's right. It's not my promotion, but rather Jesus's proclamation on behalf of his father, my father, our Father—the one who adopted me out of my dysfunctional family into his family of God. The one who calls me down to play and often joins me. My best friend forever.

2014

BLUETOOTH BATHROOMS

Saving Waste With Technology

Excuse me, I have to go to the bathroom. This might take awhile—not because I have a plumbing or digestive problem; those things still work fine for me. It's the bathroom itself that gives me problems.

It used to be that using a bathroom outside the home was straightforward: no need to think or plan after you located the appropriate one for your gender. Perhaps you've noticed that things have changed. Technology has crept into restrooms, and unevenly so. This is what makes for unsettling confusion.

It started some years ago with the restricted dispensation of paper towels near the sinks. At first, the hand crank on the towel dispenser became stingier, rolling out one sheet at a time and making you wait (and work) to crank out another paper towel. I am not profligate, but it often takes three or four of these towels to get my hands dry. Some bathrooms switched to air-blowing dryers in place of paper towels—a cool idea, unless you place your hands too close to the blower and risk a burn in the effort to dry your hands. (Those blowers *seem* to take a long time.) The air blowers do dry the hands, but somehow are not as satisfying as wiping with towels. They are supposed to be more sanitary—but what about the large silver button that everyone's hands touch to start the air blow dryer?

These days, many of the air blow dryers are motion activated by placing your hands under the sensor. That helps, but it seems that bathrooms vary widely in the innovations and instruments they install. This makes for confusion. No doubt, you've noticed the proliferation of motion activated faucets at the sinks. Again, cool… but sometimes not warm enough to satisfy my need for a really warm hand-washing. And haven't you noticed that some sinks require that you press a button, and some that you place your hands *just so* under a sensor you cannot see? In both cases, the stream of water is metered out so that one stream is rarely enough.

Adding to the confusion are the soap dispensers. Each time I visit a bathroom, I have to figure out or remember: do I press on the soap dispenser or just wait with upturned hands like a surgeon in a scrub routine? Often I stand waiting with wet hands facing upward, expecting soap or perhaps the Lord's acknowledgment. Eventually, I figure out that the dispenser can't read my mind or sense my hands. I press the knob and get rewarded by a pink glob. There seems to be no coordination among bathroom appurtenances. Are there design consultants for public bathrooms?

I am all for conservation. I get it: we need to be conscious and ecological in saving resources. But the whole bathroom "movement" in this regard is confusing and disconcerting. I cannot tell or predict what I'll be required to do or not do once I enter the lavatory. The latest innovation seems to be motion sensitive lights. This is a great invention for hands-free illumination and is also another potential savings on the proliferation of germs. Doesn't stop me from banging on the wall next to the door, though, especially on my way out. I wonder how many others slam the wall switch out of habit or frustration?

And yes: the toilets themselves! How did we ever live without self-flushing toilets? Here's where it gets a bit personal: forgive me for boldly approaching the scatological, but Number 1 and Number 2 are sacred and sensitive rituals. I detest having motion sensitive (*too sensitive*) toilets whoosh away my waste before I am ready, simply because some unaccountable distance was sensed between it's eager mechanisms and my privates. And if I happen to not be *finished*, then we are not saving water after all. I confess to occasionally getting even with the self-appropriating toilets by approaching and backing away repeatedly in order to have a sense of control with cause and effect flushing. It's childish, I know, but I do get a kick out of it. I'm like a boxer in the stall, feinting, ducking, daring my opponent to swallow in impulsive reaction. *Float like a butterfly, sting like a BM.* Remember a generation ago the big silver buttons on the back of the toilets that you kicked in order to flush? Now that was weird (and satisfying).

So the public bathroom situation is perplexing. I find myself frequently standing in front of an appliance, waiting for it to flush, blow, rinse, or light. I feel stupid about this and also technologically challenged about these "bluetooth bathrooms." If we have to go the way of hands-free, I'd like some consistency and standardization. I'm tired of tentatively approaching a fixture that used to present no issues, often to be unexpectedly sprayed, squirted, blown, or—worse—ignored as I fumble around looking for a lever, a switch, or some mysterious invisible sensor.

I suppose that "hands-free" will be the new norm and gateway into the ecological "handling" of our waste. Less product, more infra-red, and more Bluetooth wireless. We are increasingly used to that with phones. It's still unnerving. Picture me standing at a urinal next to a man gesticulating and shouting feverishly, "It's okay—I'm *handling it,* okay?" Frightened initially, I quickly realized that he was speaking metaphorically into his earpiece while talking on a cell phone. I trusted that he was handling the manual aspect of his business at the urinal. (Okay, I borrowed that one from humorist Dave Barry. But Dave has no doubt been frightened in many bathrooms and stolen that line himself.)

I know I will adjust. Technology brings mostly good things and convenience. But going to the bathroom should be as private and personal as can be. What could be next? Motion sensitive zippers? I am a bit apprehensive about the possibility of Bluetooth jeans.

2011

TISSUE OVERHEAD, TISSUE UNDERNEATH

The woman sobbed as she sat across from me. Instinctively, I leaned forward and handed her the box of tissues that she grabbed with a desperate admixture of appreciation and embarrassment. Several minutes into her weeping, the tissues ran out. Her plaintive pleas and confessions sputtered on as I listened solicitously. I became distracted, though, by the parade of tissues emerging from the box to escort tears in the processional across her lap and trailing off the couch. With growing concern, I watched the tissues disappear as the woman fumbled into the box, sniffling and emotionally exposed. In a moment of quizzical tension she stopped and looked to me in appeal, the awkward discomfort palpable as if a magician had suddenly run out of tricks.

There were no more tissues, and so, temporarily, the act was interrupted. This was my theater, the environs of the therapy office: I, the master of ceremonies, producer, audience, and critic all at once—a mesmerizing mélange of roles supervised with paternal compassion.

In that awkward moment when the tissues depleted, I mused silently over the mainstay prop that had for so long depicted my profession. Traditionally, tissues were the overhead of therapists, the gauze for staunching the flow of emotional wounds upon the compassionate ears of the putative healer.

Cotton tissues: a sparse costume and cheap overhead indeed for the esoteric art and dance of catharsis and healing. As the tissues become soiled, absorbing the conflicted confessions of weepers, the transformation occurs: besotted mucus escorts unveiling the liberated smiles of knowing insight and resolve. Or so we hope and even pretend.

The paper tissues of catharsis are readily consumed and must be replenished; the therapist serves as the vendor of relief, the receptacle of sorrows, and the purveyor and modulator of emotional equanimity and dependence. It is tough and wearing work, and terribly inefficient also, somewhat like tailing a person learning to ride a bicycle, making sure he doesn't fall.

In its contemporary mainstream incarnation, symptomatic relief is also dependent and disposable: drugs and medicines propel and brake the nervous system, and the external tissue box is replaced by the pill box. It is a system of palliative respite where cause and effect remain mysterious, circumstantial, or fabricated.

As a psychologist, I deal daily with human emotion and behavior, with the abstract depths of motivation and intent, and with the surface pragmatics of habit, frustration, destructiveness, and conflict. I practice—in scrambling parts—the salvage of the past, the repair of the present, and the architecture of the future. I play the courier of the mind, content and context, a persuader and comforter, an inspirational security who blends sales and science to nurture hope and effective change in my confidants. In so doing, I've discovered I need more than tissues in my toolbox and insight as my guide.

For decades, I've utilized the emerging discoveries and tools of neuroscience to bolster and supplant the pearls of wisdom that counseling supposedly provides. Though human nature stubbornly prevails, the methods of managing its complexities have evolved. (As a parallel, the elegance and utility of language continue intact, but quills and typewriters have yielded to digital communications using the same symbols and meanings, but with different transmissions and distributions.)

To access the tissue underneath—that is, the matrix of neurons and cells within the brain and nervous system—we use technology. The brain performs via timing mechanisms and electrical impulses that modulate chemical interactions and action potentials, which are the trigger mechanisms that determine the inhibition or activation of behaviors including thoughts, feelings, motor actions, perceptions, attention, and even hormonal secretions. These timing mechanisms can be influenced and modified by computers interacting with a person's conscious and subconscious flow of attention and electricity. The practice of training the brain in this manner—monitoring and modifying the EEG—is called *neurofeedback.* Training via this modality alters and restores the brain's capacity and efficiency to regulate itself, thus relieving and diminishing frustration, impulsivity, anxiety and depression, and other symptoms resulting from or associated with nervous system irregularity or dysfunction.

There are other advanced methods of rapidly and dramatically eliminating illogical and typically inaccessible and recalcitrant disturbances such as phobias and traumas. For example, Thought Field Therapy quickly eliminates negative emotions by determining and targeting the codes by which the body and brain store and retain associations that maintain unpleasant symptoms. By identifying the code sequences—most efficiently through the voice using Voice Technology—and tapping precise sequences along the body's meridians, we can deprogram and unlock the alarm system that keeps traumas, fears, anxieties, and emotional blockages (even resentment, lack of forgiveness, anger, and procrastination) stuck and debilitating in its victims.

Ironically, even as this "symptomatic" and physiological approach to treatment relieves a broad spectrum of anguish, it opens the way to developing insight, perspective, emotional sentience, flexibility, and self-awareness—the very goals of insight-oriented or cognitive behavioral "talk" therapy. The treatment is self-sustaining in the manner of other acquired and self-reinforcing skills like driving or riding a bicycle.

It is hard to find a downside to these described neuroscientific methods of accessing and capitalizing on the brain's inherent plasticity—unless you are invested in consumer dependence and disposable chemistry. In light of the dynamic and effective neuroscience methods of retraining the brain, perhaps the pharmaceutical industry should collude with the makers of paper products to produce recyclable rags—stem-cell Kleenex to fortify the therapist's arsenal.

There will always be the necessity of human touch, comfort, and connection in relationship as healing transpires. But we need not cloak this natural process in the vestments of psychoanalytic theory or chemical control. It is enough to be there as a person and a guide and facilitate nature doing its work.

Examining and auditing the past can become an obsessive trap, like inspecting and interpreting the spewed wet tissues for some phlegm-blot clues to unlock the shackles of dysfunction. Instead, we need to focus on the present and visit the dynamic processes of the tissue underneath; for it is the circuitry of brain function, the bits and bytes of storage and transmission that hold the keys to release from habit bondage and into the flexibility of meaningful behavior change. The science and chemistry that gave us disposable tissues is also giving us disposable traumas.

The paper tissue still consoles the tears of sorrow that accompany this complicated life. But the undergirding healing comes from changes in tissue underneath, the sweeping software upgrade and debugging that transforms our ways of processing information and interacting with the world. The tearing wounds will sew themselves as the brain rebuilds its unity and wholeness, much as skin stitches itself anew when allowed the proper environment and protection to do its job.

The weeping patient sheds the soiled pulp tissue and reconstructs the tissue underneath, weaving an improved and strengthened fabric of existence. It is the smile of sunshine replacing the rain.

1990

RAISING GRADES AND CONTROVERSY

My topic this month will probably irritate some readers, especially those with a vested interest in the educational status quo. Critics will probably concede, however, that my suggestions on the topic of grading could be implemented next week without one cent of additional cost.

Grades may wield more power and cause more conflict than any other educational issue. Grades influence family communications, student self-esteem and motivation, teacher control, and an array of restrictions and opportunities for students. Despite this importance, grading practices are woefully inconsistent and lacking in validity and justification.

In order to make sense of this, we must examine grades in light of several criteria:

1. For what purpose(s) are grades used?
2. What is the method by which grades are assigned?
3. How are grades matched with student performances?

Grades are supposed to reflect student performance. Technically, the value of any grading system rests in its function of measuring the extent to which students master instructional objectives. However, grading practices typically address concerns that are tangential to measuring academic learning. These concerns involve controlling students, discriminating among students for selection or admission, and describing the extent to which students have satisfied their teachers' demands.

Conventional educational theories recognize several systems of grading: norm-referenced (competitive), criterion-referenced (absolute value), mastery (pass-fail, pass-incomplete), and written evaluation. Most teachers can describe their bases for assigning grades; on the surface, many descriptions seem sensible. However, when asked to explain which model their grading practices fit and exactly how such practices best evaluate their students' achievement of instructional objectives, most teachers will evade reasonable answers.

Even when grading systems reflect sensible educational concepts, there remains the persistent problem that, in practice, students and parents are unaware of the relationships among performance, expectations, and grades. Typically, students do not know what grade their performances are earning until the report card comes—often with surprise!

Can you imagine working at a job without knowing how much you will be paid, when you will be paid, or what exactly you must do to earn more? Picture your paycheck docked because someone spelled words better than you did. If it sounds ridiculous, consider that this is how most contemporary grading practices treat our children. Besides their irrelevance to the main purpose of evaluating student achievement of instructional objectives, contemporary grading practices undermine equal opportunity by discriminating arbitrarily among individuals. In addition, typical grading procedures are based on the assumption that everyone cannot or should not succeed in each course—an unethical assumption in a country in which the school's purpose is to give each child the basic skills and attitudes that will allow him to define success for himself.

For those readers who believe strongly in the virtues of our present educational grading practices, I have a suggestion: let your children or students grade you on your parenting or teaching; send those grades into the DMV, and have the DMV affix your grade to both your driver's license and your license plates. Only those adults with As will be permitted to drive independently.

1995

BILATERAL EDUCATION

Integrating the Third World of Logic with Indigenous Hemispheres

There is a story about a cat that protected her kittens from a prowling dog. Upon the dog's advances, the cat barked ferociously until the dog backed away. Returning to her kittens, the cat instructed, "It's good to know a second language."

The animated arguments over bilingual education bend logic with similar requests for breaches of reality. The assumptions imposed are convenient to circumstances. In its stereotyped extreme, this divisive rhetoric would classify learners into different and exclusive species. Such logic is specious, of course. More importantly, the bilingual education controversy displaces a truly relevant educational issue that pedagogy seldom acknowledges and rarely accommodates: *bilateral education*—the teaching and development of both sides of the brain in accord with measured individual differences and curriculum-equated modifications.

Despite ideological and methodological differences, bilingual education and bilateral education share a common departure from curriculum-as-usual. Each approach features a rationale suggesting that sustained and systematic learning will be effective only to the extent that it occurs within the context of the students' needs, orientation, and entering behaviors. Bilingualists vehemently evince language as the central focus; for bilateralists, it is the corpus callosum. For bilingualists, hemispheric pertinence is cultural; for bilateralists, it is anatomical. Bilingualists recognize a third world denoting people of color from developing nations. Bilateralists are concerned with the gray matter of developing brains and the integration of both hemispheres with the third world of reasoning, logical analysis, and cause-and-effect thinking.

The bilingualists' vocal prominence and the growing filibuster and infiltration of bilingual education merit a consideration of the arguments, which basically involve the following:

1. Its soundness in principle and effectiveness in producing desired learning outcomes
2. Its financial viability and merit as policy worthy of resource allocation

Advocates for bilingual education claim that children who lack English fluency suffer the deprivation of skills acquisition when in mainstream American society.

The arguments are reminiscent of whether it is better to learn to drive with the steering wheel on the left or right, with a standard or automatic transmission, etc. Realistically, these particulars are more stylistic idiosyncrasies than they are relevant determinants of competent driving performance. From a practical or monetary standpoint, a student driver may well have to learn in his own circumstances and later make the transition to a different vehicle or set of road rules. Alternatively, he will likely have to adjust to the conventions of his immediate surroundings. The overriding principle is that he must learn a set of techniques and then adapt them within a framework of rules to a variety of changing conditions. How adept he is in this process is a function of variables more significant than where the steering wheel or transmission is located. Ergonomics may be helpful but are rarely determinant. Whether driving or learning in a native or foreign situation, those with flexibility have an easier time of it and usually perform better.

Like the driver in our example, the learner needs a variety of specific and combined skills. He must be alert, understand signals and symbolic meaning, anticipate and plan, attend to relevant stimuli, negotiate time and space, know consequences and limits, and compensate for the mistakes of himself and others.

Individual differences characteristically reflect a distribution of relative successes among life's variety of demands and challenges. Ability levels, neurological makeup, brain organization, and reinforcement contingencies are far more predictive of successful learning outcomes than are language or cultural curriculum.

The plaintive rhetoric of *Why can't Johnny read?* balances its counterpart: *Why can't Jose find his homework?* The answers probably lie more in the way their brains work than in the political expediency of familiar educational policies. Johnny may have trouble reading because he is dyslexic or attention-deficient, and traditional teaching methods and curricula do little to help him work around this problem. Jose may lose his homework because of visuospatial processing weaknesses that make him disorganized and prone to overlook or misplace things.

The bilingualist argument that a limited English-speaking student cannot participate in an English class discussion about literature presupposes that such a student's verbal and inferential skills would permit him to do so in any language. Yet the overwhelming evidence is that cognitive abilities (differential abilities and neuropsychological intactness, not merely IQ) determine success at assimilation and adaptation.

Advocates for minorities often trumpet the assertion that limited English masks the display of intelligence and results in discriminatory assessment. Ironically, bilingual services would facilitate the detection of disabilities, mainly those affecting language and symbolic functions that are usually housed within the left cerebral hemisphere, regardless of culture. Although multilingual fine-tuning in the assessment of linguistic abilities would be useful, such allocation of resources simply defines more clearly the educational challenges facing teachers and students in any tongue. Expertise in assessment and cognitive development already allows us to reliably measure abilities in culture-fair terms. This is true for the domains of verbal, nonverbal, and global abilities—for English and non-English speakers alike.

Proper individual assessment (a vital part of any education) diminishes ethnocentrism with respect to the data that tend to show abilities and deficits distributed with more variability than can be explained by language or culture. The remaining challenges are those of teaching normal and abnormal, English-speaking and non-English-speaking individuals how to think—critically, sensibly, and with perceptual accuracy and discerning judgment. Formal schooling ought to foster the mastery of skills that are critical for efficient thinking, and these skills are taught only in English. They contend that children could learn academic skills more quickly and completely if these skills were taught in their native language over a period of years as the students gradually become better English speakers. According to this theory, youngsters would grow into their English acquisition with a more fully developed set of academic tools honed in their native language before English fluency materialized. Bilingual education proponents claim that it saves money by making third-world students more productive and more independent.

Opponents of bilingual education maintain that it isolates students, impedes English development, hampers assimilation, and reinforces negative stereotypes. They cite generations of immigrants who acclimated to English-only education, despite poverty and different native languages. These immigrants managed to learn skills and English simultaneously, and many of them accelerated to outperform American peers and achieve notably in many areas of learning and effective functioning in everyday life. Among these are:

- Registration of incoming stimuli and understanding of auditory verbal communications
- Ability to attend to relevant stimuli and screen out nonessential stimuli
- Competence in following verbal and written instructions

- Development of abstraction, reasoning, and memory skills
- Accurate comprehension of recurring similarities and differences among objects and events
- Establishment of cause-and-effect thinking
- Ability to develop and apply organizing principles in problem solving
- Ability to generalize and think logically
- Intuitive apprehension of visual and nonverbal stimuli (necessary to picture, sequence, or construct outcomes, as well as to understand how things fit together)—necessary for appreciating the symbolic significance of "people" messages, emotions, and feedback
- Ability to function efficiently in space and time
- Integration of cerebral hemispheric functioning

Bilateral education involves the systematic development and transmission of these basic and required life skills, the underpinnings of any meaningful academic achievement. It is a methodology consistent with human nervous system development, a century of educational, psychological, and behavioral research, and with social conscience and pragmatic need. It is a nonpartisan, scientific, fiscally sound approach that will work in any language and culture (because it is in large part nonverbal and wholly based on biological brain development).

Language is a fundamental and integrated component of human communication, learning, and efficiency—emphasis on "component" and implication of the integrated "whole."

A poorly scripted movie does not fundamentally change when it is dubbed or subtitled. Such language modifications make the movie accessible only to the extent that the plot makes sense and the viewer is able to follow and comprehend the story with its sequences, relationships, and subtleties.

American education is a poorly scripted production—in black-and-white or colorized. Despite a few classics, the education industry relies on illusion and special effects. As in entertainment, budgets influence education, though with little predictive correlation between scale and quality.

At stake are the futures of our pluralistic population and of our society. Special interests compete for the investments of an educational industrial complex that has lost credibility and focus. It's time to teach survival skills in the most basic and productive terms. Cats don't need to bark, but they must do other things. And drivers must mind the road rules, whatever the language or direction.

Without sound methodology for teaching people in accord with their learning needs and abilities, the "bilingual" cat will have no advantage in protecting her kittens. The animals in that story will all be run over by poor drivers on both sides of the road.

2007

FORTUNE COOKIE

Read and Pray

-Amid the hullabaloo over the recent scare about lead-contaminated toys from China, an important threat has been overlooked. This hazard involves another Asian import. First, it was the bird flu, then leaded toys, and now it is the peril of leaching fortune cookies.

Yes, emerging scientific research has uncovered a health hazard from the print on the paper strips inside fortune cookies bleeding into the cookie itself and thereby, unfortunately, into the digestive tracts of unknowing consumers. Though this may seem strange and incredible, new evidence has pointed to the fortune cookie's responsibility for the illness symptoms (and bad fortune) traced to traditional post–Chinese-meal syndrome. This is shocking and disconcerting, since the fortune cookie is as American as Mom, apple pie, baseball, and MSG. Nevertheless, the health risk is great, and the offending agents must be purged.

There appear to be two types of contaminants leaching from the fortunes inside these innocent-looking sugar crisps: toner ink and actual lead. The vast majority of fortune cookies are mass produced and delivered to Chinese restaurants via the wholesale process that gets the myriad delicious and inscrutable ingredients through the back doors of the kitchens so that they can be cooked, assembled, and partitioned into columns with English category headings and alphabetic letters. These cookies come prefabricated with the sugary dough baked around paper strips bearing vague, general, and sometimes syntactically awkward one-sentence harbingers. That cookie fortunes today gravitate toward successful business predictions rather than health and longevity may reflect either the growth of the Asian food industry or the proliferation of gastric accidents and lawsuits. Nevertheless, one is more likely to find "Your next business move will be bold and successful" rather than "You are destined to be happy and healthy."

The real concern, however, is that the nesting of these fortune strips has resulted in the bleeding of toner ink into the cookie itself. Whether it is heat from shipment and storage or the natural decay of cheap printer toner, samples of fortune cookies taken from diverse geographic regions have revealed alarming levels of graphite in the crisps nonchalantly munched by diners as they ironically absorb the same graphite with their eyes that is also filtering through their stomachs.

As if the seemingly innocuous trend of graphite migrating into our guts were not disconcerting enough, the CDC has alerted us to the more disturbing menace of *lead-laced* fortune cookies! This is not the jury-rigged sabotage of terrorists, but rather the handiwork of stylized culinary artisans who personalize their products by hand-printing the fortune strips. Thus, the lead from pencils imprinted upon the strips finds its way into the cookie shell and eventually accumulates in the cells of millions of unsuspecting patrons who repeatedly savor Asian meals.

The rising furor over shoddy standards in the imported toy market has spilled over to the combination plate of a venerable institution: the Chinese meal punctuated by fortune cookies is as dangerous to people of all ages as the Christmas toy is to the child consumer (quite literally).

US administration security departments have diverted attention to the potential threat, heightened at the peak of holidays and gift-giving season. The erstwhile government covert operation of filtering e-mails has shifted to deciphering potential clues contained in fortune cookie messages. Flagged for suspicion were such improbable phrases as "You were born to read" and "All work and no pray not make you happy."

Conspiracy theories aside, we cannot stop the influx of Asian products, people, and influence. Our government should relax the security alert from orange to yellow, since the Asian presence brings unarguably more culture and economy than it does danger. We must not permit any escalation of xenophobia. Still, the risk of lead or graphite-tainted food is not acceptable. Thus, the conundrum of potential solutions carries the familiar morass of stereotypes and political correctness. Should we ban fortunes inside cookies? Alas, the American diner would be miffed, hurling allegations of stinginess and cheating at the Asian merchants. Perhaps have the fortunes printed on the meal checks? This would eliminate the leaching, but how would the multiple fortunes be distributed to all? Separate checks? (How Dutch instead!) What about the Asian characters depicting the food served? Meal checks with English fortunes below Asian dinner items would be a tacky paradox indeed. Also, syntactical errors on the checks could lead to skeptical Caucasians haggling over misspellings on Chinese characters.

Such scenarios are complex and difficult to contemplate. Perhaps an easy, though radical, solution would be to eliminate dessert altogether. Americans, it could be argued, would do well to dispense with the larding of extra calories and sweets. This scandalous suggestion would, however, tamper with a precious American custom and entitlement.

Face it: we are far too hooked on the tradition of fortunes inside cookies to do more than add the lead and graphite issue to our list of worries. The levels of contamination are disturbing, yet their effects remain to be measured. This may just be another scare that fills the court dockets behind the pending cases of secondhand diabetes acquired through those candy cigarettes.

For now, the sage advice might well be: Look for a good fortune at the end of your meal. Crumble the crisp curl and follow your dream. Discard the sugary treat and wash your hands. Above all, "Pray with toys and eat less read."

2006

THE PUNCH LINE

Hitting Bottom and Laughing

My younger son, Jeremy, said years ago, "Dad, you are *really* funny! But Uncle Lee makes people laugh."

These words stung me with their truth. In the innocent and spontaneous bluntness of his pubescence, Jeremy had hit the nail on the head. Proud of my cleverness, quick puns, and sophisticated humor, I've lived a sideshow as a social comedian. It has its rewards: people appreciate my wit and marvel at the repository of jokes and apt retorts I bring rapidly to most situations. However, they don't always laugh. The jokes may be brilliant, creative, or time-tested winners delivered well—but the punch line can leave a devastating gap in the connection between me and my audience. In the lingo of stand-up comedy, I can *die* out there when the crowd doesn't join me and do its part to complete the routine.

The punch line is the payoff for the work of the setup, construction, delivery, imagination, mock truth, and willingness to connect. Without it, there is no satisfaction—only an awkward embarrassment and desire to escape. The punch line is the art, the joy, the fruit of labor and desire, and the rush of climax.

In switching from comedy, my avocation, to leadership, teaching, and guidance—my truer roles in life—I notice a similar dynamic between laughing out loud at the punch line and understanding intellectually its clever logic. People can appreciate the sage advice I give, and they can gain insight and understanding from imparted wisdom. Yet, if they don't act and apply this wisdom readily to their own betterment, then I have simply been clever, but I have not made them laugh.

Most comedy is talk. In life, however, we must walk the walk, not just talk the talk. I measure my effectiveness by how well those whom I influence walk the walk. There are fine lines between the healthy mentoring role of motivating, teaching, and supporting the ones you care about and the insidious trap of accepting excuses or the responsibility that others should engender for themselves.

It is easy to become convinced by the stories of our own complexity, rightness, and meaningful experiences. Each of us has tales to tell and music to play. It is necessary to broadcast on wavelengths the audience can receive. Moreover, the message and the signal quality matter little unless the listeners laugh and get up and dance.

Frustrating as it is to disconnect and to miss the mark so many times, I strive for my efforts to move people. I don't just want to be funny; I want them to laugh. I don't just want to be exclaimed for articulation or recognized for insight; I want them to hear the music and to sing and dance. I want the talk to make them walk. In the comic's lingo, I don't want to *die* onstage. I want to *kill*—so that others may *live*!

This, then, is the nature of commitment and intention—to press on when the message falls flat, when the punch line misses or they just don't get it, and to reconsider when they simply don't laugh.

> *Do not merely listen to the word, and so deceive yourselves. Do what it says. Anyone who listens to the word but does not do what it says is like a man who looks at his face in the mirror and, after looking at himself, goes away and immediately forgets what he looks like. But the man who looks intently into the perfect law that gives freedom, and continues to do this, not forgetting*

> *what he has heard, but doing it—he will be blessed in what he does.*
>
> —James 1:22–25

To reach this level of effectiveness, I must put aside my ego, my selfishness, my clever pride, and my ideas about what others should appreciate. Above all, I must care for and relate to my audience. As the apostle Paul stated:

> *If I speak in tongues of men and angels, but have not love, I am only a resounding gong or a clanging cymbal. If I have the gift of prophecy and can fathom all mysteries and all knowledge, and if I have a faith that can move mountains, but have not love, I am nothing. If I give all I possess to the poor and surrender my body to the flames, but have not love, I gain nothing.*
>
> —1 Corinthians 13:1–3

A life of quick one-liners and acerbic retorts is not for me. Neither is a career offering the carefully buffed edges of sarcasm. The appeal for popularity in the name of self-protection amounts to deceit. My retirement is going to be based on the royalties of good humor well delivered, remembered, and retold. I want to be funny *and* I want people to laugh. But jokes told at the expense of others have too high a cost. Ultimately, pain isn't funny and dirt isn't beautiful.

I want my punch lines to comfort and entertain, to tease and embrace, to teach and to care. If I am effective, they will laugh and tell others, many times over.

CATCH 'EM DOING GOOD—HIDDEN OPPORTUNITIES

It may seem strange to address building good behaviors in children by talking about marine air horns—but an episode in my own family highlights a principle that escapes many people earnestly trying to praise the positive and reward good behaviors.

Twelve-year-old Jeremy has been faithfully trying to train his dog. Though we've had the dog a few months, his (the dog's) lack of cooperation and the training frustration (Jeremy's) are quickly growing old and rigid. This unpleasant situation led to the eventual addition of an air horn to our family arsenal of communication. You can purchase a marine air horn at a sporting good store. If you own a boat, an air horn is a necessity. The seas are vast and loud, and you need such a tool to announce your presence and ward off danger. Houses, however, are much smaller; and, smaller yet, is a wire-haired miniature dachshund. We've learned the biological truth that you can't determine listening capacity by the size of the ears.

Enter the air horn—my son's not-so-secret weapon in the war on bad behaviors. Jeremy crouches behind doors and furniture, coveting the hope of catching his dog in a vile act so he can blast him with the air horn. This aversive surprise will supposedly teach the beloved but unruly dog a lesson.

It doesn't work. Jeremy's frustration increases as his dog senses him and blithely, lovingly, innocently carries on without infraction. My son's indignation churns at the dog's unwillingness to follow the script, thus denying Jeremy the opportunity to punish. The air is charged with silent expectation, and I wait with cowering sensitivity for my son's infliction of the piercing sound he thinks the dog deserves.

I break the tension with a comment about the disadvantages of punishment. Jeremy sneers at this interruption, regarding it as a distraction from the inevitable indiscretion he awaits. "Rewards don't work with him, Dad," Jeremy intones. "I need to catch him doing wrong and punish him so he won't do it again."

I wonder if Jeremy knows the irony in his declaration. After all, he is a child on the receiving end of countless corrections in the trials of growing up—hopefully, with the successful and benevolent administration of positive influences from me, his psychologist father. What is it, then, that impels people to gravitate toward what goes wrong and to concentrate on (and thereby strengthen) unwanted behaviors?

After years of observation and experimentation, I have discovered why people focus on the negative, even when it is decidedly to their detriment. Disregarding for the moment the individual differences by which some people are negative, perfectionistic, or faultfinding and the universal tendencies we have to want to be "right," the overriding force that makes us focus upon unwanted behaviors is that they are very attention getting.

Is that it? You may ask with incredulity: the startling discovery that undesirable behaviors get our attention…what else is new? Actually, some very important points, although they are not new. Almost everyone, however, routinely disregards them—and that makes the difference between success and failure.

There is a paradox that goes like this: we think we choose what we want, yet we attribute independent power to things, people, and events that displease, annoy, or irritate us. "How can you ignore that teasing (tone of voice, disrespect, etc.)?" is a common refrain. We respond to undesirable behaviors as if they are stronger than our power to choose responses, and so they draw our attention, which then becomes unwitting and under the control of the uninvited behaviors.

Another huge mistake is assuming that we know what is rewarding for another person. Actually, the operative principle is *reinforcement* rather than reward. The difference between them is that reinforcement strengthens behavior (makes it occur with greater frequency, duration, or intensity), whereas reward simply feels good (without necessarily changing behavior). Rewards often are reinforcements—that is, they are inducements to change behavior. The problem is that very frequently what *seems* like it should be worth working for does not actually change behavior in the desired way. Hence, the "rewards don't work on him" conclusion—but it is false, because you simply haven't found the right rewards. How do you find the right rewards? Look at what changes the behavior! It sounds backward, and it is. But people do things for their reasons, not yours. Their "reasons" often involve consequences that affect their behaviors in ways you would not have predicted. Add to the mystery the notion that you probably would not be motivated by those same consequences.

You may offer your child a treat in return for cleaning the dishes or doing homework. Both you and your child may claim that the treat is desirable for him—it is a reward, and he wants it—but if it does not serve to improve the behavior you desire, then it is not relevant. This is a difficult concept for most people. We think we know what rewards are and what others should want. However, we must observe whether this conforms to reality. Otherwise, we will conclude that rewards don't work, we will feel resentful and powerless, and we will remain at the effect of unwanted behaviors clamoring for our attention. In the name of discipline, many of us will stake out territories, air horns in hand, waiting for some derelict behavior upon which to pounce with punishment—because, you see, the dog didn't respond well to our notion of rewards.

How to avoid the snare of the air horn dilemma? Well, observe and experiment, as I have for years. It won't take you that long. I have researched many behaviors and situations, and have extracted the common threads. Individual application is much quicker, and the results are seen almost immediately.

Here are some pointers:

- **In order to find the right "rewards," pay attention to what consequences follow behaviors that reoccur.**

  Consequences aren't always rewards or desirable aftereffects. They are simply events that happen in connection with given behaviors that may affect the probability of those behaviors happening again. If you enter a room and flip a switch expecting a particular light to go on, your expectation of that switch will be influenced by what happens. If the light does not go on, would you conclude that switches don't work? What if a different appliance turned on when you flipped the switch while expecting that light? You would understand that the switch was wired to a certain appliance. Activating it produces a different effect, but a predictable effect nonetheless.

  Behaviors work similarly, though you have to observe more carefully and systematically.

  Sometimes, the lure of negative attention will trigger a behavior. The "reward" is criticism—not an intentional or pleasant reward, obviously, but a positive (yes, positive, as in reinforcing) influence upon the behavior, making it more likely to occur again.

  Alternatively, a consequence you might not think especially fun or rewarding can have powerful effects on behaviors. For example, recording and charting activities is tremendously motivating for people. Adults abound with their lists, and when children are asked to mark down or check off good behaviors (even "inconsequential" ones), these behaviors tend to increase.

If the dog likes chewing an old sock and that improves his housetraining, do use old socks for that purpose. That chewing an old sock doesn't appeal to you has no bearing (besides, you are already housetrained!). If the dog gives you what you want, give him what he wants. Such exchange is the basis for teaching, learning, and mutually satisfying relationships. Though the currency varies, the principle works as well for children and adults.

I once had a young patient who loved to collect stickers. She had binders full of them, and she proudly displayed these to everyone who would look. She earned stickers by increasing her appropriate behaviors, a system that worked well until we tried to redeem her stickers for actual prizes. At this the girl rebelled, and her behavior deteriorated. She didn't want our "prizes"; she wanted *stickers.* Once the adults working with her learned and accepted this, she behaved well. Stickers were her rewards in themselves, though the adults tried to impose a different reality. Allowing her to choose her consequences and acknowledging their legitimacy improved both her behavior and her sense of independence.

- **Become aware of high-probability behaviors (HPBs). These are activities (desirable or otherwise) in which your child engages frequently of his own accord.**

  By this simple power of observation, you can gain several advantages. Firstly, HPBs are, by definition, already reinforced. The attraction is there for your child, since he is already doing these things regularly. If you can discover what is "rewarding" these activities, you can adapt the reward/reinforcement to other behaviors you are interested in strengthening. Most of the time, the HPBs are inherently rewarding.

For example, suppose your child is in the habit of returning home from school, dropping his backpack in the way, and turning on the TV. Although this habitual HPB may not please you, there is a hidden and useful opportunity here. This behavior most likely makes the child feel comfortable, unburdened, and "free" of the day's demands. If that is its pleasurable and reinforcing value, then you can use conditions of comfort and freedom to shape your child's other behaviors—whether or not these rewards involve TV or letting him leave his backpack where he wants.

Secondly, because HPBs occur regularly, you can introduce other rewards that are more likely to assume higher value when they are affixed to a likely behavior that is already in place. Were you to give your child a treat for dropping his pack or watching TV, you would be associating the treat with a behavior that already has sufficient strength. The advantages are twofold: you can introduce, test, and strengthen the reinforcement value of a new reward, and you can gradually use the reinforcement to shape and strengthen a behavior that is slightly different from the one that is already his habit. You can unobtrusively *shift* the behavior. After several incidences of rewarding the typical HPB, you can reward him for dropping his backpack, turning on the TV, and then retrieving his backpack. After awhile, you can hold out the reward after he turns on the TV, but before giving it to him, ask him to check what is on several other channels. This method would increase his repertoire of behaviors *under your influence* with little likelihood of resistance (because the shift is so subtle and nonthreatening).

With proper observation and planning, very soon these shifts will reshape your child's HPBs.

Thirdly, you can schedule HPBs themselves to reinforce lower probability behaviors (LPBs). Do this by making the exercise of HPBs conditional or contingent upon the completion of a lower probability behavior (one you are trying to teach). The HPB has a natural attraction, or reinforcement effect, and the determinant of its success as a teaching tool is the before-and-after scheduling of the contingency: first, perform the LPB, and then you can engage in the HPB. Implemented in this manner, your child may only watch TV and drop his backpack *after* he has taken out the garbage, etc.

- **When it seems like nothing appeals to your child, allow choices as incentives, and consider sanctioning HPBs as reinforcers.**

Children who feign indifference to rewards are usually playing (and winning) a power struggle with their parents. The child's rewards are 1) frustrating the parent and 2) choosing to do without goodies because this seems preferable to the "work" of changing behavior.

There are two interventions that will compromise this mischief and get the child on track with your agenda. First, you must take away the reward value of frustrating the adult. This may be challenging for you; however, it works, it is necessary, and it will produce huge rewards for *you.* When your child learns (through demonstration, modeling, and repetition) that you are neither concerned nor emotionally set off by his lack of interest in rewards, he will change his tune. Everybody wants and needs things; after all, children are dependent upon adults. Your child takes for granted things, privileges, and services he does not recognize as items for the bargaining table.

> Second, when your child is not forthcoming about what he values and what he will work for, create choices for him, and tie the choices to a particular behavior with a response cost attached if he fails to perform. For example, you might tell him that in return for taking out the garbage and cleaning the dishes, you will offer him either his choice of dinner for the next two days, a movie rental, or fifteen minutes of cleaning up (of his choice) that you will do for him. If he doesn't choose the reward within two minutes, you will make the choice for him. If he doesn't perform the task on his own, you will *make* him do it (by insisting and watching him do it) and he will sacrifice TV (one of his HPBs) for a day.
>
> Alternatively, if you can't stand his habit of watching TV, consider giving him your limited but overt approval in exchange for doing chores. Many children and adolescents prize being left alone to their recreational choices.
>
> Another useful tool is giving a disenchanted child a "stockpile" of extras (things he likes and uses—also could be money) that must be maintained and released exclusively through performances you designate.
>
> Many unenthusiastic children become motivated to keep their fortunes rather than watch them dwindle under the "response cost" control of their parents.

The insights and practical strategies will help you take advantage of the many opportunities to "catch 'em doing good"—the effective way to shape and strengthen the behaviors you want.

On the other hand, in the other hand, you can hide an air horn, and wait for the chance to blast 'em.

Now, where is that dog?

2002

YOU OUGHTA HAVE YOUR HEAD EXAMINED

1-800-EXPIRED

Imagine my displeasure when 1-800-CONTACTS contacted me to apologize that they could not fill my contact lens order because my optometrist informed them that my prescription had expired and was, therefore, invalid.

Now it's true that I had not had an eye exam in a year and half—but why had my prescription "expired"? I've been wearing the same prescription for at least ten years. This "expiration" seemed like a thinly veiled demand that I come in for an eye exam. My optometrist is a good guy, competent and all, and I've been "under his care" for nearly two decades. Nearly every year, I have an eye exam. I miss one, and my prescription has expired and is invalid. My optometrist has never been to see me for an exam. I don't know if he's been to any other psychologists, but I doubt he's been in to have his head examined with anywhere near the regularity he requires of his own patients.

Don't get me wrong: eye examinations are important. I believe in them, and I undergo them routinely, notwithstanding my recent tardiness. But the pressure to comply under the threat of expiration amounts to professional racketeering. And it's not limited to eye doctors. Try missing a teeth cleaning for six months: the dental delinquency team will be in touch personally. Even without them, the commercials are enough to inspire guilt. (At least you can buy toothpaste without a prescription.)

Think for a moment about the many gateways, requirements, and pay stations to which we must routinely capitulate: school immunizations, driver's licenses (there are tests for that, including a basic vision test), dental and medical checkups (including X-rays and blood tests), insurance physicals, vehicle smog certifications, home inspections and appraisals, college and professional applications and exams, and credit reports (yes, these are tests—indeed, the more frequently you get them, the lower your scores; each time a credit report is run, your credit score is lowered by two points), all of which we pay for with a zero-tolerance policy for resistance or challenge toward those in charge.

Then, of course, there is the ultimate prescriptive gateway, the one that delivers psychiatric drugs. We *should* require such exams and, in the bargain, demand more rigor and thoroughness. When do psychiatric prescriptions expire? When new medications arrive on the market, when intolerable ill effects are reported for the ones prescribed, when the patient reports subjective complaints or exhibits behaviors that bother others, or when the doctor decides it's time for another visit.

For the most part, mental health professionals—even the top-notch psychiatrists—don't get to summon people for visits. In our society, you are presumed mentally fit unless circumstances get you in for an exam. Such circumstances may involve legal scrapes, life traumas, behavioral transgressions, or just plain old misery creeping up on you. Even then, visits to the shrink are largely voluntary. Still, most people don't want to go. If mental fitness is the norm, why are people so avoidant of examination or even contact with the mental health profession? The stigma notwithstanding, the vast majority of psychiatrists make their living by prescribing medications—so, there are an awful lot of visits and recall exams nonetheless. But the patronage of psychiatrists palls beside the visits to dentists and optometrists.

Most of us have most parts of our head routinely examined—except for our brain! We even visit the (sometimes specialized) physician who checks our nose when we contract a cold. And we regularly visit the barber or hairdresser who examines another aspect of our head while cleansing us and improving our (hygienic and social) fitness and self-esteem.

Keeping ourselves up does require maintenance and the routine "pound-of-flesh" sacrifice (please pardon the metaphor) to the coffers of professionals. Much of this repeated homage is coerced, even legislated, for our own good. After all, you put contact lenses *into* your eyes, right? True. But can I be trusted on what I put in my stomach (without a prescription)? Imagine being denied a meal because your "prescription" for that food has expired! Do people need prescriptions for shoes? For high heels? Arguably, we could render ourselves all manner of damage by our unsupervised or ill-advised choices. The mass market and the Internet have made access and poor choices all the more ready and threatening.

The plain truth is that there are people driving who are dangerous (and not for lack of vision or driving skills), and there are people parenting though ill equipped, and we don't check on these folks or require exams until they make big mistakes. The misfits drive and make other people crazy, though I am not advocating a detection frenzy. The vast majority—people considered well adjusted by themselves and others—struggle privately while stress, that relentless cannibal of health and happiness, eats away inside them. Few of them get exams, and fewer are called.

We get our teeth cleaned, our hair cut, our eyes checked and remediated—why don't we get our brains cleaned? Think you don't put stuff in your head that isn't good for you? Stuff that affects your mental vision, your values, your judgment, your common sense and ability to think clearly and effectively, even your physiological functioning? Think you were born balanced and fly frictionless to the pull of your own imperturbable gyroscope?

Most people support the prescriptive monitoring of children and the planning of their education, diets, and social and recreational activities. Few of these supporters bring their children for mental health or developmental health checkups unless something goes obviously wrong. Taking this a step further, even fewer adults willingly get themselves checked—even *once*—despite the massive array of evidence that minimal examination and intervention can prevent disaster and greatly improve the quality of life.

So, what's this about "brain-cleaning"? A simple two-step procedure, really. Check yourself out, and tune yourself up. Find out how adequately your brain is regulated and whether the way you see the world is realistic. If you need one, get a prescription for clearing your mind and functioning more effectively. You can improve quickly and immensely through the challenge of brain-training (neurofeedback) and/or the guidance of a professional who will challenge or validate your perceptions, give you feedback and useful recommendations, and enable you to function with more control, productivity, and satisfaction.

Perceptions do expire. The lenses through which we view the world may distort. Views once effective can become invalid. We need to learn new things as we develop and change and as the world around us changes. This is a natural process, and it doesn't mean we are messed up. It does mean that we need attention and temporary professional assistance—and sometimes a new prescription.

Anyone who doesn't understand this ought to get his head examined—but will have to wait in line behind those who already do. Self-sufficiency expires, but that doesn't make you invalid. Mental health is not just for some people, and you don't have to be sick to get better.

Some professions have a ransom net on recall visits. Mental health tends not to be that way. However, don't be surprised if you get on the Internet one day and are asked for your prescription. Some monitoring is necessary to protect the public and ensure that what you put in your head (and what comes out of it) is right and good for you. After all, computers (and even some TV cable and satellite services) allow parental controls. Why not a professional password prescription? Think of it as psychological protection for your well-being.

Haven't had your head examined lately? Not to worry—you're probably fine. If you forget your password, however, you may get the message "PRESCRIPTION EXPIRED! CALL 1-800-EXPIRED."

Do call. I'll give you an appointment just as soon as I return from the eye doctor.

2002

ADD DEMYSTIFIED: WHAT YOU REALLY NEED TO KNOW

The Problem

Almost everyone has heard of ADD/ADHD. Most people have opinions about it; some have very strong, even militant, opinions. It is common to know people with ADD or to find out that someone you know has ADD. Whether communicated by relieved announcement or decried through hushed whispers, ADD tends to stir emotions and attitudes in those who live with it or around it. This condition—ostensibly a deficiency of attention—draws ironically to itself a remarkable amount of attention, as if to make up for its namesake. There are ADD organizations, ADD pharmaceuticals, laws about ADD, treatments for it, diagnostic guidelines—yet there little agreement (in the broad consensus) about what ADD is, how to diagnose it, and how to treat it.

Those who take issue with the assertion about consensus are camped in the medical mainstream, where the pharmaceutical monolith has prevailed, along with dogma necessary to justify the prolific drugging of the populace. Despite the comfort in numbers (both acolytes and sales figures), the medical model still embraces a naked emperor with regard to the rigors of identifying a unitary entity called ADD. The reality is that the conglomerate of impairment and marginalized function lumped into the ADD diagnosis has been evident for a very long time, subsumed under different labels and targeted by numerous and sundry attempts to control it, deny it, or minimize its impact.

The problem with defining and identifying ADD is that the brain has little regard for our attempts to classify it. It simply does not follow the rules of publication in the psychiatric manuals. Symptoms, behaviors, and personality patterns "leak" and "creep" across brackets of diagnoses and categories. This recognition is fortuitous; aside from its fidelity with the reality of individual differences and brain functions, the cross migration of symptoms across diagnoses parallels the discovery that treatments designed for one condition are often very effective for others. This holds true for many mental and developmental conditions, as well as for treatment interventions including pharmacological, behavioral, neurocognitive, and energy-based approaches.

ADD doesn't care what you call it. Those afflicted just want to feel better and function better. Fortunately, a model exists for understanding and simplifying ADD in a manner consistent with and true to its essential characteristics. This characterization lends uncanny accuracy and practical utility without compromising medical theories, oversimplifying the diagnosis, or generalizing the disorder to the point of overinclusion. Happily, the model also lends itself to practical solutions for the problems of ADD.

This model is known as the *disregulation model.* The essential common denominator that characterizes all ADD/ADHD and that manifests in such a variety of seemingly disparate symptoms and diagnoses is *disregulation.* This term refers to the uneven, inconsistent, sporadic, or irregular management by the brain and nervous system of the internal housekeeping functions of the body and mind.

Disregulation is the touchstone for the relevant and distinguishing characteristics of ADD/ADHD. It is also the fundamental underlying mechanism by which we can control and improve mental functioning and behavior. The core characteristics of ADD/ADHD (underpinned by disregulation) can be relieved and the brain regulated through the vehicle of EEG neurofeedback training.

These characteristics are:

1. Disregulation of the arousal system

Just as the human body has systems for respiration, digestion, circulation, cell rebuilding, etc., it also has a system for managing arousal. Arousal refers to states of excitation and relaxation that are in constant relationship with each other. Think of picking up a cup and then setting it down and letting go. Your muscles must tense to grip the cup, and they must relax to release your grip. The nervous system performs similarly with regard to excitation and relaxation. This continuous feedback loop is described technically as the activity of the sympathetic and parasympathetic nervous system. This activity controls states of attention, wakefulness and sleepiness, impulsivity, mood, awareness, and inhibition/disinhibition.

The arousal system manages or regulates a person's appetites, perceptions, and abilities to control, soothe, gear up, and modulate oneself. It may be likened to a biological thermostat that regulates internal housekeeping. When this thermostat malfunctions or works only intermittently, the resulting glitches in the continual and automatic adjustment of arousal functions give rise to symptoms and functional disruptions.

This fluctuation and irregular management of arousal is at the core of ADD, and it results in a variety of behavioral, emotional, and physical symptoms (such as anger, moodiness, difficulty concentrating, anxiety, sleep problems, etc.). It also leads to inconsistencies in performance.

The aspect of arousal regulation is so important that all of ADD revolves around it. Indeed, a more precise term than attention deficit disorder would be arousal disregulation disorder.

Neuroscientists describe brain function in terms of activation. A brain that is calm, alert, and processing functionally is said to be activated. A deactivated brain exerts less differentiation over its electrical activity, its neurotransmission, and, consequently, its self-management and outward responses. A disregulated brain has trouble activating and resting, recognizing and shifting from a deactivated state.

ADD is characterized by disregulation in brain activation, often reflected in the activation management of the EEG. Although the EEG may not typically show morphological abnormalities (marked deviations in the type or structure of the brainwaves), the EEGs of ADD people are often less differentiated, less activated, and less responsive to internal and external cues requiring shifts in activation states.

2. Poor integration with environmental demands

A common complaint about ADD children is that they do, in fact, pay attention, but mostly to what interests them. Usually they can sustain attention for prolonged periods when they are engaged in activities of their choice. Perhaps you've heard or echoed the refrain, "It's amazing how he can sit and play video games for hours, but he can't pay attention to his work for more than two minutes!"

Disregulation of arousal predisposes people to become drawn to (possibly fixated or "stuck" on) highly stimulating, novel, and even risky activities because the activity stimulates their brain and makes them feel involved, even more normal. (This is also why stimulant medications work to make people pay better attention.) When the nervous system is underaroused, substances or activities that boost arousal become desirable and may become addictive.

People with ADD have atypically inconsistent performance. This is due to fluctuations in arousal management. By contrast, what is notable is their consistently better performance on tasks they select and on time schedules that suit them. Realistically, most of us are more interested and involved in activities we prefer. The difference with ADD folks is that their performances on tasks they choose is markedly better than on those delegated to them. This selective attention factor (so entwined with arousal) also reflects in the difficulty ADD individuals have with schedules, deadlines, timeliness, and conformity. People with ADD tend to function at much higher levels when they choose what they will do and when they will do it. Schedules, specifications, and demands imposed from the environment (even routine cues like bedtime and waking time) can present huge problems in handling daily life.

Parents and teachers often notice that ADD children have trouble transitioning or shifting from one activity to another. This, too, is a manifestation of disregulation—taking cues from the environment and integrating its demands requires fluidity of arousal. The brain has to shift gears and modify brainwaves—something usually quite difficult for the ADD person.

3. Perceptual focus problems

A hallmark of ADD is distractibility, the faltering of attention and its ready disruption by random stimuli unrelated to the intended focus. Many ADD people are overly sensitive to sounds and other stimuli that intrude in their consciousness and vie for their attention.

Whether or not distractibility is an overt problem, the disregulation that underlies it invariably causes perceptual differences that throw the ADD person off track. Thus, novel stimuli or unique components elicit selective attention. While this can result in refreshing creativity and original perspectives, it frequently leads the ADD person to focus on unconventional, less relevant, and less productive aspects of a situation or problem. This leads to greater peripheral activity and reduced goal attainment.

Disregulation sponsors idiosyncrasies in perception that make less important details seem salient. It promotes a perceptual style that predisposes the ADD individual to attend to the urgent rather than the important. It can cloud judgment and boost impulsivity. Perceptual anomalies can also color information processing and make it more arduous and inefficient.

Perceptual distortions are much more likely when you study postage stamps from across the room or you watch a movie with your nose pressed to the big screen. Though these may seem like metaphorical exaggerations, they typify the perceptual idiosyncrasies to which the ADD mind is prone.

We refer to this phenomenon as the "zoom lens malfunction." On a video camera, the zoom apparatus allows you to zoom in for detail and zoom out for the bigger picture. Our brains have to do this, too. Otherwise, we lose perspective, overfocus, miss important details, miss social and nonverbal cues, and leave ourselves at risk. Get the picture? Most ADD people struggle mightily with the zoom lens function.

4. Stressed brain syndrome

A very familiar scenario is repeated routinely for those with ADD: the person applies himself to a task…and gets stuck! Some people freeze up, some become frustrated or angry, some give up easily, some redouble their efforts. The effect is ironically similar: the harder the person tries, the more his brain stresses and the less efficient his performance becomes. (This has been documented repeatedly by medical imaging studies of the ADD brain under challenge conditions.)

This is indeed a defining characteristic of ADD. However, since the average person can't see this relationship, its repeated occurrence often brands the ADD person as lazy. This is both tragic and inaccurate. The reality is that normal brain function depends upon the intermittent recurrence of the resting response within a period of exertion or challenge. Because the ADD brain has not learned to rest when challenged, it goes into overdrive and stalls or freezes. People who recognize this episode sometimes term it "brain lock." Most ADD people simply experience the discomfort, restlessness, and shame of not measuring up to the challenge. Then the avoidance or release mechanisms kick in, and the task gets abandoned while the person gets criticized.

5. Compromised flexibility

Flexibility involves the ability to change set or perspective, to view things from different vantage points, to shift gears when necessary, to vary one's repertoire. It is essentially "the ability to drive at the speed appropriate for the conditions."

By definition, flexibility involves making adjustments, and making adjustments presupposes a functional frame of reference and adequate monitoring and evaluation. Disregulation throws a monkey wrench into these works. When the gearshift gets jammed, it's hard to make timely adjustments. This is the situation that poorly regulated ADD people face every day.

One tool and one speed will carry you only so far in a world with plentiful variation, complexity, changing circumstances, and demands. Compromised flexibility is a liability that the ADD person can ill afford, but usually has.

The Solution

In dealing with ADD, it is vital to correct the disregulated condition. When the brain becomes organized and self-regulated, symptoms from seemingly disparate origins ameliorate. Behavior improves, concentration and focus increase, sleep normalizes, and moods become more even.

What a marvelous testimony to the innate flexibility and plasticity of the human brain! These inherent capabilities can be activated through brainwave training, known as EEG biofeedback or neurofeedback.

2002

SHOPPING FOR THERAPY

Would you shop for food at the hardware store? Hopefully not. Maybe a few canned goods or bulk staples in a pinch—but generally, a market is the place to buy groceries. What about buying tools at the supermarket? Beyond a screwdriver or batteries, you'd be better off at the hardware emporium. And how about letting the jeweler look at your teeth, or the dentist brighten your whitewall tires? In light of this silliness, consider the recourse many people choose when emotional, psychological, or behavioral woes darken the doorway: counseling psychotherapy. We are virtually programmed to rely upon counseling, or "talk therapy," to solve problems ranging from relationship conflicts to mood swings to attention and behavior deficits or neurophysiological disorders.

In our age of crossover shopping (where the computer megastore sells arrays of candy and dry goods, and where physicians use antipsychotic drugs to treat attention deficit disorder), both specialization and cross application are commonplace. Ironically, when it comes to human needs, consumers shop almost exclusively at the pharmacy or the couch of the talk therapist. All too often, the expectations are inappropriate and the results disappointing. The quest for solace and relief ends up like shopping for groceries at the hardware store. Traditional therapy stocks only limited goods for human error and suffering.

Therapy—as in psychotherapy—has a stigma in American society. Though we perceive ourselves generally in this culture as open-minded, we remain secretive about personal problems and leery of seeking help for them. Self-consciousness and emotional sensitivity and insecurity engage with rational skepticism in discouraging many people from pursuing interventions that could provide relief or change their lives.

The stigmatization of hurts, illnesses, and frustrations in the "mental health" realm is truly unfortunate. Perhaps some of the stereotypes are attributable to the misguided efforts of therapists and mental health professionals over the years in the provision of treatments that are largely ineffective and expensive, as well as sometimes degrading and painful.

In mental health, an uncomfortable collusion has evolved among professionals, the lay public, and health care insurers. It is tacitly assumed that psychological, mental, emotional, or behavioral problems:

a) Occur separate from the body medical (as in: categorized and administered separately with reduced benefits by insurance companies)
b) Take a long time and much therapy to heal, improve, or incur long-lasting change
c) Require insight and understanding of deep-seated and historical material (and/or repressed memories) in order to change
d) Are caused by underlying biochemical imbalances that require medications

On the one hand, these assumptions imply that meaningful improvement will occur only through lengthy treatment (expensive therapy or lifelong medication) at the direction of professionals. On the other hand, these "problems" are tossed back in the laps of sufferers as their own responsibility—not medical problems worthy of attention, measurably effective treatment, and reimbursable health coverage. They are medically necessary when it comes to doctors' orders (and please be compliant!), but not medically necessary when it comes to reimbursement.

In this collusive system, we all lose: consumers, health care professionals, and society at large. Social and economic costs multiply, therapists provide treatments that fall far short, and people, by and large, lose confidence in purported treatments that aren't really helping.

So what are savvy and earnest consumers to do? How can you evaluate and select treatment interventions that will do the job? The marketplace brims with offerings clamoring for your attention and your dollars. Claims for success abound, and the burgeoning competition for sovereignty in efficacy has consumers scurrying their mice over the Internet in the spiraling production of more confusion. When you need help, where do you turn and how do you decide?

Here are some suggestions:

1. **Clarify the job you want done**—Whose behavior and feelings are supposed to change and what specifically are the targets? Do you want a traditional DSM (psychiatric) or ICD (medical) diagnosis? Formal assessment? Intervention and treatment? Most therapists don't do formal assessment (testing), and many do not understand its contributions to treatment. Some psychologists only assess, but don't treat. Who is being treated, and why? Do you need intervention or assistance outside the office—advocacy, coordination among professionals, educational intervention?

2. **Question your assumptions and beliefs about how people get better (and worse)**—Such assumptions form the foundation for treatment approaches and expectations about improvement, motivation, responsibilities, communications, and evaluation. For example, do you think that someone needs to believe in a psychological treatment in order for it to work or work better? (Compare this with taking an antibiotic; does belief matter?) What do you and your therapist think about biochemical imbalances, and what role might this play in treatment options? What is the impact of spiritual life, and how do your beliefs about the symptomatic "condition" integrate with your notions of choice and free will?

3. **Get your expectations in line with what is achievable in treatment**—Paradoxically, people are often skeptical of therapeutic promises and claims, but they harbor great inward hopes and expectations. When the therapy does what it's supposed to do, but doesn't solve all of life's problems, disappointment can ensue and clients can overlook true benefits attained because of their misconstrued expectations. At the beginning of treatment, clients may not be aware of their true expectations, only to have fantasies subsequently dashed in the light of realistic gains. At least some of the "talk" in therapy should be about what lines the aisles in a particular therapeutic market.

4. **Select benchmarks for measuring progress**—Entering behaviors, symptom baselines, and progress should be documented and reviewed. Both objective and subjective measures are useful; the important point is to keep reference measures in order to guide treatment, make appropriate modifications, and adjudicate progress with expectations. Progress measures are also critical for factual communication between client and therapist.

5. **Set boundaries and parameters for your engagement with treatment**—It is crucial and helpful for you to understand the logistics of your therapeutic arrangement: costs, frequency and duration of treatment, your responsibilities and those of the therapist, expectations of follow-up, and the forums for communication between you and the therapist.

Despite the pitfalls, variability, and expense, therapy should and can be a targeted, reasonably limited, satisfying intervention that results in alleviation of the original symptoms and positive side benefits of growth and flexibility. Discuss the appropriateness of the treatment methods to the presenting needs and complaints in terms of costs, benefits, and standards of success. Otherwise, the "talk" in "talk therapy" is cheap, but the bill from the therapist is expensive.

2004

DOWNSIZING ECONOMY, SUPERSIZING GASTRONOMY, FITTING AUTONOMY

Adapting Technology to Its Makers

For many Americans, the new millennium has brought changes is size and scale. Our paychecks have become leaner, our girths wider, and our temperaments and outlooks meaner. In the job marketplace, downsizing has become an ugly fact of life. In a taunting irony, the food industry, particularly the fast-food industry, has accelerated portion size—as if some weird combination of consolation comfort and food manufacturing is compensating us for what technology does fast—innovate—and people do more slowly—rebound. And we, as sensitive individuals, are caught in the imbalance.

Yes, we make and consume speedy chips: circuits in the workplace, and corn ones with cheese on top as we dash between tasks in the valley of survival. In this fast-paced lifestyle, we can barely keep up. And the chips for many of us, believe it or not, are really down. We are depressed and worried, and mad about it, and worried some more, and pressured; some of us are addicted and falling off the wagon. We are afraid of falling off our car payments, and we grip the steering wheel in tenacious defiance of the maddening traffic and our tenuous sense of self-control. Stress and tolerances are no longer jargon for civil engineers. They are mantras for our moods, and we are barely civil about the increasing unrest in our personal lives. In many ways besides financially, the downturn ravages autonomy beyond economy.

That the consequences of a sour market should gut the most innovative sector is, perhaps, cruel fate. Yet there is a serendipitous paradox: in this stretch of unparalleled stress, there is a technological solution to mend many of its unseemly effects. We can attach the computer directly to ourselves as a healing medium for our physiological troubles and our worrisome woes. That miracle agent—the computer chip—which we have ridden in temptation, swashbuckling conceit and to destitute crashes on the slippery market floor, can rescue us from the bipolar havoc wreaked upon us.

The fact is we can train our brains to function better by using computers to condition our brainwaves. Sleep better, beat the blues, banish anxiety, relinquish destructive cravings and habits, work more efficiently, concentrate, and let go of puckering obsessions about unreasonable bosses, overwhelming odds, and ridiculous circumstances.

It's high time for the tech community, our sacred vanguard, to embrace the blessing it has bestowed on the populace. The shoemaker may not sport the best style, though he outfits and repairs royalty. We created, manufactured, miniaturized, expanded, and cheapened the technologies that have changed the patterns of life. Cycles of misfortune have changed our patterns of life, and we need to use our familiar resources to rebound—emotionally, psychologically, cognitively, and socially; the financial collateral will follow. Through the combination of scientific rigor, computer technology, and biological realities, we can literally reconnect ourselves with our spawned technology in a self-regenerating manner. The vehicle is EEG neurofeedback (or EEG biofeedback), and it uses the combined mechanisms of software engineering, operant conditioning, and neurotransmitters. And—get this—the "job" is to play video games with your brain as a stepladder to better heights of performance and well-being!

This is not a commercial for computer training skills at the local college mill. It is the high drama of actual reality, that of tuning up your brain. This interesting marriage of technology and biology has birthed the capacity to change one's mind in response to self-directed programming. It harbors the essence of autonomy for those at the behest of pressures and annoyances. The freedom to be yourself can unfold in a matter of hours from your CPU, keyboard, and your head—and, uh, a set of electrodes.

The very bottom line is that by training your brainwaves with a personal computer, some peripherals, and exquisitely fine-tuned software, you can get rid of a plethora of irritating symptoms, improve your attitude and performance, maintain consistency, overcome bad habits, sustain clarity of mind and focus, and enhance your relationships and productivity.

How does this work?

For the end user, it's simply a matter of training about thirty minutes at a time by playing a specially designed video game while tethered to the apparatus by some electrodes. The equipment monitors and digitally filters brainwaves while transforming the different signals into elements of the video game. You will neither find the addictive complexity of *Everquest* in these games nor the adrenaline rush of a kill. There's no blood (either on the screen or on the player) and no weapons. Only the relentless mélange of messages about what your brain is doing at the moment. Therein results a special kind of victory—a conquest through observation and self-modification. It is a kind of "Zen-hacking" process whereby you have access to the inner workings of your electrical mind. As it turns out, these electrical patterns are fundamental to what is known as *self-regulation*—the process by which the brain and nervous system control and correct the balances and imbalances responsible for daily functioning. Self-regulation is like a human operating system. When it runs smoothly in the background, things are fine. But when there are bugs or glitches or irregularities, the system hangs up. Disregulation can result in symptoms as disparate as erratic concentration, moodiness, poor sleep, stress, headaches, overeating, cravings, inability to relax, obsessive thinking, brooding, diminished work capacity, and poor rebound from overwork.

Amazingly—and scientifically—the simple act of repetitively witnessing one's own brain activity allows and encourages instinctive subtle changes in cortical electrical frequencies that positively effect mood, cognitive functions, and behavior. Praise technology! Just as the computer has reformed the ways we manage our own information and exchange with the world around us, so does brainwave training revamp our resources and efficiency in managing our internal affairs and the ways we relate to others. A brave new world, indeed, but one with auspicious outcomes for us who intrepidly reengage with our computers in a novel and self-gratifying way.

Of course, you'll need some tech support at the beginning: this comes in the form of clinical supervision by an experienced neurotherapist. In a matter of hours, though, you can be up and running on your own with a home system under remote supervision.

The ins and outs of EEG neurofeedback training are documented in a new book, *ADD: The 20-Hour Solution*, by Mark Steinberg, Ph.D and Siegfried Othmer, Ph.D. Don't let the headline of ADD distract you. Though neurofeedback is nearly miraculous for attention deficit disorder, its virtues apply to the high-functioning veterans of our competitive adult world battles. You don't need an attention problem to struggle with the stressors of a bad economy, raising kids, difficult managers or coworkers, continuing resentments, and unreasonable demands.

Training brainwaves has been increasingly scientifically validated over the last forty years. Like many technologies (including the Internet and the space program), it started with a government effort to propel toward its goals, and then the by-products filtered down to the individual consumer. The distinguishing aspect of this technology is that the increased speed and lower prices of personal computers have allowed ordinary scientists, entrepreneurs, health care providers, and consumers to get a piece of the action. It's hard to build your own rocket ship or monopolize a mainframe, but a personal computer and your own brain are private, individual, and economically viable.

So why haven't you heard all about this before? One reason is that the pharmaceutical industry has big plans to sell you drugs for the rest of your life. It wants to manage your emotional life and package a browser in as many people as it can that will point directly to its products on the pharmacy shelves and in the medicine cabinets. Among the most alarming problems with this trend is that the upgrade path leads to more symptoms and dependence, rather than autonomy and freedom.

Another reason that this is new to you might be your strenuous devotion to the production and distribution of technologies that enable others to program our collective habits of consumption. You have been very busy feeding scientific data to the mass market, perhaps barely taking time to nourish yourself. In creature comforts and self-indulgence, bigger seems to signal better—even as, in electronics, the chips get smaller and the signals faster.

One sign is fast approaching: if we are to continue to live off the fat of the land, we must replenish the land and self-indulge in other ways. It's time to turn our great technology resource directly upon ourselves. From the ravages of sickened economy, palliative junk consumerism, smoldering resentment, and an almost forgotten tech sector, we will become prominent and prosperous again.

Then, as now, we just may let it go to our heads.

2001

WHAT DRIVES ME

Working in Reverse

Fifty years ago, my mother gave me life. Tonight, I put more life into her and, in turn, became more alive myself.

She called me from her home, three thousand miles distant. She was upset and humiliated. On this very difficult day, Mom had failed her driving test for the third time in recent efforts. After numerous cerebral strokes during the last year, she has fought to regain her functioning. The last time I visited her, she was relearning to dress herself. Her speech has gradually improved, and tonight it was clear: she wants to get back into life, but reality has dealt her some harsh blows. After waiting two hours at the DMV, she froze with anxiety and failed her driving test.

"I was so nervous. I put the car into reverse, but it wouldn't work. The guy just looked at me and I froze." She starts to cry. My protector is hurting.

This is the same woman who drove me lovingly to baseball games and relentlessly to achievement. Mom was my model for how to handle the world through words, action, spirit, and sheer force of will.

Now that confidence is shattered, and she seeks to recover from emotional and physical trauma. Three nights ago, she fell and split her lip. They sutured her wounds at the emergency room, but we know that her pride was left unstitched, gaping at the vulnerability of her life as an impaired senior citizen. Her anguish multiplied at the thought that she would not be able to drive herself to jury duty, an extant calling she considers an honor. My mom loves people and loves to serve others. Dad is nearly blind, and his progressive glaucoma has found a bedfellow with emotional myopia. My parents are outcasts; though married for fifty-one years, they have become estranged from their bodies, divorced from the social mainstream, and married to their memories.

And I am a continent away.

I consoled my mom. Ignoring the carboned pattern of communications that encrusts so many of our child-parent conversations, I challenged Mom. I told her that she was entitled to know why the examiner failed her and that she was responsible to distinguish between poor performance, anxiety, self-pity, and traumatic memory. You see, Mom was an educator, a veteran teacher and high school administrator. In her retirement, she is a prize-winning painter. She understands expression, drive, and leadership. But lately, her brain has been under attack, as has her pride and independence. In defense and support, I turned upon her and challenged her yet again. Yes, I consoled her, but with an apogee of exhortation to rid herself of anxiety and bad feeling. I told her that she needed to determine realistically if her driving skills were up to par. After all, the lives of others are at stake, too. (This is the woman who stayed up waiting for me to come home so she could fall asleep, knowing I was safe. Mom used to tell me that she trusted me—it was the other "nuts" out there on the road she had to worry about!)

Now the roles were reversed, and I had to wonder if Mom was reversed, too. I explained that I could treat her with Voice Technology before her next driving test so she wouldn't be so nervous. She seemed eager, and said she probably should practice the tapping (a good sign!). I said okay, how about now? She agreed. What was Mom feeling?

"I want to be over this humiliation."

Eventually, "I will be completely over this humiliation."

I will, she will, my will, she drives, she drives me…

What drives me is the complete will to relieve suffering, to achieve, and to celebrate. The daily complications and invitations of life are so vast, so infinite. We are hungry, and driven, and power-hungry, and when we find a power to relieve the hunger, we are driven to use it. I heard Mom's voice in her womb, and I heard it now again. Time has been tamed by Nature.

Mom was humiliated at a level of ten. Ten, as in "tender." Ten minutes later she was a one. One, as in, Mom and I are one again—talking about the incidentals of our daily lives, about work, and Dad, and the grandchildren, and, of course, the weather (yes, Mom, I am dressing warmly enough, wearing the sweaters that, by definition, are what you don when Mother is cold).

My mom is really never cold, but sometimes, when the world is frosty, she must be bundled and wrapped, trundled and tapped.

Mom tapped into my caring and met her need through the gift of TFT. We are both more alive because of it.

"So, Mom, how do you feel?"

"I'm fine, Mark."

"Do you feel humiliated?"

"No."

"Think of the driving test. You failed."

"I feel better talking to you. I love you. How are the children?"

"We're fine, Mom. Do you remember that ten minutes ago, you were at a ten, feeling humiliated about failing your driving test?"

"Yes."

"But you don't feel any humiliation now?"

"No."

It's amazing to me how people forget. Even though they remember cognitively, they forget emotionally—those are the lucky ones, who remember that they forgot. Many sufferers try to forget cognitively, but they recall emotionally.

But I don't forget. I remember with poignant clarity and vibrant emotion. It's what drives me.

2009

CAN YOU MAKE MY CHILD NORMAL?

Every parent wants the best for his or her child. Traditional ambitions in the past decades of our country's growth were for children to do better than their parents. Parental efforts and sacrifices were exerted in the hope and expectation that their children's opportunities, achievements, and income would exceed the previous generation. To live a better life would mean more money and less strife and hardship. It is so difficult for parents to let children make their own mistakes and—these days—cope with a tougher world. Our society is much more expensive and competitive: oh, to get into a good school, get a job, buy a house, afford a family, launch and sustain a career!

But that is for normal children—the ones who develop the skills, ambition, and mettle to compete and make their way. Yet what of those strata of children who have great trouble in growing up? The ones whose development and adjustment and achievement deviate significantly from the norm? What is the future of these children, their parents wonder. At the most personal level, a parent asks, "What will become of my child? Can my child be normal?"

The fears and heartbreak of parents with difficult children are often underscored by the daily challenges of living with them. Parenting is stressful and expensive enough with any child. The high-maintenance or special-needs child can drive parents to the brink. When these parents bring their child to yet another evaluation or therapy, there is an undercurrent of hope and doubt that accompanies the commitments, the decisions, the striving to understand what is wrong and to believe it can be fixed. It is the unstated theme of worry and the seminal question that begs for reassurance: *Can you make my child normal?*

Parents routinely ask me this question, along with variants: "Is he really responsible for what he does? Can he help himself?" "Will she become independent? Am I going to have to support her indefinitely?" "Can he be like other children?"

What Is Normal?

It is worthwhile, therefore, to discuss normality in light of the anguish and hopes of dedicated parents and the many children who struggle and seem to exist on the fringes of belonging. *Normal* has two interpretations:

1. Acting, appearing, performing, or conforming like most others on commonly observed measures
2. Being physically, mentally, and emotionally healthy, and progressing according to natural developmental principles

Normal is a statistical concept, defined as including 95 percent of the observed population and stretching two standard deviations on either side of the mean (middle) of a numerical distribution. That is meaningless gobbledygook for most people, though it is a fundamental principle in statistics. Perhaps the "95 percent" caught your attention—that's a lot of inclusion. Here's an example: if the average height of a grown man is five foot nine and the standard deviation is three inches, then 95 percent of men would range in height from five foot three to six foot three. Does that mean men who are six foot four or five foot two are abnormal? Yes, it does. It doesn't mean they are weird or dysfunctional; it simply means they are beyond the normal range on the variable called "height."

We could measure lots of people on many different characteristics and determine where they fit in and where they do not. So the strict sense of being normal means inclusion within the range that comprises 95 percent of the people you are measuring on that characteristic.

However, there is another meaning for normal, one relating more directly to the concerns of parents. That meaning of normal connotes the state of being physically, mentally, or emotionally healthy, or conforming to a usual or accepted standard. This interpretation of normal differs from the lay meaning of normal, which is more like "typical." Some things that may occur typically are still not considered normal by large segments of the "normal" population. Using marijuana or other drugs may be considered a normal (typical) rite of passage for college students; however, there is much evidence to controvert its adaptive value and normalcy. Crime or violence or aggression may be normal for some cultures, populations, or neighborhoods, but few would argue that such perpetrations are normal in the moral or health sense. Even divorce is considered by many to be an aberration from expectations, though it occurs frequently.

Relating these concepts to the concern for making difficult or errant children normal, we must distinguish between normal as a *statistical and descriptive* function and normal as an *adaptive and developmental* function. Of course, parents really want their children to fit in, to be like others, to not be hampered or burdened in ways that will deprive or exclude them from the opportunities and benefits afforded to most kids. Despite this worthy aspiration, most people overlook the natural effects of individual differences and the fact that conformity to a social standard or adherence to a value is not equivalent to being the same as everyone else.

Clearly, the leaders who run our top institutions are abnormal; they are in the top 2 percent in achievement, intelligence, ambition, and a host of other qualities. That statistical distinction does not make them moral or wholesome; it simply delineates their difference in capacity on certain attributes. Conversely, there are individuals at the other end of the "ability" spectrum who are loving and moral and more "normal" than corrupt leaders will ever be.

What Parents Want

The kind of normal that parents want their kids to be cuts across the two types of normal I've outlined. That kind of normal includes finishing homework and getting good grades, respecting others, showing awareness, empathy, and consideration, controlling oneself and refraining from strange or impulsive behaviors. Sadly, children's variations in genetic and developed abilities slip the minds of parents and educators alike. The humorist and author Garrison Keillor described the mythical Minnesota town of Lake Wobegon, where "all of the children are above average." In reality, half are above average and half are below average. Believe it or not, an eleven-year-old sixth grader who reads at a fourth-grade level and who has a mental age of nine is not only normal, but also within the *average range.* This is factual and unbiased. Statistics trump political correctness every time.

Therefore, children will range in achievement and adaptive proclivities according to natural variations, *even with intensive interventions.* Just as some children will do better than others with the same exposure and opportunities, some children will benefit more from special interventions more than other children will. This is frustrating to parents whose expectations are high (and possibly unrealistic), based upon the reports of a particular treatment efficacy for large groups of children. It is reasonable to expect both that children who learn faster will show improvement more quickly and that children who are behind the curve of developmental sufficiency will benefit more from the appropriate intervention (in much the same way that proper nutrition will help the healthy child function even better and could make the difference between functioning and not functioning for a less-than-healthy child).

For example, I treat a wide range of problems and neurodevelopmental irregularities. The very bright kid who has a concentration problem is likely to respond more quickly and more adaptively than the kid who has moderate autism. However, the one with autism will progress with nonlinear benefit, even if he doesn't catch up to those who blend more easily into the average profile. Perhaps more significantly, the child with greater handicaps or disadvantages is likely—with effective intervention—to correct course with regard to development. This means that he will veer toward normal and healthy development that will accelerate over time. The role of proper intervention must include that "course correction" as well as the relief of symptoms as goals.

Symptom Relief and Developmental Progress

Most parents and professionals are aware of basic developmental stages and principles. These occur throughout our life-span, but they are most pronounced during what is known as the developmental period (birth through about age twenty). It is during this prolonged period that we learn to care for ourselves, to think, and to interact with our environment. We also develop the basic self-regulatory mechanisms that enable us to balance our bodies and minds and the experiences that shape our world views.

Aging gracefully is more than a pithy reference to good looks or acceptance of limitations. It is a process of managing the pings and insults of life and staying on track toward one's growth and developmental potential. When parents see their children hurting, acting strangely, or falling behind, they intuitively know that something is wrong beyond the immediate and distressing symptoms. All children have setbacks, injuries, and traumas. However, some (including adults) live in a world of embattlement with symptoms and lack of direction and progress. It is these folks who draw the most concern and often the most exclusion.

It is a luxury to wax philosophical about developmental life-spans and statistical frequency distributions. But I work in the trenches daily with families in trouble. These people need fast relief, guidance and direction, and evidence that there is light at the end of the tunnel. The treatments and interventions work dramatically for many, sufficiently for most, and not enough for some. How, then, to rationalize the different outcomes and foresee the next steps? (In statistics, this is known as accounting for variance.) What's there to tell the parent who still wonders and worries about the child's present and future?

The Bottom Line for Normal

There is good news, even for those whose children lag behind with severe problems. Almost every child can respond well to appropriate interventions and challenges that will make him more normal. The three critical factors to keep in mind are:

1. The interventions and challenges must catalyze developmental growth and the orienting toward normalcy. That is, they must facilitate the child's "healing" and ability to progress toward more adaptive functioning.
2. Expectations should align with the realities of individual differences. (The short kid in second grade [like me] grows taller, but the other kids grow taller, too. Eventually, everybody attains full height—and some people will be tall and others will be short.)
3. Time is a nonlinear factor. Just as the acorn's growth into an oak tree has periods of dormancy and periods of acceleration, children's growth and progress occurs in spurts—some through genetic unfolding and some by virtue of timely interventions.

Time does not heal everything. One has to judge when to intervene, how to assess progress, and when to change course. However, properly fitted educational, developmental, and medical interventions will set in motion a process by which the child can progress more normally for years after the intervention ends. With the right engagement, time becomes an ally instead of a critic.

With EEG neurofeedback, we set in motion a process by which the brain corrects itself. The vast majority of clients experience symptom relief within a short time. However, some people get better, but normal is a long way off for them. Almost everyone seeking treatment wants relief and improvement soon, and they expect to know that the treatment they paid for provided it. For most people, that improvement comes quickly, yet the real advantages, even for the early responders, reveal themselves over time as acclimatizations to normality become easier and broader. People improve for years to come, because the brain is truly capable, especially if shown efficiently what to do.

There is an old story about someone drawing a bucket of water from a well. A rope suspends the bucket, which hangs very deep in the well. The person cranks the bucket upward for a long time. Thirst and expectation drive his efforts, but fatigue and disappointment overcome him. He leaves without water, not knowing that the bucket hangs just inches beneath the shaft of light eclipsing the deep vertical tunnel.

The message here goes beyond the encouragement to not give up. We have found that people come in for treatment to relieve their symptoms. They leave with their symptoms gone, but also with a newfound transformation. That transformation may unfold a long time after intervention. The bucket holds steady until someone comes along and cranks it into the light. Wherever a child may be on the normal curve, he thirsts for development and for someone to crank up his bucket.

1996

REDUCING STRESS—PART ONE

The many demands of life in the 1990s make stress management a growing need for most of us. When we look beyond the buzzwords, the hype, the guilt, and the advertising, the reality is that so many people are simply overwhelmed. There are pressures, expectations, and responsibilities in an environment that is increasingly more crowded, toxic, and overstimulating. When we are "stressed" by lack of time, money, understanding, assistance, etc., our coping abilities are affected.

There is a significant difference between a *stressor* and *stress*. A stressor is a stimulus or condition that intrudes and demands a response. Stress is a maladaptive response pattern to stressors that we must deal with routinely in life. Stress is more than being "uptight" occasionally or having a bad day. It is a recurring imbalance resulting in the daily wear and tear on the body and mind that leads to dysfunction or breakdown.

The reason stress is harmful is because we are unconsciously creating it, and we become accustomed to sustaining it. Unfortunately, we accept stress as a "normal" part of life, and even rationalize that some stress is good for us. This is a misperception, like thinking that some headaches are good for us.

Much of what we do to cope with this problem focuses on the symptoms but does little to relieve the underlying condition or cause. This is because stress is not a "thing" like a germ or virus or broken part. It is a pattern of maladaptive responses. Think of the warning lights on an automotive dashboard. When they light up, it signals a condition that has reached breakdown. Pouring oil into the crankcase, for example, will usually not remedy the problem of low oil pressure. The system needs repair so it can maintain regulation.

The same is true with stress. To reduce it, we must restore an internal balance of self-regulation. Specifically, this means a balance between *arousal* and *inhibition*, two basic functions of the nervous system. To the question "What is the proper speed to drive a car?", the answer is "It depends on the conditions." Managing stress involves regulating one's internal responsiveness to ever-changing conditions.

In "Reducing Stress—Part Two," I will outline some practical examples.

REDUCING STRESS—PART TWO

Stress is a prison built by maladaptive habits, attitudes, emotions, and response patterns. To relieve and reduce stress, we must modify our internal regulation of *arousal* and *inhibition. Arousal* is the relative state of alertness, stimulation, energy, interest, and heightened emotional and physical responsiveness. Arousal is necessary to interact effectively with people and events around us. It is the mechanism by which we receive and exchange information and action for the functions of living. In the extreme, arousal results in the "fight or flight" response. *Inhibition* is the relative state of inactivity, drowsiness, rest, and relaxation. It is necessary for sleep, digestion, replenishment, and "recharging" of our biological batteries. It is the "reloading" component of effective and purposeful interaction with the world. Inhibition causes our nerves to stop transmitting messages, as brakes cause a car to slow down or stop. Just as safe driving requires the coordinated use of acceleration and braking, self-controlled living involves the proper mixture of arousal and inhibition. Arousal is managed by the part of our nervous system called the *sympathetic* nervous system. Inhibition is managed by the *parasympathetic* nervous system. The interplay of these nervous system parts is vital to stress management.

Various things we do, both intentionally and subconsciously, affect the way our nervous systems manage the braking and acceleration of responses. Habitual mismanagement causes the brake or accelerator responses to get stuck in the "on" position for too long, and this is what we experience as stress. For example, overarousal often results in anger, argumentativeness, difficulty unwinding or relaxing, fear, suspicion, anxiety, restlessness, tension, headaches, and digestive problems. Underarousal may cause attentional problems, depression, pain, PMS, fatigue, and boredom. Many people are chronic victims of overarousal or underarousal, and some people suffer from the symptoms of both. Besides the obvious unpleasantness of symptoms caused by stress, the continuation of these imbalances leads to disease. To relieve the discomfort, many people develop unhelpful appetites and habits to compensate the imbalance—substance abuse, overeating, and other addictive behaviors, thrill-seeking, avoidance, "shutdown"—however, these temporary fixes end up reinforcing the imbalances they once relieved.

There are many healthy and effective ways to manage the arousal and inhibition that control our internal "housekeeping" functions. Diet, meditation, exercise, sleep, and prayer have long been touted as staples in stress management. Music, hobbies, and vacations also work when they allow us to reset and readjust our internal rhythms.

One of the best ways to self-regulate our arousal/inhibition thermostats is through EEG biofeedback, the discipline of brainwave training. EEG biofeedback improves performance, decreases stress, and reduces symptomatic discomfort by teaching people to automatically regulate the brainwave states associated with arousal and inhibition. The result is a natural acceleration and braking appropriate to changing conditions.

2002

WHY EVERY CHILD SHOULD BE INDIVIDUALLY ASSESSED

Would a patient with severe stomach pain receive surgery or medication without obtaining an evaluation? Hopefully not. He probably wouldn't consent to surgery unless the doctor had some tests to confirm its necessity. In the dental office, X-rays are considered fundamental in determining the extent of decay or deterioration. And most of us certainly wouldn't buy prescription eyeglasses without an eye doctor's examination to determine correct visual needs. Yet in education, instruction and intervention *without* diagnostic assessment are the norm. People routinely submit their children to years of education without the benefit of an individually administered examination to determine readiness, learning needs, styles, and limitations.

This is astonishing, especially in light of the evidence that learning and developmental disorders afflict nearly 20 percent of the school-aged population. In addition, many more children with differences struggle to meet curricular rigors or adult expectations that are inappropriate to their abilities, maturity, or neurological functioning. Every child should be individually assessed to monitor development, identify basic personality and learning styles, plan suitable instructional and motivational strategies and environments, and to detect learning or emotional problems for early and effective remediation.

Assessment is *a time-limited, formal process that collects clinical information from many sources in order to reach a diagnosis, to make a prognosis, to render hypotheses about the person's condition, and to determine instructional and other interventions.* Although it includes "tests," assessment is a broader process that integrates numerous measurements with professional clinical interpretation specific to an individual. Assessment may result in diagnoses, but its greater goal is to identify combinations and interactions of strengths and weaknesses in aspects of human functioning that have particular relevance to learning and problem solving (both academically and interpersonally).

Why Aren't Children Routinely Assessed?

Generally, children (or adults) are assessed only when there is a perceived crisis or when symptoms are manifest that perplex others.

The lack of routine individual assessment is attributable to four factors:

1. Financial constraints
2. Skepticism and fear about educational and psychological testing
3. Ignorance about the purposes and needs for assessment and misinformation about tests
4. Absence of crises or noticeably disturbing symptoms or blanket denial that anything may be wrong

For children at risk, off-track, or in trouble, none of these factors justifies the years of frustration, failure, and family heartache that competent assessment can avert.

According to the California State Department of Education and the budget act under Proposition 98, the average per-pupil expenditure was $7,002.00 for the 2001–2002 school year. In 2002 dollars, this means that the average child's entire public education (K–12) costs $91,026.00.

Given the thousands of dollars spent each year per pupil on education and the tens of thousands spent over the course of each child's education, it is quite sensible to spend a small fraction of this sum on the individual assessment that provides direction and effectiveness for the time, money, and effort spent educating each child. Consider for a moment: Would it be sensible to buy a Mercedes-Benz and not afford insurance or snow tires? This, then, is the analogous paradox of spending vast sums to educate children without providing the guidance, direction, and preventive protection afforded by individual assessment.

Don't They Test Children at School?

Children must indeed submit to many tests in school—however, such testing rarely constitutes individual assessment. Most of the testing administered is pencil-and-paper *group* testing, which yields much information about the conformity of groups of students to a standard curriculum but relatively little useful information about the capabilities, learning styles, motivations, and differences among individuals. In general, schools give two types of tests: standardized achievement tests and teacher-made tests. Standardized achievement tests (e.g., CTBS, CAP, Stanford Achievement) are normed on large numbers of students in California or nationwide. They are curriculum-bound in content, yield general information about students' mastery of curricular material, and are intended for use in comparing the relative standings in academic achievement among *groups of students*—that is, *schools.*

Teacher-made tests are given to students to measure the extent to which the children have "learned" the material taught in class and to provide feedback about students' progress. Unfortunately, many teacher-made tests are notoriously unreliable, do not provide accurate and timely feedback to improve learning, are often used in coercive and punishing ways, and supply little (if any) diagnostic information targeted to help the student improve. Additionally, the group testing system uses only a pencil-and-paper format and has inherent biases that tend to reward the good test-takers and penalize the poor test-takers, irrespective of actual achievement or ability.

What about Individual Assessments?

Public school districts employ trained specialists who can administer reputable and useful individual tests. Federal and state laws mandate that the schools identify children with exceptional needs and provide free and appropriate education. School personnel often initiate the request for individual assessments; however, parents may also make the request. In either case, the school must legally follow through with assessments, written reports, and meetings within a specified time (usually fifty days). Although these services are available, it is important for parents to realize that mobilizing them requires a suspected disability that adversely affects a student's education. There are many instances where parents want specific information on their child's functioning, yet school districts have become more stringent and discriminating about the circumstances when they deem individual testing warranted.

This often leaves parents with the choice of struggling against the schools or obtaining a private assessment. An independent private assessment is a wise course of action on several counts. First, a competent and experienced practitioner (especially someone with a background in educational psychology) will usually provide a more comprehensive and targeted assessment. Second, the private practitioner is not biased or restricted by the administrative agenda and policies of the school. Third, the private assessment information can be selectively used to assist the school staff in teaching the child; in situations where disputes exist between the educators' and the parents' views about what is appropriate for the child, the independent assessment can shed light (and evidentiary data) on appropriate decisionmaking and services.

What Should a Competent Assessment Include?

Assessment has purposes beyond labeling and diagnosing. Comprehensive assessment uses a scientific methodology that compares thousands of data points to distinguish among conditions that would account for the same sets of data. The job of the examiner is to guide you and your child through this process and turn up with information that can alert you to difficulties and help you achieve defined goals.

Have the assessment done by someone appropriately trained and licensed (preferably with a doctoral degree). Assessment is a clinical process and should investigate all areas of development relevant to your child's functioning or suspected difficulties. Tests, observations, records, and interviews are tools—but there is no substitute for experienced clinical judgment. When a child manifests symptoms of significant underachievement or maladjustment, a differential diagnosis is necessary to pinpoint the source of the problem. Proper assessment (just like medical diagnosis) uses scientific techniques to "rule out" different disorders that can present similar symptoms.

The assessment process should include a consultation with you, a written report of the results, and specific recommendations for implementation in your child's learning and home environments. Don't settle for some test scores you don't understand plus a statement about whether or not your child qualifies for special services. Look for the following information in your child's assessment:

- Intellectual capacity for school
- An equating of school achievement with intellectual potentials
- An alert to reading, spelling, arithmetic, listening, language, memory, or writing problems
- Measurement of perceptual-motor capacity
- Discovery of dominant learning modality: auditory, visuospatial, kinesthetic, mixed
- Determination of developmental grade level and discrepancies in standard score terms
- Insight into cognitive style: convergent and divergent
- Assessment of factors affecting development, family/peer adjustment, and school performanceself-esteem, motivation, anxiety, depression, anger, and other emotional indicators

- An alert to developing attitude problems and contribution of stressors
- Identification of temperament, interpersonal strengths and weaknesses, and influences on learning

After the assessment is completed, you may want to apprise your child's educators of the results and how they influence your child's learning, development, and achievement. Getting school staff to implement thc results and recommendations can be tricky, but advocating for your child is a major role you can play in modeling responsibility and ensuring a suitable environment for growth.

Levels of Assessment

It is understandable that tests are intimidating to many people. Perhaps our culture and our professional community have erred in the interpretation and meaning often assigned to tests, as well as the agendas they have served. Regrettably, tests are sometimes used to exclude people or to weed out some from opportunities for which they are deemed unfit.

When used appropriately and diagnostically, tests can save time, pinpoint areas of need, and greatly guide diagnosis, description, and meaningful interventions and recommendations. I have used tests strategically and invaluably for twenty-seven years in providing assistance to children and adults. It is simply good professional practice.

However, most of the public and much of the professional community misunderstand or misjudge fundamental elements and principles of testing and assessment. Unfortunately, the competitive applications of testing have obscured the broader scientific bases for the measurement of individual differences.

Most testing (and the general perception of testing) is based on an expectation and familiarity with a mode known as *level of performance.* Though level of performance is only one facet of assessment, it is the aspect most people recognize. Let's review the larger picture:

1. Level of Performance

Level of performance testing encompasses how well the subject (examinee) does. This is measured either in reference to a similar population (group of children the same age, for example) or to a criterion standard (e.g., number of words spelled correctly). The vast majority of tests yield information only in the level of performance domain. Norm-referenced, criterion-referenced, and mastery-referenced scoring systems all compare performance levels, though how they compare them varies. This information is basic and useful because it assesses competencies and shows them in reference to known or assumed standards.

Intelligence tests, academic tests, personality tests, etc. reveal information about how a person performs relative to the performance of others. You can think of level of performance as measuring the height, for instance, of all fourth graders, or measuring how many push-ups each child does, or reading levels of all the students. One could then rank order the scores and judge a particular child's demonstrated competency or position within the group.

What this information does not reveal is whether the performance shows abnormalities or anomalies with respect to the individual's own self. For this, we need to use other neuropsychological techniques.

2. Occurrence of Specific Deficits (Pathognomonic Signs)

Pathognomonic sign testing is concerned with errors and performance deviations that occur almost exclusively among certain populations. For example, as a medical analog, consider tuberculosis or AIDS. Although the blood and skin of people differ, positive markers for AIDS or tuberculosis would only be expected to occur in people carrying these diseases. In a population comprising people with and without these diseases, we could gather lots of measurements across which people with and without the diseases would differ. However, specific signs would distinguish the people with tuberculosis or AIDS because these signs do not occur in others.

Pregnancy is another example. Though it is not a pathological condition, pregnancy is a good example of the principle of pathognomonic sign testing. You (women only, please) can be a little or a lot pregnant, but as far as pregnancy testing goes, the main consideration is whether you are or are not pregnant. Only pregnant women have certain blood and urine characteristics.

Let's take this a step further with regard to behavior. Would you ever expect to drive into your neighbor's driveway thinking it's your own? Or put your key into your neighbor's door lock, mistaking it for your own apartment? Or confuse a sink with a toilet? Hardly. These silly examples give a sense of the breach represented by specific deficits. In neuropsychological testing, the breach occurrences are subtler, but they are highly significant.

3. Patterns and Relationships among Test Scores

As Mark Twain once said, "There are liars, damn liars, and statisticians." Test scores alone can be misinterpreted. A scientific guard against this is the clinical and mathematical analysis of combinations of scores and patterns and relationships among the sores and performances. The old saw "where there's smoke, there's fire" must be subjected to the rigorous scrutiny of comparing performance variability with known profiles of deviations in brain function.

Does the examinee show striking variability in scores on different tests that fits a pattern with regard to the known functions of the two cerebral hemispheres or areas within the cerebral hemispheres? An example: Two children the same age can have Full Scale IQ scores of 98. These are average IQ scores. However, these two children may be far from the same or even similar. Child A might have a Verbal IQ of 98 and a Performance (nonverbal) IQ of 99. His "scatter" or variability among the subtest scores could be minimal—no conspicuous weaknesses, strengths in moderation and balance. Child B could have a Verbal IQ of 78 and a Performance (nonverbal) IQ of 123 with variability ranging between the fifth and the ninety-eighth percentiles. Child B would probably have significant language learning and academic problems along with superior abilities at nonverbal learning. Such a child would undoubtedly excel at spatial and mechanical tasks but would struggle with the codes of language that suffuse reading, spelling, writing, and listening. (Interventions for this child would likely include procedures and strategies targeting specific training of the left hemisphere.) All composite IQs are not the same. Patterns and relationships among scores are critical in properly assessing brain function.

4. Differences in the Adequacy of Motor and Sensory-Perceptual Functions on Two Sides of the Body

Neuropsychologists and neurotherapists are very interested in the integrity of and relationship between the two hemispheres. Are they different in the way they function? Do they work together to enhance performance? Are there specific deficits in either hemisphere that are correlated with compromised performance?

In neuropsychology, such findings are known as lateralization—disparities between left and right sides of the brain that go beyond expected limits for examinees with normal brain functions.

When administered properly, even brief screenings contribute valuable information about your child's neuropsychological makeup that can guide expectations and interventions, indicate deficits needing further attention, and provide predictive information on treatment length and outcomes. The process is complex, however. As wonderful and malleable as the brain is, we need to give it adequate information. Part of the sequence is to gather relevant information in a methodical and translatable manner. That is the essence of assessment.

General Assessment Model

The following assessment model encapsulates an overview of assessment and may assist you in appreciating its value:

ASSESSMENT MODEL

The following notations describe the components of comprehensive assessment from the perspectives of diagnostic methodology and categorical information yielded as an outcome of assessment:

- **Levels of performance**
  - compares and quantifies
  - *interindividual*—compares performances with those of others
  - measures functioning in relation to others at same age or grade level

- **Clinical / descriptive**
  - identifies preferred styles of learning, behaving, perceiving
  - *intraindividual*—compares strengths and weaknesses shown by examinee
  - identifies indicators of distress and potential or manifest disturbance

- **Achievement / mastery**
  - specifies what the person knows or can do (knowledge, skills, performance)
  - assesses achievement of developmental milestones and readiness for learning
  - criterion-related (relative to task mastery rather than relative to performances of others)

- **Differential diagnostic**
  - process of *ruling out* possible disorders
  - uses scientific methodology of hypothesis testing
  - tests for presence of specific deficits that differentiate conditions
  - identifies factors that sustain or hinder performance
  - interprets why some performances are elevated and others reduced

- **Predictive / prescriptive**
  - prescribes recommendations, interventions, treatments
  - offers prognoses, expectations
  - predicts probable outcomes with or without interventions

ASSESSMENT MATRIX

Abilities	1	2	3
Strengths	4	5	6
Weaknesses	7	8	9
Styles	10	11	12
	Coping/ Inhibiting	*Applicative/ Stunted*	*Adaptive/ Maladaptive*

1. Do the identified abilities integrate in the person's coping mechanisms or do they interfere?

2. Is the person able to apply his abilities to everyday demands and real tasks?

3. Are the abilities used toward adaptive or maladaptive results?

4. Are the strengths properly channeled or overextended?

5. Are the strengths advantageous in getting practical tasks done at levels commensurate with abilities?

6. Do the strengths attain adaptive purposes or do they result in manipulation and self-sabotage?

7. To what extend do the weaknesses predominate? Do they exert balancing or humbling effects?

8. Does the person try to use skills beyond what he has in those areas?

9. Are the weaknesses and vulnerabilities controlled and compensated?

10. Do the problem-solving styles provide advantage or do they get in the way?

11. Are the styles efficient and well matched to the challenges, or are they ill suited?

12. Do the habits, talents, idiosyncrasies, and processing mechanisms facilitate adaptive functioning?

2011

WHEN PEOPLE ARE DIFFICULT OR MISTREAT YOU

Surely daily life presents struggles and trials. Along the way, we run into difficult people whose intractable and selfish behaviors are frustrating and hurtful. Expecting that we will face rejection, mistreatment, and even betrayal is not pessimistic, but rather it is realistic. It is a part of life.

Being treated worse than you deserve or expect confronts you with the challenge of adjusting to life on its own terms and adapting effectively when you don't get what you want or need or should receive. I spend much time and effort helping people recognize how these realities affect them and how to deal with them effectively.

In more than thirty years of professional practice and nearly double that in life experience, I've discovered some truths that make it so much easier and more satisfying to cope with the many situations when things go awry and especially when people are difficult, mean, selfish, or unfair. In fact, this area of life is so crucial that I've written a book containing strategies and perspectives to prevail when people are difficult or mistreat you. These principles and techniques are covered in detail in *Living Intact: Challenge and Choice in Tough Times.*

Here is a summary of the proper responses and attitudes when these situations occur:

1. Love the ones who mistreat you.
2. Eliminate your negative emotions and trauma.

3. Forgive them their trespasses.
4. Pray for them.
5. Set limits and boundaries on their behavior.

You've probably learned that if you skid while driving a car, the safe action is to turn your steering wheel in the direction of the skid. Although this is counterintuitive—because your instincts tell you to turn away from the skid—steering in the direction you are skidding uses physics to your advantage and safety. Similarly, when people are offensive, it is tempting and natural to respond instinctively, usually with disadvantageous repercussions. When you learn to counter that instinct by using conscious choice, natural cause and effect, and the instructions from God, the result will yield and reflect saved lives.

2011

YOU CAN'T TELL THE HEART WHAT TO DO

In matters of love, we see both the transforming power that supersedes linear reasoning and the vulnerability that can make us sensitive, fearful, compassionate, foolish, determined, and even mean.

Woody Allen has said, "The heart wants what it wants." My wife says, "You can't tell the heart what to do." Woody Allen married his adopted daughter; my wife married me, so I trust her more. However, I am not content to accept the maxim that you cannot tell the heart what to do. Passion is intoxicating, but I can do without the hangover.

True, you cannot tell the heart what to *feel.* But feelings and actions are different and, though they can and should be related, running one's life based upon feelings as captain surely leads to shipwreck. The wonder of adventure and sensation needs the guidance of a plan and safeguards.

If musical melody and rhythm are like feelings and lyrics like reason, then there are times for each and optimal blendings for enhanced meaning and pleasure. But sometimes, one must turn down the volume or modify the beat. If art draws upon emotion, it should be tempered by reason that evaluates the message and the price.

Art, literature, and history have continually testified to the greatness and foibles of human passions. There are spiritual lessons as well and divine directives that guide us in matters of the heart. God says that you can tell the heart what to do, and he instructs that you should. He commands us to love other people whether or not we feel like it and whether or not they act lovable. Plain and simple, yet oh what a challenge!

If you can tell your heart to swell with compassion and love, even in the face of circumstances and facts that would justify and validate the opposite, then can't you negotiate, discuss, and even overrule the desires of your heart that may lead you astray? Aren't prudence, judgment, wisdom, experience, commitment, and reason necessary ingredients to temper the intensity of desire?

Analytic psychological theories and empirical studies show that individuals develop distinct styles of problem solving and dealing with the ambiguities of life. Some individuals are given to intellectualization and rationalization, while others are prone to make decisions based upon emotion. Just as most people have a preferred dominant handedness, it is most effective to use a predominant psychological style. However, the lack of the other hand or the other style may cause an imbalance that handicaps effective functioning.

You *can* tell your heart what to do while honoring the nature and capacity of the human heart. There is a saying that the longest distance is between the mind and the heart. Perhaps the struggle between good and evil, between wisdom and foolishness is determined along that path.

2000

THE WORLD ACCORDING TO MARK—PART 1—TFT ROUNDED

Bee Brave When Life Stings

Recently, I eliminated a bee phobia plaguing an eleven-year-old to the point where he had to leave summer camp. His parents brought him to me with a variety of complaints about his compromised functioning and poor adjustment.

He was a demanding child of high intellect, defensive and argumentative, without friends and bereft of personal responsibility. Previously diagnosed with ADHD, this boy took (during the school year) fifty milligrams daily of Ritalin, which he hated.

After some initial assessment, examination, history taking, observation, and discussion, I confided to the parents my doubt that their son had ADHD and my evidence that his brain and nervous system were functioning within normal limits off medication. His father, a physician, professed his openness to trying a nonmedication approach. They seemed relieved about this part of my diagnosis, since the sole treatment of Ritalin had done nothing to improve their son's relations with them or with the world. Still, the parents were perplexed and in need of guidance about raising their son.

So, after experiencing the wonderful benefits of TFT, this family was eager for input and suggestions to improve their situation. In discussing with them a context for engaging my services, I outlined the beliefs and philosophy that govern my approach to working with people. Here is a summary:

1. **Growing up presents essentially similar challenges for everyone**—There are many stages and tasks that we move through to know and master our own bodies and their relationships with the world around us. Achieving progressive levels of mastery; discovering how to meet our own needs; sacrificing to meet the needs of others; making decisions about how friendly, favorable, and receptive the world is; and learning to live life on its own terms—these are challenges we all face. Learning to take care of ourselves (and others), finding our strengths and weaknesses, finding our value and values, regulating affect and impulses, delaying gratification, adjusting to work and effort, weathering rejection, practicing self-control, partaking in negotiation and compromise, coping with loss and disappointment, tolerating differences and ambiguity—these are among the many tasks awaiting the resourceful folks and the limited ones alike.

   I find traditional nosological diagnoses contribute very little toward helping people. It is a professionally convenient, sophisticated form of name-calling, more suited to the competitive puerile egos of children than to the practice of healing. Unfortunately, the populace has followed the professional lead in seeking meticulous diagnoses, purportedly in the service of effective treatment. This heightened analytical search often loses sight of the goal, capitulating instead to worship of the method. I have seen so many families exhaust all their resources and energy trying to establish the correct diagnosis that effective intervention eludes them. It is reminiscent of a story about a man walking in circles at night on the banks of the River Thames in London. A policeman approached this suspicious-looking gent and asked what he might be doing.

"I'm looking for my keys, officer," replied the man.

The bobby watched the man feverishly pacing a tight circle outlined by the streetlamp's glow, baffled by the activity around a patch of lit sidewalk with no keys to be seen.

"Well, I say there, did you lose them here recently?"

"Oh, I didn't lose them here at all. I'm quite sure I lost them about a mile down the way."

Muttered the bobby, "Then why, for bloody sake, are you looking here?"

With a poker face, the man replied, "Because here is where the light is."

In my practical world, there are only two diagnoses: the Easy Ones and the Hard Ones. All the rest is just name-calling.

Certainly, some people are more limited or impaired than others. That the ease and rate of achievement among people varies greatly should not blind us to the basic necessity of meeting each individual at his level of readiness and progressing from that point. Throughout many developmental domains, the challenges for those with "special needs" are equivalent to those faced universally. Some people have to work more or differently in certain areas than do others. Excising these challenges to a diagnostic list stains life in unrealistic specimens. For example, impulsiveness, distractibility, and disorganization are often characterized as hallmarks of a disorder. Such symptoms may feature prominently among poorly functioning individuals. But let's not forget that a big part of maturity is the regulation of impulses, the curtailment of selfish desires, and the development of abilities to get important things done when so many stimuli vie for our attention and so many temptations beckon.

The normal developmental challenges (surmounted gradually) and exacerbated symptomatology interweave among individuals whose trajectories of maturation go smoothly and those who are impeded. When appraising the problems, let us beware of labels and remember that growing up is not easy for the Easy Ones and is harder for the Hard Ones.

2. **Hold people accountable**—When you label people with the history of their actions and causation, you hold them accountable. This does not involve diagnosis or accusation, nor does it imply blaming, interpreting, or attributing motives. It simply means linking people with what happened because of them in specific, readily observable, and neutral terms. Editorializing and criticizing are different from holding people accountable.

   When you distinguish these differences, you gain a major advantage in reality.

   Holding people accountable does not imply or exclude forgiveness. It does not preclude your reactions, nor does it obligate you to them. It does not mean that people are necessarily "responsible" for their actions or that they "own" them. It simply describes a reflection of empirical events that pairs people with what they did, what they caused, and what happened as a result of their involvement.

Holding people accountable is a reference necessary for consensual reality, the making and sustaining of agreements, and is the basis for enabling people to evaluate effectiveness and make adjustments.

Holding someone accountable allows separation of the worth of the person from the effects and desirability of his particular behaviors. We have all heard the admonition, "Criticize the behavior, not the person." This becomes possible only when behaviors are *seen* separately from the blend of associations that form personality styles and emotional reactions.

When you hold someone accountable, you tie him to the reality-based events from which truth emanates and reliability accrues. Accountability builds your own credibility, as well as the ability of the other person to see himself realistically and make flexible modifications.

Most of us cheat. We are not naturally good observers of ourselves, and we garner perceptions of our actions and interactions to conform to a consistent self-image, favorable or otherwise. Also, there is an unwritten system of social grace by which most humans operate. It goes like this: if you won't call attention to my mistakes, inconsistencies, and hypocrisies, I'll overlook yours. As long as we observe this unstated agreement, neither of us will be embarrassed or hurt.

Nice try, but it doesn't work. Most of us do it anyway because it is expected and because we are not sure whom and when we can trust. This is the antithesis of accountability. It is a make-believe system of mutual self-delusion. Ironically, accountability allows us to trust because it reports and reflects our behaviors as they are, unfiltered by and independent of the needs and opinions of others.

When you hold people accountable, you give the gift of independence, allowing others to exist separate from your needs, reactions, and expectations about you. You give the feedback that others need to make informed decisions about change and trust.

3. **Make good bargains**—People do things for their reasons, not necessarily yours. If you want to motivate people and have them interested in meeting some of your expectations, then create situations in which they can win (i.e., get what they want). Making good bargains isn't bribery (which connotes an illicit temptation or deal), and it doesn't involve coercion. It does involve the structuring and negotiation of behavior exchanges so that each party gets at least some of the outcomes he wants. It often involves compromise and always requires a careful consideration (listening and observation) of what is meaningful to the other person.

   Making good bargains is different from making people offers they can't refuse. The latter causes resentment, while the former fosters independence, responsibility for decision making, the sense of competence, and the general expectation that the world is an equitable and rewarding place.

   A good bargain means that *you* get something out of it, too. Don't simply be a nice guy. Make deals you can live with. I am reminded of the story about the man who is hiking up a mountain when he encounters a snake. It is hot and dusty, and the snake asks the man if he can hitch a ride on the man's shoulders.

"You walk so much faster than I can slither," whined the snake, "and it is hot and I am tired. I don't weigh much. I'll keep your neck and shoulders cool, and I promise I won't bite."

"All right," said the man, generously, "climb aboard."

So, the snake curled around the man's upper body and freeloaded a ride up the mountain. As they reached the top, the man said, "Okay, we're atop the mountain, you can get off now."

Suddenly, the snake bit the man viciously then slithered away. The stunned man fell down, shocked as the venom overtook him. As he lay dying, he called out to the snake, "You promised you wouldn't bite me. I was nice to you. I carried you up the mountain. How could you do such a thing?"

The snake laughed. "I'm a snake, you fool. Snakes lie and snakes bite. That's what we do."

A good bargain implies honor. Know what you're giving and what you're getting. Keep your word, and expect the same. The payoff for win-win is more than the situational prize. It is knowing you can adapt and survive in varied and conflicting circumstances. Teach it to others through repeated examples.

4. **Tell the truth, emotionally and behaviorally**—Amazing things unfold when you tell the truth. What does it mean to tell the truth? It means confessing your emotional experience and honestly reporting that which makes a difference between you and others. Telling the truth does not mean you voice every thought or that you inveigh absolute or relative truths for the approval or benefit of converts. Telling the truth lets others know

where you stand, what is important to you, and how the actions and intentions of others affect you.

Telling the truth is saying what is so, as best you can earnestly discern it. It is characterized by “I” messages, rather than by editorials about others. The truth is how you feel, not how you think you should feel or how others make you feel. By the way, I am not extolling feelings as paramount; indeed, feelings are vastly overrated. It's just that your feelings are a lot more relevant and pressing than most of what we rationalize about them.

Don't mistake telling the truth for giving people “permission” to exceed boundaries. Permission implies sanction and too often leads to the selfish manipulation of reality. Telling the truth is the acknowledgment of reality, a candor that connects you reliably and responsibly to others. It leads to respect, not exploitation.

One of the truths revealed in my work is that parents frequently do not like their children. They *love* their children, but often distinctly and fervently disdain their habits, motivations, values, and manners in conducting relationships with the parents themselves and others. Moreover, they find their parenting roles arduous and unsatisfying. Telling this truth does not give parents permission to abandon their children or their duties, but it does create a context for reformation of limits and expectations, and this sets a foundation for improved outcomes.

One of my truths is that children owe their parents a major contribution toward the satisfaction of parenting. This contribution is not measured in rent or honor or respect, but rather in the gratification that parents experience as a result of their efforts in raising children.

Offspring have a kind of indefinite homework, graded by the competence and rewards experienced by those who rear and provide for them.

Some might proclaim this view as unfair. As my wife used to tell our children, "The fair is in August."

Whether something is fair necessarily implies comparison with some set of rules or standards. Telling the truth requires a discussion of the rule(s) by which someone's complaint or allegation is considered. Unfair means that a rule was broken or that someone acted outside the boundaries (as in "Foul ball!"). Proclaiming that something is not fair may actually be an attempt to justify a personal distaste for an outcome, not a violation of justice.

The truth may sometimes hurt, but telling it is never offensive and always contributes to healing.

5. **Act like a model whom the camera is always recording—** It is human nature to learn vicariously, as well as through demonstration, copying, and practice. The transmission of information and experience need for survival is etched into our culture through family, teaching, work, recreation, and entertainment. Technology has bred some warping of appropriate sources of modeling, but its advent does not negate the survival pattern endemic to man: we learn how to live by watching, copying, and apprenticing others.

   Children have subcultures, and we can barely understand them. However unusual their fads and departures may seem, young people still must learn from those who went before them how to engage and master the myriad of daunting challenges and complexities that independent, effective living requires.

> People are watching you, even when it is not obvious. This is a call to pride and responsibility, not paranoia or guilt. There is a maxim for circumventing hypocrisy: do what I say, not what I do. I say that if there is a hypocrisy to your life, let it be this: *do what I do, not what I say*. In other words, let your life shine with examples of self-corrections, improvements, and growth. Saying one thing and doing another is the foible that snares us all. Do you not think that others (including your children) have also caught themselves in this snare? Talk about your mistakes, not romantically, but with gratitude and understanding. Live life as though you have learned from mistakes. Modeling is the gift that we must bestow carefully and lovingly.
>
> You are an actor in a show whose end is better than its beginning. Most people will not walk out if there is the hope of improvement, surprise, and identification. Give these gifts, take it seriously, and enjoy the role.
>
> Jesus was the ultimate model, baring himself for all scrutiny and example for all time—and the world has not been the same since. Though you and I are not without blemish, let us act our best, as if we are always on record—for indeed we are, by the All-Knowing, and by those who know less, but who look upon us for example and direction.

Among the miracles offered by TFT are those made possible when anxieties, fears, and other negative emotions disappear. Then the fun begins; it's time for favorite things. I love the words from the song "My Favorite Things":

> When the dog bites, when the bee stings, when
> I'm feeling sad,
> I simply remember my favorite things, and then
> I don't feel so bad.

Actually, when life stings, I do TFT—then I don't feel bad, and *then* I remember my favorite things.

One of my favorite things is another type of TFT: I call it Talk-Filled Training. It is the forum for the guidance, redirection, and skills training that help people get back on track and employ the success strategies that make life worth living. It is training, not therapy, and it occurs *aprés-symptoms.*

This pleasure is TFT of a different nature. Unlike Thought Field Therapy (Th-F-Th), it is Talk-Filled Training (Ta-F-Tr). I cannot call it TFT^2 or 2(TFT), so I'll call it TFT-R-rounded the use of TFT to eliminate negative symptoms and maladaptive responses to clear the way for relational guidance and training in building adaptive behaviors and shaping positive life attitudes.

2002

THE AROUSAL PARADOX AND THE CHALLENGE OF CHANGE

As we embark upon the challenges of the new millennium, few of these challenges are as daunting as the crucible of mental health. The combination of dwindling resources, multiplying stressors, increased demands and expectations, and the frustration of intractable psychological problems that detract from the quality of life all impose a huge burden on those who are hurting and those who purport to heal them.

Psychological healing and the development and maintenance of stable mental health now embrace and depend upon the fusion of physiological brain science with traditional knowledge detailing how people become robust, resistant, and able to weather setbacks and handle the demands of life. Maturity, stability, and responsibility—those paragons of healthy adjustment—are increasingly seen as functions of effective self-regulation of arousal and the corollary increase in the ability to master challenges at many levels of internal biology and external environmental demands and changes.

From this perspective, we view mental health, developmental, and other disorders as reflecting malfunctions in self-regulation and arousal; therefore, the most direct and effective interventions are aimed at developing and restoring stable, functional, and flexible arousal. EEG neurofeedback is a significant tool in this process.

In working with various dysfunctions, we may deal with people whose nervous systems are underaroused, overaroused, or unstable (mixed underarousal and overarousal). Typically, many conditions reflect poor functioning at low levels of arousal. This refers to brainwave and physiological activity associated with theta bandwidths (4–7 Hz) and sometimes alpha bandwidths (8–13 Hz). Often, people with ADD, depression, trauma, compulsive behavior, or addictions do not function well, tolerate, or transition through these low arousal states. Much of their symptomatology reflects this nervous system mismanagement and attempts to relieve, escape, or substitute other physiological activity for the poorly tolerated low arousal states.

Paradoxically, the low arousal states that cause so much difficulty can also facilitate the healing process and the maintenance of relaxed alert functioning. The key to achieving this is the structured presentation of incremental challenges to the brain, much along the lines of the physical exercise model: challenges that are at first formidable become—through gradual, incremental, repeated practice—an automatic, relatively effortless part of the repertoire.

Basic and Advanced Training

EEG biofeedback is initially directed at conditioning the neurophysiological responses of the brain and nervous system. As the brain learns to respond to the momentary challenges of perceiving and correcting brainwaves, it becomes flexible, stronger, and more resistant to stressors and impositions. The initial training (first twenty to forty sessions) is known as "eyes-open SMR/beta" training. (SMR—sensorimotor rhythm—and beta refer to frequency bands of brainwaves that are reinforced.) We may think of this conditioning as "basic training"—almost like conditioning a skater, whose competitive sport involves higher-order skills, but whose success certainly depends upon a reasonable level of fitness and automaticity with basic rudiments of skating. So it is with brain and neuronal functioning. Once this is under control (or moving predictably in that direction), we are able to accelerate the healing and growth process by using another type of EEG neurofeedback called alphatheta training.

Alphatheta (also called deep-state training or EEG hypnosis) emphasizes achieving a relaxed, open state of mind and helps direct the trainee to produce brainwave patterns that promote deep relaxation, reflection, and the spontaneous imagery of the subconscious. Alphatheta training is extremely helpful in dispelling negative self-talk, releasing the grip of past traumas, and rescripting compulsions and unproductive behavior patterns within a comfortable mental state. This training allows people to move mental and emotional blockages toward optimal mental performance.

Though alphatheta neurofeedback has been used successfully for decades with adults suffering addictions, alcoholism, or posttraumatic stress disorder, it is gaining popularity as a successful intervention for ADD/ADHD youngsters. For almost everyone who tries it, the alphatheta experience is a delightful journey inward that results in profound relaxation, pleasure, and new or enhanced ability to "lighten up," relinquish bad habits, and experience different points of view with more empathy and less defensiveness.

For the ADD child, alphatheta can be a revolution in the ownership of experience and responsibility. Typically, only a few sessions will produce noticeable changes in the child who has for years been fiercely attached to his sense of being unduly victimized or wronged.

Low Arousal and Extinction

Alphatheta teaches people to feel comfortable in low arousal states. This is crucial for two reasons:

1. Most trauma is reinforced and kept active in tandem with elevated arousal. In other words, when people think of events that have caused great unpleasantness and discomfort (such as the constant negative environmental feedback hurled at the ADD child), they pair-associate the event with

a nervous system overarousal that fuses the memory and the emotional displeasure—thus, constantly and intermittently reinforcing that connection. Remember that when you pay attention to a behavior, even a thought, you reinforce (strengthen) it. In trauma or other negative patterns, what gets reinforced is the overarousal associated with the event. It is as though the person is reliving the actual experience (certainly on neuronal and emotional levels). By inducing low arousal states, alphatheta trains the mind to disengage or disassociate the memory (and impact) of unpleasant events from the negative emotions that have been bonded to it. Freedom from negative emotions is freedom indeed! Alphatheta sessions are a real pleasure for ADD/ADHD kids because they can experience themselves apart from threat.

2. Alphatheta is good for ADD/ADHD for a neurological reason: it allows the frenetic and irritable brain to experience and learn relaxation in a controlled brainwave state that had been previously uncontrolled and excessive. Most ADD/ADHD children have excessive theta or alpha (or both) brainwaves emitting rampantly in disorderly fashion in the brain. Alpha (brainwave frequencies between approximately 8–12 Hz—cycles per second) and theta (brainwave frequencies between approximately 4–7 Hz—cycles per second) are normal parts of brain function. However, excesses of these patterns, particularly in the frontal parts of the brain, are abnormal; such excesses interfere with concentration, planning, organization, and mood stabilization. Too much of this slow wave activity makes people foggy and/or irritable. Because these foggy, irritable states are inherently unrewarding, people plagued with them unconsciously and habitually engage in behaviors (neurological and overt) to escape and compensate for the dysfunctional low-frequency state. Overtly, such behaviors include stimulation-seeking, risk-taking, hyperactivity, provoking others, and, eventually,

self-medicating with drugs or alcohol. Inwardly, the nervous system avoids experiencing the discomfort of irritable low arousal, but also, tragically, the inner resources, renewal and rejuvenation, and the spiritual awakenings that require looking inward. By carefully guiding the client to experience the low arousal state as natural, pleasant, and refreshing, the neurotherapist allows the child's brain to discover its innate capacity to relax and to summon its "safe" resources.

Low arousal states can be transformationally healing. As such, they have been a part of Eastern medicine for centuries. The ADD/ADHD child is typically self-absorbed and focused inward due to excessive and irritating slow wave activity, but paradoxically does not experience the awareness and relaxation that low arousal and inner experience can generate.

By training the brain toward stability with neurofeedback, we are able to train the brain both to function at a high level and to maintain stability under challenge conditions. This training strengthens the apparatus of brain self-regulation so that a person is not so readily upended by events. The trained brain will be capable of more resilience under challenge. It will sustain a more robust "self." The threshold may be raised on the level of stress at which a person becomes symptomatic.

The ADD Loop

A very familiar scenario is repeated routinely for those with ADD: tThe person applies himself to a task...and gets stuck! Some people freeze up, some become frustrated or angry, some give up easily, and some redouble their efforts. The effect is ironically similar: the harder the person tries, the more his brain stresses and the less efficient his performance becomes. (This has been documented repeatedly by medical imaging studies of the ADD brain under challenge conditions.)

This is indeed a defining characteristic of ADD. However, since the average person can't see this relationship, its repeated occurrence often brands the ADD person as lazy. This is both tragic and inaccurate. The reality is that normal brain function depends upon the intermittent recurrence of the resting response within a period of exertion or challenge. Because the ADD brain has not learned to rest when challenged, it goes into overdrive and stalls or freezes. People who recognize this episode sometimes term it "brain lock." Most ADD people simply experience the discomfort, restlessness, and shame of not measuring up to the challenge. Then the avoidance or release mechanisms kick in, and the task gets abandoned while the person gets criticized.

Awakening the Rest

This framework is seminal for ADD/ADHD, but goes beyond a set diagnosis to incorporate the model of mental fitness that incorporates structured and strategic brain challenge as a method of fortifying, growing, and expanding.

The paradox of arousal is that identical levels can produce either functionality or dysfunction, depending upon flexibility and appropriateness of circumstance. Changing toward adaptive responses to challenge is the mechanism by which our brains simulate and practice neurologically the abilities to meet the demands of life. Improving upon arousal modulation and learning to welcome and meet challenges creates stronger, more flexible brains, individuals, and societies.

2002

GRAVE MATTERS

My father died last week. I delivered the eulogy, and after the burial, my family began a week of ceremonial mourning known in the Jewish tradition as *sitting Shiva.* (If you are interested in a copy of my eulogy and poetry for his death, please backchannel me. I would consider it a contribution to his honor.)

Interestingly, a Jewish custom at the grave site is for the immediate family members to shovel three loads of dirt upon the lowered casket. It is supposed to be done with the back of the shovel to symbolize hardship. As I shoveled with the back of the shovel, I thought about reversal and death being the reversal of life. The only correction for that reversal was the Resurrection.

Shiva involves a week of mourning where you sit on wooden or cardboard boxes and grieve. Mirrors are covered, there is no TV or music, and there is lots of food (contrary to what you may think, death is no reason to stop eating, at least for Jews). Relatives and friends of the family and the deceased visit to pay condolences and join in the mourning.

It is a time of sadness and relief, of support and loneliness, of boredom and interest. Sitting on boxes for a week is quite boring. Relatives are both boring and interesting. It's interesting and emotionally provocative to spend time with people who have known you your whole life, yet they don't really know you. We talked about my father, of course, alternately roasting and endearing him for his virtues and foibles in life and for his bold abandonment of departure. He was eight-six, older than anyone else living in the extended family, but we don't excuse him on that basis. He simply left, and the banter between him and my mother over who would drive whom to the cemetery is finished.

"Did you hear the story about the couple who bought adjacent cemetery plots?"

"No, what happened?"

"As the story goes, one of them dies, and the plot thickens."

In the hearse on the way to the cemetery, my father's sister swore that he was already laughing at us. Perhaps this was her testimonial to his controlling nature and peculiar expressions of independence. My own opinion is that my father could not bear to live without my mother, his companion of fifty-two years. When she began to have strokes two years ago, his decline and panic accelerated. He always was the first one out of the stadium when he thought the game was decided. He hated crowds, and bugs and rain as well.

In my mother's living room, we reminisced and reissued my father's jokes. Everyone present has heard them too many times, but we were a captive audience. Here's where I came in: it's no longer a competition, because I am the only one to maintain this library of heritage. Genes pass on among themselves, but humor requires human effort. Even groaning takes practice. The relatives constantly traded comments about how much I look and act like my father and a cousin. For me, it was mortifying and scary. If this be the result of discovering identity, I'd rather look for myself elsewhere.

The psychological aspects of this experience are what I'd like to share with you. *Sitting Shiva* is a kind of psychotherapeutic hell. First of all, there was lots of past trauma revisited and compiled with the present difficult circumstances. Imagine sitting in a room, day after day, and listening to stories of your childhood—rather like the accused hearing what transpires in the jury room. I recused myself to the bathroom repeatedly to tap and treat myself. The bathroom was a popular place, for several of my revered elders now wear diapers. No matter what they've done to you, how much they've embarrassed you, it's really hard to hold anything against someone who wears diapers.

In addition to my own traumas, the traumas and problems of my family were on parade. My severely depressed step-aunt lauded the competence of her newfound therapist. To the approval of the clan, my aunt described what a long cry she had in therapy. This result was apparently the standard by which the therapist's competence was confirmed.

In turn, my relatives vented and described their personal agonies. I felt invisible. I wanted to tap them all into peace. It is so frustrating and exasperating to have this wonderful therapeutic tool and to witness so many people ignoring it, not taking it seriously, not even trying it. I am not bashful. Perhaps I even command some respect with regard to therapeutic knowledge. But I am still a fool when it comes to suffering. I am captivated by its hold on us in much of life and by our responses to it. To be thwarted in healing is indeed a difficult feeling. Sometimes it is better to be quiet, but suffering is difficult to witness, as well as to experience.

There is the story about a man in Naples, Italy, who went to see a doctor about his melancholia. In between this man's sobs, the doctor told him to visit the theater as a means of relieving his distress. "You ought to go across the piazza and see a show featuring the great Carlini, for he is known to make even the saddest souls brighten with laughter. It will lift your spirits far higher than any tonic I can give you." The despondent man waved away the doctor's suggestion, lamenting that it would be of no help. "You see," he wailed, "I *am* Carlini."

I have learned that sometimes it is more appropriate to join people in suffering than to relieve it, even if I think it can be relieved. That frustration and deliberations are also aspects of suffering. And so the cycle continues. Death, of course, is irreversible, a bittersweet certainty that absolutes do exist in an oft confusing world. Sometimes we tap, sometimes we play taps, sometimes we listen to taps.

I hoped that this would be a touching story.

2010

JUSTICE AND MERCY

In our postmodern world, we still struggle with opinions, misgivings, and decisions about punishment, leniency, clemency, and holding people accountable. The media and daily experience pummel us with brash outrages and personal suffering. Criminal acts, corporate greed, backroom deals, and brazen transgressions cry out for justice and retribution. Yet each of us wants to be forgiven for ignorance and questionable behavior in those "What was I thinking?" moments. When caught for the act, we want desperately to be treated with mercy and given a chance to move on.

The balance between justice and mercy is played out regularly in personal relationships, especially those within the family. Though we may not be able to individually control the banks, administrative leaders, or sociopaths, we should be able to control and influence our children—right? It's a huge job with demands that grow as the rules change with development and societal complexity.

The core of parental responsibility and effectiveness involves teaching children rules and methods pertinent to survival and decent living. For most parents, holding children accountable and keeping them sanguine and motivated takes center stage, but this balancing act is supported by the backstage team that coordinates and resolves the conflicts between justice and mercy. That team is composed of your mind and your heart, the forces of logic and practicality versus emotion and compassion.

Justice requires that the demands of rules be satisfied. When people misbehave or violate norms or the rights of others, there must be consequences that teach them to obey and act within limits. Mercy, conversely, is *not* getting what one deserves for transgressions.

How does one balance these two vital lessons? The most important tip I can relate is this: when you get control of yourself and the principles of effective behavior change, you can blend justice and mercy more naturally and effectively. Many parents complain to me despairingly that they routinely punish or rescind privileges, even though they see it doesn't work correctly. They feel compelled to enforce consequences that are ineffective, simply because they don't know what else to do, and they fear their authority will otherwise be undermined.

In this situation, parents need professional help. Competent and successful direction will enable you to train your kids to mind and follow rules, allow you to be merciful without guilt or self-doubt, and free you from the burden of being a heartless enforcer.

1995

ONE FLEW UP TO THE CUCKOO'S NEST

Interval Training for the Birds and Other Creatures of Habit

Once upon a time, there was a boy who hated doing homework. His parents thought that homework was very important. They knew that their son was smart, and they held up high standards for his performance. The boy supposed inwardly that homework was probably important (although he overtly rebelled and scoffed at the meaninglessness of his assignments). Although he understood most of the work (at least when the teacher explained it), sitting down to review, practice, and complete assigned work was torturous. The boy was bright and talented, but he wasn't very organized or disciplined. He was persistent and effective at things *he* wanted to do. But when it came to satisfying the demands of others (particularly on *their* timetables), he often fell short.

Predictably, there was much conflict and angst between the boy and his parents. The homework war stretched on and on, with battles and skirmishes almost nightly. His parents nagged him with stern looks of disapproval. They often worked up to a fevered pitch of exhortation, holding the boy in custodial confusion with reminders that he was smart, but that he was going to be a bum. These associations built very negative feelings in the boy about schoolwork and himself (not to mention his parents and teachers) and helped him develop firm and resistant behaviors of avoidance and guilt. Naturally, this state of affairs did little to coerce improved work and learning habits or productive motivation. The boy pretty much gravitated toward the default option of gaining pleasure from what he liked to do.

One of his favorite attractions at this time in his young life was a cuckoo clock in his room. It hung high above his bed, tethered by the long chains and suspended weights that sustained its mechanical life. The boy was fascinated by the carved, stained wooden house perched loftily above his reach. He was especially infatuated with the little cuckoo bird that lived in the house and emerged periodically. This bird became the boy's imaginary friend, their relationship enhanced by the bird's appearances on the hour and half-hour. As in any love relationship, barriers to closeness became painfully apparent, and so it was that the boy grew frustrated with obstacles separating him from his adored friend. One obstacle was the height of the clock. The boy could only reach the clock by jumping on the bed. After repeated trampoline efforts, the boy's face could just about reach the cuckoo's door; even then, his closeness to the bird was transitory—a moment of exhilaration, tormented by the frustration of gravity. Like a smitten Romeo, the boy often stood forlornly on his bed, lonely and exposed in his longing for the chick on the veranda towering above.

Each half-hour brought the cuckoo out for a tittering unitary tease. Although the boy knew that half-hours delivered but one ephemeral chirp, he felt compelled nonetheless to visit his friend whenever possible. These trysts were governed, of course, by the relentless schedule of time. Whatever the cuckoo's limitations, it was certainly punctual—that is, as long as its regulatory mechanisms remained adjusted.

Alas, the cuckoo did not remain regulated, for the little boy interfered with its schedule. He wanted the bird to cuckoo more frequently, at *his convenience* (much as the adults in his world insisted on frequent performances from him). So the boy began to fiddle with the long chains and suspended weights that controlled the clock's timing and, in turn, made the cuckoo work.

Around this time, it so happened that his parents were becoming helplessly frustrated with the boy's lackadaisical performance and with their ineffectiveness at changing it. Deciding that professional help was warranted, they took him to the doctor. Though ordinarily the boy didn't like visiting doctors, this time the experience was different. The doctor didn't give him any injections or explore him with instruments. Actually, the doctor spent hardly any time with him at all, but mostly talked with the boy's parents. After the visit, the boy had to take medication to help him do his homework, behave better, and listen to his parents (or so they said). Although the boy couldn't understand how pills could make homework any better or make him listen to his parents if he didn't want to (and he didn't, because they endlessly disapproved and nagged him), he swallowed them anyway. He had to, because his parents insisted; so the boy followed the usual pattern of resentfully yielding to his parents' demands and getting back at them in other ways.

In response to these pressures, the boy became tenacious and rigid about getting his way. He had an unarticulated, emotionally staunch resistance to other people imposing their will on him. He felt jilted, "done to," or violated, as adults might say when given the chance and clarity to comment on their victimhood. The boy had no words for these uncomfortable feelings about his enforced passivity in treatment. Had he been asked, he may have just told the grown-ups to go away. As it was, the medication made him feel peculiar, and he thought of himself as a lab experiment that wasn't going very well. He tried to stay away from his parents and their world of frowns and demands, and he preferred to take charge of what he could. He needed some control and rewards; since other people were controlling him, he would find ways to make them stop and to turn the tables. Quite predictably, the boy turned to the cuckoo clock.

He decided to make the cuckoo appear more frequently—at his whim, if it could be arranged. The boy fiddled with the long chains and suspended weights. Sure enough, he made the cuckoo emerge and chirp as if it were in training. As he manipulated the clock's mechanism, the boy experienced an odd mixture of sensations: joy at seeing his cuckoo, the mysterious thrill of power, the familiar fear that something bad would happen, and a compulsion to control his bird ever more intensely and obviously. At first, the bird communicated obediently as the boy pulled the chains. Soon, however, the weights became quite imbalanced; the cuckoo chirped very slowly, the time was wrong, and the boy grew anxious, angry, and impatient. Eventually, one chain was suspended at full altitude, just below the clock where the boy could not reach it. The clock had stopped with the cuckoo stuck in the out position, its silent plastic mouth open and its painted tongue dangling disabled over the boy who, by now, was writhing in disgust and medication rebound on the bed below. A solo circus of ornithology hung suspended over childhood in bas-relief.

After a long, painful time, the boy's mother entered his room and surveyed the situation. Because he was asleep, she stifled her reaction (which was to blame the boy for breaking the clock). Finger-pointing and reproof would have to wait until he was awake to appreciate it. She covered him and kissed him, and she shook her head in dismay as she regarded the cuckoo. Sadly, she left the room.

His parents knew it was time for a change, so they took the boy to another doctor—this time to a counselor. This doctor talked with the boy for a long time, asking all kinds of questions about what the boy enjoyed and what he liked to do. The doctor listened and even joked; after awhile, the boy hesitantly shared the situation about the cuckoo. The doctor listened, asked some questions, then listened again as the boy talked and cried. He felt surprised, embarrassed, helpless, and relieved as the doctor listened to his stories and his sobs. The boy was slightly afraid and felt very guilty. He suspected that he would never see his cuckoo again, just the punishment he deserved. The doctor smiled, patted him on the shoulder, and tousled his hair. Then the boy waited while his parents met for a long time with the doctor.

They stopped giving him medicine. Much to his surprise, his parents didn't scold him. In fact, they promised him that they would get the clock fixed, and this enlivened his spirits. On the way to visit the doctor the next week, they stopped at the repair shop and picked up the clock. The boy's excitement grew as he anticipated seeing and apologizing to his bird.

The doctor was friendly. He kidded around with the boy and used examples and stories to explain to the boy how to improve things for himself. He told the boy that life had rules, and that it would be much more fun if the boy learned what the rules were, how to follow them, and how to win—just like in a game. The doctor showed the boy how to relax, how to breathe more smoothly, how to concentrate, and how to control his thoughts and moods. He showed the boy some really cool ways to observe and monitor what his brain and body were doing.

His father hung the repaired cuckoo clock back on the wall above the boy's bed; this time he positioned it lower so the boy could look directly at the cuckoo's door when he stood on the bed. The boy appreciated these efforts, and he felt grateful and relieved to see his friend chirp regularly again. From this point forward, he vowed to be more careful and respectful of the cuckoo clock. His renewal was tinged with anxiety, however, about his mistakes and his eagerness to see his cuckoo and maintain self-control. He felt a little sheepish around his parents, and he experienced a strange admixture of remorse, resentfulness, embarrassment, helplessness, and dependence. He really wanted to get along and to do well, and he still yearned for his rewards and independence.

Fortunately, his parents had learned quite a lot from these miserable events. Committed far more to positive results and their son's well-being than to their own pride and opinions, his parents set up a system to gradually change the boy's habits.

They learned this from the new doctor, along with some attitudes and expectations that made sense and felt really wholesome: They began to accept that their son responded to their emotions, though not in the way they consciously intended. Over the years, their impatience, yelling, anger, and disapproval had relentlessly conditioned the boy to avoid them. In turn, his avoidance accelerated their negative responses, which heightened until the boy acknowledged that they meant business. The only recognizable signal that it was time to perform was his parents' observable wrath! Moreover, through these repetitive episodes, the boy subconsciously associated "responsible" behaviors with unpleasant emotions—and so, because he was bright, he quickly learned to avoid the emotions and responsibilities as best he could. Coupled with this learning, the boy had developed spotty work habits, a poor reputation, and the gnawing inner sense of being driven away. He responded to instinct and consequences and could not explain or justify the repertoire that perpetuated his guilt and meager performance.

His parents also acknowledged their feelings and frustrations. They learned in counseling that these feelings were expected and allowable, but that keeping them separate from the implementation of rules, schedules, and consequences would yield much better results.

They also grew to understand and experience the mysterious wisdom that altering minor elements of behaviors often results in remarkable changes in feelings. (They used to believe that people only did, could, or should do things if they *felt* like doing them—anything else would be dishonest! Naturally, the boy absorbed this belief; though he didn't feel like doing homework, he clung to his feelings of sincerity about the issue.)

After several sessions with the new doctor, the mother and father approached their son with some ideas very new to their family. They apologized for nagging the boy to do things that he did not value, simply because adults directed him to do so. They spoke of respect, consideration, and responsibility as a two-way street, and they suggested that they needed to do their part by providing incentives. They apologized to the boy for their prolonged demands and disapproval, and they even mentioned that they could understand his point of view in not performing where there was no payoff. (Here the parents were feeling slightly dishonest in stretching their conciliation—indeed, they felt uncomfortable and somewhat phony with this whole new approach—but the doctor had swirled their perceptions of "honesty" and had rehearsed and reassured them that new behaviors usually felt unnatural at first. The important point was that they stay focused on the intended outcome and monitor the small steps toward that end.)

They asked the boy what he wanted in return for quality performance. They helped him make a list of rewards worth working for. The list was headed by activities involving the cuckoo. His parents recognized the cuckoo as (in the doctor's words) a high-probability behavior. They explained that from then on, the boy would get to visit with his bird only at certain times and only *after* he had completed homework and chores according to specified standards. (These were the boy's low-probability behaviors; the doctor had explained to the parents how to make low-probability behaviors more frequent by making high-probability behaviors *contingent* upon the performance of certain low-probability behaviors.)

Thus arose the condition that the boy could visit his cuckoo only after his homework and chores were completed and inspected. Whereas previously the boy had been sent to his room for infractions, now he was kept *out* of his room until he performed. His father hung window shades from the ceiling slightly in front of the cuckoo clock and on its sides. As long as the boy accomplished the minimum requirements, the shades stayed rolled up to the ceiling. When the boy refused or forgot or did a sloppy job, down came the shades, veiling his beloved bird behind the opacity of his own insufficiency.

All was not rigor and restriction, however, for the boy was allowed liberties with his paramour never imagined! When he performed well, without complaints, and of his own initiative, the boy was given a stepladder and allowed to consort with his cuckoo on a new level of intimacy. And another *coup de cuckoo* ensued when his father mounted a microphone above the bird's door. The mike was connected to four awesome-sounding speakers that amplified the dainty chirps into strident and startling announcements. This arrangement was a special privilege, as the mike was activated only after the boy had demonstrated consistent and outstanding performance.

The boy was eager and motivated. His parents saw striking changes in his behavior. They mused about whether he was more keyed into the rewards of his cuckoo or the challenges of accomplishing his tasks. Logic and a veteran cynicism persuaded them that their son's fervor was maintained by the prospect of rewards—but he seemed so energetically *dedicated* to the dispatch of his tasks—so the parents wondered...and they also marveled at the change.

The boy was influenced by the allure of one particular reward: he was allowed to visit the cuckoo on the hour after he had fulfilled a targeted amount of work during the preceding window of time. Although the cuckoo trilled with timely precision, the boy's access was determined by his performance during the arranged interval. This contingency proved especially successful in getting the boy to manage his time and become organized.

His progress was truly impressive. Besides improving his grades, the boy found interest in routines that were once intolerable. His parents noticed cautiously, at first, and soon with mounting delight. Eventually, they replaced their image of him with higher (but realistic) expectations. His resistance and contumacy faded in memory. People treated him better because he behaved better. As he was treated better, included more frequently, respected for decisions, and granted increasing autonomy, the boy grew to really like himself and adhere to high (but usually realistic) standards.

All of this took place rather gradually and naturally. Things got so much better that the platitudes offered by his teachers and relatives seemed almost plausible: "He *has* matured"...

"It was just a rough stage"..."See, I told you there was really nothing wrong."

His parents put it behind them, secure in his accomplishments and nascent relative conformity. They were less stressed and less vigilant, yet they maintained their attentiveness to providing reinforcement and focusing on specific positive outcomes. Despite their many problems, the parents were happier, for they now had a boy who was bright *and* functional.

The boy was not naïve. This period of his life made a profound impact on his identity and self-direction. He abandoned crankiness but remained idiosyncratic. He could get away with individualism because he had learned about modifying the environment and himself when circumstances warranted or demanded. Over many years, whenever the demands grew heavy, his mind would fly back to the cuckoo—once and forever his reward, inspiration, and nest of assurance—to ground himself in the knowledge that he could adjust with self-control to the rhythms of regulation and new habits.

His old friend, the cuckoo, was an interval of respite, never an end in itself nor an object to be possessed. Because of this close association, his mind flew up to the cuckoo's nest after a job well done. And when he thought of his beloved cuckoo, it was...well, it was when there was an important job to do.

III

POEMS AND SONGS

1996
A lighter side of neuropsychology.

BRAIN IMPROVEMENT TRAINING EXPERIENCE RAP

Mark Steinberg, Ph.D.
The*rap*ist

Refrain

The Brain Improvement Training Experience Rap
Is a story 'bout improving potential to tap
The gifts in your head
Which you thought might be dead
Till discovering that they are just taking a nap.

They send ya to school and they tell ya the rules
They keep ya there for years and make ya feel like fools
Cause ya can't learn what they teach
And they can't teach what ya need
They make ya feel dumb if ya don't know how to read.

They put ya in pain when they try to explain
Whatcha can't understand, 'cause they don't know how to train
Thinking skills ya must use
If ya don't wanna lose
Out on life 'cause you been playing educational blues.

Blues, blues, educational blues,
Education in America is not such good news
What we need in our nation
Is some cognitive salvation

From a program that has real developmental foundation.

Refrain

The Brain Improvement Training Experience Rap
Is a story 'bout improving potential to tap
The gifts in your head
Which you thought might be dead
Till discovering that they are just taking a nap.

A man named Ralph Reitan had a prominent notion
Which became his life's work and passionate devotion,
He met Deborah Wolfson who is also very smart
Together they composed a model having these parts:

Sensory input is the gateway into you
Ya got to pay attention and have memory too,
The stimulation gets into your hemispheres
Which process information from your fingers, eyes, and ears.

Sometimes it's your left brain, and sometimes it's your right
They need to work together, so that you can see the light,
Because, in effect, ya can't just have sensation
Life don't make sense unless you understand relations.

Brain improvement training can teach you to respond
To task demands and people in a way that's beyond
The random acquisition of behaviors, facts, and fears
To make the most of what the Lord has put between your ears.

The Brain Improvement Training Experience Rap
Is a story 'bout teaching the brain to adapt
By using methodology
To learn developmentally
You navigate the skills for which your mind has a map.

1999

I JUST CAN'T THOUGHT ABOUT IT ANYMORE

THOUGHT FIELD THERAPY RAP

Mark Steinberg, Ph.D.
The*rap*ist

Think about it, think about it, get yourself zapped,
Negative emotions in a thought field trap.
Liberate yourself with some selective taps,
This is the Thought Field Therapy rap!

Therapy, therapy, I've had my fill.
They promise the world, but I tell 'em to chill.
Cause my problems weren't susceptible to kill
Until I used the Thought Field Therapy drill.

"I want to be over this problem," I declare.
I tap a little here, and I tap a little there.
I roll my eyes and I hum a little tune.
Amazingly, I feel much better pretty soon!

Thought Field Therapy makes very little sense
The apex problem makes its doubters real dense.
What's undeniable is the problem before
I just can't thought about it anymore!

Refrain

Thought Field, Thought Field Therapy rap,
You gonna feel better when you know how to tap
The most effective cure on the whole darn planet
Once you've run through the entire gamut.

Perturbations, perturbations, gimme a break.
My energy field is beginning to ache.
My problem is irrational, but I can't shake
Reactions that continue for their own sake.

Talk about it, talk about it, does no good,
Guilty that I oughta, and knowing that I should.
Feeling pretty hopeless, but if only I could
Make myself feel better, I surely would.

Healing people tell me there's a measure of pain
In order to improve I gotta sustain.
With mostly discomfort and very little gain,
I tell the healing people their system is insane.

Refrain

Thought Field, Thought Field Therapy rap,
You gonna feel better when you know how to tap
The most effective cure on the whole darn planet
Once you've run through the entire gamut.

The method upon which Thought Field Therapy draws
Eradicates the problem's fundamental cause.
Removing perturbations and reversing flaws
According to natural energy laws.

Think about it, thought about it, feel upset.
With most interventions, such is what you get.
With Thought Field Therapy's quantum core
I just can't thought about the problem any more!

Refrain

Thought Field, Thought Field Therapy rap,
You gonna feel better when you know how to tap
The most effective cure on the whole darn planet
Once you've run through the entire gamut.

2009

DIGITAL REVOLUTION
(AKA. THOUGHT FIELD THERAPY RAP REMIX)

Mark Steinberg, Ph.D.
The*rap*ist

Hey—Whassup, whassup?
It's my SUD that's up.
I gotta bad feelin'
And my mind is reelin'
What can bring relief
Is sho' 'nough appealin'.

Remind myself that my fingers can tap
And text to my brain a smoother rap.
I don't have to be depressed,
I don't have to yield to cravings,
I can get over this
And have energy savings.

I think about the problem
And I wanna take a pill
Or drink or smoke or cut or poke
To make myself chill.
Then I remember what I really wanna kill
Is not myself, but the bad feelings that fill.

Let's get busy and tap upon my bones,
I'm gonna be happy and get rid of my Jones.
I tap under my eye and then under my arm,
Under my collar and I'm doin' no harm.
The stuff I been through ain't like the gamut on my hand,
I follow the procedure and my problems disband.

Fourteen points that I gotta realize
Will help me feel better 'cause the body never lies.
I play the algorithms and then I can lyricize
Thought fields that feel good as I reach out for the prize
With bold confidence because my mood is on the rise.
So getcha fingers ready and let me summarize:

Announce you wanna rid yourself of problems that you fight.
Either side will do, use your body left or right,
Karate chop your fingers and reversals take flight.
Tap upon the cheekbone that is right beneath your eyes
Where your eyebrow meets your sinus, without shyness tap the orbit,
Tap the top rib on your side about four inches from your armpit.

It's time to tap the soft spot right beneath your collarbones,
It helps release the anger and it vanishes the Jones.
Cheekbone, armpit, collar
With the eyebrow in between,
Get ready for the gamut
As we change tapping scenes.

I'm tappin' on the gamut while I'm rollin' my eyes,
I'm hummin', countin', hummin' 'til it's no surprise
My bad feeling's tankin' and my optimism's bankin'
On the calm that's overtakin' where there used to be a shakin',
I'm correctin' the reversals and it's gettin' like rehearsals
For the chill I can will to drain swill that I despise.

Parents, teachers, lots of strife,
I even get it from my peers.
It's getting hard to live my life—
Addictions, worries, moods, and fears.
But TFT will save the day,
'Cause I can tap distress away.

Get down, get down,
My SUD is gone and so's my frown.
I'm tappin' and I'm rappin' and I'm slappin' down the fear.
Problems have solutions with the digital revolution.
Get the message, quit the balkin', let your fingers do the talkin'
'Bout the peace that comes 'cause TFT is here.

2007

HIDE AND SEEK

Peek-a-boo, where are you?
Come out, come out, wherever you are!
No one can see God,
Yet everyone can find him.

Where can I find God?
I find him in the smallest things and the biggest obstacles,
Like the dust bunnies in the corner
And the overwhelming problems I face all life long.

I find him in the blue skies, impenetrable by my eyes,
In the wisest truths and his forgiveness of men's lies
He screams in storms, and when it rains, I hear his cries
Pitter-patter, energy and matter all around me
As I wonder about what really matters.

I find God in the trees so green
And in the memories heard and seen
Across my planetary days, I plan my ways,
But he diverts me to eternity; you, Lord, I praise!

God comes out of hiding with every baby born
And every death that leaves loved ones forlorn.
The sun rises and sets aimlessly, except at his direction
Everything on earth and mind and spirit that has ever been
Is caused by him and under his detection and inspection.

And his reflection is the light I chase
To glimpse a heaven where sin is erased.
Meanwhile, my salvation is a taste
Of perfect being, nothing gone to waste.

The animals, the arts, the cultures that we trade,
Pleasures of the senses, sex, awe, fantasy, friendship, relations all around,
Learning, and the pain of yearning, deprivation, agony,
Senselessness, confusion, darkness—all these God has made.
Hide and seek endures, for God is playful and he wants to be found.

God is everywhere; he manifests elation, yet appears to grumble
At my prideful crossing of his ways; but when I'm humble
He rescues me from danger and despair.
He comforts me, and has enough for everyone, infinite to spare.

I find him in the food I eat, the mess I make, what I excrete,
I find him in my search for better things in life
Entwined in intermittent conflicts, suffering, and strife.
He finds me when I'm too preoccupied with selfishness,
Indignation, conflagration, lack of patience,
Challenges at work and struggles with my wife.

Formerly, I tried hiding from God
By pretending that he wasn't there.
Where? Why, everywhere!
But, God created sand and creatures to hide their heads in there.
I am not one of them, plunging into burial without a care.
Instead, I seek him with each thankful breath of air.

Peek-a-boo, where are you?
Come out, come out, wherever you are!
Aha! I found you!
Embrace me, Hallelujah!

2006
Ode to my wife.

GIULIA

A wonderful woman named Giulia
Said, “I’m real, what I feel won’t fool ya.
You see what you get,
My intentions are set.
In the matter of love, let me school ya.”

With playfulness that of a kitten
She pounced on my heart—I was smitten.
Determined to marry,
Few moments to tarry,
Lest Lady Luck leave me just sittin’.

Her manner direct and straightforward,
Magnetic charm drawing me toward
Her beckoning hips
And her full truthful lips.
With this woman I’ll never be bored.

Personality big as a stadium,
A temperament active as radium.
She’s bright as the sun
And immeasurable fun.
Safe and healthy to touch as God made ’em.

She comes from a different nation
With females of three generations.
For family she cares
And her lustrous red hair
Lights my passion for love's new creation.

Though romantic illusions can rule ya,
Reality's intrusions will cool ya.
Rare jewel that I've found,
Remain upright and sound
Please be who I think you are, Giulia.

2012
For my beloved wife, Giulia.

I LOVE YOU BECAUSE

I love you because
Of the way you are
And how you tolerate me.
I love you because
You are good to people
And when I look at you
My heart melts.

I love you because
You love me back
And forward in life together.
You cling to me and also lead
In our journeys through
Routine and unknown
Bonded in fear and fun.

You are beautiful
As I've said many times
Your loveliness endures
As does my wanting you.
I love you because
You raise excitement above the boredom
And salve the hurt that otherwise abounds.

I love you because
That is what you deserve
Because you're vulnerable
And need protection
Because you're admirable
Upon reflection of God's gifts
You are a treasure whom I adore.

2003
Anticipation of my son, Neal, leaving for college.

I WILL MISS YOU

I will miss you when you leave and go to college.
Listening for the rumble of your skating, echoing in my ears.
I'll remember when I worried with the knowledge
That you'd fall—and stumble into tears.

Now I'm the one who fears this fall
From childhood when you amble away
To independent living in peer-filled fray,
And I shall grace the sidelines scraping memories that stray.

Oh, the glare of what I tried to reinforce
When you were young and I could press my way
To stay upon intended course,
But nature had to have her say.

So, son, you grew and drew the source
From which you sprung into your independence.
I behold you with no remorse,
Just vivid pride and piquant loss at your descendence.

The dearth of MTV will give my eardrums rest.
Downstairs the kitchen reeks, a food-stained mess;
And still I rant my vain prerogatives for what is best,
I know that when you're gone…I'll have so much less.

Your music fills my head with rhythms loud
Enough to burst the membranes' generation gap.
Your artful skew of limits makes me very proud
Of how you vest your energy into maturity to tap.

When you depart from home, this womb of habits that we've spun,
You might review our parenting and counsel with disdain.
You may not see the chrysalis transforming and begun
To morph your freedom from the sinews of our heritage and pain.

I celebrate your youthfulness and dreams and straining toward the world.
I wait with diffidence and confidence for accidents to counter what you know.
You have a history and destiny about to be unfurled.
The stark reality is that when you go, my son, I'll miss you so.

2013
Written after my son's untimely death.

THINGS NEAL LIKED

Seeking attention and knowing what's true
Debating, arguing, and conquering you
Questioning God and being a Jew
These are the things Neal liked to do.

Coffee at Starbucks and coffee at Peet's
Pizza with pesto and sugary treats
Chinese and pasta and burgers with cheese
These are some things Neal liked to eat.

Physics, philosophy, math, and science
Cosmology, autonomy, and lack of compliance
Challenging authority and passive defiance
Neal would admire intellectual giants.

Skateboards and sports and athletic pursuit
Snowboarding, glowsticks, Asian girls he found cute
YouTube, Reddit, and Internet memes
Neal's curiosity flourished, it seems.

Mountain moguls to snowboard, hockey goal shots to slap
Hip-hop and trance music mixing to rap
Running and biking and taking a nap
Neal liked neurofeedback and learned how to tap.

Playing with pets and playing guitar
Neal's moods could swing wildly, his mind would range far
The thrill of speed, martial arts to spar
Neal knew so much about all kinds of cars.

Calculus, string theory, nuclear fission
Solving equations he did with a mission
Neal was a talented academician
But he could take days to make simple decisions.

Neal loved to read, he craved movement and speed
Japanese racing bikes followed his lead
His keen smell collected arrays of colognes
He preferred socializing over being alone.

Neal enjoyed life, he valued his many friends
He practiced good fashion, was conscious of trends
He shared thoughts and feelings, could talk to no end
About certain topics, your ear he would bend.

He liked his neck rubbed, his back massaged, too
He loved watching movies and giving his view
His charm and his brilliance could make people swoon
Neal, we miss you! You left us far too soon.

2004

COMFORT ZONE

I like to be in my comfort zone,
That spacious noose of freedom.
Instead of risking parts unknown,
I much prefer familiar tedium.

It's not that curiosity
Won't risk a dance with life afraid,
I just have no velocity
To leave the comfy bed I've made.

Others may think my world too small.
Take opportunity and grab it!
I'm guard and warden of the walls
Of princely prisons I inhabit.

I've ventured forth to exercise,
To strain, stretch, and accommodate.
Life's challenges have flexed me wise
To comfort zones in which I sate.

Birds fly the air, fish swim the sea,
The lion stalks his jungle.
There is a habitat for me
Beyond which I might bungle.

My programs and my practices
Build spider webs of steel
Supporting bridges with the axes
Lands connecting me with real.

I can be reached by mail or phone
And various forms of interaction.
But don't entice me from the zone
Where comfort binds my satisfaction.

It's said we each will force our way
And cling to habits we amass
When life won't match the rules we play,
We figure: This part, too, shall pass.

The comfort zone is not routine,
For some, it's all about what's new.
Variety and challenge screen
The sameness driving those askew.

The problem, then, is not the style,
But limits that usurp us,
Deterring us from work worthwhile,
From meaning and from purpose.

It feels good in my comfort zone,
Prevailing with the things I know.
The cost of letting habits hone
Is less of helping others grow.

LOVING TONGUE

When I use words, I fly
Across mountaintops
Liberating leaps
Advantaged mind
Off gravity of shackled thoughts
A plenary of motion and emotion
That finds its fancy flight
Unbounded while in other minds it's caught.

When I write, I try
To capture foreign lands
And free the people and geography
Topography of my experience
Edit terrain and history.

I'm captain, so I steer
Through elements of nature
With alphabetic rudder
Turning phrases toward adventure
Eventually safe harbors of expression.

Language takes us everywhere
Where masters of the code
Rule by draft and ode
I reign in my abode
Of languid letters lilting here and there
In intercourse
Poetic embryos.

A rocketeer, I have no fear
Of unimagined speed
Linguistically I seed
Unbuckled on my steed
Of sentences as spaceships clear
Of friction as the diction
Dockets here in paragraphs
Ideas become my creed.

Through litanies of light I ride
My tongue a rudder
Phonically I utter
Laser focus of a mind
Seek and find
Combinations, variations
Semantic and romantic
Pen as sword
Words I hoard
Keyboard console does console my soul
The loving tongue of language makes me whole.

COULD NOT LOVE YOU ANY MORE

Could not love you any more
Like God, whose love is limitless.
Even though you make mistakes,
I choose to love you nonetheless.

Fallout follows sinful flesh,
Selfish desire breeds events.
Reality becomes enmeshed
With ineluctable consequence.

I look beyond my skin, my wants
To ascertain the truth of things.
Yet history and desire haunts
Abilities that prayer brings.

Temptation clothes itself in works
To earn and promote privilege.
Being and doing better lead to perks.
Grace and mercy bring eternal edge.

Could not love you any more
Like God, no matter how you fail.
I will not love you less, nor
Base your value on the price of sale.

God thinks about you as his child,
Protectively, without condition.
Mistakes and imperfections filed,
Inheritance still your position.

Why should I think differently
From God, his love and judgment fair?
I choose to love magnificently
Those who share my equal heir.

FORGIVENESS

Light dust settles on dark surfaces,
Dark particles contaminate the light.
Overwhelm and guilt are my companions,
Loneliness penetrates the night.

Mistakes pervade the air like water,
Invisible as vapor, torrential as rain.
Breaths I take, errors I make, survival fought for
Trail tellingly with modern Eden's pain.

Every act potential imperfection,
Deeds of others garish as mine pall.
Criticism worshipped as a deity of detection,
Accuse, convict, eviscerate the innocence of all.

What's the answer to this burning question:
What method can eradicate hurt and fault?
Heaven sends a glimpse, a taste, aroma, and suggestion
Forgiveness is the salve in the salvation being called.

Moth and rust cannot destroy,
Nor thieves break in and steal
The Spirit's treasure God deployed
By making absolution real.

To be washed clean without guilt showing,
Canceled debt and free to live,
The gift to give and pay without owing
Is to love manyfold and repeatedly forgive.

Forgiveness acts like magic,
Making dirtiness, sin, and guilt disappear.
Forgiving is God's way of starting over after tragic.
God speaks the answer—can you hear?

CONSECRATED CONFISCATION

I love the God who gives me things and reasons,
Who gives me things without reasons,
Who gives me songs and seasons.

I hate the nature forcing me to give up things I want—still want—when I'm not ready,
Willing or steady in resolve to be okay,
Complete in confiscation.

Take away, take me away, don't punish me with abstinence.
Lift my burdens, hear me say
That emptiness is nascent.

Consecrate this forfeiture instead of wresting trauma.
Give up the entitlements without the trenchant drama.
Oh God, I'm awed with fortune, how you populate my life
With work and food, conflicting moods, with children and a wife.

Yet in the end, around the bend, it all becomes rescinded.
I run the race and find my place, the trek has left me winded.
Remaining breaths appreciate the time and matter left to stay,
For soon enough, it is enough,
And then God takes away.

2013

GRACEFUL DANCING

Step forward, step back
Move lightly aside.
Dance confidently,
But lacking in pride.

Know when to step in
And when to step out.
This choreograph
Takes practice, no doubt.

At times you engage,
At times you detach.
The timing of each
Is often the catch.

The music may sway,
The lyrics add reason.
The rhythms of progress
Each have their season.

You want to embrace
As passion envelops.
Leave room for the space
That problems develop.

You can't always hold on
To partners that fall.
You must be emboldened
To bend, yet stand tall.

To move in life's dances,
To lead and be led,
Have faith in life's chance
For which you were bred.

Be grown up to loved ones,
Be childlike to Father.
Defer to above ones,
With worry don't bother.

Mature in reflection,
Flee evil divisions,
Succumb to protection,
Be wise in decisions.

Swim and paddle with zest,
Also go with the flow.
The Director knows best
Who scripted the show.

Dance with a flourish
Give freedom to talents
Gracefulness nourish
While keeping your balance.

Everyone missteps,
Performances stumble.
Life's gravity is left
To keep us humble.

2007

MUSINGS

You can choose your views and you can voice your choices, but remember God knows all that you chose.

Foolishness is misrepresenting self-justification as insight.

Desire is attraction to something with the expectation that its attainment will bring satisfaction.

Conflict is the frustration of desire or a disagreement in the context of opposition or competition.

Lack of compassion is the global warming of the nervous system.

2004

TEACHING TAPPING

Teach a man, so he problem-solves
Tap him so his problem resolves.
Teach him to tap, he controls his feelings—
Tap him to teach, a lifetime of healing.

MY MENTOR

My, my, my,
My mentor's quite a guy
His guidance meant and means so much
For healing lives with loving touch
Under his leadership and watchful eye.

My, my, my,
My mentor's conquered sorrow.
He's tamed emotions' willful churn,
Genius exposed to storming spurn,
Though it will reign tomorrow.

My, my, my,
My mentor teaches knowledge
With skills precisely tactical
And methods quite more practical
Than those I learned in college.

My, my, my,
My mentor voices class
With scientific proof to show
He challenges the status quo,
Though kissing nothing crass.

My, my, my,
My mentor sets the tone,
With nature's painless restoration
Sans long-winded explanation
In person or by phone.

My, my, my,
My mentor works with courage,
Emerging as a pioneer
In overcoming wrath and fear,
He leads the new entourage.

My, my, my,
My mentor is a model
For tapping self-sufficiency
In place of helpless effigy.
Self-pity he won't coddle.

My, my, my,
My mentor's very wise.
When sharing his experience,
He graces it with common sense
And insight that applies.

My, my, my,
My mentor meant to understand
Anxiety that plagues the land.
Discovering what he never planned,
He gave the world a helping hand.

My, my, my,
My mentor's found a code
Propounding nature's healing wisdom,
Founding its therapeutic system
He's deserving of this ode.

My, my, my,
My mentor changed my living.
Tolerance of suffering dwindles,
Quest for truth and health rekindles,
I thank him for his giving.

MENTOR WHAT I MEANT

Love is more than dinner
And caring through the years.
To help you become a winner,
I've labored sweat and suffered tears.

To foster your allegiance,
I've paved the way and paid
The cost of raw intelligence,
Experiences strayed.

Now you've come of age to choose
The paths that map your future.
Mistakes I can't be there to soothe,
New wounds to kiss and suture.

I trust in your resilience
As new phases you will enter
And flourish with your brilliance,
But I'll always be your mentor.

GOD NEVER LOST

This is God's body
I use for awhile.
This is God's joy
Expressed in a smile.
This is God's sorrow,
The tears when I cry.
My being in God
Endures when I die.

This is his universe,
Stars, sun, and moon.
This is his will,
Past, present, and soon.
This is God's present,
Mercy and grace,
Gifts that he sent us
With troubles to face.

God made us promises
God doesn't lie
In keeping his word
Ours mustn't defy.
God gave us danger,
Fatigue and unrest.
God is our ranger,
Protecting what's best.

Often I worry
What choices to make,
Plotting and scheming
Escape from heartache.
God knows my inside,
God plans my out.
Foolish to think
I could leave him without.

This is his edict:
"Fear me, don't sin."
This is his will
I strive to live in.
All his commands
Are models I choose.
This is God's love
That I'll never lose.

LOST PUPPY

Hello there, little puppy…
Where do you belong?
You look so lost and innocent,
Could you be headed wrong?

Sniff, sniff, I need some comfort,
I'm out here on my own,
Have strayed from home and master,
And now I'm Satan's bone.

Yes, play with me and scratch my head
And feed me what you might.
Invite me right into your bed—
I won't put up a fight.

Now, sit and I will feed you scraps
And teach you tricks pedantic.
Though while you eat and take your naps,
Your true master is frantic.

I've wandered bold to not be bossed,
A world of scents inducing.
Shall I grow old while staying lost
All common sense reducing?

Here puppy, let me stroke your neck
And lead you by your appetite,
Seduce you with my call and beck
And take you far from what is right.

I trade my birthright for a meal,
My nose is cold, I need a pack
Adventure seemed like quite the deal,
But now, I want my mommy back.

It's okay, puppy, you seem lost
And needy, unprotected hound.
Your master's love will pay the cost
To seek and search until you're found.

Too tough out there, they growl and bite.
My dominance is waning.
I'll wag at home, bask in the light,
Protected by my training.

2012

QUESTIONS AND ANSWERS

When the birds build their dwellings in trees
When the cows give up milk to make cheese
When the rain falls away to soft breezes
Then I'll love you the way nature pleases.

When the fish in the sea do not drown
When the children grow up and not down
When a smile turns around from a frown.
Then I'll make you my queen with a crown.

O why does the sun set at night
And how can dark see without light
Explain to me gravity's pull
My empty with you becomes full.

Some animals crawl while some fly
Babies and sad people cry
Indolent folks may not try
But you turn my low into high.

Lightning may partner with thunder
And mysteries highlight the wonder
Of clues to a universe under
God's love that won't leave us asunder.

Which is the road I should travel
When will life's secrets unravel
From this truth I never will wander
Your lovingness makes me grow fonder.

BIB OR APRON

I wore the bib of expectation,
Shielding me from soil,
Then donned the smock of dedication,
Fitting me for toil.

The apron strings of servitude
Accept the body splatters
With remnants of the gratitude
For work that surely matters.

A natural consumer
Of goods and favors I deserve.
It costs me more to humor
Those whose needs I deign to serve.

It's time to shed the baby bib—
Entitlement has left its taints—
And climb instead outside the crib
To heights where aprons clothe the saints.

FIVE QUESTIONS

How does my heart know thee?
In fullness and time before the beginning,
You chose me and led me to be free
Eternally from the start to shed the bonds of sinning.

Why did you select me?
From myriad of souls who live in desperation
Your spirit did detect me
And lift me out of darkness into light of expectation.

When was I conceived?
Was it through my parents or before the world arose?
The trail I followed 'til I first believed,
Truth camouflaged by counterfeit and evil to oppose.

What method did you use
To pick the people who would rise,
Accept your calling, message, gifts, and choose
To follow and fulfill your invitation to reject the lies?

Who are the fortunate?
Among the stars, the glitter, riches, sickness, beauty, nondescription,
Who gets the gifts with enduring benefit?
How blessed are the souls created with your loving divine encryption.

2012

JESUS HAS PAID

I was scared not knowing
Then I was healed, God showing
Grace and mercy, my not owing
Anything, for Jesus has paid.

Took too long not yielding
I was wrong for shielding
My heart and soul from wielding
Forgiveness, for Jesus has paid.

You may live, not believing
You may give, not receiving
You may suffer with grieving
Let go, for Jesus has paid.

Troubles come and add burdens
Seems like I'm always hurtin'
Sorrow hangs like a curtain
That's lifted 'cause Jesus has paid.

Righteousness was hard to encourage
My debt had ballooned much too large
But the father said, "Son, there's no charge
Rejoice, for Jesus has paid."

I could yearn for worldly resources
And accumulate wins over losses
But there are no greater riches attained
Than the blessings for which Jesus paid.

2012

HEARTBEAT

Words cannot express
Beat, beat, a bloody mess
Words can just confess
Beat, beat, a heart's distress.

Squeeze, pump, then let go
Beat, beat, a bloody flow
Faster, slower, hearty show
Life sustained by cardio.

Beat, beat, expand, contract
Every tick another act
Beat, beat can mean to win
Or stray erratic into sin.

Constant pumping, every breath
Beat, beat, until my death
Squeezing pounding, silent rest
Beat, beat, within my chest.

Beat, beat means to compress
To subjugate or to defeat
Beat, beat, but no attack
Abundant blood, though battles lack.

Constant work through joy and ache
Beat, beat, but never break.
Feel life's essence, swish and thump
Beat, beat, prime the pump.

Swell my mind, contain my soul
Beat, beat, and keep me whole.
Skip no rhythms, just repeat
Keep me pure and beat, beat.

STRANGER: THINGS HAVE HAPPENED

The universe is full of vast empty spaces
Bodies, light, gases, energy, momentum, nothing
Stranger: things have happened
To connect our orbits, plight of interlaces.

We catapult upon uncharted map and
Travel for awhile together, pushing, pulling
Helping, yelping, exploring math and aftermath
Stranger: things have happened.

All the formulas, timing, and circumstance
Occur for us to star just where we are
And carry fortune forward, but not too far
Stranger: things have happened not by chance.

Propinquity and probability collide in cosmic bet
Stranger: things have happened yet
Who knew the details, riddles solved, steps for us to dance
And history was practicing until we met.

2011

MADLY IN LOVE WITH YOU

Once upon a time we met
Our lives forever changed
Sparks alit, permissions let
Our future rearranged.

I left my parents, you left yours
We fell enamored and enmeshed
Our loins entwined, our legs were four
We grew together as one flesh.

Pledged in good times and in bad
Until death solely do us part
Though boredom, conflict, traumas had
Afflict sanguinity of heart.

Some habits may exasperate
And choke the breaths of tenderness
But choosing not to irritate
To compromise is best, I guess.

I love you madly, cherished mate!
I'm smitten with your soul
Devotion to you won't abate
I am complete—with you I'm whole.

Some flames may flicker, cooling douses
Affairs, divorce may highlight fashion
We too may bicker, as do spouses
But you're my source and light of passion.

Pleasing you remains my theme
That keeps my love refreshed and active
When I hold you in high esteem
Is when I find you most attractive.

Many fantasies excite
And sameness tempts some minds to stray
You are my treasure and delight
I'm madly in love with you to stay!

2003

BEAUTIFUL LINING

There is a beautiful lining in this mortal coil,
Smooth, soft, rich, and intricate with gratitude and mercy.
Sown in hope, cut through suffering, sewn again by love, lathed and turned by life's toil,
Sanded down and burnished by penitence, made more worthy.

A splendid work transpires inside,
Unfinished, but ready to show
Any audience and reaching those who bid low,
A proud creation leaching all its pride.

Outside, where quills of trauma seek to puncture arrogance,
The calm is oft betrayed by truculence or militants,
Or self-defense, or diffidence, or incidents eroding confidence,
While inside, the beautiful lining cushions life's events.

Stitched together, woven in my mother's womb,
Catapulted out throughout development toward a tomb,
I wonder wistfully as my mother grows old
And realize that, because she does, my own maturity unfolds.

Living three times, but dying only twice:
Birth, death to fleshly sin, spiritual rebirth, physical death, resurrection.
The lining of this vessel ages supply, stretching to suffice,
Transforming and renorming, a chrysalis of confirmation.

2003

WITH THE LOVE I GIVE

Song for My Son

Watching you make big mistakes
Generating huge heartaches,
I cannot approve your style,
Living life that's not worthwhile.

With the love I give you
Can find the way to live true.
One thing that you must do:
Believe in me who trusts you.

Your choices often offend
And repeat to the selfish end
Of a road that leads to demise.
But you're precious indeed in my eyes.

Transgressions have cast you aside
With an attitude hard to abide.
Intemperate defiance rejects
The acceptance it somehow expects.

With the love I give you
Can find the way to live true.
One thing that you must do:
Believe in me who trusts you.

You challenge my loyal approval,
Yet precipitate logic removal.
You want things your way without reason
And objections are treated like treason.

Love overlooks without keeping score,
Defends less and forgives even more.
It's only possible making it through
With the love I give you.

With the love I give you
Can find the way to live true.
One thing that you must do:
Believe in me who trusts you.

2010

TIME WITH GOD

When I spend time with God,
He reads to me from His Word.
I am loved and comforted
And closer to Heaven.

Some say I make this up,
Imaginary God because I'm needy.
How do they know? Do they relate?
For they are right about being needy.

God is real and always present,
The same yesterday, today, and forever.
How do I know?
Because of forgiveness, sacrifice, and second chances.

Physical reality is harsh and unforgiving.
Scars are with me always, even when they hurt less.
Outwardly, I waste away, aging toward expiration,
While inwardly I am renewed, day by day.

Spending time with God, I love and contribute,
Experiencing loyalty and promises and keeping one's word,
Security, discipline, modeling, and tenderness,
Joyful in hope, patient in affliction, faithful in prayer.

THE GIFT

Giulia, my beloved,

You are a gift
As a daughter to your mother,
A prize, one and only,
Devoted to keep from getting lonely.

You are gifted as a mother,
Nurturing and loving,
Protecting and detecting
What girls need to know and show.

You're a gift to your husband,
Supportive and endorsing,
Affectionate and challenging,
A loving best friend to the end.

You are gifted in your talents—
The keenest eye
A beauty to behold
In the eye of this beholder.

2010

TIDES

The days move on relentlessly,
Like the lonely repetition of the tides.
Anonymous footprints and personal sand castles
Imprinted on the beach with purpose,
Routinely swept away, forever gone.

Those imprints on the sand,
Important marks of individuals
With goals, feelings, joys, burdens, and intent.
Yet, who remembers them?
Not the stretch of empty shore.

The snoring next to me,
Persistent bursts of air against obstacles,
Despairingly monotonous and constant, like tides.
Slight variations in a pressing pattern,
The ebb and flow sustaining life.

Across isolated mountains and teeming cities
The wind blows, the rain falls, the sun shines.
People come and go as plants watch.
No one knows why, we all advance the mystery.
We form concepts, measure, study, and still don't understand.

Feelings drive the physics of motion (they are emotion).
Without them, there remain just rules,
Like relics in a game without players.
Reason is the compass guiding progress
Toward destinations in the land of character.

The tides repeat – their beauty and security
Inspire comfort and provoke respect
For nature and power grander than imagination,
A swirling journey through time, a place for me
In sequence and in parallel—who can fathom?

I ebb and flow, advance, recede,
Foam and furl within the limits set,
Rise up and crash,
Cascade imposing postures that fall formless,
Returning aimlessly in rhythm, cycles until when…?

There is comfort in the tides
The certainty of yesterday, dominance of today,
The likelihood of tomorrow.
Human tides have swelled me in their midst.
I must remain connected to the source.

2009

YOU CAN'T GO HOME AGAIN

Or,

The Pizza Doesn't Taste as Good as I Remember It

Beyond the setbacks and disappointments,
The troubles that controvert anointments
Are twinges that emerge surprising,
The absence of expected joy rising.

It's not the creeping claws of anhedonia
The panic or self-pity of feeling alone
Discovering instead that what was formerly delightful
Has come around to be mundane, allure no longer rightful.

They say you can't go home again, for things have changed
And memories of what was tasteful and secure become deranged
When I was a child, I thought that way and acted out of magic
Now I am grown, perceptions stable and tempered, the comfort somehow tragic.

Why don't the foods I long for taste as special?
The cherished places I revisit lose their wonder
Friends I thought were soul mates flaunt their foibles
My memories of treasures cast asunder.

Now childish ways are put behind
Attachments yield to present views
Reality not always kind
As fantasy, with much to lose.

I can't go home again to the past
I've changed; the past is set, though tainted
I long for former joys to last
With hues my memory has painted.

Now and here I have good sense
To welcome what presents anew
To fairly judge and recompense
Development of what is true.

Pleasures I seek out again to savor,
Revisited can often lose elation
There's nothing wrong with me, and yet lost flavor
Must yield to growth and changing expectations.

TURNS

When things are going well,
I give almighty God the credit.
With gratitude, my fate His story,
A tale that I can only edit.

And when events are frustrating,
Each day pain and despair,
I ask God for His mercy
As a substitute for what is fair.

When challenge brings adversity
And weakness takes its toll,
My sufferings surrender to
God's being in control.

I live with stubbornness and pride,
The scars of imperfection.
The failures of the self I've tried
Defer to ways of God's selection.

It's natural to order life
Interpreted to favor me.
Yet better to reduce the strife
By looking at what our Lord sees.

I can't escape the ups and downs,
Cycles and turns that don't make sense
When laughs and smiles yield cries and frowns,
I turn to God's benevolence.

I'm not the measure or the limits,
Nor can I invent the rules.
Creation is from God, with Him it's
Following to crown and jewels.

Relinquishing entitlement,
Embracing holy ways,
I strive to live a life that's meant
To follow what God says.

2009

BETRAYAL

There once was a thief named Madoff
Who made off with the devil a trade-off.
In exchange for his soul
He pursued lofty goals
And caused many hard workers to be laid off.

Where's your moral compass, Bernie?
You're pompous, but with good attorneys
You'll end up in jail
For your deceptive sales
Instead of spread out on a gurney.

Even though your dreams were myriad
Don't you know Jews no longer build pyramids?
For your hurtful invention
You'll rot in detention,
Your Ponzis and cons will end, period.

ECONOMY

They say it's the economy
That preoccupies the mind.
My worry is autonomy
And falling farther behind.

We're in a deep recession
And more in debt embedded.
Incredulous at their profession,
The financiers get more discredit.

We seek relief through leaders
From the pressure never ending.
Our infrastructure teeters
As the government keep spending.

With faith placed in democracy
And hope in Barack Obama
To save us from hypocrisy
And end this melodrama.

We teach our children to behave,
Response cost through economies token.
But securities lost, king becomes knave
Our trust and Wall Street both have broken.

Of the people, for the people,
By the people, our government—
My faith is placed under the steeple
Solutions must be heaven sent.

2009

HUMBLE

It's said that into every life
A little rain must fall.
Dripping hardship, soaked with strife,
I must have hit a squall.

When skies are gray and overcast
Or full of rain or sleet
I get the blues about wet shoes
Until I meet someone without feet.

Life's troubles make me grumble,
Complain, criticize, and sigh
Yet when I see those struck who tumble
I say, "There but for God's grace go I."

Overwhelmed by stress and storm,
Frailty makes me stumble.
My character challenges form
And surely make me humble.

2011

ONE FELL SWOOP

One fell swoop
Jesus paid the price for me
Fled the coop
The devil has no hold on me
Endless loop
Confession and forgiveness be mine
His blood on the cross was a sign
The Lord's sacrifice will outshine
My darkness with his spirit divine!

Once I lived in foolish pride
Often had great sins to hide
Failed with the techniques I tried
To fill up the emptiness inside (me)

Mostly blame I saw because
I was using mankind's laws
To highlight others' faults and flaws
So I could draw the audience applause

Never then occurred to me
That life was more than I could see
That what I thought and did would be
Remembered, judged, and bound up eternally

Misunderstood and felt denied
I sought others to take my side
Thought revenge was justified
Each battle won prolonged the great divide

Belief that I was on my own
Resulted in a hubris grown
Reaped the weeds of poor deeds sown
My self-image misshapen and overblown

Finally reached my end of rope
Realized that I couldn't cope
Desperate and bereft of hope
God reached down and pulled me from that fatal slope

Now I see that I was wrong
Denied, defied for much too long
The truth I tell you in this song
God's family is the place to belong

ROARING LAMB

I pray an answer greets who delves
Inside a most perplexing riddle.
Does God help those who help themselves
Or does conducting make God second fiddle?

I live inside a paradox
To pray on knees or prey and seize
Lay like a hen, pounce like a fox
Which is my place, and whom to please?

The suitable response often eludes,
To trust, leave consequences up to God
Conflicts with taking charge and restlessly occludes
Where ownership, initiative get the nod.

Determining a proper course of action
Is difficult when logic starts to breach
And I am trapped and pressured in contraction
Encapsulated in figures of speech.

In meekness and surrender I need guidance,
But willfully independent still I am
A startling combination of submissive stridence,
The character befits a roaring lamb.

CHANCE

Some think that circumstances happen just by chance,
That universe events occur at random.
I know a God who wills his plans advance
Creation wisdom operates with him in tandem.

Many hold that faith is blind
And doubt the facts they cannot see
Faith is vision viewing what's behind,
It sees the forest, not a single tree.

Life has tricky tests and arduous trials
With hidden topics, teachers, and a judge
Whose mercy transcends evidence and files.
Belief yields hope and faith that will not budge.

Those who doubt rely upon their reason,
Gambling life by leaving it to chance.
Self as center of the world is treason
To a God who give so many chances.

2007

SHOW ME, FATHER

Father, what is your work for me to do?
What is my work, from me to you?
What is my role, what is my mission,
What ought be my godly position?

Teach me and guide me, so I can learn
Through my frustration, through what I yearn.
Redeem me from sin, relieve stress that churns.
Give me the wisdom and will to discern.

Move me to prayer, give me supervision,
Condition my heart to fulfill my decision.
Show me the life that surpasses all dreams,
Keep me protected from Satan's cruel schemes.

Bless where go as I follow your lead,
Bless those around me and let them take heed
Lest the burdens on earth stampede and trample
Salvation that rises from one true example.

Father, this day, my commitment is noted,
To follow your way I am solely devoted,
To live justly, love mercy, humbly in prayer
For your children and precepts to faithfully care.

2007

MISSING PICTURE

What's missing from this picture?
I ask patients on the test.
Do you know important details
That connect with all the rest?

In my own life, I've forgotten
Something—wistful oversight,
To include you in the times begotten,
Without you, nothing's right.

I brought along my camera,
Clicked and shuttered for your eyes.
At day's end I searched and stammered,
Shuddered and realized

I had no good connection
To upload these memories
What is worse, upon reflection
Is that you're not here to please.

Through my digital obsession
I have images to share.
There is lots of good expression,
But one's absent from the pair.

What's missing from this picture
Is neither clarity nor care
The only flaw and structure
Is that you're not here to share.

2006

INTIMACY

How can we get close
Without becoming smothered?
Calm confidence to separate
After years of being mothered.

The strange truth of development
Is fight for freedom and release.
But years ahead, the sacrament
Is that attachment nurtures peace.

How can we get past the fear
That launches fight-or-flight alarm?
By settling neurons poised to hear
The soothing rhythms that disarm.

With interest piqued, so we can sense
Our mantra of espousal
To regulate the fine balance
'Tween soothing and arousal.

To recognize the vulnerable,
With empathy entrain,
Takes training on the well-worn path
Between the heart and brain.

Life hurts with pain and soothes with pleasure
Yet we all must suffer.
Intimacy is the treasure
Serving as the buffer.

How can we grow intimate,
Connect in loving fashion?
Eschew aggression, let it abate
Embrace instead compassion.

2006

ROOM FOR GOD

There is room for God in my mind
Uncluttered, like an open field or mostly empty highway.
Unlike the crowded filth of slums and tenements of obsession,
Instead, psalms make unwanted thoughts fly away.

A placid vacancy within,
A sign outside inviting passersby to bunk here with the spirit.
A dwelling where God routinely cleans, the view of heaven clear
And proverbs pave the landscape, echoing the Word for those who hear it.

God is welcome in my mind
A place hospitable, a chamber suitable for worship
Caverns receptive for the truth to seep and steep inside skin walls,
The gospels' haven from the selfish prideful worldly hardship.

Our history of wandering, the Israelites and I,
Has led to peace and safety amid the roiling throngs of clamorers and tyrants.
The homelessness has ended, even shy of residence eternal yet
The room for God inside is vast, expanding with its vibrance.

VERGE OF DEPARTURE

You are leaving son, growing away,
To college you depart.
Though I know you couldn't stay,
Your absence pulls my heart.

My little boy has disappeared,
A fledgling man arrives.
To tell me Jeremy's still here,
It's just that he's switched lives.

When you depart to weave your life,
Tethered only by my cash,
I'll miss supplying you with strife
About taking out the trash.

The verge of separating homes
As age exerts its mission
Intends that progeny do roam
Toward genetic fission.

I'll have to learn to love you now
Respectfully at distance
And watch while you discover how
To meet the world's resistance.

Remember as you spread your wings
Above new roads to travel,
Our flesh and blood share many things
That time will not unravel.

2006

INTONATION

I learned to speak your language so I could survive
In the jungle of predation where my instincts would revive.
Interpret what's important in this culture of confusion
To get by and satisfy the blend of immigrant collusion.

It is primitive where language lives, especially when foreign,
Where I'd lived, derivative of economics barren,
Economy derivative from richer cultured nations
Begin to speak your native tongue with stranger intonations.

Push comes to shove, communicate the distances to cover,
Conjugate the grammar, for acceptance is my lover.
I make mistakes, my syntax aches for want of smooth expression,
Yet make my point, accent anoint this human intercession.

For we must speak from heart to heart, not only wagging tongues
And move beyond the symbols smart that bellow from our lungs.
Cultures brag of differences, their labels are disparate.
More basic is a common theme, and we should learn to share it.

We wander much as aliens 'til we learned to claim our home
Some of us don't settle 'fore the miles we have to roam.
Inflection yields detection of the land from which I came,
For the things that really matter, you and I are much the same.

2006

WHEN YOU'RE NOT HERE

When you're not here, an empty space,
A mattress unimpressed, a vanished face,
A void to fill with colored memories
Of indentations in my life with you in place.

No rhythmic breath syncs, alone the pillow rests,
The warming cover sinks, no body there, a flattened empty nest.
Though I have room to flail about and exercise my soul,
I find whatever shape I'm in without you is not whole.

The days' activities flow by like currents with their silt,
Diurnal tides recede and wash away the dreams nights built.
Trade winds delivered you like foreign spices, climate of romance.
When you're not here, the ships are gone, my port's no longer filled.

I fete myself, take care of me, and last not worse for wear,
I welcome when you come to me and celebrate the things we share.
When you retreat and I recede, electrons disappear,
No oxygen with hydrogen, it's dry when you're not here.

CONTINUITY

Thinking about you day and night,
Too tired to love, too weak to fight
Feelings that course through my veins
Blood red when exposed to light.

A history of my temperament
Would read like a gory crusade
Eras of wreckage rebuilt in self-control
A retrofit of earthquake damage made.

The cracks in armor long since shed
Lay glinting in the sunlight splayed upon our bed
I send you messages, words, e-mails, telepathic pathos
From a land remote where I live inside my head.

Round and round the images go
Musical thinking that ends in woe
When the melody stops and the lyrics pop
While one doubt stands out in the repeating show.

How can I know that this spiritual sinew
Will survive the mundane and profane and continue
To grow and withstand the cheating erosion
Life soil too familiar, yet mined with explosion?

For you, my inmost yearnings will bear
With tears and fears and phlegm to share.
To carry our burdens distributed fairly,
To revere trust and treasure it squarely.

Courtship delivers behavior at best.
But in you, I want my soul to find rest.
In me are no secrets to keep, and in you
My hope, faith, and love want to grow and continue.

COMPLAINING TOGETHER

There is a joy I share these days
With a winsome red-haired lady whose ways
Bring me comfort whatever the weather
For we have joined in complaining together.

We mimic each other while taking cheap shots
At the folly around us, as we laugh lots
At metal detectors and airport insecurity,
Public safety lectures and false purity.

While mocking slow service with faux despair,
I catch the quick wink of my friend with red hair,
My partner in crimes of sarcastic flair,
We suffer small insults with umbrage to share.

Pretending annoyance at petty offenses
We chirp to each other and heighten our senses
To balk at the world outside our cocoon
Mundane detractors from our habit to swoon.

Long lines and delays, shoddy things and high prices,
Entwining the days with a myriad small crises,
She matches my well-practiced sniveling disdain
Charismatically mimicking playful refrain.

A stage polymorphous with acts every day
I ogle my partner and copy the way
She flies through the world, we're birds of a feather,
Nested and invested, complaining together.

We're not arrogant or condescending
It's magnetic attraction that seems never-ending
We bind in the game that strengthens our tether
By thinking alike and complaining together.

WHO IS THERE?

Who is there?
A history of maturity's abduction.
Life unfair—a mystery,
Insecurity's obstruction.

Through your eyes,
A witness to surprise,
An apparition wise.
The camera never lies.

The years unseen revealed,
With passions finally unsealed.
The secrets spilling out,
Emotion telling all about

My inner life spelled out
Loud, with urgency to shout
And scream with sinner's strife
The sting of panic and the dreams of better life.

Captured and suspended,
A prodigy enlarged and charged with artist's flair,
Tweaked with shadows and enlightened,
My image gradually discharged—but who is there?

Speckled convolutions of beard and hair,
Expressions of intrigue and intimacy to share.
The artist baits, contemplates, manipulates, relates with flair.
Yet, ultimately, as fate's impression airs—who is there?

There is a quizzical perplexity,
A pompous epidermal complexity,
The pixels emphasized convey concern and care.
But, 'neath the ink, the feel and think still ask: Who is there?

TOGETHER

Equal heirs, different hair
Two bodies with one flesh
Inequities resolve as fair
Vivid attraction makes us mesh.

I'm in your body, you're in my mind
In ecstasy we come united
Growing together is better I find
Than loneliness or love unrequited.

Aromas mixing in the air
Scents and senses bright and mingling
Thoughts and feelings, touch we share
Spark nerve ends, light and tingling.

Routine moves in and settles down
Flush excitement dwindles
We still regard each other's crown
Passion yet rekindles.

In this life's path we are a pair
For worse or weak or better stronger
You bless my soul, arousing care
I travel lost no longer.

2006

HALVES

You are indeed beautiful
And when I watch you sleep
I feel the exhale
Of a life breathtaking.

The in-and-outness of our goings on
And comings to and from
The up-and-downness of our moods
Are halves that sum.

A whole lot of everything
Begs and bewitches when broken
When a man cries in despair, or sheds a tear,
It splits reality in half, as if a tree had spoken.

My tears run down your back
In rivulets of separation.
And I am back on track
In you, and you in me
Halves joined in true elation.

I walk into a room and vent
Words leaping off my tongue to paint the labels
You dance between my hands in rhythmic comment
A visual context deepening our fables.

You are my eyes, the rods and cones
That color inference, move beneath the lyrics' laugh.
Absorb me deep inside your bones,
Broaden marrow, not as clones
Complementing beyond praises
Melody to sing the phrases
Nourishing in myriad ways
The lovely face that is my other half.

We are two minds, with organs, souls, and brains and pains disparate.
Incredible to find, repeatedly, ideas to bind
And stumbling over ironies and art and songs and troubles so abundant
That we naturally want to share it.

Initially, I sped to you, succumbing to a logic lapse
Surrendered flooding chemicals, your surge too oversexed.
Then pleasure's plume excited so much mating in each synapse
And I belong to you like text to context.

2006
For my mom on Mother's Day.

MEASURELESS

There are miles to measure countries.
There are bushels, too, for wheat.
There are fathoms for the oceans,
Degrees to measure heat.

There are years to measure ages,
Light years for stars above.
But no way has been discovered
To measure a mother's love.

SIGNALS

Since we met, some things are racing:
An elevated mood, a heavy and depressed accelerator,
As if to track down happiness, whose rights I have been chasing
For unity that would, that should, come later.

When I am not with you
Life sits on hold, a restive limbo waiting at red light.
Anticipation frames activities in lieu
Of facing you, embracing you in bed at night.

You drive me to the heights of love's arousal
And make restored the heart that has been worn.
Request escaped my lips for your espousal,
When you said yes, a life anew was born.

At that moment, I felt something dawn,
A bond experienced only once before,
When I first held my first-born son,
A gift for life to treasure and adore.

You are the signal that my path has rearranged.
Without you, noisy traffic made me slow.
Then you appeared and signals quickly changed,
Your light insists that forward we shall go.

2006

MAGNETS ARE NEVER AFRAID

Don't be afraid of life and love falling,
Hark, the music we've made!
Welcome the song of the siren calling,
Caution—but don't be afraid.

If it should happen that we grow together,
Fly with me, build us a nest.
Should we become like birds of a feather,
Soar with me above the rest.

Tentative pawing and pecking and gnawing,
Sniffing and licking for worth,
Emboldening soon with instinct exploring,
Coveting treasure of soul to unearth.

Breaking the stallion and training his power,
Riding the passion of disciplined steed,
Timing advances to capture the hour,
This is the moment you answer my need.

Courage announces the goal of intention,
Calls into being what's said.
Wariness tethers desire's ascension,
Watchful—but don't be afraid.

You are my magnet and I am attracted
Swept and pulled in by your field.
Chance led us near so that forces enacted,
Joining together in nature we yield.

Oh! How the instinct propels our attraction!
Biology won't be mislaid.
Electrons and hormones in passionate action,
Magnets are never afraid.

2006

WITHOUT YOU

If the earth were not round,
My breath wouldn't quicken, my heart wouldn't pound.
If the sky weren't blue,
Perhaps I could carry on heedless and needless of you.
I could live in a world
Without you.

If babes were born old
And history's future were easily told.
If lies could be true,
If wishes could make it so hearts were see-through,
Even then I would struggle
To live without you.

(Refrain)

Without you,
Love would just be lust.
Without you,
(Crescendo) May would become must.
Without you,
My efforts to whom would entrust
(Andante) My mood would be blue,
My heart could not be true
(Lentissimo) Without you.

If you were my lover
And yearnings for joining my soul mate were over
I'd savor each minute,
Embracing and living each second within it.
Each new day invite me to joyfully begin it,
But not without you.

If pain would be gone
And suffering vanish so I could move on
To live in a world with compassion and caring,
Replacing the cries of the hurt and despairing,
Effacing the pride and the folly of daring
To live without you.

(Refrain)

	Without you,
	Love would just be lust.
	Without you,
(Crescendo)	May would become must.
	Without you,
	My efforts to whom would entrust
(Andante)	My mood would be blue,
	My heart could not be true
(Lentissimo)	Without you.

NATURE

I'm strong and sturdy as a mountain,
Tough and seasoned as a hide,
Refreshing as a summer fountain,
Sensitive as sunburn inside.

Who are you? A mystery!
Surround me like the weather.
Reveal and join our history
Perhaps to bond and tether.

Human nature will confound
Desire battles reason.
Hope and fantasies abound
For symbiosis without treason.

You and I encounter magic
Sleight of fate in drama's dance
Stepping over traumas tragic
Destiny eclipses chance.

First we must explore terrain
Seeded with hidden danger
Thirsts to quench, goals to attain
Friendship becomes no stranger.

SYMPHONY

I sit here near sixty
Listening to the symphony
Too old to rock and over
I will not lie
Too young to lie under a rock
I will not lie

The audience is bald and gray
In proper harmony they say
Maturity with silent voice
Viagra is the drug of choice

The music stands the test of time
Through centuries composers watch
Orchestration blends sublime
Percussion, winds, and strings attached.

Acoustics fill the concert hall
Emotion at its basest
Instruments collide to call
The heartbeat of the bassist

Music is a global language
Uniting different nations
With common hands, lungs, and tongues
In sweet communication.

BUTTERFLIES

Absent the time to find a mate
Would loneliness become my plight?
You swirled sublime, a twist of fate.
Hope set aloft, my heart took flight.

Enrapture me with blue sky charm
And shutterbug me sharing light,
Eyes capture me, lens to disarm
The butterflies that lift my sight.

A humid mist, a musky scent,
Gardens of dazzling flowers,
Excursion to where heaven spent
A Thursday's earthly hours.

Please share with me more days like this
With pictures, touch, and praise to utter.
Transform my life, a chrysalis
Smile, spread like wings, about to flutter.

2006

STAGES IN A MATURING RELATIONSHIP

No God.
Oh, God.
Where's God?
Listen, God.
Speak to me, God.
Where, God?
Yes, God.
Speak through me, God.
Thanks, God.
Praise God!

Go away, God.
No way, God.
Hey, God.
Say, God.
Pray God.
Way to go, God!

Cussed God.
Bust God.
Fussed God.
Must God.
Trust God.

2006

THAT GUY THING

Liking sports and beer and tools,
Aggressive competition,
Getting past the broken rules
Are guy things by tradition.

Barbecuing on the grill,
Basting life that's in the way.
Testosterone can make us kill
What feelings cannot make us say.

It's true, no doubt, you recognize
Such global maudlin stereotype.
Yet guys stay geared to legends' size
Performance, achievements, possessions, and physical hype.

Grilling, building, chilling, guilding
Hunting, bragging, punting, sagging.
Manhood flaunts with ego wagging,
Taunts the rest with tissue tagging.

Though women train equality
And social senses quintessential,
Guys take pride in equity,
That tag of tissue makes us special.

2005

MY FAVORITE GUY THINGS

(Sung to the Tune of "My Favorite Things")

Face hair and chest hair and tightly formed muscles
Solving tough problems and winning at tussles
Taking hot showers where I loudly sing
These are a few of my favorite guy things.

When my team wins, it gives me elation
When I have sex, I get good penetration
Not doing laundry or decorating
These are a few of my favorite guy things.

(Refrain)
When the women nag
When the boss rings
When I feel at all
I simply remember my favorite guy things
And then I stand strong and tall.

Facing new challenges, daring and willing
Keeping my scrotum from underwear spilling
Hiding my faults and my fears and feelings
These are a few of my favorite guy things.

Having erections and casting off shaving
Getting my way and sometimes misbehaving
Strutting opinions and delegating
These are a few of my favorite guy things.

(Refrain)
When the women nag
When the boss rings
When I feel at all
I simply remember my favorite guy things
And then I stand strong and tall.

2005

APRÈS DIVORCE

(Written While Eating Fish–Which Barbara Never Liked)

From the moment we met,
It was you I wanted to protect.
But destiny in time was set.
Eventually, you would defect.

My heart began to tear
As we sank into despair.
For I no longer could attract
You and our union became sacked.

Though I was faithful, no reward
Accorded our progressive discord.
My sacrifices you would hoard
And pierced me more than my resources could afford.

O, why am I conflicted when you cheated,
Withheld from me until I was defeated.
I care for you despite your cowardly escape.
My character compels this love agape.

2005

WHEN YOU'RE IN LOVE

When you're in love,
Everything becomes brighter.
Like laughing gas
Without the crash
It seems inane,
But it's all really sane,
Just lighter.

Routines carry on
Reliably mundane
The secret's not kept
But by two entrained.
Sleepover giggles
Turn-on wriggles
Trust ingrained.

When you're in love,
Life is a cage,
You've reached the age
Of release
And the peace
Of a satisfied sage
Pollinated to engage.

Love is seeking
And peeking
No hiding or reeking
Excuses for tweaking
Magnetic attraction
Forcing the action
For consummate strength and conjugal peaking.

Oh love is just a drug
That raises those we know
Sweeps you high, below
The mundane drag must go
Beneath the freeze-frame climax
An emotional Imax
Finds the common ground of bliss we know.

2005
For my mom on her eightieth birthday.

NEVER LET ME GO

This stage in life, applause greets your arrival.
A star of sorts, your own one-woman show.
An octopus of decades suctioning survival,
Now history will never let you go.

When you were young and I was even younger,
I rarely sung a melody that ventured out solo.
You edited, then credited with being my expunger
Of life's lyrics that were unfit—my supervised echo.

The years accrued and I would brood,
You tilled the soil and plowed the toil
Of family farm to harvest grades as well as food.
From omelet substitutes and egging on I would recoil.

I yearned for fun, my brain would run
To pleasure centers barred for Jewish sons.
You rescued me with lassoed apron strings,
Instructed me on dangers independence brings.

In additive, now we have lived about as long as Moses.
Like desert parched and Red Sea marched, we passed through tragedy.
The promised land is out of hand, our lives no bed of roses,
Dysfunctional, we clamber on, and cling to anguished family.

A wise thing happens as years flow:
Development takes separate routes.
Then currents bring us back in tow
Like water parks with roundabouts.

When separately we navigate,
Then reengage, we realize
That though we individuate,
The ties that bind are quite a prize.

Far from childhood's stern protection,
Four score years have let you be
More loving in your life's reflection
Toward everyone, including me.

Maturity is ever endless
Though children grow up overnight.
Family leaves you never friendless
Bound by nature's sense of right.

Independence has a lure:
Human enticement to be free.
In middle age, I'm much more sure
Of me and liking your company.

Sometimes we run away and sometimes toward.
Fear, pride, and hubris filter what we know.
Regardless, we are always moving forward.
On my life's journey, never let me go.

2005
The first marriage disintegrates.

LEAVING

Moments became hours, hours became years,
The status quo hypnotically deceiving.
I settled for disgruntlement to calm my fears.
I'm over it—entitlement—I'm leaving.

Leaving memories of you behind,
Wishing plaintively I could,
And keep the soundness of my mind
Preserving all remembrances of good.

An animal emerging from the tangle
Of survival in the wild with battle scars,
Resurging from the wily traps to dangle
Free and vigorous to tattle trauma's horrors.

More than you I wrestled with a quitter,
Fought the phantom yet alive but grieving,
Settled to acquit the babysitter.
You taught the bantam to survive—I'm leaving.

2005

SIMILES IN THE BRAIN

Trying to discern intricacies of the mind
By using logic to divide
Is like taking your bicycle into the sea
Because you know how to ride
And want to use this tool to help you swim.

Do you not know how to breathe?
Slap then on your baby rump,
Dip you underneath the surface
Only for a moment—FEAR!
Catch your heart within your lungs
And then a sigh of sadness or relief.

If I explain in detail how
To carve a roast beef with a screwdriver,
Then I am neither carpenter nor chef
And we are hungry poets starving on linguistics.

The person who enjoys music
Or savors a tasty meal
Is party to cuisine and audience to concert
Without creating, understands creation.

First recognize, then harmonize,
Yet improvise and proselytize,
Observing, then observant
Quite subservient to growing wise.

The monkey climbing bars within your mind
Needs exercise and playful hide-and-seek.
The simian is brimming with connection
And a need for close affection
And social intercourse and humorous inflection
All tweaks, of course, before you get to sleep.

I tell you: Watch your brain,
Don't ask what you should see!
Whatever I profess will leave much left,
Whatever you discover will be right.
Motivation serves sensation
And eyesight fades behind insight.

2005

BE MY FRIEND

A Poem for JuliAnne

When I look in the mirror, I mostly see
Someone who doesn't reflect the real me.
The person who shows is not who's inside
The mirror and life have repeatedly lied.

I could suck in my stomach, smile, and pretend,
But whom would I fool and to what good end.
It seems that whatever message I send,
There might still be no one to be my friend.

People are pushy, and they want to be right.
My dog's love is mushy and he doesn't bite.
I want to be hugged, but not too tight,
And sometimes it's scary to lie down at night.

Grown-ups act sure when they say what to do.
They don't endure what I have to go through
Whom to believe, and whom to eschew?
It's so hard to tell what's nonsense and what's true.

People around me don't hear what I'm saying,
Lack of support, my complaining and braying
Fall on deaf ears, but when I keep praying,
God listens, and I feel like obeying.

Be my friend, please—if you don't I'll be hurt.
My inside and outside are having a fight.
The mirror may tease and people desert.
Your friendship would turn my despair to delight.

I get so lonely, no one understands,
My crying face only hid by my hands.
I feel no one wants me, except for their use
Anxiety taunts me, frustration breaks loose.

When I doubt that people will like me at all
And mirrors won't flatter, their harshness won't bend,
Continued endurance begs for a call
To provide reassurance—won't you be my friend?

TRANSITION

You led me to the mighty river,
Threshold of the land of milk and honey,
Brought me love and set my heart aquiver
Anticipating gilding with reward greater than money.

Let me cross the chasm now
Sail from years of barren thirst
Show me life and living how
To cross the loss where cross is first.

Leave the locusts far behind
Escape from devastation's path
Help me seek and let me find
Safe shelter from the vengeant wrath.

Hold me in your warm embrace,
Shift outlook, new position.
When I behold your smiling face,
I'm moved to make transition.

Lift me from the water's plume,
Bathe me radiant sunlight.
Make my days from now resume
With purpose from transition's plight.

2005

THE HEART IS A QUANTUM PLAYER

You have rescued me
From the shipwreck of loneliness.
Islands of the past left behind.
Substitute for the destitute,
No second-guessing or need to rewind.

The heart is a quantum player,
Wanting its wants and jumping
Its checkered chest while pumping
Toward destiny's best consumption
Of vested prayers.

You've lifted my heart.
Invisible surgery taking apart
The tragedies flogging and clogging my soul.
Memory etchings of when I was whole
Disappear in the swallow, engulfed by a cardiac black hole.

The heart is a player whose score catapults
Beyond reasonable share of predictable pulse.
A quantum tear multiplies the results
Of your influence on my caring
For your heart, persuaded to sharing.

Caprice and power and moral resolve
Defer to the hour forgiveness absolves.
The heart may grow sour toward those it involves,
Then rebound with romantic flair,
For the heart that is sound is indeed a quantum player.

I LOVE YOU

I love you for listening
When you have much to say.
I love you for seeing
When you can't have your way.
I love you for accepting
My offering today.

I love you for bearing
Unimaginable pain.
I love you for wearing
The sackcloth of shame.
I love you for sharing
This day again.

I love you because
You will live under yoke.
I love you, though loss
Of such freedom's no joke.
I love you, of course,
Through the words that God spoke.

BODY OF CHRIST

Your hands and feet aloofly shake
Your presence shakes the future
Of myriads of souls at stake
Because you make the Master tutor.

Corporeally, what once you could
Becomes progressively what can't
Embody what the will says should
Accompany the covenant.

Your body, just a vessel empty
But for spirit's occupancy.
Nerve cells shoddy, quite unkempt,
Endear eternal divine clemency.

Spirit willing, flesh does weaken
Crave mobility some more.
You have been the spirit's beacon
Brave nobility, body's door.

Sorrow haunts the physical,
Pain chaperones the fleshly thorn.
Practical taunts mystical.
Through Christ the body is reborn.

Thank you for your perseverance,
Character and faith outstanding,
Leadership and truth adherence
Carrying all our burdens demanding.

The body may desert direction,
Winding down in disarray,
You've ordained heavenly protection.
Christ will have the final say.

GOD'S MERMAID

Suffocatingly aquatic, human in complexion,
Your origin unknown, familiar face.
God's mermaid agonizing for connection,
Swimming still away from truth's surface.

All creatures mill in venal circumstance.
What odds we should collide!
Old cliché: No accidents by chance,
Gambling loss if we should be denied.

Your presence peels the darkness like a decal off the land.
Dawn highlights shape of days, a silhouette in bas-relief.
Terror fades, the storm recedes, visions of a mermaid stand,
Embodiment of fantasy, challenging mind's reef.

You have been baited by so many seamen,
Landed in their boats as trawlers' prey.
You wiggled free, returned to sea with demons.
God, save this mermaid—don't let her get away!

Creator wrought the food chain, and stocked it well with fish,
An ordered competition buried deep.
Chasing for survival and revival with transforming wish,
Transfiguring a mermaid leaps a bridge across belief.

Don't contaminate the waters,
Boundaries for the lapping tides
Reach to you, my son, your daughter,
God-man, mermaid, father-bride.

Swim ashore, for I shall drown
If crossing barriers forbade.
You can carry kingdom's crown
By crossing over, God's mermaid.

2005

MARRIED LOVE

(or the Getting Up to Pee song, because I wrote it during the night in crepuscular half sleep, and it awakened me, one stanza at a time)

To married love
I do subscribe.
Our culture's sex is set to hex with lurid bribes.
I want no part of one-night stands, affairs divide
My heart's security, no fantasy, my bride.

In married love,
Indulge in flesh,
My nature drives me to combine Spirit enmeshed.
With earthly lust, commitment to my soul at rest
Inside my bust, with swollen trust, enjoy the best.

(Refrain)

Our world is seductive,
Temptation dancing undressed.
But sin is unproductive
(It's Satan's kin
Though hatin's "in")
Love wants the best.

With married love,
Togetherness.
We'll share the rights and privileges if you'll say yes.
This man and woman recapitulate what's right
When first we pledge ourselves before the wedding night.

For married love,
It's worth the wait.
The right relationship my heart will satiate.
I've looked around, rejected other substitutes,
For married love's what joy's made of, my faith salutes.

(Refrain)

Our world is seductive,
Temptation dancing undressed.
But sin is unproductive
(It's Satan's kin
Though hatin's "in")
Love wants the best.

Selfish reasons
Breed liaisons.
Sex out of wedlock hurts adults, daughters, and sons.
Vexing the bedrock of security with fun,
Enduring romance, married kind's the only one.

Forever mine,
Not just a line.
Eternal unity, our love will grow and shine.
I've left the offers of alternatives behind.
For you and me, great married love's the only kind.

2004

DON'T SHIRK WORK OR YOU'LL GO BERSERK

Joy becomes my blessing as it follows hard work
Partners like digestion/appetite.
If not for this relationship, I'd grow more like the jerk
Who fancies leisure as his own birthright.

Love and marriage, horse and carriage, couplets we assume
Belong together, bringing satisfaction.
Joy and work can harmonize and tune
With rhythmic rest and energy contraction.

I'm lazy when my efforts seem like work
Habitual indulgence: my forte,
Expect results from elbow grease I shirk
When mellow is the flavor every day.

The yin and yang and zen of endless striving,
What peace derives from finishing my work.
Accomplishment the fuel itself for driving
In safety from collisions with berserk.

2002

FOR BETTER OR VERSE

He who heeds the poet's call
Must let the grass, the weeds grow tall
The healing bard who hears the song
Must barter healing all day long.

For time is money, efforts made
To heal the hurts pays off in spades,
Mind is matter and energy
Threads healing and creativity.

Patience shrinks and patients grow
With busi-ness, it helps to know
That eloquence will have to wait
While suffering patients perturbate.

From head to toes, from heels to nose,
The healing heads off painful throes,
Ambivalence the healer knows
As patients, patience, comes and goes.

2004

POLITICAL POETRY

Poetry is politics linguistic
Receiving letters, representing states
Running for the office, bard as mystic,
Inspired till the cause for words abates.

Symbols and ideas recruit their leaders
With promises and pledges to protect
Free associations and their readers
From narrow definitions words elect.

This grass roots rising of semantic fashion
Words worth matching in rhythmic liaison
Verbal conjugal romantic passion
Till meter peters out of rhyme or reason.

The poet freely speaks, recruiting gerunds
And other figures from speeches he totes.
Campaigning wildly with grammatic errands,
Liberating adjectives for votes.

He canvases the language of his people
For images and urges to give voice
To visions from atop inspired steeples.
The keyboard is his messenger of choice.

The candidate invokes poetic rhetoric
The consciousness with words expression heightens
Debating prose and cons with measured metric
Parameters allowed by sovereign license.

COOL SIDE OF THE PILLOW

I turn to the cool side of the pillow
Like turning a page of life from repetition hoary,
Leaving the sweat and rage and strife,
I dream a new chapter in my story.

Mountains of cotton obscure my vision
Fabric of life seems real,
Perspiration precipitates the feel
Of swamplands swallowing imagination's keel.

Upheavals in environmental texture—
The room sways and sheets of air revolve
Cotton clouds settle and dissolve.
Rest comes peacefully, temperature absolves.

The cool side of the pillow
Is a respite always there
Solace beneath my hair,
A dry reprieve of access through the axes of my bedroom air.

2004
About to become my ex-wife.

SHE LIVES ALONE

She lives alone, surrounded by men
Who love her dearly, but even then,
She feels unsupported in her life
An uneasy parent, a frustrated wife.

Sheltered from love, exposed to sin,
The stormy weather rages within.
Protection can serve as a two-way filter
And alter relationships out of kilter.

Defense and denial are mind's martial arts,
The marital shield against intimate starts.
The scything of feelings before they erupt
Can decimate dealings in truths quite abrupt.

She claims she has problems with me being right,
But fails to provide more encouraging light.
She dashes the thought that she's possibly ill,
Dismissing as well the effects of her will.

Lost in a maze of relative values,
Entrapped in the prison of guilt-ridden "Shall yous."
Blaming the world and herself for despair,
Her soul is too busy to come up for air.

If love and acceptance cannot be received,
Belonging and worthiness won't be believed.
She could be my queen reigning high on the throne,
Instead of a sad drone who's living alone.

I KILLED THE MAN YOU LOVED

I killed the man you loved, dear wife.
His person ceased to be.
A higher spirit rose to life
Inhabiting new me.

We shared bipartisan attraction
Based on false agreement,
Enjoyed sensual satisfaction
Bound in sinful cement.

I carried you; you towed my sloth,
We looked askance at purpose
Until commitment's behemoth
In challenge did usurp us.

We were one flesh until I died,
And now you're free to choose
Between the myths 'bout which we lied
And misery to lose.

The knight you rode so many days
Is gutted, gone—he's finally slain
To welcome with celebrant praise
Replacement for the years of pain.

The man who stole your youthful fancy
Vanished into selfish passing.
Turn away from necromancy
Build instead liaison lasting.

My passion killed the man you loved.
I loathed the competition.
The egotist whom you betrothed,
Consumed by great contrition.

I hope you can forgive the death
Of one you knew so well.
He had to go, or my last breath
Would take me straight to Hell.

If you can't love the murderer
Of sinful partner, my dear spouse,
Then future mocks the past interred
And we'll not build our spiritual house.

If you, however, rise with me
Above our past to please forgive,
This suicide will set us free,
True matrimony thus will live.

1997

WHY CAN'T YOU MOVE IN HER HEART?

You have the strength to move mountains and cancers,
You made the world from the start.
You founded love with all questions and answers,
So why can't you move in her heart?

Living like lyrics parched without melodies
Love is a burdensome art.
Feeling satirical, shadowing jealousies,
Why can't you move in her heart?

Miracles I dream, etched in reality,
Counter it seems life's fateful finality.
You stepped in, helped me to win
Transformed my joy from without to within…

Misted with tears, flooded by memories,
Clinging, yet falling apart.
Wistful of years full of efforts to please,
Why can't you move in her heart?

Loneliness magnifies hurt without measure,
Growing as we grow apart.
Aching inside with a yearning for pleasure,
Why can't you move in her heart?

Miracles I dream, etched in reality,
Counter it seems life's fateful finality.
You stepped in, helped me to win
Transformed my joy from without to within...

I must return with my wounds and my burns
To the healer who maintains my chart.
Pray for relief, yet this lovesickness churns
Why can't you move in her heart?

I miss her so, I pine by the hour
Pierced by self-doubt's stinging darts
Yet I have faith, awaiting the power
Why can't you move in her heart?

Miracles I dream, etched in reality,
Counter it seems life's fateful finality
You stepped in, helped me to win
Transformed my joy from without to within...

Peacefulness settles like dew on the hillside
Loving's no longer as hard.
You made the pain and the anguish subside
Thank you for moving her heart.

On this glorious day, as I kneel down to pray
Clouds lift and I feel blues depart.
Gone are notorious days when I'd say
Why can't you move in her heart?

2004
The painful last stages of an unhappy marriage.

EMOTIONAL HUSBANDRY AND WIFE IN THE GHETTO

My wife is an emotionally absent landlord
Less friendly from her distance than demanding
Her due plus what else I can afford,
Our home in disrepair with little understanding.

Grievances and gripes reside in-dwelling
Dissatisfaction eats beneath our roof.
When harmony moved out there's little telling,
The tenants of this shanty shack up aloof.

Displeasure stacks congealed upon the dishes
Served with more resentment than with spice;
While discontentment rudely piles up wishes
For getting even even more than getting nice.

Utilities are paid with little balking,
So power struggles on throughout the nights.
Seeds of conflict grow instead of talking
The grass cut down like disrespect maintained by fights.

This marriage is a duplex squatter tenement
A termite-riddled hovel that I would
Abandon with less complex hotter sentiment
If I could find a better neighborhood.

Awhile ago delight and love evicted,
Now loyalty and duty pay the lease.
A substitute arrangement interdicted,
Proposing child support to keep the peace.

So why do I endure this acrid ghetto
Cohabit with a slumlord and her rules?
Because I pledged my life and do a debt owe
For children we conceived as family jewels.

Offspring fill our household, needy renters,
Abode for child protection carapace
Parental ownership emotion centers,
Shell out for kids' well-being, saving grace.

NORTH AND SOUTH

Once ago, you snuggled up against me
Like iron filings clung 'round my magnetic pole.
Then, ironically, you struggled quite against me
As if repelling opposite my very soul.

The story of attractions and repulsions
Writ large in human history and affairs
Replays the blessed union, harsh expulsions
Between Creator and created wares.

North and south encompass life's directions
The winds of change blow 'cross the east and west.
To weather love's allure, requite rejections,
The laws of magnetism do behest.

Like motors set in motion, push and pull
Ambitions revved with memories in a dance
To energize and make life flush and full
When spinning combinations mate with chance.

Our past trajectories have caught the magnet
Amalgam of our harmonies entwined.
Our forces changed, alone I cast a dragnet
Attracted to whatever fate may find.

2004

FIRST HAND, SECOND CHANCE, THIRD TAKE, FORGIVE

Life is not vicarious
Experience first hand
The joys and traumas various
To reinforce a stand.

Errors and misfortune
That may circumstance advance
Terrors that importune
For a privileged second chance.

First hand, second chance, third take, forgive
Blessings that make it worthwhile to live.
Suffering diminishes, much to relieve
Buffering challenges just to believe.

Natural birth, sin-self demise
Spirit reborn awake,
Thrice passing cycles acting wise
To play out the third take.

Don't take umbrage, forgive the rage
Forget mounting offense.
To take accounting as a sage,
First, second, third, forgive, repent.

First hand, second chance, third take, forgive
Blessings that make it worthwhile to live.
Suffering diminishes, much to relieve
Buffering challenges just to believe.

2004

PERFECT WORLD

A perfect world would harbor no mistakes.
Reliability of life accedes to one.
Community of body-mind lacking in aches,
And everything that's done gets done—with fun.

A world where standards set by everyone
Collectively and singly all are met
Eliminates all doubt and risk to shun
Embarrassment when errors lead to debt

In a perfect world, I wouldn't need a voice
There'd be no conflict, grief, or pain to salve
In this coil mortal yet I still have choice
Which with imperfect life is all I have.

2004

LIFECYCLES

When I work out at the gym,
It's 90 percent unpleasant strain and 10 percent transient liberty.
The clock and biologic limits trim
My victories o'er ever-vigilant gravity.

It looks as though I'm winning
One scant minute out of ten;
Fat moving, sweat precipitant, wheels spinning,
Muscles grooving, yet time spiteful even then.

After exercise, I feel tired, thirsty, calm, relaxed, and soothed,
Successful, clear, and level-headed.
Later in the day, my food tastes really good, digestion moved.
I sleep even better when I'm bedded.

The next day, I'm stiff and sore,
My body uncooperative,
My sense of saddles weighted even more,
My muscles and mobility less operative.

The day after the gym, if you asked me to return,
I'd think suddenly about killing you.
Recovering from yesterday's burn
The last thing I would want is exercise renewed.

The day après the sweated reps
I focus consciousness upon the stairs
And count the motions even climbing steps,
My body much in need of gross repairs.

Two days beyond the workout if you called
And beckoned me again to spin the wheels,
I'd beg and plead more respite, less enthralled
To challenge yet so soon the way my body feels.

The third day after rending fat and calories expunged
I'm ready once again to take on gravity,
Deftly moving mass through air in pushes, pulls, with squats and lunges
Battling through the cycle of my own depravity.

2004

SUNDAY MORNING DREAMING

In morning, dreams recede like the tides
Withdrawing their secrets in hidden deep.
The dawning conceals what night drama confides,
New day confiscates shrouded covers of sleep.

Earth turning quickens, light shakes me awake
To escape that subconscious torpedo
Which prowls the thickened buried heartache
Of yearnings, revenge, and libido.

Mind theater is dark, its night players gone
Horizon progressively lightens.
Time meter parked; gear up to move on
In limbo, incipient plans heighten.

Morning is quiet, tuning inside,
Rehearsing my part in the orchestral play,
Echoing phrases my night muse has tried
To prepare for performance throughout the day.

Coping and moping and groping and hoping,
Diurnal clatter and scatter of plight.
Daily pleas to appease backed by frenetic roping
Of anchors recharging in silence of night.

Evening connects what the morning will find
Though intention delivers the colorful ride.
Nocturne interprets perplexes of mind
Worth mention: Perceptions reflect what's inside.

Productions of life invoke scenes and acts,
Stories prevail upon plots and themes.
Reality pivots round tangible facts,
Creation requires the magic of dreams.

Surface to land, as the sky lights the day,
Become clear as to what, where, and when,
Energies spent on the world's work and play
Drive submergence in nether's sweet embrace again.

LEAD BY GOD

God sees us with precision
All lighting and direction.
Divine x-ray vision
Trumps all other protection.
Lead by God.

Some churches bear stained glass
With rivulets of inset lead.
The window's body lets light pass
With silhouettes of how God bled.
Lead by God.

Painting history's coverage old
When land was threshed by oxen
God's children ate the manna fold
Colored, suffused with toxin.
Lead by God.

The preacher leads with sermon
Etched from scripture's hallowed stencils
Believers heed, determined
Taking notes, inspired pencils.
Lead by God.

BLEED ON GOD

Bleed on God when I feel this way.
Ooze my trouble and despair upon his presence.
Hemorrhage on him of age, as if to say
On this day, don't stay away, but heal me with your essence.

Seed on sod, life burgeoning when trampled.
Rub my being in the dirt, inter my breath
Till season favors rights to blossom ample
Reason in the light 'til God confers my death.

Wind me up and wind me down.
Wound around the senses, even odd
That I should find my fickle feelings sown
In soil and toil sin-sickled, bleed on God.

2003

COFFEE OR TEA

The tea leaf and the coffee bean were having quite a row
Determined to determine who is more popular now.
The bean did boast that he was present always at a feast
The leaf did vainly claim to be the drink of all the East.

When coffee claimed economy it boosts for all it's costin'
The party tea reminded us of history in Boston.
They both lay claim upon us to our taste buds and our nerves,
But which of these proud beverages asserts superior verve?

They each exert profound effects upon our lingual muscles
Propounding us to explicate about life's daily tussles.
Tea drinkers talk about themselves, while coffee sponsors others,
So stimulate libation's palate according to your druthers.

2003

INTOXICSOMNIA

I had a toxin, and I simply cannot sleep.
Thought patterns race around my mind I'd really like to bleep,
Tried so hard to drown them out with mantras in my head,
Instead I'm swimming vainly in the sweat upon my bed.

With many trials and problems I am wrestlin' and boxin'.
The conflict deep within me is just actually a toxin.
My inner battles have exhausted many, many rounds,
I'm refereeing perturbations leaping out of bounds.

When something's bugging you, they say you have to flush the system.
Nemesis: Emesis, catharsis is the wisdom.
I need to find ways more effective to relax
When toxins enter me and everything attacks.

In seven seconds, I can have a simple answer.
It may not end world wars or be a cure for cancer.
I merely want myself to shut up and shut eye,
Therefore, the seven-second treatment I apply.

Because inside I truly am a breather and a sweater,
I squeeze and tap myself until I do feel much, much better.
Intoxicsomnia distorts my consciousness of time.
The cure retorts subconsciousness and restfulness sublime.

When I eat something tasty that for me is not so good,
My heart rate varies less than healthfully it should.
Using this principle to keep myself in line,
To sleep, perchance to dream, invite such blessings to be mine.

MANNA

So many times I could have perished.
Then manna fell from the sky.
Cascades of opportunities to cherish
Rescued me to flourish, not to die.

Cats with nine lives are cheated
Compared to my fortune evident.
Another chance escape repeated,
Manna of speaking, provident.

Out of my voracious need
Expels a world of motivation.
Yet failures multiply to seed
The plummeting of expectation.

Desperation floods my land,
Then aridly evaporates.
Propitiate my grasping hand
With resources that faith awaits.

God helps those who help themselves—
The saying prompts one's druthers.
But Spirit, angels, saints, and elves,
Pitch in when I help others.

In sparse and Spartan circumstance
Might manna blessedly descend,
In self-defense, with common sense and confidence
I do my best, and then depend.

2003

DIFFERENCES

The difference between me and Jesus
Is in my nature.
It's sin, my nature.
Death-defying arrogance
Until life ceases.

The difference between me and Jesus
Is in full living.
It's sinless dying.
Self-denying fragrance
Fulfills and pleases.

The world rates me and Jesus less than great
In differences apparent.
Indifferences a parent
Senses differences in parity,
But covenants with clarity strategic fate.

The world regards me similar to Jesus.
Easy to reject,
Is he to reject?
Those who won't accept the word
Follow what they heard except the shepherd.

The world berates me brutally, quite like Jesus.
Believing us odd,
Be leaving us, God.
It separates our history, excerpts the divine mystery
Creates a story ending God then seizes.

The world tries me and Jesus with its lies
Different sells for
Different cells or
Common ad campaign to proselytize
The same temptations leading to demise.

The differences between Jesus and me
Debate 'bout will and won't and do and don't and faith and truth and right.
Though arguments have lessened since the lessons made me see
That darkness does surround me, but where Jesus is the light.

2003

DISAPPEARANCE

My wife has disappeared into our history.
She is here, but not present,
Imprisoned by distress,
Captured by dissatisfaction.

We are like chessboard pieces,
Taken without give,
Familiar with forsaken,
Strangers to forgive.

I am seared by the pain
Of utter aloneness
In the midst of being crowded out
With no reward and no gain.

It seems insane
That what we had exists no longer
Succumbed to time and something stronger
Than our pleasure from each other could entrain.

Our love has made a disappearance.
Reverse magic in emotional implosion,
Indeed an unintended gradual erosion,
An end of season clearance.

2003

RHYME IS UP

Violence leads to increased rhyme
Punishment to vengeance
Comic relief leaves too much time
For punch lines in the sentence.

In former days a smoother thug
Would touch you for a loan
But now the rappers tap your mug
And smash your collarbone.

Therapists are often psycho,
Rarely do we bludgeon
We racketeer, but not with FICO
We analyze curmudgeons.

Put down your insight, take your fingers,
Tap upon your gamut.
With rhyme, no reason, be a singer
Write a poem and slam it.

Violent rhyme is on the rise,
Expressing great frustration,
Anger knows no gender bias
"Whoa-man"—tap for elimination.

2003

LANGUAGE FOR MEN

The appeal of lascivious pictures
Will stimulate lustful male nature.
But jiggling the word rules and strictures
Teases tingling linguist nomenclatures.

Pulchritude pleases the juices,
For men are visual creatures.
Yet the beauty of language adduces
That words are superior teachers.

Though producing ephemeral climax
Pornography generally debases
Language, too, can control how the brain acts
Through the visceral message of phrases.

With the antics that spur the male native
I can play with myself, quite compelling.
Rather master semantics and bait the creative
Romancing my grammar and spelling.

Admittedly, sex is alluring,
Each picture a thousand words.
A turn of good phrase more enduring
Than orgasms not read or heard.

Females can capture us sensually,
Mighty phallic with pen and with sword.
Surrender and sway come eventually
To *italic* influence of the Word.

PLEDGE YOUR EYES

Progeny, you grow to clone,
Reaching toward the future.
Find yourself, possession's own
Teaching my imprimatur.

Borrow not my household tools,
Pledge your eyes elsewhere.
Steal my words and capture fools
Be wise in wisdom's lair.

Lionize your father's rules,
Copycat these proverbs.
Confiscate my household tools?
Be banished from the suburbs.

Where's the wrench, the spatula,
Scotch tape, and calculator?
Is that the stench of ancient food—
Your room to clean up later?

Plagiarize my words of wit
Borrow my pithy sayings.
But pledge your eyes far from my bit—
You'll do a different braying.

To watch you imitate my lessons,
Fragrant and refreshing.
Refrain from my possessions
And you will have my blessing.

2003

JOURNEY FOR JOY

Where is the future for which I have strived?
You were deceitful, and so you contrived
To leave me in ruin; you cheated and lied.
I knew not who you really were inside.

You captured my heart and let me confide
My secrets and dreams; you punctured my pride.
You brought disappointment along for the ride
On the journey for joy where hope and faith died.

Coupled together, promised to care,
Seeded for pleasure, committed to fair
Playing by rules we couldn't quite share,
Our journey for joy headed into despair.

You had my worship; I cherished your word.
That current attraction distantly absurd,
You have absconded, the last I have heard,
Attempted escape from the debts you've incurred.

Feeling resentful of choices you bossed,
Respect I was owed, but discredit you tossed.
Hitting the road and paying the cost
On a journey for joy that somehow got lost.

1996

HE WANTS TO LIVE WITH US FOREVER

A man came knocking at our door the other day,
Sweetheart;
Said he wanted to come in.
I opened the door at his insistent clamor;
Seems I've met him somewhere before.

He didn't want to impose, he said, unless we were willing.
I took him at his word, and suddenly felt warm and peaceful.
He didn't say his name just yet—
He did say, though, that he had been everywhere.
I thought that most peculiar.

He wants to clean our house,
He claims,
So he can live here
Too.
Talked of vanquishing
The cobwebs of unrighteousness.

I told him he could have a room
For awhile,
As long as he didn't require my time, or cost us trouble or money.
He said, "Thank you, that will never do; for I want all of you both.
Verily, I give you My Word
That I am He."

He? Who? Oh, Him. God.
Just when I was beginning to own and manage things, He comes to confiscate—
The Great Corporate Head from above.
"No, my child," He said, "I came to substitute, for yours which rusts,
That which will never tarnish."

I said, "Okay," although,
Sweetheart, I thought of checking with you first.
We've built some longtime habits
Of selfishness together.
He said, "I'll wait."
I replied, "It may be long before our decision.
We've only a little bit of space."

He smiled,
As there was yet sun and thunder in the sky.
He said, "I'll wait, for I have forever.
Do you?"

He wants to live with us, my dear—
Forever, He says.
And clean and crowd us out of every filthy sin.
We cling to habits and things
He promises will turn to dust.

He claims He is a carpenter, and will rebuild our house.
Eventually, He'll take us to His palace.
He wants to live with us
Forever. How strange! Why us?
What will the neighbors think?

We should let Him in, dear,
After all, we're nice,
And open-minded.
Aren't we?

He knows it's a mess inside;
He doesn't mind;
Really, He cares.

He asked especially for you,
My darling.
I wonder how He knew
That you are troubled.
He says He's loved you for a long time.
Funny…
I felt no jealousy, just intrigue.
He wanted my acceptance before He came to you.
He asked me to intercede for Him,
My darling.
He wants to live with us forever.
Remarkably, He wants just what we have.
He'll give us more, He promises,
In return for our allegiance.

I told Him it was up to you,
For you.
Though I will live with Him always.
He's in our house, my love, and wants permission to stay here,
Forever.
Won't you welcome Him?
The three of us inseparable,
A trinity of life.

2003

OMELET GOD DO IT

Afraid, but not chicken
To put eggs in one basket,
Though provender spoils in my kitchen,
Restored when providence will ask it.

Most times I stash new eggs,
A nearing feast to scramble,
My plans get smashed, I beg
For fearing hunger's ramble.

The shells mysteriously pierced,
My breakfast gone to ruin.
My pride imperiously fierce,
Fate plays another tune.

Divine nutrition makes appeal,
The broken eggs replaced.
God substitutes another meal,
Impoverishment erased.

Whenever I waste eggs of hens
Through cooking I intuit,
I humbly seek the food God sends
Omelet God do it.

MY LOVER

Passion in the night invades my dreams
Stimulating glands, and then it seems
We should be the way we were before
My lover wouldn't love me anymore.

I remember holding you so close
Folding limbs from fingers to our toes
Making love together brought such bliss
You are the lost lover whom I miss.

Why can't I still fit in your embrace,
Fastened by the magic of your face?
Memories of what we had adore
The lover who won't love me anymore.

(Refrain)

Fill my abyss with the love that I miss,
Be the one lock for my key.
Our combination is hard to resist.
Lover, please come back to me.

Mornings wake me with your smell aroused,
Wishing our relationship was housed
In the bed our passions used to soar
Before you wouldn't love me anymore.

2003

YOU ARE THE SECRET

(Refrain)

Never leave me without your love,
Always watch over from heaven above.
I can do nothing worthwhile on my own,
Share in my burdens so I'm not alone.

You are the secret that I have to share,
Telling your truths brings relief from despair.
Yours is the promise that I have to keep,
Loving you nurtures a trust ever deep.

I went a long time without having fun,
Inside my own cave without seeing the sun.
Then I surrendered to needing you badly;
Now I dance in the daylight while loving you gladly.

It was apparent that I hit the wall,
Driving myself and my people to fall.
Chasing desire, to bleed and to flecce
Feet to the fire, I sped without peace.

A roadblock you set with your bold sacrifice,
I collided with you, like a roll of the dice
It seemed like good fortune that chances had tossed
You to turn me around (praise that luck had me found) so I wouldn't stay lost.

Pity the travesties hurt in my past,
Dangers enshrined in mistakes that I cast.
Trinkets, indulgences that brought me pleasure
Pall in the wealth of your love that I treasure.

You are the secret that I have to share,
Telling your truths brings relief from despair.
Yours is the promise that I have to keep,
Loving you nurtures a trust ever deep.

2003

BALLAD OF THE BEST-SELLER

The words lie mute in folded phonics,
Sentences tied quietly at rest.
Messages delayed for deeds ironic,
The seller can't communicate his best.

The story of a calf that's sent to market,
An innocent that's taken from his field,
Absconded at the whim of those who hawk it,
Gristle for as much as it can yield.

Dissect the guts and edit out the fluids
Trim the fat, but leave the heart for now.
Marketers distribute it like druids
Sales and exposure feed the sacred cow.

Experience and wisdom laid on pages,
The ballad and the drama set to print
The writer and his craft defer to sages
To sell the book for which they have no hint.

Pray, Pulitzer, you dangled aspiration
To win your grand approval for myself.
Though first my work must garner publication
To reach the public's fingers on the shelf.

2003

APOTHECARY GARDENS

Your touch makes organisms grow,
Your skills bring hope those sick.
Your presence casts an earthly glow,
Expressions phototropic.

You work beneath the surface where life rumbles
With breath of life, fecundity of soil.
The sustenance of health in challenge humbles,
To organize immunity, you toil.

Blood runs red with scalpels of incision,
The craft of coaxing organs ill to heal.
Organic grafts pruned, carefully made decision,
Bandaged with leaves and veins of chlorophyll.

Cultivate, and while you wait,
Apply your thumbs and potions to the pain.
Excavate, and seek the fate
Of Eden's loss to sprout toward mankind's gain.

The healer's knowledge checks all nature's systems,
Examination more than cursory.
When bodies have responded to her wisdom,
The doctor smiles and tends her nursery.

Walk among your wards of charges fragile,
Nurture them, recant the heart that hardens,
Fill the cells with protoplasm agile
To blossom in apothecary gardens.

2003

LOVE ENOUGH

Like you, I've searched for reasons why things happen as they do,
A world of sense with sense of self at center.
In lieu of seasons passing on what's really true,
I've jangled keys of many rooms to enter.

Discerning outlines that converge, I've scurried to assemble
The living puzzles, contours feel so rough.
Those pictures that emerge do most resemble
A life in which I haven't loved enough.

My mind works all the time to find solutions
To problems of reality's design
In circling back through logic's false collusions,
I'm left with explanations only mine.

To do what hopes to leave some lasting blessing,
To polish my behavior more than scuff
Is due acknowledgment that I've been messing
More with neediness, but haven't loved enough.

Observing what has grown and what has withered
In gardens seasoned from the watch above,
Serving from the weather patterns dithered,
The healthy plants flourish from constant love.

I scout around and find repeated failure,
Elusive wind most efforts lead us chasing,
Engage with our desires by derailleur
In gear with cycles morally debasing.

What works, what grows, what lasts, what knows—
In truth, the spirit blesses more thereof.
Reaping exceeds what weeping sows
When seedlings trampled sprout with enough love.

Love is patient, love is kind, love is all the things I find
So hard summon from within when life's deficient.
So with dread, I crawl inside, consoling hurt, embracing pride
Instead of facing who had died and proved sufficient.

Endorsed hope often vies with dreams envisioned
The outcomes reconciled with plans that bluff
To force the future based on vain decisions
That don't include the planner's love enough.

SPIKE ANGLED SCANNER

A Cranial Anthem Ahead of Its Timing

What say can you see
From my QEEG
O'er the tracings we detailed
At my brainwaves' last streaming.

Whose broad bands and sharp spikes
Formed a map of the likes
That our country had not seen
Neurosoldiers start training.

And the Z-score's harsh glare
From beneath my scalp hair
Gave proof left and right
That red flags were still there.

Or

And the Z-score's red glare
From beneath my scalp hair
Confirms day and night
That my talent's imbalanced.

O say does that spike angled scanner
Yet save
Data from the symptom-free
And suspicious brainwaves.

THE RELATIONSHIP

(I Miss You)

Why do I miss you when you are here?
Is it because the you I know and love and want has disappeared?
Pieces of memories surround my soul to feel and hear and smell and see
As I try to rebuild the you that makes up so much of me.

Such longing fills my imagination
While day-to-day life promotes our separation.
Like motives of a rip tide tease and scare
And pull me farther from the place where you repair.

Relationship is one in reference to another.
When my desire alights, the counterpart delights in flames to smother.
No wonder, then, I burn in deep remorse for damage rendered,
And pine for your forgiveness and restoration tendered.

What have we here between us growing stranger?
Familiar ways cling toward comfort, but bring forward danger.
I miss you so, and argue thus with history
That we may grow, or let our past remain an unsolved mystery.

I ONLY WANT TO BE LIKE GOD

Far, far away, as if in a dream
I break the leash of gravity and fly to heights of power
Where I prevail o'er Nature, or so it seems
Forsake depravity for moral rectitude in which I tower.

I only want to be like God,
All-knowing and benevolent and totally understanding
This regalomania may seem odd
A fantasy of Icarus fated for crash-landing.

Stiff competition for the Captain's wheel
From all the crew who want to be in charge.
Humanity itself has come to feel
Entitlement to life divinely large.

Who dies with the most toys wins
Pretends to canonize the hierarchy
Such lies emboss the ploys to cover sins
And aggrandize the self with pure malarkey.

The tide of people reaching toward Heaven
For airlift from the swell that threatens drowning.
Royal rescue those beseeching and then even
Desiring fellowship as well as crowning.

I only want to be like God,
Cast miracles and copy how He lives
Such imitation turns out hard
To replicate how He forgives.

God says that I *can* be like Him,
Leave decay behind and rise above
Ascending to the company of angels
Requires rising up on wings of love.

Commanding elements of earth and people's wills
Is my idea of how the Lordship rules
His different sense of how to garner thrills
Provokes me to the use of other tools.

God shows me how to love and embrace
Those who rebel, hurt, and reject.
Thereby the countenance of His true face
My likeness will reflect.

2002

LIMERICKS

There once was a company climbing,
Its products repaired the brain's timing.
But its time wasn't right
For the principals' fight
Ended up with each other's sliming.

The company landed in scandal,
Its ownership banded by vandals.
The company split,
Its assets worth shit
And relationships no one could handle.

An entity, EEG Spectrum
Had computers with brains to connect them.
Their signals went wild
Like an unruly child
Who got mad at his toys and then wrecked them.

We're feeling abandoned so often,
The voice of affiliate orphans
We offer our dues
But continue to bruise,
Can't you give us some corporate endorphins?

2002

SELLING PENCILS

I spend my time selling pencils to God,
Like a beggar in the street
Who has little with which to navigate the world,
But won't give up in defeat.

I offer my cup
In mute supplication.
God lifts me up
From self-denigration.

God needs my pencils less than I need a baby's grip
To pull me to standing position.
My infantile needs and childlike dependence strip
All pretense, as lead is sharpened to fruition.

I offer pencils, proudly demonstrating how to make letters.
He accepts them, writing my story across eternity, showing me better.
Pencils I sell with proud, restless, independent determination,
Rescued from Hell by the author of my character who saves me from damnation.

Shamelessly, I push pencils at my maker
When He accepts them, it is I who am the taker.
Extolling virtues of my cache, I meekly scribble.
God illustrates a canvas vast, and who am I to quibble?

He is my manufacturer, architect, artist, engineer, and supplier,
And I sell pencils to the maker of the trees that made the pencils, also graciously the buyer.
God plays my customer, requiring not my sacrifice in trade,
Rewarding both my effort and discovery that in His image I am made.

Pencils and pride—these are my sole wares.
Empty inside—so my buyer knows and cares.
Soon my cup empties its lead weight and outer shavings
And I am left bereft of offerings beside my desperate cravings.

Who thinks he is, this beggar, mute, blind, deaf, and tasteless?
Impudent, bold, yet needy, stakes his territory baseless.
God is kind, and trades His treasures for the trinkets that are given.
He gives instead a passage out of penury and into heaven.

2002

I NEED A FRIEND

I need a friend who will listen,
A friend who's not too busy
With his personality.

I need to talk about the truth
As I've lived it,
And where my sorrows went astray.

Where is my company—
Compatriot for my soul?
I need someone to confirm that I am whole.

I need a friend to listen to,
To give my compassion,
A person who will keep my secrets openly.

There is a soul mate searching for me,
And we will find adventure
Looking for each other.

EVEN THOUGH

Even though your heart is hardened
And we've drifted far apart,
In my heart and mind, you're pardoned,
Free from rancor on my part.

You can live without a balance,
Interest-free on borrowed love,
Not indebted to the dalliance
With commitment's treasure trove.

I'll honor you as half of me,
Respect you even though
With sustenance I offer freely,
Growth may never show.

And even though we now share less
As if we've lost our pact,
Your distance doesn't make me careless
About keeping love intact.

GOD'S FRIENDS

My friend Peter is friends with God,
His agency long-standing.
But sometime when he's well downtrod,
He feels God's too demanding.

God said, "I'll teach you how to pray
And lead the needy churches.
Just keep on doing what I say,
And heed not what besmirches."

So Peter led for many years.
So many thought, A job well done.
God never doubted Peter's tears,
He shouted, "With you, I'm not done, Son.

"I'll shake the earth (including you),
I'll cause mountains and nerves to tremble.
When I speak, there'll be no dearth
Of listeners who will assemble."

Peter cried and begged and prayed,
And God received his stark despair.
When Peter preached, his pain was stayed.
The hearers knew that God was there.

Our thanks to God for all His grace
In guiding us with gifted leaders
Who show divine and human face
Through services lifted like Peter's.

The light of truth illuminates
When someone makes the circuit
Though God designed the path of fate,
His servants need to work it.

Continue Peter in your quest
With reason and connection
To seek and give God's very best,
Expressed through resurrection.

Though individual bodies fail
And corporal energy dwindles,
The corporate body swells to hail
Revival as our strength rekindles.

Count not each irritating thorn.
God lets us overcome intrusions.
We are His garments, some well worn
To cover others from sin's illusions.

2002
Written upon the death of my father.

DEATH IS SO INCONVENIENT

Death is so inconvenient,
It happens into whatever you're doing
Death is so persistent,
It won't go away.
Death is so personal,
It involves you.
Death is so present,
So distant from life long ago.

2002
Upon my father's passing.

LAST TANGO
When the Music Stops

The end-of-life tango is often ungraceful
Awkwardly stepping on many loved toes.
Dancing and music becoming distasteful
Prancing to pratfalls as sustenance goes.

Gasping for breath 'fore the singing abates,
Barely the strength to continue.
Tallying up life's loves and hates,
Summoning spiritual sinew.

Death ends a life, but relationships last,
Proving connections enduring.
Marking our meaning and ties to the past
While the future proceeds from our mooring.

We are mere handbreadths who stay for awhile
Searching for fun and pretending
That we will prevail in our hubris and guile,
Forgetting that we have an ending.

Youth is a gale gathering force for a party
Robustly seeking the journey.
Age becomes frail with efforts less hearty
Destined to land on a gurney.

The last tango is a most difficult dance
With the balance of life careening,
The bandstand offering one final chance
To saunter life's exit with meaning.

When it comes time to release the baton
And relinquish the race to successors,
The peace that ensues from life moving on
Makes its limits not greater, but lesser.

The anguish in leaving the stage alone
Punctuates our last choreographs.
In truth, it's the memories of what we have done
With partners that leaves epitaphs.

2001

IT'S ONLY THE LOVE OF JESUS

When we walk on the hot coals of torment
And sin and temptation tease us,
The grace of salvation's not dormant,
It's only the love of Jesus.

In the wake of our ongoing needs,
Selfishness and despair he eases
For the spiritual hunger he feeds,
It's only the love of Jesus.

(Refrain)
The sound of his name
Exceeds all other fame
The victorious blessing that frees us.
Without fear or shame
We are proud to exclaim
It's only the love of Jesus.

Let the guidance forever continue
As he nurtures behavior that pleases
To replace the old sin we knew
It's only the love of Jesus.

Watching us all through our days
With omniscient vision he sees us
What harmonious music he plays,
It's only the love of Jesus.

(Refrain)
The sound of his name
Exceeds all other fame
The victorious blessing that frees us.
Without fear or shame
We are proud to exclaim
It's only the love of Jesus.

We call out his name in dependence
Our personal sovereignty ceases
No longer the same in transcendence
It's only the love of Jesus.

(Refrain)
The sound of his name
Exceeds all other fame
The victorious blessing that frees us.
Without fear or shame
We are proud to exclaim
It's only the love of Jesus.

200

AM I MY LIFE?

Sometimes my life seems far larger than me
As I scurry hither and yon to its boundaries,
Caroming from one crisis or obligation to the next
Stretching to fulfill the skin that defines me.

My life at other moments is a part of me,
A multifaceted reflection of who I really am,
Expressed one need, one gesture, one action
At a time while I observe the contents.

Am I my life? when life is too much?
When life is more than I can handle,
Is that me? No match for my life?
More or less, or someone else entirely?

When I die, will I stop being me?
My life a history of memory,
Even now, there's lots of me that's gone,
Faded into past oblivion—though I live on,

I've died already, many times,
The parts that I've disowned, a new life honed
Dead to sin, alive within
Is that not life after death?

Which life could I be?
The life I struggle to contain?
Or the life contained within me?
Am I my life? Or lifeless am I yet me?

2001

STEINBERG CHRISTMAS

'Twas the night before Christmas
And all through the dwelling
The dachshund and children were set to gift smelling
They circled the tree
As if they would beg,
But didn't they pee
Or dare lift a leg.

They won't stay in bed
And they make too much noise
And Santa don't know
If they're good enough boys.
Their mama set limits
On what could be spent
But she ain't got game on what Santa sent.

The thing to remember
On what Santa rules
Is that in December,
There's protocol yule.
If they wake too early
Their folks will be surly
And might treat them to April Fools.

The morning of Christmas
Is eagerly awaited
But Father's deep snoring has hardly abated,
The children had better their presents forebear
And never too early the wrapping to tear
Or Papa will capture their spirits to spare.

2002

THE CALLING

I wasn't called to harvest grain,
To forage land or scour oceans;
Instead, to cultivate the brain,
To harness strengths of man's emotions.

I've not the skills to fix, replace,
Produce those things material.
I labor for those in disgrace
Whose needs are more ethereal.

Commercial trades, inventions ventured—
Amid the concrete contributions
I am called, indeed indentured
For healing, teaching spirit-willed solutions.

I've often wished for wealth and fame
And trappings influential.
But those good fortunes aren't the same
As winnings more essential.

My work is saving human souls
From ever constant falling,
And helping folks toward worthy goals,
A blessed, noble calling.

BROKEN AGAIN

Fixed for awhile, broken again,
Time after time it's the same old story:
Living in style, pretending 'til when
Spiritual crime wrests imagined glory.

Help me, O Heaven, I'm terribly broken,
Wretched this state like a garment ill fitting.
Inflated by leaven, appearances token,
Battered by fate toward disarmament quitting.

Captured by forces and dashed into pieces,
Busted and wasted, broke and diminished,
Tempted to courses that passion releases,
Led into ruin 'til it's seemingly finished.

Cast away, shattered, beleaguered, and broken.
Who wants this vessel in need of repair?
Listen, O sufferer, His word that is spoken,
Restored forever in heed of His care.

Where is the courage to witness the future?
Attitude break that is torn from the past.
Looking to God for my essence to suture,
Worthy to make, to adorn, and to last.

Broken again, rendered backward by nature.
Humbled, fumbling, my soul decomposed.
God has spoken again through His own nomenclature,
The stumbling beyond which Creation grows.

I WISH, I CRAVE

I wish I could share with you joys of the day.
If I opened up to you, what would you say?
No room for argument, blocks we have practiced,
Deep in our history, bondage we've accessed.

Bondage or bonding: What is our scene?
Actors in transit, our script's turned obscene.
Clinging to hope frail as gossamer wings,
Silently battling comments that sting.

Habits entrap us, emotionally fused;
Called on to love, though routinely abused;
Consciously casting aside what went wrong,
Desperately seeking to whom we belong.

Life makes us winnow the wheat from the chaff,
Ferreting separately tears and the laughs.
Seeking much wisdom, forgiving each knave,
Your friendship and loving are what I most crave.

2002

WHAT IS LIFE ABOUT?

Who am I? What is my life about?
I am a whisper, trying to shout,
A sapling lost in the forest,
Full of yearning, potential, and doubt.

Why am I here? And why not there?
Why do I metabolize, mobilize, and even care?
I must be here to share and find out where
I belong, though life is not fair.

Why am I given fleeting life?
To struggle toward eternity amid this earthly strife?
To plunge with desperation beneath the surface smiles and laughter,
Trading intermittently between now and the hereafter.

What is life about that we deride and yet we sing?
Expressions that would indicate a purpose that we bring
To mark upon existence and a history that rings
With echoes evolutionary, more than just a fling.

I go about, and live without
Much certainty—the jury's out
With evidence, mistakes are rife.
Indeed, the judge could give me life.

Have I done what I said I'd do?
Or has life offered something new?
Distracted me from setting out,
Enticed to find what life's about.

Who *am* I? What *is* life about?
I'm a vapor in a veil of tears,
Condensed to moisten those dried out
And make sense of my finite years.

POETIC JUSTICE

I believe in the sun, even when it isn't shining.
I believe in love, even when I cannot feel it.
I believe in God, even when He is silent.

In the end, all I have of ultimate value is my word
And His Word.

I choose them carefully.
Yet my beliefs and mistakes abound
In a universe where justice prevails.

Let me be judged by my choices,
Not by the voices of condemnation
Shouting down errors
They cannot see in themselves.

Reality has rules whose breach does not go unnoticed,
Each violation creates a debt that must be paid.
All of life a striving toward this balance,
Frenzied futility, apology, pretense, denial,
And seeking of forgiveness and mercy.

The universe is just and accountable.
We seek formulas
God has the answers.

Let me love and be loved, even when it goes unnoticed,
And if my feelings and beliefs and vain wonderings
Figure into the solution,
Cast them as adornments
To the ledger of mercy and justice.

Along the journey of life
The longest distance is the foot
Between the heart and the head.
Step forward into the separation of powers,
And travel into eternity.

2002

IF

If I could reach across the conflict that divides us,
I would.
If I could navigate the mischief deep inside me,
I'd be good.
If I could love you more than cater to my pride,
I should.
If I could overcome the loneliness that hides me,
I'd be understood.

If you would choose me from among your many options,
I'd be thrilled.
Install me as your valuable adoption,
I'd be filled
With honor and devotion and my fear of fading
Would be killed.
Replaced with nurture and compassion's inundating
Loving gild.

If we could draft our actions from a level roster of emotions
And choose
The players from the schemes of willful limbic notions
And use
The best of logic and of balanced biologic potions
Infused

With good intention activate our loving game without dissension
And never lose.

O where is the bard who settles disputes of the mind?
(He's fleeting.)
How can I summon his peaceful persuasion and find
(Entreating)
The suitable prayers and right supplications to blind
(Overheating)
The glare of exposure to hurt that makes life so unkind
(Indeed, defeating).

If only the rules could be bent and transgressions be sifted
From laws.
And logical reason meander unchallenged, effects lifted
From cause
The world's circumvention of justice could blithely be shifted
To flaws
Of an innocent nature, while the spirit unblemished and gifted
Soars.

1996

ACROSS TIME, DOWN THE AGES

Thoughtful As you're Waking
Mindful Aware of Aching
Graceful Conscious Stretching
Open Receiving Joy

Youth Means Might
Dreams Bring Rest
Age Many Bless
Beams Light Things Best

Happy Birthday 48
Happy Birthday Celebrate
Happy Birthday Not too late
Birthday Girl Awakening

2002

THE COLOR OF THE SKY

The color of the sky pours down on me
With the bright blues of day and the nightly dark.
Embrace of the season, shade of the tree,
Calming urban din like a city park.

Foliage is green as the Lord decrees,
Vision ensconced in memory traces;
Knowledge abstract as a temporal breeze,
Reality captured as times and places.

People evolve into what they admire,
Miracles launching ideas with power;
The universe seems too awesome to tire
Let earth spin, gravity dance, sky colors shower!

1978
Written upon the death of my grandmother.

DARK SECRET

Death in the darkness of January,
Lights glint off snow that buries
Cities not very bright.
Gloaming weekend—plans unnecessary;
We will lower Grandma after another night.

All childhood's memories
Scream within the quiet platitudes
Of adult reserves.
Previous movies and tapes rerun stealthily—
The cranial theater filled with blood, lymph, nerves.

Very soon, my grandma, before they've all forgotten,
You'll be back among us in some form.
I hope for you it's easier next time
Perhaps another life
For you will glow more warm.

Earth will mount yet on your grave anew
And future footprints will erase but
Never smear the pain which you've grown through;
Yet there's a secret that's for us to share
Just we two, Grandma, we kindred Jews.

Because you cradled me in younger days,
Then socialized me in the proper ways,
My tears for you, now welling with emotion,
Embrace clandestine whispers heralding devotion;
Everything I'll do has part of you in me.

This knowledge that we're one hath set us free.

1978

I was asked to share with you this poem that I wrote to express my feelings when I realized that my grandma, Rose, was dying. It's called, "Grandma, Why Can't You Live Forever?"

GRANDMA, WHY CAN'T YOU LIVE FOREVER?

A summery June day
Cached in the sunlight of yesteryear;
The afternoon glitters with memories,
Lengthening shadows yawn dolefully
At my thoughts of you and I through the years—

Or was it, you and me, Grandma,
Back in the days when all was
Me, Me, Me, Me—
And only "Me" mattered.
Forgotten shrouds of egocentric babyhood,
When you were there,
Protecting me from too much mothering.

I watch respectfully in kitchen
Undaunted sunlight bleaching orange juice in a glass
Happily, helplessly; unwaveringly—
That glass sits near a window
Much the kind by which you sat
With me, Grandma;

You watched with me, Grandma,
As time scuttled past that window
Endlessly, mercilessly;

As only family can, you watched me grow,
Fearlessly—
And you loved me
And cherished what was to be my joy
In a future when I'd realize who you are, what you mean to me,
How you loved me—
I didn't know till now!

Grandma, why can't you live forever?
Are the fruits of your destiny but seedless glory of a past
When neighbors recognized you in the street,
And piety satisfied the meat of your existence?

I know you must dissemble, Grandma;
Humanity returns in cycles,
The wheels of life spin for eternity.
Each of us rides shortly.
We beget
And forget
The pain and sorrow of a world filled with miracles.
The mirror of my childhood
Will always reflect your goodness;
Immortality exists—
Grandma, why can't you live forever?

GRANDMA, WHY CAN'T YOU LIVE FOREVER? (EULOGY)

Almost two years ago, when Rose took seriously ill, I felt the stinging shock of realizing that Grandma really would die; the imminence of this thought was stifling—so I wrote those words in an effort to understand the significance of human growth, development, and, ultimately, death. When I wrote the poem, I *knew* Grandma would have to die, but I could not *understand* it.

Over the past nineteen months, I have reflected deeply about the meaning of physical and psychological change and development. I have studied such change in my work, and I have watched it taking place in myself, my friends, and my family. While Grandma Rose became infirm and less comfortable, her grandchildren grew stronger, healthier, and more comfortable in a world to which she lovingly helped to introduce them. I have had time to prepare for Grandma's death; so at this tender moment I feel not only the awareness that she has passed on, but I understand it; yet more than understanding, I appreciate what Grandma Rose has contributed to my life and the way in which she will continue to be a part of me.

Rose was a religious woman and is a spiritual being. Owing to respect for the wishes of the deceased, there was some question, on the part of my family, as to the propriety of presenting this eulogy. In discussing this with my family last night, it seemed to me that the only relevant question to ask is: Would Rose want such a sharing of feelings among her loved ones? I believe strongly that she would approve of any desire to express oneself, providing it is done respectfully and with true conviction. In this manner, Grandma Rose has always been an indomitable spirit and will, indeed, live in our hearts forever.

Mark Steinberg
presented at the funeral of
Rose Bergwerk, January 8, 1978

1996
Inspired by a patient.

ODE TO A NODE OF NEUROPHILOSOPHY

It feels like you're carting a cache of parts
So the doctors can treat you dis "organ" ized
Without understanding the soul where it starts,
A feature not medically realized.

Treating and healing begin with the heart
Where the will to go on is sustained,
While gradually shifting through science and art
To the actual source of the pain.

Let us proceed to work with your mind
Being mindful throughout of your wholeness,
Accomplishing tasks of a cognitive kind
While reducing your sense of aloneness.

Myriad functions persist in the brain
Creating unique convolutions.
Connections and modifications we train
To result in adaptive solutions.

If only the caring would sharpen their skills
And technicians would sharpen their caring
What healing would flourish beyond need for pills
When techniques and spirit are sharing.

1996
When my sons were young.

SCIENCE STORY

'Twas two days before turkey
And all through the house
Not a creature was stirring,
Not even a mouse.
The family was out on the prowl for some fowl
...And Golden was out and about.

Grammy had returned for the boys, just to see 'em
They whisked her to Frisco's Exploratorium.
To find out the ways in which science does work, we
Build appetites for learning, before the Big Turkey.

Their dad made a promise to give a reward
For each science story the boys could record.
To tape what they're seeing, and later to write,
The boys would earn *special* desserts that night.

To further the progress of science is great
But first to discover how things operate
Is the method of scientists who note and record
And whose interest in science keeps them from being bored.

Children can study and earn themselves prizes
Despite their young brains and their often small sizes
It's noble to learn and Nobel to prize (sorry Barnes!)
For science is truthful, and not about lies.

Those who return before Thanksgiving and share
Scientific principles they learned while visiting up there
Will earn some rewards, and learn a principle of living:
That to get what you want, you must also be giving.

1998
For the Clintons, et al.

MORE LIMERICKS

A woman named Monica dated
A Government Bill she inflated.
Publicity leached
While the man she impeached
Had his career officially castrated.

Did the president really unzip
His pants and his paramour's lips?
Now he's got an agenda,
But not to defend her
From sporting embarrassing slips.

A Washington intern named Monica
Befriended Bill Clinton platonic. A
Brouhaha ensued
Over whom he had wooed
With the stories appearing ironic.

A diligent lawyer named Starr
Sought Clinton with feathers and tar.
Would his comings and goings
Reveal secret knowings
Of a president who went too far?

The accusations are choral
That our president is immoral.
He defended his honor
By swearing upon her
Relations with him as just oral.

A DREAM POPPED OPEN

A dream popped open, understood
Enamored of your mystery
Invited by temptation's mood
To reenact our history.

Once you shone upon me
With the sunlight in your hair
Enveloped me with love's delight
Sequestered in your lair.

Hand in glove we spent our youth
Caressing every surface
In middle age we grasp at truth
More frayed, but not as nervous.

Pulled apart by toil and sweat
The hand and glove have weathered
Inverted lining won't push back
The way it once was tethered.

Calmly, we manipulate
The memories of pleasure
That let us rehabilitate
Commitment to our treasure.

Nights I've lain beside you, much
Vulnerable and tired
To know your presence, feel your touch
Was what I most required.

Life's solitary separation
Beckoned me like slumber
I entered and a dream popped open
You appeared with wonder.

I lie awake, in truth I dream
Remaking what is broken
Reality you have redeemed
For me, a dream popped open.

1997

THERE ARE TIMES

In the stillness of the night
There are times
I want to wake you
And share the chatter in my head,
Spill the drivel that accumulates from life.

Absent sufficient light
There are times
I want to soak you in my dreams
So I won't drown alone.
Submerged in darkness and symbolic meaning floating by.

Earlier than dawn's less fearful light
There are times
I rotate, writhe,
Fatigue impales my roasting body
Mind and spirit heated, though less bright.

In the search for what is right
There are times
I need your guidance to determine what is real
Amid declension and fanciful flight
With myriad conclusions up for grabs.

When I desire to cling tight
There are times
I ask who you are and if it matters,
How I matter in your sight.
Who are we and who else each of us might be?

Through the calmness and the fights
There are times
I wonder why we are together here—Who found us each other?
Such musings conquer separateness and
There are times
When loneliness is severed for respite.

1999

FIREWOOD

Give me fire,
I'll give you wood.
Order and desire
Misunderstood.

The hearth rests blankly
Quite unlit.
The heart seethes frankly
Toward a fit.

The man incensed
By lack of flame.
No recompense,
Himself to blame.

I'll heap your fire
With logs to spare.
But first require
Ignite the air.

That order's wrong,
Nature exclaims
The sacrificial song's
The same.

You feed me wood,
I'll build you fire.
Work and faith should
Follow desire.

And sacrifice
Precedes reward.
Things very nice
Worth working toward.

The universe
Makes little sense
Till you rehearse
Precise sequence.
I promise fuel!
First billow blazes.
You silly fool
Whom truth yet hazes.

First you yield
What Nature asks.
And then you field
The fruit of tasks.

The pride is fired,
I've piled in wood.
Hubris expired,
Now order's good.

Job dignity
With faith extended
Affinity
With Nature mended.

Flames dance
Firewood's due heat rises.
Perchance
Woodfire's name reprises.

1998
For my mother's friend, Ellie, who turned ninety-five!

NINETY-FIVE

Across nearly fifty years and fifty states
I behold you near the millennium,
First verging on ninety-five
Eyeing ninety-five.

I-95 runs north and south
I-80 runs east and west.
You've eyed eighty and passed that test.
Time to look ahead, I-95, eye the best
Friend south of ninety-five on I-95—
Seventy-three southern Pearls of wisdom.

Crisscross the nation, generation
Of energy for celebration.
Your mind is clear, your vision here
And hearing no cessation
Of experience this century.

Almost a Century
Village of experience
Best friends "vill age"
Along vith you und your experiments
Of living life so fully,
Centenarian.

In middle of this race
For age, I stop in place
And contemplate my middle age and race
Origins and connections, verstehten?

How can I connect with you
Who knew
Me in diapers.
I know!
You northern Yankee,
Love the Yankees,
Me too!

You knew me when I was a wee Yankee
In cloth with pins
Instead of pinstripes.
I took a whack at life
And got on base.

But you have lived beyond the broken records
And stranded runners.
You remember the Babe
And other babes with home run potential.

You've watched the players grow,
The innings shuttle.
And now you're ninety-five.
The twentieth century you've connived
By managing to stay alive
And thrive.

1998

SECOND HAND, SECOND CHANCE

Wait a second,
Second hand moves
Relentlessly
As time marches forward
Experience garnered
Definitively.

Go back
Move in reverse
Perspectively
As life is construed
After facts are reviewed
Collectively.

Who will second
My choices
Or counter my moves
Defensively
As life lurches on
Toward conclusions foregone
Inevitably.

Time seconds or minutes
Or larger chunks
Incrementally
Mistakes will accrue
As I stumble through
Apprehensively.

Just a second—
Hand life unfolds
Deferentially To a leadership mold
Understood from respect
Consequentially.

Second time
Second chance
Forgivingly
The teacher with love
Corrects from above
Comprehensively.

Many seconds
Many chances
Electively
Second chances bequeathed
By the One who second to none
Everlastingly.

POTTER'S GOLD

Dear God,
You are the Potter,
I am the clay
You make the rules
Whenever we play.
I take the form of
Whatever You say.

Shaped by Your will,
Crafted to last,
You know my future,
Have molded my past.
Into Your image
My nature is cast.

Of Your creation
I am a product.
Filled with sensation
I harbor my conduct
Toward Your service
I am aligned.
Like potter's gold
I appear unrefined.

Take me, perfect me,
Subject me to fire.

Spare me the wrath
Of judgmental ire.
Gird me with strength
In Your heavenly crucible,
Kiln me with grace
For Your purposes usable.

Play with me,
Stay with me,
Make me yet malleable.
You are the Master
Whose love is infallible.
Leap to discover
My value is savable
Dear God Who died for me,
What more to ask?
Die for me, die me for
Something to last.

1996

AMERICAN MOM AND APPLE SAUCE

Don't feel bad about your homemade apple sauce
When cooking for us seems a total loss.
Though I pretend to be a fussy gourmet,
Your efforts are appreciated anyway.

Food not eaten may rot and stink;
The dirty dishes pile up routinely in the sink.
It might help you to know that the kids and I think
That you provide the family with a vital link.

Mom supplies treats just like Santa's elves;
Mom reminds us sternly to put things back on the shelves;
Mom often works and plans past when the clock strikes twelve
To manage us and make sure we take care of ourselves.

2000

MOMENTS OF CLOSENESS
PSALM 151

Nothing I do is good enough.
Always there is someone who wants more,
Different, something to criticize or
Someone who has it better.

I strive for recognition,
But there are those ahead of me.
I trumpet my petition,
Failing, railing, paling behind the ones chosen instead of me.

All fall short of glory,
And, at some point, share my story.
Who among you has not tried
Yet cried out lost, unsatisfied?

Amazingly, I'm noticed every day,
Among the throngs who cavil in my way,
By God, He listens, speaks, gives
Moments of closeness where He lives.

I live in the moment, by the moment, for the moment
Of closeness with One who understands my fanciful renown,
Who lifts me up, exposes my nothingness
And loves me completely with true greatness, compassion, and royal crown.

The company I keep in moments of closeness
Sustains me and shows my importance
To those who trample me in their hurry
To run faster than the earth spins.

Notice me and celebrate my feats!
The battle cry of competition
Which is not even close
To the moments of closeness I know.

1995

HELEN'S LIMERICK

I once had a friend named Helen,
An artist who took up sellin'
The work she created
Through markets she hated
The stress that ensued was tellin'

She's coped with the tension 'til now
She's even displayed her own show
She's hung in the galleries
Sung to infallibly
Praised as the cat's meow.

ABOUT THE AUTHOR

Dr. Mark Steinberg is a licensed psychologist with expertise in clinical, educational, and neuropsychology. He appears regularly on television to offer his psychological expertise on topics pertaining to health, behavior, and living a more satisfying and productive life. He treats children, adolescents, and adults, offering a range of services dealing with attention and mood disorders, behavior problems, family and communication issues, developmental disabilities, educational and learning problems, parenting challenges, habit change, addictions, and neurological disorders (including headaches, seizures, and sleep disorders).

Over the course of his practice, Dr. Steinberg has administered over fifty thousand evaluation and treatment procedures.

By blending the latest technological advances with traditional and scientific methods, Dr. Steinberg improves functioning and eliminates problems that have persisted for years. He is well-known for his pioneering work with EEG neurofeedback and Voice Technology, the treatment that eliminates negative emotions in minutes.

Dr. Steinberg has made many appearances on local and national television. Widely consulted as a medical expert, he has won local and statewide awards. He is the author of three acclaimed books: *Living Intact: Challenge and Choice in Tough Times, Staying Madly in Love With Your Spouse: Guide to a Happier Marriage,* and coauthor of the popular book, *ADD: The 20-Hour Solution.* He offers seminars and consulting services as well as individual psychotherapeutic services.

His clinic, Mark Steinberg, Ph.D. & Associates, is located in Los Gatos, California and San Francisco, California. For information, call (408) 356-1002 or visit www.marksteinberg.com.

Made in the USA
Middletown, DE
27 January 2015